NORTH AMERICAN INDIAN MUSIC

GARLAND LIBRARY OF MUSIC ETHNOLOGY
VOLUME 5
GARLAND REFERENCE LIBRARY OF THE HUMANITIES
VOLUME 1440

GARLAND LIBRARY OF MUSIC ETHNOLOGY

JAMES PORTER, *Series Editor*

ETHNOMUSICOLOGY RESEARCH
A Select Annotated
Bibliography
by Ann Briegleb Schuursma

TRADITIONAL ANGLO-
AMERICAN FOLK MUSIC
An Annotated Discography
of Published Sound Recordings
by Norm Cohen

CENTRAL EUROPEAN
FOLK MUSIC
An Annotated Bibliography
of Sources in German
by Philip V. Bohlman

JAZZ RESEARCH AND
PERFORMANCE MATERIALS
A Select Annotated
Bibliography
Second Edition
by Eddie S. Meadows

NORTH AMERICAN INDIAN MUSIC
A Guide to Published Sources
and Selected Recordings
by Richard Keeling

North American Indian Music
A Guide to Published Sources and Selected Recordings

Richard Keeling

Garland Publishing, Inc.
New York and London
1997

Library of Congress Cataloging-in-Publication Data

Keeling, Richard.
    North American Indian music : a guide to published sources and se-
lected recordings / by Richard Keeling.
        p.   cm. — (Garland library of music ethnology ; 5) (Garland
reference library of the humanities ; vol. 1440)
        Includes bibliographical references and indexes.
        ISBN 0-8153-0232-0 (alk. paper)
        1. Indians of North America—Music—History and criticism—Bibliogra-
phy.   2. Indians of North America—Music—Discography.   I. Title.
II. Series.   III. Series: Garland reference library of the humanities ; vol.
1440.
ML128.F75K44   1997
016.78'089'97—dc20   96-41847
                                                          CIP
                                                          MN

Printed on acid-free, 250-year-life paper
Manufactured in the United States of America

SERIES EDITOR'S PREFACE

Dr. Richard Keeling is superbly qualified to undertake this bibliography of Native American music. Having gained a B.A. in anthropology (UC Berkeley, 1966) and M.A. in music (UCLA, 1975), he earned his Ph.D. in music (ethnomusicology) from UCLA in 1982 with a dissertation on the music of the Indian peoples of Northwestern California. His book *Cry for Luck: Sacred Song and Speech among the Yurok, Hupa, and Karok Indians of Northwestern California* (1992) was published by the University of California Press, which also published his *A Guide to Early Field Recordings* (1900–1949) at the Lowie Museum of Anthropology (1991). Dr. Keeling has also edited two useful collections of essays: *Music and Spiritual Power among the Indians of North America* (Berlin, 1992) and *Women in North American Indian Music* (Ann Arbor, 1989). His articles in major journals address problems of comparative Native American history, the transcription of Indian singing style, and culture change. He has contributed six articles on California Indian peoples to the *New Grove Dictionary of American Music* (New York, 1986).

Dr. Keeling has won several major research awards for his work, including a Fellowship for University Teachers (National Endowment for the Humanities, 1987–1988), a Fulbright Senior Research Fellowship (1991–1992), and the Ida Halpern Fellowship (Society for Ethnomusicology, 1994–1995). He has been active in the Society for Ethnomusicology, reading papers and organizing panels on major topics in the field of Native American music, such as "Gender in North American Indian Music" (1987) and "Historical Dynamics of Indian Music" (1994). From 1983 to 1986 Dr. Keeling was Senior Museum Scientist at the Lowie Museum of Anthropology, UC Berkeley, and since 1988 he has been appointed Visiting Associate Professor in the Department of Ethnomusicology, UCLA, where he teaches courses on North American Indian music, American popular music, and the anthropology of music. This guide to Native American music, the result of Richard Keeling's careful and wide-ranging research, is a testimony to his unusual breadth of knowledge and scholarly insight.

James Porter
Professor and Chair
Department of Ethnomusicology and Systematic Musicology

Contents

Preface

The present volume contains references and descriptive annotations for 1,497 sources on North American Indian and Eskimo music. As conceived here, the subject encompasses works on dance, ritual, and other aspects of religion or culture related to music, and selected "classic" recordings have also been included. The coverage is equally broad in other respects, including writings in several different languages and spanning a chronological period from 1535 to 1995. The book is intended as a reference tool for researchers, teachers, and college students. With their needs in mind, the sources are arranged in ten sections by culture area, and the introduction includes a general history of research. Finally, there are also indices by author, tribe, and subject.

This is the first fairly comprehensive bibliography of Native American music which has been published to date. Several other, less inclusive bibliographies are listed here, but the only previous work to provide similarly extensive coverage was unfortunately never published. I am referring to Joseph Hickerson's "Annotated Bibliography of North American Indian Music North of Mexico," an extraordinary piece of scholarship which was submitted as a master's thesis to Indiana University in 1961. Hickerson's thesis was enormously useful in early stages of preparing the present volume, and in all honesty I am not sure that I would have undertaken this project without knowing that I could use the earlier bibliography as a foundation. The extent of my reliance and departures from the approach used by Hickerson are discussed in the introduction which follows. Here, let me only add that I assume full responsibility for any errors of fact or omission in the present volume.

Joseph Hickerson has served as the Head of Acquisitions at the Archive of Folk Culture (Library of Congress) since 1974, and when I called to ask his permission he not only gave his blessings to the project but also offered to supply me with xerox copies of articles which might be difficult to find. I took him up on that and he later sent copies of about thirty of them. Other colleagues who provided copies of articles or useful bibliographic information were: Beverley Diamond, Steven Elster, Judith Gray, Orin Hatton, Dell Hymes, Leanne Hinton, Thomas Johnston (deceased, 1994), Victoria Lindsay Levine, Bruno Nettl, and William Powers. In closing, I would only reiterate that any errors found here are entirely my responsibility. I know full well there will be regrettable omissions and apologize in advance to any authors I have unintentionally slighted in this manner.

Introduction

The music and dance of North American Indian peoples have been
described in travel diaries, mission records, and other writings of
European and American observers dating back to the earliest periods of
exploration in the New World. By the turn of the last century, it was
generally assumed by anthropologists and others that these cultures
were rapidly disappearing and needed to be documented before they
became completely extinct. Over the decades which followed there was
intensive research in Indian communities all over North America, and
these were the studies from which American anthropology emerged and
developed its initial orientations. The field of comparative musicology
(as ethnomusicology was then known) was also shaped to a great extent
by research on Native American music, and in the years from 1890 to
1940 fieldworkers using the Edison-type phonograph managed to
collect more than 17,000 cylinders containing recordings of songs and
spoken narratives from tribes of various regions. In recent decades—
since the late 1960s—our presumptions about the survival of Indian
peoples and standards for cultural research have changed dramatically,
but articles and books have continued to be published at an impressive
rate. And as a result the historical evidence for current research on
Native American music and culture is more complete and more detailed
than that of any comparable area of indigenous music in the world.

Because of this extraordinary legacy those who study American
Indian music are also by necessity bibliographers and historians, not
only in ethnomusicology but also in anthropology, folklore, history, and
linguistics. This has gradually tended to balkanize a field which was
already intrinsically complex or variegated because of the number of
cultures involved. There are hundreds of native cultures and languages
in North America, and the musical styles are quite diverse, yet in earlier
decades it was not at all unusual for leaders in the field to publish
studies on the music of various tribes and areas. Over the past thirty
years however, research on Indian music has become much more

specialized. Today (with the exception of introductory writings intended for students or other general readers) many of us publish only on the music of one tribe or region, and those who claim expertise in more than one culture area are very rare indeed. Assuredly, this owes to several factors, not the least of which is a conscious reaction against the analytical biases and oversimplifications of previous comparative research, but it also reflects a collective regard for the bibliographic difficulties involved. Nowadays, particularly because recordings and manuscripts in archives have become more accessible, we find ourselves all but overwhelmed by the musicological resources in our own areas of specialization, and the prospect of mastering the literature and available recordings from other culture areas seems very intimidating indeed.

All things considered, it is perhaps not surprising that a comprehensive bibliography has not been published before, but one is surely needed at this point in time—not only to make the field more accessible to newcomers but also to encourage more experienced researchers to broaden their perspectives and more fully utilize the inheritance provided by earlier pioneers in the field. For many years, specialists have relied upon an excellent work prepared by Joseph C. Hickerson submitted as a master's thesis to Indiana University in 1961. The present volume incorporates much information from Hickerson's bibliography while also including recent publications and some new perspectives on the older ones. While Hickerson's goal was to produce an all-inclusive list encompassing all manner of publications, this bibliography is more select in some respects and mainly intended as a practical guide for professional researchers and college students. More specific information concerning the format and rationale for the present volume will be given in sections to follow, but first it seems useful and important to sketch a general history placing some of the major personalities and developments in North American Indian music research in chronological perspective. This is only an introductory survey, not a detailed history, thus it omits the contributions of many important authors whose writings are listed in the regional bibliographies which follow.

General History of Research

For the sake of convenience and in order to emphasize the continuing evolution of attitudes, concepts, and methods relating to the subject, I have divided this history into five periods. But these are certainly not intended as definitive, and readers of the bibliographies which follow will surely notice exceptions in which books or articles representing a particular viewpoint have appeared before or after the time limits indicated. Additional information and other perspectives on earlier developments can also be found in similar historical surveys by Densmore (1927a), Herzog (1936b:3–44), Hickerson (1961:2–48), and Rhodes (1952b).

1. Period of Earliest Encounters (Before 1880)

In the centuries following Columbus's first voyage to the West Indies, the continent of North America was invaded by explorers from various European nations (most notably Spain, France, Great Britain, the Netherlands, and Russia), each of which laid title to certain territories by right of discovery and sought to consolidate the new holdings as best they could. Then, in later periods, the United States and Canada also sent expeditions which ultimately searched the remaining territories and developed these regions for settlement by whites. These colonial enterprises generated an extensive literature in the form of travel journals, natural histories, mission records, and similar writings which provide the earliest images of Native American life and culture as documented by Euro-American observers.

Generally speaking, references to music and related topics are scattered and incidental in the original works, but some find their way into secondary sources and reference books such as the well-known *Dictionnaire de Musique* by Jean Jacques Rousseau (1768).[1] More than twenty of these sources are discussed in a historical survey by Hickerson (1961:4–10), the earliest being an *Histoire de la Nouvelle France* by Marc Lescarbot (1609).[2] Two later essays by Stevenson (1973a, 1973b) discuss this literature in greater detail, including numerous musical examples and translations of music-related passages from the original Spanish and French. The earliest reference identified by Stevenson (1973a) occurs in a natural history of the West Indies which was first published by Fernández de Oviedo y Valdéz in 1535.[3]

The importance of the colonial sources for providing information on earlier forms of Indian music is illustrated by any number of quotations found in Stevenson (1973a). Thus, for example, he includes the following account of rowing songs sung by Natchez warriors as witnessed during the late-1500s by Garcilaso de la Vega (1539–1616). The extraordinary Natchez war canoes were occasionally large enough to hold 75 or 80 men, and Vega writes

In order for all to row simultaneously and in rhythm, the Indians have composed various songs to different tunes, short or long depending on how fast or slow the canoes are moving. The texts of these songs tell of the deeds in war of their own or other chiefs, the memory of which incites them to battle and to triumph. The canoes of the rich and powerful come painted within and without even to the oars, in a single color, be it blue, yellow, white, red, green, scarlet, purple, black, or some other hue. Also the oarsmen and oars, as well as the warriors to the last feather and thread and the last bow and arrow are tinted with that same single color. Spread out over the broad river, the canoes made a magnificent sight.[4]

Stevenson's essays (1973a and 1973b) give many other examples which are equally rare and inspiring to the imagination. Some of these early references and others from Hickerson (1961) are listed in the bibliographies which follow, but many have also been excluded from the present volume because they are considered marginally relevant or difficult to obtain.

As some have noted, writings of the Spanish and French observers typically seem more respectful and objective than the English-language sources, which are often rather ethnocentric and condescending.[5] The English and American authors may occasionally convey a sense of astonishment, even admiring certain aspects of the "savage" temperament, but the music itself is generally dismissed as a succession of grunts or noises and seldom described or analyzed in detail. Thus, for example, the American journalist Stephen Powers describes a Yurok shaman he observed in 1871 as "squatting down like a dog on his haunches before the patient, and barking at him like that noble and faithful animal for hours" (1877:26). And in speaking of songs performed by Twana and Clallam Indians in 1875, Myron Eells informs his readers that "music among these Indians consists more of a noise, as a general thing, than of melody or chords" (1879:249).

Despite the obvious limitations, these sources provide our earliest glimpses of Indian music and dance in a world that was rapidly changing, and they often include specific details that can become very useful for historical interpretations. For example, even a seemingly gratuitous comment like that of Powers can become meaningful for the student of Yurok music, as it seems most likely that the "barking" he noticed may correspond to the type of vocal accompaniment sung by men in a curing ceremony known as the Brush Dance. Thus, despite the insulting comparison, Powers (1877) provides highly significant information on a type of shamanistic vocalizing which has been extinct for several generations and was never adequately documented.

2. The Beginnings of Musicological Research, 1880–1920.

It is generally agreed that "serious research" on American Indian music began with the publication of Theodore Baker's dissertation, *Über die Musik der nordamerikanischen Wilden* (1882),[6] and this certainly was an important milestone. Besides the data that Baker collected from Senecas of New York and at Carlisle Indian School (Pennsylvania), this also contained information from more than forty earlier sources, and it remained the most comprehensive work for decades. But while the beginning of this period might seem easy enough to define, the next forty years would see the emergence of some very diverse trends and personalities. In short, this was a period of marked transition—theoretically speaking, and to the extent that there was a unifying concept it was a general commitment to documenting songs and other aspects of Indian culture before they became extinct.

The expectation that musical traditions and other aspects of Indian culture would become extinct is expressed in numerous writings of this period, and indeed the early collectors did manage to document many types of songs and performance styles that would no longer be obtainable in later years. Among the most notable early figures in this area was Alice Cunningham Fletcher (1838–1923), who began collecting songs of the Omaha and Dakota tribes in 1883. Initially, Fletcher notated the melodies by ear, having them sung repeatedly until she was satisfied with her notated rendition. But a major advance occurred with the invention of the Edison-type phonograph, which was patented in the United States in 1877. Interestingly, this revolutionary device was not used for ethnographic research until 1890, when Jesse Walter Fewkes (1850–1930) collected 31 cylinders containing songs and spoken texts from the Passamaquoddy Indians of Maine. The phonograph not only made it easier to collect musical data (and spoken narratives), but also made the processes of transcription and analysis much more efficient. The Edison-type recorder had its heyday in ethnographic research from 1890 until around 1930, though it continued to be used even later, and before it became completely obsolete an estimated 17,000 cylinders were recorded in North American Indian communities.[7]

The most prolific of the early fieldworkers was Frances Densmore (1867–1957), who collected some 2,112 cylinder recordings from various tribes and areas while working in association with the Bureau of American Ethnology during the years from 1907 to 1941.[8] But while Fewkes and Densmore deserve to be singled out as the earliest and the most industrious of the early recording pioneers (respectively), there were scores of others who played major roles in collecting what now comprises our earliest recorded evidence of Indian music. In many cases these cylinder collectors were not primarily musicologists at all but anthropologists, folklorists, and/or linguists who collected songs as an adjunct to their other studies. Among the most well known of these non-specialists were Franz Boas (1858–1942), Alfred Kroeber (1876–1960), Edward Sapir (1884–1939), and Edward Curtis (1868–1952). Kroeber and Curtis typically had their musical recordings notated by colleagues. Boas and Sapir often did the same but also published their own transcriptions on occasion.[9] In many cases the cylinders never were transcribed and remain today as untapped resources at the Library of Congress, the Archives of Traditional Music (Indiana University), and other repositories in the United States and Canada.

One important exception to the trend described here was Natalie (Curtis) Burlin (1875–1921), who began collecting songs among tribes of the southwest in 1901. Obviously a skilled transcriber, Burlin used the Edison phonograph initially, but soon came to regard the device as "inadequate and unnecessary" (Burlin 1907:xxii). Her major work, *The Indians' Book* (1907), is a general survey of music and folklore containing 149 musical examples from 21 different tribes. These appear to be excellent transcriptions, despite having been notated by ear without mechanical mediation.

As suggested previously, this was an era marked by extraordinary progress in theory, though the advances may be obscured in retrospect by the tenacity with which obsolete notions and practices would persist in certain quarters. European and American perceptions of tribal peoples were dominated by evolutionist concepts during the late 19th century; thus, it was natural that Theodore Baker and the other early writers on Indian music initially tended to accept certain presumptions as axiomatic or self-evident. There were three basic assumptions: (1) that humankind had progressed through various stages of development, (2) that western civilization represented the highest level of cultural achievement, and (3) that existing "primitives" could still be observed or studied as living examples of the earliest stages in human evolution. The postulates of evolutionism found various expressions in musicological research, but none seem more remote from modern sensibilities than the highly influential ideas of John Comfort Fillmore (1843–1898).

Primarily a professor of western music, Fillmore developed an elaborate theory concerning the origins of all music and the stages through which music passed in evolving from "primitive" expressions to the pinnacle of the art in European harmonic counterpoint of the Romantic era. Basically, he postulates that music followed certain general laws which govern all physical and mental activity. It was his position that in producing musical tones the singer's voice naturally tended to follow a "line of least resistance" which found its ultimate and most perfect manifestation in the major and minor scales of western art music. From this perspective all music had a "natural harmonic basis," even though "primitive" musicians might only be aware of the fact subconsciously. These ideas are outlined in several different articles, but for present purposes the implications are particularly clear in his paper entitled "What Do Indians Mean To Do When They Sing, and How Far Do They Succeed?" (Fillmore 1895). Here he argues that Native American singers, like any untrained amateurs, often fail to sing the notes they actually intend to sing. In trying to find the true melody, Fillmore would actually sing along with the native informant and confer with him directly as to how the notes should be corrected. He specifically criticized the use of the phonograph for research, in favor of his own interactive method (1895:138–139). The most common problem, in his view, was that the Indians often sang "neutral" thirds which had to be replaced with major or minor thirds. Having corrected the thirds and other intervals, Fillmore would then take the Indian singer to a piano and perform the melody with full (triadic) chords that fit its natural harmonic basis. The Native American singer would then be asked to repeat the song as accompanied by Fillmore on piano, a process which Fillmore states almost always resulted in the elimination of doubtful intervals (1895:140).

Surprising as it seems in retrospect, Fillmore had considerable influence in his day. He collaborated rather intensively with Alice Fletcher and Franz Boas during the early 1890s, even supplying a report on "structural peculiarities" in Fletcher's earliest major publication on Omaha Indian music (Fletcher and LaFlesche 1893:59–77). These ideas were supported in a review by Boas (1894), and it was only after Fillmore's death that Wead (1900) and others began to criticize his theories as unscientific and ethnocentric. Fillmore's dominance during this period is probably best explained by the lack of conflicting theoretical concepts and the vehemence with which Fillmore expressed his own ideas. Nonetheless, his influence did remain highly significant even after his death in 1898. His theories were supported in early papers by Frances Densmore (1905, 1906), and they also lived on in the work of composers such as Arthur Farwell (1872–1952), who wrote pieces based on Indian themes with the goal of creating an American national music. The manifesto of these composers and their reliance on Fillmore's theories are outlined an essay entitled "The 'Idealization' of Indian Music" by Charles Wakefield Cadman (1915).

Even during Fillmore's heyday, a strikingly different interpretation had begun to emerge from the writings of Benjamin Ives Gilman (1852–1933). A lecturer on the psychology of music at Harvard University, Gilman was asked to study and analyze two sets of cylinder recordings that Jesse Walter Fewkes had collected among the Zuni and Hopi tribes in 1890 and 1891 (respectively). In analyzing the Zuni cylinders he used a phonograph and carefully attempted to measure the actual pitches that were sung with the aid of a harmonium. In commenting on the (nine) transcriptions, he concluded that the whole concept of musical scales was alien to Indian music. In his words, "What we have in these melodies is the musical growths out of which scales are elaborated, and not compositions undertaken in conformity to norms of interval order already fixed in the consciousness of the singers. In this archaic stage of art, scales are not formed, but forming" (1891:89). Not to be upstaged so easily, Fillmore responded in a review (1893–1894) by criticizing Gilman's failure to understand the "harmonic" nature of Indian melodies, and he illustrated the point by retranscribing three of Gilman's examples.

Gilman's later analysis of the (nineteen) Hopi songs (1908) was even more detailed and continued to focus on the difficult question of intervals and intonation. Here he writes: "The singer's musical consciousness seems to be restricted to a few intervals of simplest vibration ratio approximately rendered, and to melody sequences formed by their various analyses and syntheses and rendered with a certain loose fidelity" (1908:5). From these quotations it is clear that Gilman was still operating well within the sphere of evolutionist thinking, but his interpretation was much less ethnocentric than Fillmore's and his concern with the variable intonations so typical of Native American musical styles raised an issue that would continue to interest scholars for generations.[10]

Further advances in theory would emerge from the writings of German scholars working at the University of Berlin during the same general period. Their involvement in research on Native American music began in 1886, when Carl Stumpf (1848–1936) published a paper describing nine songs performed by a group of Bella Coola Indians who had visited Germany the year before. The musical examples in this early paper were transcribed by ear, but Stumpf and his colleagues would later employ the newest technologies and soon established a Phonogramm-Archiv which enabled them to study cylinder recordings sent to them by ethnologists from all over the world. The major theorist of the group was Erich Moritz von Hornbostel (1877–1935). Inspired by the cents system of pitch measurement developed by the English scholar and acoustician

Alexander J. Ellis (1814–1890), Hornbostel gradually developed laboratory methods which allowed for precise tonal measurements and conceived a set of descriptive (analytical) concepts which could be uniformly applied to virtually any style of world music. The methodology is beautifully illustrated in a study of 43 Thompson River Indian songs that were recorded in British Columbia by Franz Boas (Abraham and Hornbostel 1906). In this paper, the precise tonometric measurements and detailed scalar analyses are basically intended to show that any deviations from western intonational norms are not accidental but entirely purposeful and stylistic. Thus, despite the obvious limitations of "armchair research" focusing on music-sound entirely divorced from its social context, Hornbostel and his colleagues deserve much credit for being among the first to extend the emerging concept of cultural relativity to studies of North American Indian music.

Clearly the single most important influence in breaking the evolutionist paradigm was Franz Boas (1858–1942). Born and educated in Germany, Boas did extensive fieldwork in the Arctic and Northwest Coast regions during the 1880s and 1890s (respectively), and as teacher at Columbia University he trained an entire generation of scholars who would define the basic standards of American Cultural Anthropology in the years from 1900 to 1940 and beyond.[11] Boas was the first to speak of "cultures" in the plural sense, and his respect for the mentality and character of native peoples was evident even in his early reports of fieldwork among the Central Eskimo in 1883.[12] The presumption that human cultures had passed through uniform stages of development was refuted by Boas in a classic paper of 1896 ("The Limitations of the Comparative Method in Anthropology"), and throughout his career Boas would insist on the need for intensive fieldwork and collecting of detailed ethnographic information before attempting any reconstruction of local culture histories. Boas' position as the father of "scientific anthropology" (Mead 1959:35) is widely recognized, but less well known is the extent of his contributions to ethnomusicology.

Music was important to Boas. This is shown by the fact that he addressed the subject in more than twenty publications and corresponded with virtually all the major figures in Native American music research throughout his career. It is also shown by the work of his students, and here I am referring not only to the distinguished musicologists George Herzog and Helen Roberts, but also to Alfred Kroeber, Edward Sapir, Frank Speck, Leslie Spier, and many others who are best known as anthropologists or linguists. These others not only collected important recordings but also published song texts and other valuable information on the contexts and functions of music, often describing rituals, dances, attitudes, and beliefs relating to music in some detail. This was partially done for the sake of thoroughness in ethnography, but it was also motivated by the Boasian concept of culture as a unified whole.

At a time when others were thinking in less integrated terms, Boas was among the first to recognize that various aspects of culture— "religion and science; music, poetry, and dance; myth and ritual; fashion and ethics"—were all "intrinsically interwoven" (Boas 1904:243). This not only reshaped current thinking with respect to the nature of culture itself but also suggested fascinating possibilities for music as a vehicle for interpreting cultural attitudes and symbols. In a few cases the results were spectacular: thus, for example, Edward Sapir's essay on "Song Recitative in Paiute Mythology" (1910) seems to me vastly ahead of its time as a study of musical semiotics or symbolism. More typically, information relating to the meanings and functions of music in culture was only documented and left for future musical specialists to interpret.[13] Thus, while Hornbostel and his German colleagues were focusing on music-sound, Boas and his students were beginning to explore the cultural correlates of music, impelled by concepts that were not so very different from those motivating later scholars of the 1960s and beyond. In retrospect, we are generally inclined to view this as a period dominated by ethnocentric and evolutionistic notions, nor should this be minimized. But it was also a period of extraordinary progress, and failing to recognize the advances that were made—scientifically and humanistically—would perpetuate a modern bias that is all too prevalent in our discipline.

3. The Period of Classic Comparative Studies, 1920–1945

The decline of evolutionism in anthropology led to an emphasis on more empirical studies which sought to explore historical relationships by studying the geographical distribution of various inventions or other cultural traits that were presumed to have spread from one culture to another as a result of borrowing. Among Europeans, the new diffusionism led to broad-based studies focusing on the world-wide distribution of trait-complexes or "culture circles" (*Kulturkreise*). In the United States, the influence of Boas and relatively convenient access to indigenous populations whose cultures were strikingly diverse fostered genres of comparative and historical research that were far more intensive and detailed in character. The central problem of classifying Native American cultures by "culture area" was repeatedly addressed with increasing sophistication in works by Wissler (1926), Kroeber (1939), and various others. But the period also produced a gamut of other studies dealing with related issues such as the diffusion of traits or trait complexes from one tribe or region to another (Wissler 1923), the problem of delineating boundaries between "cultures" conceived as aggregates of disparate traits or "elements" (Driver and Kroeber 1932), and the classification of Indian languages into historically related language families (Sapir 1928).

As would often be the case, developments in anthropological theory established new goals for research in the smaller and more specialized field of musical ethnology, and it was during this period that the discipline we now call ethnomusicology began to be known generally as comparative musicology or *vergleichende Musikwissenschaft*.[14] Working under the influence of European diffusionist concepts, Hornbostel (1923) and Sachs (1929) published some very significant findings concerning the broad characteristics of Native American music as viewed from a global perspective. But despite their analytical sophistication, the Germans would always be viewing Indian music from a vast distance, and their ultimate contribution to the field seems minimal by comparison with that of American scholars during these years. The latter not only rubbed shoulders with the singers they studied, but they were also stimulated by fairly momentous advances made by anthropologists and linguists studying the same Native American cultures as they were.

Would they succeed in developing comparative and historical methods comparable in sophistication to those of Kroeber or Sapir? In retrospect the answer is clearly negative, but considerable progress was made, especially considering the difficulties involved, the relatively naive state of American comparative music theory when the period began, and the fact that individuals with appropriate training and interest in American Indian music were so rare. Many were collecting recordings and related information during these years, but the major developments in American comparative musicology can be sketched through the works of only three individuals: Frances Densmore (1867–1957), Helen Heffron Roberts (1888–1985), and George Herzog (1901–1984).

Of these, Densmore is the most difficult to place historically for various reasons but chiefly due to the fact that her career was so long and productive. She had begun lecturing on Indian music as early as 1895 and first conducted fieldwork among the Ojibwa (Chippewa) of Minnesota in 1901. During the decades which followed Densmore was not only the most energetic collector of Indian music but also established herself as the most prolific author on the subject. In the years between 1910 and her death in 1957, she would produce more than a dozen books and about one hundred shorter articles related to the study of Indian music in one way or another.[15]

In her earliest period Densmore produced short articles of a popular nature and others which seem to have been influenced by the evolutionistic theories of John C. Fillmore.[16] Quite soon, however, she would tend to avoid theoretical generalizations of this sort, and her own approach is best shown in a series of monographs on the music of various particular tribes or groups of tribes. These were mainly published by the Bureau of American Ethnology, and they probably comprise her most important contribution to the literature. Her methods would change somewhat over the years, but the basic style is already established in the two-volume work on Chippewa music (1910–1913) and in another similar study on music of the Teton Sioux (1918).

Typically, Densmore's monographs are ostentatiously data oriented or empirical in character. The study of Teton Sioux music (for example) contains individual notations and analyses for 240 songs, but the musical examples are also juxtaposed with fairly detailed descriptions of the ceremonies or other contexts in which the songs were performed, and Densmore also provides other information on musical instruments, the singers themselves, and the processes through which the recordings were collected and analyzed. As Kroeber notes in a review (1918:448–449), Densmore seems to be juxtaposing her analyses with ethnographic information out of a conviction that the style of the music is influenced by the context or function. This is her method in virtually all the monographs, reflecting an approach in which musical analysis is firmly grounded in observed musical behavior.

Beyond this (descriptive) level of analysis, however, there are also tables through which Densmore attempts to compare various musical styles in a statistical manner. The tables focus mainly on melodic content (especially tonality and intervals used) and on rhythmic features of the music, and they are employed in successive monographs as a uniform methodology for comparing different regional musical styles. Thus, in the Teton Sioux monograph (1918) Densmore's tables compare her 240 musical examples with 360 songs previously published in the study of Chippewa music (1910–1913), and in the next book (1922) she uses similar tables to compare 110 Northern Ute songs with the 600 songs she had analyzed previously. Gradually, she would develop a statistical compilation based on more than 1500 songs, and for Densmore this represented a statistical norm for American Indian music as a whole.

While this method was clearly intended to be "scientific," its value was severely limited by the fact that Densmore's understanding of scales and intervals was essentially based on western music theory.

Some of her tables seem objective enough, as for example when she measures the melodic range of the songs or counts interval progressions upward and downward. But others classify the songs according to western key signatures, number of accidentals, relation of prominent tones to the (presumed) tonic, and other measures which clearly imply European concepts of tonality. This ethnocentric approach was already obsolete before the earliest monograph was written, but Densmore would continue in a similar manner throughout her career. As Rhodes would state decades later, "Densmore has been familiar with the studies of von Hornbostel for many years, but it appears doubtful whether she ever understood or agreed with his principles and point of view" (1952:37). This tendency of hers to ignore the work of others was already commented upon by Kroeber in his review of the Teton Sioux book (1918). Thus while Densmore would go on to publish vast quantities of useful data well into the 1950s, her methods of analysis remained ethnocentric and dated throughout her entire career, and indeed it was these very shortcomings which seem to have inspired the early writings of Helen Roberts.

According to a memorial biography by Frisbie (1989:99), Helen Roberts began her studies of comparative musicology in 1918 at the suggestion of Franz Boas. Her initial orientations—and most probably the influence of Boas—are revealed in a review of the Densmore book on Teton Sioux music (1919). Here, Roberts suggests interviewing the song-makers in order to understand their own ideas relating to form and tonality (1919:523). She also points up the need to revise our notational techniques in order to develop a "universal, concise, and accurate system" through which the pitches, durations, and other aspects of Indian music could be designated in a less biased manner (1919:524). And finally she notes the importance of analyzing the form and structure of songs in order to understand the indigenous logic of the music, retranscribing two of Densmore's examples and discussing the results at length (1919:526–532).

These are issues that Roberts would address in other major publications of the 1920s and early 1930s. Her paper "New Phases in the Study of Primitive Music" (1922) might have had an anachronistic title, but it was also a fairly revolutionary call for more objective and incisive modes of analysis, raising issues she would address later in articles dealing with concepts of tonality in Indian music (1932) and the interesting phenomenon through which vocal styles are "patterned" by the ritual or dance contexts in which they are performed (1933). Echoing the concerns of her colleagues in anthropology, Roberts (1922) also emphasizes the potential of music as a vehicle for comparative and historical interpretations. This—she argues—should be a major goal for future research, and in closing remarks (1922:157–160) Roberts criticizes earlier scholars whose work she considered mainly descriptive in character (Densmore, Fletcher, Gilman, and Curtis) or based on old-fashioned presumptions relating to the evolution of world music (Burton).

Roberts was very active in collecting field recordings during these years, particularly in California and the Southwest, and she also collaborated with anthropologists and linguists who had collected musical materials from other culture areas. Ultimately, this broad experience enabled her to produce the first summary of Native American musical styles by culture area. This work, "Musical Areas in Aboriginal North America" (1936), was assuredly too brief to be comprehensive (41 pages), and a youthful Bruno Nettl was probably justified in calling it "unsystematic" and "impressionistic" (1954:vii). But it remains one of the four or five classics that every serious scholar in the field needs to own. Most of Roberts's generalizations have stood the test of time, and even in its occasionally casual style the monograph raises a variety of issues and problems which have never been resolved and remain highly interesting even for students of Native American music in the 1990s.[17]

For all that Roberts accomplished, comparative research on Indian music reached still greater sophistication in the work of George Herzog. Beginning his studies of *vergleichende Musikwissenschaft* under Hornbostel in Germany, Herzog later came to the United States to study anthropology with Franz Boas in 1925. This ideal background was reflected in his best work, which combined German analytical know-how with research methods shaped by the close-grained descriptive standards of American cultural anthropology. The results are already apparent in his earliest major publication, a study of Yuman Indian music produced in association with Alfred Kroeber (1928). Here, the musical analysis is clearly more systematic than that of earlier American scholars, and Herzog also separates himself from the others by placing considerable emphasis on the vocal quality or "manner of singing" (1928:190–191). Herzog's initial optimism concerning the possibilities of music as a vehicle for comparative and historical research is shown in a brief four-page paper on "Musical Styles in North America" (1930). But in fact this is little more than a tentative statement indicating the diversity of Native American musical styles, and it's intriguing in retrospect that, for all he did accomplish during the 1930s, Herzog never would end up publishing an overview of musical culture areas comparable to that of Helen Roberts (1936).

One possible explanation for this becomes apparent by looking at a few of the classic studies that he did produce. In "Plains Ghost Dance and Great Basin Music" (1935a) Herzog defines the basic style of songs associated with the Ghost Dance and traces its dissemination (along with the dance) from the Great Basin to tribes of the Plains and other areas. His analysis equates the Ghost Dance musical style with that of the Great Basin generally, but by showing that these particular songs also entered the musical repertories of other culture areas—areas whose predominant musical styles were different, Herzog (1935a) shows that historical events tend to prohibit or complicate any straightforward classification of musical culture areas as such. A similar problem with defining musical boundaries emerges from another paper comparing songs of the Pima and various Pueblo tribes (1936a). In this lengthy study, originally his doctoral dissertation, Herzog finds some basic distinctions between the Piman and Pueblo musical styles (1936a:288–308), but he also notes that the "corn-grinding songs" of the Pueblo women are unmistakably Piman in style and—therefore—that the overall picture appears to be complicated by historical interactions between the two groups.

In both of these papers Herzog seems to be wrestling with the problem of defining musical boundaries. While it might be tempting to presume that each tribe or culture area has its own distinctive musical style, Herzog had become concerned with the fact that the musical repertories were actually quite variegated and that the resultant multiplicity of styles presumably owed to historical interactions of a fairly complex nature. The resultant blurring of musical style area boundaries is perhaps most explicitly addressed in a paper entitled "Special Song Types in North American Indian Music" (1935b), where Herzog writes:

> It is not uncommon to find in the possession of a single group a number of styles, represented in different categories of songs; specific styles that do not seem to have any organic reason for co-existing. . . . In order to characterize the music of an ethnic group, it is necessary to separate the strains that are obviously due to the intrusion of foreign elements or to the survival of old forms from those which make up the bulk of the musical lore. The latter will be more apt to range themselves readily into the picture of a prevalent "style" (Herzog 1935b: 24).

Thus, while the well-known musical area summaries by Roberts (1936) and later Nettl (1954) focus mainly on the predominant styles of various regions, Herzog's writings during the 1930s seem to question the very possibility of defining musical areas through any straightforward (synchronic) classification. Similar problems were being discussed and even resolved by anthropologists of the day, but neither Herzog nor his peers ever did manage to develop analogous musicological solutions—concepts incorporating the subtleties of culture area theory as practiced by leading figures like Kroeber or Sapir. Nor indeed have we managed to do so since. As we shall see, some would continue doing related research during the decades which followed, but other approaches were already becoming more fashionable, and during the past twenty-five years (since 1970) there has been very little interest—or progress—in comparative research on Native American music and culture history.

4. Musical Anthropology in the 1950s and 1960s

In the period following World War II, the study of non-western music became increasingly recognized as a scholarly discipline, and the Society for Ethnomusicology was established at Philadelphia in 1955. Leaders in the field might debate for years how the term "ethnomusicology" should be defined, but any apparent confusion on this point owed mainly to the one thing virtually everyone did seem to agree upon: that the new field should encompass a variety of subject matters and methodologies.[18] Accordingly, patterns of research on Indian music became much more diversified during this period, but the new generation of scholars in this particular field did maintain closer ties to anthropology than specialists in other areas of world music, and indeed much of what was accomplished involved musicological studies patterned after trends that were already well established in anthropology by this time. The major areas included (1) continuing comparative research, (2) writings on musical acculturation, (3) culture-and-personality studies (considering music as an indicator of cultural values), and (4) musical ethnographies influenced by anthropological concepts of functionalism and social structure.

Not surprisingly, some of the most important comparative studies toward the beginning of this period were produced by two of Herzog's students, David McAllester (b. 1916) and Bruno Nettl (b. 1930). McAllester would soon go in other directions, but his first major work (originally his dissertation) was a very comprehensive study of songs connected with the (syncretistic) peyote religion in various tribes and culture areas (1949). Following strictly in the tradition of Herzog, McAllester (1949) analyzes some 80 musical examples, defining a prototypic style for peyote music, identifying regional variants, and comparing the basic style with that of Ghost Dance songs as characterized earlier by Herzog (1935a). Herzog's influence is also shown in an historical study of Shawnee music by Bruno Nettl (1953).

In this paper, Nettl identifies four distinct sub-styles or "layers" of Shawnee music and attempts to explain the diversity of styles in terms of historical contacts and migrations.

Taking a somewhat different approach, Gertrude Kurath (1903–1992) published many comparative studies during this period which focused not only on music but also involved similar analyses of dance movements and ceremonial patterns. Most of this work focuses on the eastern areas, the Pueblo tribes, and Indians of Mexico. An early paper on "Local Diversity in Iroquois Music and Dance" (Kurath 1951) actually involves quite distant comparisons of music and dance among Iroquoian-speaking groups ranging from the Seneca of New York State to the Cherokee of Oklahoma. Other articles compare the music of the Plains and Pueblo tribes (Kurath 1969) or examine Plains influences on Pueblo dances (Kurath 1958). Besides these limited comparisons, Kurath also produced some less-detailed surveys that were very broad in scope. For example, her article entitled "Native Choreographic Areas of North America" (1956) is not so comprehensive as the title indicates, but it does trace the distribution of several dance complexes according to ground plan and style of movement.

Most important of all the comparative studies produced during this period was a survey of musical culture areas by Bruno Nettl (1954).[19] Despite its relative brevity (51 pp.), this was—and still remains—the most extensive compilation of comparative data on Indian music ever produced, incorporating analyses of transcriptions from 60 earlier books and many other sources. The emphasis is on technical aspects of the music, and the methods of analysis are basically those of Herzog and Hornbostel (1954:4–6). In characterizing these repertories, Nettl deals with "Herzog's dilemma" (the multiplicity of styles) by focusing on the predominant musical features as determined statistically. And using this approach, he delineates six main areas: (1) Eskimo-Northwest Coast, (2) Great Basin, (3) California-Yuman, (4) Athabascan, (5) Plains-Plateau, and (6) an Eastern area.

What most distinguishes this from the earlier summary by Roberts (1936) is that Nettl (1954) defines musical areas strictly on the basis of stylistic characteristics, rather than relying on existing culture area definitions. Thus, having outlined musical boundaries through independent analysis, Nettl identifies areas which can then be discussed in relation to ethnographic culture areas and the distribution of Indian language families (1954:36–41). In retrospect, it seems clear that Nettl's classic monograph has some serious limitations. In some regions, the data base was still insufficient, and some of Nettl's areas seem untenable in light of later published findings. Perhaps even more importantly, this very concept of synchronic areas seems static and reductive today: it does not adequately account for the historical dimensions of Indian music, nor does it address the complexity of actual repertories or the manner in which musical genres tend to cross cultural boundaries. These are complications that could be resolved—I feel—if ethnomusicologists had sufficient concern or perseverance. But except for Nettl himself (1969), hardly anyone would continue wrestling with these problems in the years which followed, especially after 1970, and thus this monograph (Nettl 1954) has continued to exert a huge influence on scholars and teachers of Indian music, even to this day.[20]

During the 1930s and 1940s, anthropologists had become increasingly interested in acculturation, typically defined as "the effect on cultures of contact with other cultures" (Kroeber 1948:426), and this stimulated a number of studies dealing with related topics in Indian music. Frances Densmore was the first to get involved, publishing one early paper on English-language songs relating to the first World War (1934) and two others dealing with musical influences derived from Christian church activities (1938, 1941). Another early paper by George Herzog (1939) argues that the responsorial singing of various southeastern tribes may possibly be derived from African-American influences. Generally speaking, however, this did not become a major focus of research until the 1950s and 1960s. One leading figure was Gertrude Kurath, who published fairly detailed works on musical acculturation among the northeastern (Algonquian) tribes (1959a, 1959b, 1966) and other studies concerning European influences on Mexican Indian dances (1949, 1956, 1967).

Others, such as Alan Merriam (1955) and Bruno Nettl (1955, 1967), also contributed in this area, but the name most commonly associated with studies of acculturation in Indian music is that of Willard Rhodes (1901–1992). His writings on the subject were actually quite brief—indeed none is more than eight pages in length, but they touch some central issues. The first of major importance (Rhodes 1952) describes missionization and Indian boarding schools as the primary vehicles for musical acculturation; another paper (Rhodes 1960) deals with Christian hymn singing, and one (Rhodes 1963) discusses the use of English words in Indian songs as a general index of acculturation. But in addition to these publications, Rhodes also contributed to our knowledge of post-contact developments in Native American music through the series of sound recordings (and liner notes) which he produced while working with support from the Bureau of Indian Affairs from 1937 to 1951. These contain songs from many different tribes and regions, and much to his credit Rhodes included modern styles of singing in virtually every set. The recordings were subsequently issued as commercial albums by the Library of Congress, and many have been listed in the regional bibliographies which follow.

The anthropological area known as culture-and-personality involves various types of research focusing on the relationship between culture and the individual: these include processes of learning (enculturation), personality development, values or norms, and in general the means through which shared cultural meanings tend to shape personal experience and perceptions. Some of the major figures generally credited with developing anthropological research in these areas were Edward Sapir, Paul Radin, Ruth Benedict, Margaret Mead, and Clyde Kluckhohn. The earliest related publication in our particular field may well have been an essay by George Herzog entitled "Music in the Thinking of the American Indian" (1938). Here, among other things, Herzog discusses the connection of songs with dreams and visions, Indian concepts of how songs are obtained, and ideas about musical values or esthetics.

This early article was mainly intended as an overview for lay readers, but in the period considered here (1950–1970), there began to appear related studies which were far more intensive and systematic. The major pioneer in adapting culture-and-personality concepts to scientific research on Native American music was David McAllester. Writing today, one feels compelled to place the word "scientific" in parentheses, but McAllester's classic monograph on Enemyway music (1954) truly was intended as a scientific investigation of Navajo cultural values. Part One (pp. 3–59) gives a detailed description of the ceremony and also includes comparative musical analyses of 75 songs. Then in Part Two (pp. 63–89), McAllester discusses various categories of values (esthetic, existential, normative, and others) which emerge from a study of Navajo music as social behavior. Accordingly, the Foreword by Clyde Kluckhohn hails the book as a major scientific achievement. This was, in his words, "the first empirical and detailed exploration of the interconnections between esthetic values and the more pervasive standards and value-orientations of a particular culture" (in McAllester 1954:v).

In retrospect, this approach to musical anthropology seems so natural and promising that we might expect many others to have followed immediately in the same direction. But music-oriented scholars with adequate sophistication in anthropology were still very rare indeed, and in fact comparable studies of Indian music as a reflection of cultural values would not become common at all before the 1970s. Two other dual-specialists who did get involved during the period considered here were Alan Merriam and Bruno Nettl. Merriam's writings on Flathead Indian music (1965, 1967) and a set of articles on

Blackfoot music by Nettl (1967a, 1967b, 1968) certainly do address culture-and-personality issues, but it seems to me that these authors (especially Merriam) were also motivated to describe the Indians musical life in a more holistic manner than previous studies; thus, their work also reflects a clear concern with anthropological concepts of functionalism and structuralism.

The concept of functionalism as viewing various aspects of cultural behavior in terms of the contribution each makes to physical, psychological, or sociological well-being was first originated by Bronislaw Malinowski during the 1920s and then elaborated by several others in the decades which followed. Among the most influential of these was A. R. Radcliffe-Brown, who minimized the psychological and "needs-oriented" aspects of Malinowskian functionalism and focused primarily on social structure. In his later (structuralist) model Radcliffe-Brown viewed social structure as roughly analogous to the structure of an organism: both were comprised of separate parts (organs), each of which made its own distinctive contribution to the functioning of the whole system. Thus, for Radcliffe-Brown (and others who followed in this tradition) the important thing was to understand the relation between various elements of the social structure or to determine the function of any given behavior in terms of how it promoted the solidarity or well-being of the society at large.

This brand of social anthropology never would have direct application to ethnomusicology, but it did lead to more systematic studies of the functions of music in culture and the manner in which various aspects of music operate in relation to the functioning of the musical system as a whole. The earliest formal exposition of a related model for music was outlined by Alan Merriam in his textbook entitled *The Anthropology of Music* (1964). Here, Merriam not only discusses various functions of music in culture (pp. 209–227) but also develops a theory for understanding the social and cultural processes through which musical traditions are maintained. As he writes, "The model proposed here is a simple one. . . (which) involves study on three analytic levels—conceptualization about music, behavior in relation to music, and music sound itself" (1964:32). For Merriam, these "levels" were also considered to be dynamically interrelated in circular fashion: concepts and values influence behavior, behavior shapes the product (music sound), and the latter produces audience evaluations which affect future performers. "Thus there is constant feedback from the product to the concepts about music, and this is what accounts both for change and stability in a music system" (Merriam 1964:33).

While the model might seem "simple" as expressed in abstract terms, its realization in practice called for a very systematic approach to musical ethnography, and this was illustrated by Merriam himself in his classic *Ethnomusicology of the Flathead Indians* (1967). In speaking of Merriam's influence on the field of ethnomusicology in general, Timothy Rice has noted that

> The first and most immediate effect of the Merriam model was to increase the amount and prestige of work done on social, physical, and verbal behaviors associated with music. Its second effect was to set in motion a search for ways to relate these behaviors to the "music sound itself" (1987:470).

These assertions also certainly hold true in characterizing Merriam's impact on studies of Native American music in particular, but what's also interesting is that Merriam (1967) not only addresses these concerns but also includes an extensive comparative analysis of Flathead musical styles based on 138 musical transcriptions (pp. 180–315). In this respect, Merriam's book on Flathead Indian music (1967) was actually quite conservative and tended to validate a continuing concern for technical analysis of music-sound. It provided a standard for multi-leveled scholarship which would influence the form and content of theses and dissertations for decades, even though the status and authority of musical ethnography as a "scientific" enterprise would soon be severely challenged.

5. Contemporary Trends (After 1970)

As indicated before, American cultural anthropology and comparative musicology both were established as scholarly disciplines at a time when it was generally assumed that Indian cultures were disappearing and would soon become extinct. The presumption of impending disintegration continued long after the 1890s and fostered a continuing emphasis on "traditional" aspects of culture as viewed from an extrinsic perspective. But as the twentieth century progressed, this approach became increasingly untenable. In many areas the Indian populations actually increased during these decades, and nearly everywhere the indigenous cultures were becoming transformed in distinctly "non-traditional" ways.

Disparities between the academic literature and the actual lives of Indian people on rural reservations or in major metropolitan areas had become painfully obvious by the 1960s, and the absurdities and injustice of old-fashioned anthropology were forcefully exposed through the writings of Vine Deloria (1969) and other Native American activists. By the 1970s, a new and dramatically different orientation began to dominate in academic discourse on American Indians. In one paper which emphasizes the reflexive character of cross-cultural research (the extent to which our interpretations and even the data we collect are shaped by preconceived notions), Edward Bruner describes these differing perspectives as contrasting narratives or stories:

> In the 1930s and 1940s the dominant story constructed about Native American culture change saw the present as disorganized, the past as glorious, and the future as assimilation. Now, however, we have a new narrative: the present is viewed as a resistance movement, the past as exploitation, and the future as ethnic resurgence. . . . The theoretical concepts associated with the outmoded story, such as acculturation and assimilation, are used less frequently and another set of terms has become prominent: exploitation, oppression, colonialism, resistance, liberation, independence, nationalism, tribalism, identity, tradition, and ethnicity—the code words of the 1970s (Bruner 1986:139–140).

The new "narrative" had a major impact on studies of Indian music, and trends which emerged in research of the 1970s and beyond could be characterized as follows:

(1) *Positive validation of Native American musical traditions.* This is evident to some extent in all the recent literature, but particularly in writings intended for students and other non-specialist readers. For example, an article by Isaacs (1972) notes that the differences between Indian music and "Anglo" music derive from contrasting cultural values. While the latter reflects an orientation which Isaacs regards as analytical, highly specialized, inclined to overstatement, and based on feelings of superiority toward the natural environment, Native American music is characterized as relatively more holistic, subtle, and based on feelings of harmony with nature. This sort of advocacy was rare in earlier writings, but the tradition is hardly new. Natalie Burlin (1907) was among the first to describe Indian music in very positive terms, and this has been a continuing theme in more detailed studies by David McAllester stretching back to the 1950s.[21]

(2) *Increased concern with ethical issues in research and involvement in repatriation projects and other public sector activities.* In the years after 1970, researchers became increasingly aware that their work was potentially intrusive and offensive to members of the Indian communities they studied. Issues such as the proper handling of sacred (or other sensitive) materials, the necessity of obtaining permissions for certain types of research, and other related matters would often be discussed in graduate seminars and at scholarly meetings from this time forward, and the National Endowment for the

Humanities produced a Code of Ethics for research relating to Native American peoples during the late 1970s. Additionally, scholars have sought to improve relationships with Indian people by getting involved in projects which address their concerns and interests. For example, some have worked to obtain sound recordings from museums so that copies could be returned to the communities in which they were originally collected.[22] Ethnomusicologists and folklorists have also become active in organizing conferences, festivals, and other programs intended to educate the public with respect to Native American traditional arts and related issues.

(3) *Studies aimed at revising the historical assumptions of earlier traditional anthropology and ethnomusicology.* For many modern scholars, the most offensive presumption of earlier academic studies is the idea that post-contact developments in Native American music represent instances of acculturation, assimilation, or cultural deterioration and as such are somehow less "traditional" than aboriginal practices. This tends to impugn the identity of modern Indian people, especially because music and dance have become so important as vehicles for expressing cultural survival in the modern social setting. Accordingly, the entire post-contact history of Native American music is now being reconceived in a manner consistent with Bruner's "new narrative" quoted above (p. 29). This has many permutations and influences nearly every writer's work, but the trend is particularly notable in recent studies of pan-Indian (or intertribal) music and dance[23], musical revitalization movements[24], and writings which emphasize the indigenous elements in Christian-influenced singing.[25] Leading researchers such as Charlotte Heth (1984, 1992) and David McAllester (1984) have also argued that our concept of Native American music should be expanded to include various forms of popular music and art music produced by Indian artists, but these remain areas in which little has been published.

(4) *Emphasis in recent publications on emic (Native American) perspectives as versus etic (technical or comparative) analyses of music-sound* . This important trend is shown in recent books such as *Yaqui Deer Songs* (Evers and Molina 1987), *Songs of Indian Territory* (Smyth 1989), and *Native American Dance: Ceremonies and Social Traditions* (Heth 1992). All three are based on some sort of collaboration between Native American and non-Indian authors; all discuss concepts, feelings, and historical issues relating to music from the culture-bearer's perspective; and none of the three include musical notations or technical analysis of music-sound or dance movements. Instead, the first two mentioned above were published with cassette tapes containing examples of the music, and Heth (1992) is illustrated

throughout with superb color photographs. These not only show the dances, but also the people enjoying their dances, thus giving readers a sense of being in contact with the Native American experience. There is not much doubt that musical transcriptions and other technical information would have made these books more valuable for ethnomusicologists. But it is equally clear that they were intended for a broader audience and conceived from a perspective in which extrinsic analysis might seem awkward and irrelevant, if not downright offensive. In one paper which does contain a good deal of analysis (Bahr, Giff, and Haefer 1978), the authors refrain from including musical notations because they felt that members of the (Piman) Indian community might object if the songs were made accessible in this manner.

(5) *Biographical research focusing on the lives, achievements, and personal viewpoints of Indian singers and ceremonialists.* In seeking to better express the culture-bearer's perspective, some have produced biographies (or autobiographies) and other writings which focus on the lives, perceptions, and accomplishments of Indian persons with whom they worked. The earliest strictly ethnomusicological study in this genre was a brief biography of a Blackfoot singer by Nettl (1968). More extensive and influential was the book *Navajo Blessingway Singer: Frank Mitchell 1881–1967*, which appeared in 1978. This is narrated in the first person throughout, and the academic researchers (Charlotte Frisbie and David McAllester) serve mainly as editors. In this volume the reader gets a very close look at Frank Mitchell and the events in his life, while musicological or sociological interpretations are minimal. Another study which strives to present the personal perspective of an Indian person is *The Ojibwa Drum: Its History and Construction* by Thomas Vennum, Jr. (1982). Here, the writer quotes often and at length from his Ojibwa friend (William Bineshi Baker, Sr.), and these comments become a foundation on which Vennum erects an impressive study of Ojibwa ethnohistory in relation to the drum. Another important author in this genre has been Judith Vander. Her books *Ghost Dance Songs and Religion of a Wind River Shoshone Woman* (1986) and *Songprints: The Musical Experience of Five Shoshone Women* (1988) both frame their interpretations from a basically biographical perspective, but—interestingly—Vander manages to include numerous musical notations and technical analyses, thus showing a continuing concern with conventional theory and method.

And finally, (6) *The emergence of scholars who are themselves of Native American descent and teach or write from the perspective of "insiders."* The bibliographies which follow contain many recent writings by Native American individuals whose educational backgrounds and personal connections to the musical traditions they describe are very diverse. In some cases, these are non-academic culture-bearers—participants themselves in the music and cultural activities of their own local communities—whose position is more or less analogous to the "informant" of earlier periods. In other instances they are local educators with relatively close and enduring community involvements, and toward the opposite extreme they are university-educated scholars whose research methods and community connections (in terms of life-experience) are not so very different from those of non-Indian researchers. In one paper on the subject, Heth (1982) asserts that researchers of Native American descent have advantages over non-Indians, even when studying tribes other than their own. In the whole this is probably true, particularly in research on pan-Indian music or other more modern developments. But it's also important to bear in mind that the concept of the "insider" is relative: many can claim to be insiders when addressing non-Indian listeners at an academic meeting, but those who can claim to represent community viewpoints on a rural reservation are very rare indeed. In any case, besides the question of research advantages or special insights which the insider may have, there is also the (generally unspoken) issue of racial prerogative—the widespread presumption that persons of Indian descent (however fractional), simply have more authority to speak or write about Indian music than non-Indians. This is perhaps the ultimate culmination of the "resistance" narrative, and as such it reflects political and social issues beyond the scope of the present essay.

New Historical Studies

The other major development in contemporary writings on Native American music is an increased emphasis on historical research, particularly ethnohistorical studies which consider the results of contemporary (or relatively recent) fieldwork in relation to archival data and/or other information from earlier published sources. The interesting results which can be produced using this method are shown in articles such as "A History of Ojibwa Song Form" (1980) and "The Changing Role of Women in Ojibwa Music History" (1989) by Thomas Vennum Jr. In both papers Vennum compares recent musical practices with evidence documented by Densmore and others so as to describe historical transformations in Ojibwa music over a span of many generations. The ever-productive Bruno Nettl has also been active in this area, producing a record album containing historical recordings of Blackfoot Indian music spanning the years from 1897 to 1966 (1979) and also incorporating much historical data in his book *Blackfoot Musical Thought: Comparative Perspectives* (1989).

In fact—though I've singled out Vennum and Nettl, the number of recent studies in the area of "musical ethnohistory" is very great indeed. Among the most prominent contributors to the genre (in alphabetical order) are Nicole Beaudry, Charles Boilés, Beverley (Diamond) Cavanagh, David Draper, Charlotte Frisbie, Linda Goodman, Judith Gray, Orin Hatton, Michael Hauser, Marcia Herndon, James Howard (deceased, 1982), Thomas Johnston (deceased, 1994), Elaine Keillor, Victoria Levine, Maija Lutz, Craig Mishler, Richard Payne, William Powers, and Robert Stevenson.

Most important in laying the foundations for future historical studies have been projects to organize and preserve the major collections of cylinder recordings in the United States. These have resulted in published catalogues of Native American recordings at the Library of Congress (Federal Cylinder Project 1984), the Archives of Traditional Music at Indiana University (Lee 1979; Seeger and Spear 1987), and at Robert Lowie (now Phoebe Hearst) Museum of Anthropology at the University of California, Berkeley (Keeling 1991). As mentioned before, these collections include an estimated 17,000 cylinders collected in Indian communities from 1890 to 1940, and thus—studied in conjunction with earlier publications and manuscripts—they provide unique opportunities for expanding our knowledge in many areas of Native American music that are currently not well known (at least by ethnomusicologists).

The possibilities are illustrated by recent studies of Indian music in California. Not so long ago, this was regarded as a neglected field of research (Wallace 1978:648) and one of the least-known areas in all of Native American music (Vennum 1979:349). In fact, however, archival and bibliographic research conducted during the 1980s showed that literally thousands of cylinder recordings had been collected among Indians of this area and that there was an extensive body of published sources and manuscripts providing song-texts, translations, and other information concerning the cultural contexts and functions of music. For many tribes or localities, the music itself had been notated and analyzed in some detail, so that the on-going process of coming to understand California as a musical culture area has relied not so much on new field research (though this was and continues to be important) but is largely an effort to locate existing data in anthropological sources and integrate these findings into the literature of ethnomusicology. In my own recent studies of Yurok and Hupa music, much of the "new" information was actually collected between 1900 and 1927.

The motivation behind this trend toward ethnohistorical research cannot be explained in terms of theory. Like the earlier sources it relies upon, much of new literature in this genre tends to be data oriented and anthropology based, and some have undoubtedly been attracted out of a continuing concern with anthropological concepts and issues. Others—probably the majority—would reject this interpretation and point out the extent to which modern historical works tend to be critical or even revisionary in character. In fact the new historical studies encompass a variety of philosophical and theoretical positions. More than anything else, they seem to be inspired mainly by an increased awareness of the wealth of data which exists—this and perhaps also by a general belief among non-Indian scholars that they can make important contributions in historical research even though they speak with less authority on contemporary Native American viewpoints.

Comments on Content and Format

The present volume describes 1,497 sources on North American Indian and Eskimo music which were published or produced during the years from 1535 to 1995. The number of entries in each of the regional bibliographies is as follows: General or Inter-Regional (236), Arctic and Sub-Arctic (177), Northwest Coast (106), California (118), Great Basin and Plateau (78), Southwest (255), Plains (174), Northeast and Great Lakes (133), Southeast (77), and Mexico (143). The primary emphasis is on published writings—books and articles or reviews which have appeared in scholarly journals or other periodicals, but unpublished doctoral dissertations and even master's theses are occasionally included, particularly if they contain information on subjects that are not well documented in published sources. As far as possible—or practical, every entry has been annotated so as to describe the contents and/or the principal thesis or argument of the source in question. These annotations generally indicate whether musical notations or technical analyses are provided, and where relevant I have also given information concerning the dates and locations of the original fieldwork. In most cases my annotations are based on direct inspection of the sources themselves, but much information was gotten from the bibliography by Joseph Hickerson (1961) and other secondary sources such as book or record reviews.

As noted previously, the bibliographic approach taken here is somewhat different from that used by Hickerson (1961), but the latter was so important as a foundation that it seems convenient to discuss the content and format of the present volume by comparison. Hickerson's goal was to produce a very comprehensive bibliography (including all the sources he could obtain) and then to analyze the literature by type and subject matter.[26] The approach I have used is somewhat selective, particularly with respect to early sources, writings of a popular nature, collections of "arranged" or "adapted" melodies, and book reviews.

I have included many of the pre-twentieth century writings listed in Hickerson (1961)—and others not found there, but some listed by Hickerson have been excluded on the grounds that they are so difficult to obtain or because the musical references they contain were considered relatively marginal. Some early sources are given in each of the regional bibliographies, but specialists should also consult Hickerson (1961), and Stevenson (1973a, 1973b) for further information in this area. Popular writings and collections of "arranged" melodies were also often omitted in order to concentrate on sources that modern researchers were likely to find most useful. Finally, with respect to book reviews, I have excluded many of these and mainly sought to list reviews which either (a) express strong positions on theory or method in the book under review, (b) provide additional information on subject matter, or (c) seem important for other reasons.

In other respects, the present volume is more inclusive and/or intended to offer some practical advantages. Specific departures from the bibliographic method used by Hickerson (1961) are as follows:

(1) Foreign-language publications. Wherever possible, the present volume lists English-language translations rather than the corresponding original sources in Spanish, French, German, Danish, or Russian. The rationale for this is not only that English is more convenient for most readers, but also that many of the foreign volumes are difficult to obtain in the United States. In any case, many foreign titles have been included, particularly in the bibliography on Indian music of Mexico.

(2) Ethnographic or historical works containing non-musical information. Generally speaking, Hickerson (1961) limited himself to sources on music itself, concepts relating to music, and functions of music in culture. Modern research in ethnomusicology tends to broader interpretations, and thus the present volume lists many sources on dance, ritual, and other aspects of culture or religion, even though the latter might have no specific information on music as such. The method for selecting non-musical entries was not particularly systematic: these are simply sources which seemed useful and interesting in this researcher's opinion.

(3) Commercial recordings. This was an area for difficult decisions. Hickerson (1961) does not list commercial record albums,

stating that he hoped to include them in a later, published version but that the comprehensive coverage he envisioned did not seem practical for the original bibliography (1961: iii). At this point in time, the number of commercial recordings is vastly greater than in 1960— especially because any modern discography would need to include popular music and other genres not available then, and adequate coverage seems impossible except in a volume dedicated specifically to recordings. Still, I could not resist including some information in this area because commercial recordings have so much practical value for research and teaching. In selecting recordings for inclusion, I have focused mainly on "classics" which contain good liner notes and are readily available, but others are also listed. In many cases, I have listed record reviews rather than the recordings themselves, as these were easier to obtain and contain useful information in their own right. While coverage is admittedly quite limited, the present volume lists 73 commercial recordings and 33 record reviews or review essays.

(4) Coverage of Mexican Indian music. Anthropologists and others in the United States have commonly limited their coverage of North American Indians to tribes north of the border with Mexico, and ethnomusicologists such as Nettl (1954) and Hickerson (1961) followed in this practice. Certainly there are practical reasons for this, but from a comparative perspective the approach seems untenable because Indian cultures of Mexico obviously have great importance in the overall scheme of Native American music and culture history. The present volume includes a section on Mexico (and Guatemala) while excluding more southerly areas of Mesoamerica on the grounds that their cultural relationship to northern cultures seems less evident. I enlisted the assistance of Helena Simonett in preparing the Mexican bibliography, as she is fluent in Spanish and German and has research experience in Mexico.

(5) Arrangement by culture area. Finally, the present volume differs from Hickerson's bibliography (1961) because the latter provides one continuous list of references while I felt that it would be more convenient for users if the sources were arranged in separate bibliographies by culture area. The difficulties of culture area classification are well known but still merit some brief comments.

To begin with, the areas themselves are abstract entities, and various theorists[27] have defined them with different considerations in mind. Some groups such as the Ojibwa (for example) cover such extensive territories that they could arguably be assigned to as many as three areas (Sub-Arctic, Plains, or Northeast) in the scheme I have employed. Other groups occupy smaller territories but are situated on the boundaries between areas and are difficult to classify on cultural grounds.[28] In other cases the situation is complicated by migrations or cultural transformations which occurred during the pre-contact period or shortly after contact with whites.[29] Finally, even more problematic is the influence of historical developments which have occurred in the period well after contact. The removal of numerous tribes to Indian Territory (Oklahoma) during the 1830s (and later), the emergence of Pan-Indian trends in twentieth century culture—these and other historical developments greatly undermine the validity of any synchronic classification.

In the present volume, culture area classifications are not intended to be systematic but rather only a practical convenience. Readers who are interested in sources relating to any particular tribe or region should also consult the General or Inter-Regional bibliography which follows. As you will see, this became a handy repository for all sorts of books, articles, and recordings which were hard to place elsewhere for one reason or another.

References Cited

Note: Most of the references cited in the Introduction are listed in the General or Inter-Regional bibliography. Others are listed here below, even though many can also found in the regional bibliographies.

Abraham, Otto, and Erich M. von Hornbostel

1906   Phonographierte Indianermelodien aus Britisch-Columbia. Pp. 447–474 in *Boas Anniversary Volume: Anthropological Papers written in Honor of Franz Boas*. New York: Stechert and Co.

Bahr, Donald M., Joseph Giff, and Manuel Havier

1979   Piman Songs on Hunting. *Ethnomusicology* 23(2): 245–296.

Beaudry, Nicole

1992   The Language of Dreams: Songs of the Dene Indians (Canada). Pp. 72–90 in *Music and Spiritual Power among the Indians of North America* edited by Richard Keeling. *World of Music* 92(2). Berlin: International Institute for Traditional Music.

Boas, Franz

1888   *The Central Eskimo.* Annual Report of the Bureau of American Ethnology (1884–1885), vol. 6, pp. 399–669. Washington: Smithsonian Institution.

1894   Review of *A Study of Omaha Music* by Alice C. Fletcher and John C. Fillmore. *Journal of American Folklore* 7:169–171.

(1896)   The Limitations of the Comparative Method in Anthropology. Reprint. Pp. 271–304 in *Race, Language, and Culture* by Franz Boas. New York: Macmillan, 1940.

Bruner, Edward M.

1986   Ethnography as Narrative. pp. 139–155 in *The Anthropology of Experience* edited by Victor Turner and Edward Bruner. Urbana and Chicago: University of Illinois Press.

Deloria, Vine

1969   *Custer Died for Your Sins.* New York: Macmillan.

Densmore, Frances

1905   The Music of the American Indian. *Overland Monthly* (Series 2) 45:230–234.

1906   A Plea for the Indian Harmonization of all Indian Songs. *Indian School Journal* 6(4): 14–15.

1909   Scale Formation in Primitive Music. *American Anthropologist* 11:1–12.

1910–1913   *Chippewa Music.* 2 vols. Bureau of American Ethnology Bulletin nos. 45 and 53.

1918   *Teton Sioux Music.* Bureau of American Ethnology Bulletin (Anthropological Papers) no. 61.

1922   *Northern Ute Music.* Bureau of American Ethnology Bulletin no. 75.

Draper, David E.

1982   Abba Isht Tuluwa: The Christian Hymns of the Mississippi Choctaw. *American Indian Culture and Research Journal* 6(1): 43–62.

Driver, Harold E.

1969   *Indians of North America.* Second ed. Chicago:
        University of Chicago Press.

Driver, Harold E., and Alfred Kroeber

1932   Quantitative Expressions of Cultural Relationships.
        *University of California Publications in American
        Archeology and Ethnology* 31(4): 211–256.

Drucker, Philip

1965   *Cultures of the North Pacific Coast.* San Francisco:
        Chandler Publishing.

Eells, Myron

1879   Indian Music. *American Antiquarian* 1:249–253.

Fillmore, John Comfort

1893–1894   Review of "The Zuni Music, as Translated by Mr.
            Benjamin Ives Gilman" (1891). *Music* 5:39–46.

Frisbie, Charlotte (Johnson)

1989   In Memoriam, Helen Heffron Roberts (1888–1985).
        Ethnomusicology 33(1): 97–112.

Frisbie, Charlotte, and David P. McAllester, Editors

1978   *Navajo Blessingway Singer: Frank Mitchell, 1881–
        1967.* Tucson: University of Arizona Press.

Gilman, Benjamin Ives

1891   Zuni Melodies. *Journal of American Ethnology and
        Archaeology* 1:65–91.
1908   Hopi Songs. *Journal of American Ethnology and
        Archaeology* 5:1–226.

Herzog, George

1928   The Yuman Musical Style. *Journal of American
        Folklore* 41(160): 183–231.

1936a	A Comparison of Pueblo and Pima Musical Styles. *Journal of American Folklore* 49:283–417.
1936b	*Research in Primitive and Folk Music in the United States.* American Council of Learned Societies, no. 24.

Howard, James H.

1951	Notes on the Dakota Grass Dance. *Southwestern Journal of Anthropology* 7:82–85.
1976	The Plains Gourd Dance as a Revitalization Movement. *American Ethnologist* 3(2): 243–260.

Keeling, Richard

1984a	Returning California Indian Music to Its Sources. *Phonographic Bulletin* 38:44–53.
1984b	Tribal Music and Cultural Survival. Pp. 165–176 in *Sharing a Heritage: American Indian Arts* edited by Charlotte Heth and Michael Swarm. Contemporary American Indian Issues 5. Los Angeles: American Indian Studies Center, UCLA.
1991	*A Guide to Early Field Recordings (1900–1949) at the Lowie Museum of Anthropology.* Berkeley and Los Angeles: University of California Press.

Kroeber, Alfred L.

1918	Review of *Teton Sioux Music* by Frances Densmore. *American Anthropologist* 20:446–450.
1925	*Handbook of the Indians of California.* Bureau of American Ethnology Bulletin 78. Washington.
1936	Culture Element Distributions III: Area and Climax. *University of California Publications in American Archeology and Ethnology* 37(3): 101–116. Berkeley.
1939	Cultural and Natural Areas of Native North America. *University of California Publications in American Archeology and Ethnology,* No. 38.
1948	*Anthropology.* Revised edition. New York: Harcourt.

Kurath, Gertrude Prokosch

1949	Mexican Moriscas: A Problem in Dance Acculturation. *Journal of American Folklore* 62(244): 87–106.

1956	Dance Rituals of Mid-Europe and Middle America. *Journal of American Folklore* 69(673): 286–298.
1959a	Blackrobe and Shaman: The Christianization of the Michigan Algonquians. *Papers of the Michigan Academy of Sciences, Arts, and Letters* 44:209–215.
1959b	Menomini Indian Dance Songs in a Changing Culture. *Midwest Folklore* 9 (1): 31–38.
1966	*Michigan Indian Festivals.* Ann Arbor: Ann Arbor Publishers.
1967	La Danza de los matachines entre los indios y los mestizos. *Revista Mexicana de Estudios Antropológicos* 21:261–285. Mexico City.

Lach, Robert

| 1924 | *Die vergleichende Musikwissenschaft, ihre Methoden und Probleme.* Vienna: Akademie der Wissenschaften. |

Levine, Victoria Lindsay

| 1993 | Musical Revitalization among the Choctaw. *American Music* 11(4): 391–411. |

McAllester, David Park

| 1949 | *Peyote Music.* Viking Fund Publications in Anthropology no. 13. New York: Viking Fund. |
| 1954 | *Enemyway Music: A Study of Social and Esthetic Values as Seen in Navajo Music.* Papers of the Peabody Museum of American Archaeology and Ethnology, Harvard University, vol. 41, no. 3. |

Mead, Margaret

| 1959 | Apprenticeship Under Boas. Pp. 29–45 in *The Anthropology of Franz Boas* edited by Walter Goldschmidt. American Anthropological Association Memoir no. 87. Washington. |

Merriam, Alan P.

| 1964 | *The Anthropology of Music.* Evanston, Illinois: Northwestern University Press. |

1965   The Importance of Song in the Flathead Indian Vision Quest. *Ethnomusicology* 9(2): 91–99.

1967   *Ethnomusicology of the Flathead Indians.* Viking Fund Publications in Anthropology, no. 44. Chicago: Aldine Publishing Co.

Nettl, Bruno

1953   The Shawnee Musical Style: Historical Perspective in Primitive Music. *Southwestern Journal of Anthropology* 9:277–285.

1964   *Theory and Method in Ethnomusicology.* London: Free Press of Glencoe (Collier-Macmillan).

1967a   Blackfoot Music in Browning, 1965: Functions and Attitudes. Pp. 593–598 in *Festschrift für Walter Wiora zum 30 Dezember 1966.* Edited by Ludwig Finscher and Christoph-Hellmut Mahling. Kassel: Bärenreiter.

1967b   Studies in Blackfoot Musical Culture, Part II: Musical Life of the Montana Blackfoot, 1966. *Ethnomusicology* 11(3): 293–309.

1968   Biography of a Blackfoot Indian Singer. *Musical Quarterly* 54(2): 199–207 (April).

1973   Comparison and Comparative Method in Ethnomusicology. *Yearbook for Inter-American Music Research* 9:148–161.

1979   (Recording and liner notes) "An Historical Album of Blackfoot Indian Music." Ethnic Folkways (FE 34001).

1989   *Blackfoot Musical Thought: Comparative Perspectives.* Kent, Ohio: Kent State University Press.

Powers, Stephen

(1877)   *Tribes of California.* Contributions to North American Ethnology 3. Washington: U.S. Geographical and Geological Survey of the Rocky Mountain Region. Reprinted by University of California Press (Berkeley and Los Angeles, 1976).

Roberts, Helen Heffron

1919   Review of *Teton Sioux Music* by Frances Densmore (1918). *Journal of American Folklore* 32:523–535.

Sapir, Edward

1910   Song Recitative in Paiute Mythology. *Journal of American Folklore* 23(89): 455–472.

1928   Central and North American Languages. *Encyclopaedia Britannica* (14th edition). Vol. 5, pp. 138–141.

Stocking, George W.

1965   From Physics to Ethnology: Franz Boas' Arctic Expedition as a Problem in the Historiography of the Behavioral Sciences. *Journal of the History of the Behavioral Sciences* 1(1): 53–66.

Stumpf, Carl

1886   Leider der Bellakula-Indianer. Vierteljahrsschrift für Musikwissenschaft 2:405–426. Reprint. Pp. 87–103 in *Adhandlungen zur vergleichenden Musikwissenschaft*. Vol. 1 of *Sämmelbande für vergleichende Musikwissenschaft* edited by Carl Stumpf and Erich M. Von Hornbostel. Munich, 1922.

Vander, Judith

1986   *Ghost Dance Songs and Religion of a Wind River Shoshone Woman*. Monograph Series in Ethnomusicology, no. 4. Los Angeles: Program in Ethnomusicology, Department of Music, University of California, Los Angeles.

1988   *Songprints: The Musical Experience of Five Shoshone Women*. Urbana: University of Illinois Press.

Vennum, Thomas, Jr.

1979   Record review of "Songs of Love, Luck, Animals, and Magic: Music of the Yurok and Tolowa Indians." Produced by Charlotte Heth (New World Records NW 297). *Ethnomusicology* 23(2) 349–352.

1980   A History of Ojibwa Song Form. *Selected Reports in Ethnomusicology* 3(2): 43–75. Los Angeles: Program in Ethnomusicology, Department of Music, UCLA.

1982   *The Ojibwa Dance Drum: Its History and Construction.* Smithsonian Folklife Studies no. 2. Washington: Smithsonian Institution.

1989   The Changing Role of Women in Ojibwa Music History. Pp. 13–21 in *Women in North American Indian Music* edited by Richard Keeling. Ann Arbor: Society for Ethnomusicology.

Wallace, William J.

1978   Music and Musical Instruments. Pp. 642–648 in *Handbook of North American Indians, Volume Eight: California* edited by Robert F. Heizer. Washington: Smithsonian Institution.

Wissler, Clark

1923   *Man and Culture.* New York: Thomas Crowell.

1926   *The Relation of Nature to Man in Aboriginal America.* New York: Oxford University Press.

Notes

[1] An English translation is listed in the Northeast bibliography.

[2] This contains brief descriptions and notations of Micmac and Huron songs. An English translation of the 3-volume work (1907–1914) is listed in the Northeast bibliography.

[3] According to Stevenson (1973a:1), this contains a description and drawing of a musical instrument similar to the Aztec *teponaztli* which was observed by Fernández on the island of Hispaniola in 1515. Though more properly belonging to the Circum-Caribbean culture area, the source is listed here in the bibliography focusing on Indian music of Mexico.

[4] Stevenson (1973a:5) is here quoting from pp. 575–576 of *The Florida of the Inca* as translated and edited by John Grier Varner and Jeanette Johnson Varner

(Austin: University of Texas Press, 1951). The original edition of Vega's *La Florida del Ynca* was published by Pedro Crasbeeck of Lisbon in 1605.

[5] This is mentioned by Stevenson (1973b:399), who supports his argument by quoting similar comments made by Frances Densmore in a lecture delivered in 1899.

[6] For example, Rhodes (1952:33) and Hickerson (1961:11) both identify Baker (1882) as the earliest "serious" study in the field.

[7] This conservative estimate is based on the number of cylinders in only three of the largest collections. Cylinders at the Library of Congress were estimated at "approximately seven thousand" in a published inventory by Brady et al. (1984:29), Seeger and Spear (1987:2) give 6,985 as the total number of cylinder originals at Indiana University Archives of Traditional Music, and the collection at Phoebe Hearst (previously Lowie) Museum of Anthropology includes 2,713 cylinders (Keeling 1991:xi). These collections each include cylinders from other parts of the world, but they focus mainly on North America, and the total for cylinders collected in Indian communities would be greatly augmented if other collections were also considered.

[8] The figure is calculated from an inventory by Brady et al. (1984:42–58).

[9] Boas typically identified his musical collaborators, and the lack of any acknowledgement suggests that it was he who transcribed and analyzed 25 musical examples that are found in his ethnography of the Central Eskimo (1888). Sapir also relied on others (including his father, Jacob Sapir) for musicological assistance, but he explicitly takes credit for the 10 musical transcriptions in his paper on "Song Recitative in Paiute Mythology" (1910:460).

[10] The problem is perhaps most succinctly stated by George Herzog in his comparative study of the Pueblo and Pima musical styles (1936a). As he writes, "The tones themselves are subject to more variation than ours, depending on the musical, textual, and emotional context; especially since instruments with fixed pitches, which would standardize musical pitch and intonation, do not play an important role. Consequently, in musical transcriptions of such melodies a 'note' does not stand for an objective unit, an ideally constant tone, but for a functional unit, a mere average value around which the variations cluster. The scale schemes appended to the musical examples must be understood in the same way" (Herzog 1936a:286–287).

[11] Among his students at Columbia were (in alphabetical order) Ruth Benedict, Ruth Bunzel, Erna Gunther, Melville Herskovits, E. Adamson Hoebel, Melville Jacobs, Alfred Kroeber, Robert Lowie, Margaret Mead, Paul Radin, Edward Sapir, Frank Speck, Leslie Spier, and Clark Wissler.

[12] Thus he writes in a diary or letter dated December 23, 1883: "Is it not a beautiful custom that these 'savages' suffer all deprivation in common, but in happy times when someone has brought back booty from the hunt, all join in eating and drinking. I often ask myself what advantages our 'good society'

possesses over that of the 'savages.' The more I see of their customs, the more I realize that we have no right to look down on them. Where amongst our people would you find such true hospitality? Here, without the least complaint, people are willing to perform *every* task demanded of them. We have no right to blame them for their forms and superstitions which may seem ridiculous to us. We 'highly educated people' are much worse, relatively speaking. The fear of tradition and old customs is deeply implanted in mankind, and in the same way as it regulates life here, it halts progress for us. I believe it is a difficult struggle for every individual and every people to give up tradition and follow the path to truth. The Eskimo are sitting around me, their mouths filled with raw seal liver (the spot of blood on the back of the paper shows you how I joined in). As a thinking person, for me the most important result of this trip lies in the strengthening of my point of view that the idea of a 'cultured' individual is merely relative and that a person's worth should be judged by his *Herzenbildung* [roughly, 'education of the heart']. This quality is present or absent here among the Eskimo, just as among us. All that man can do for humanity is to further the *truth*, whether it be sweet or bitter. Such a man may truly say that he has not lived in vain" (quoted by Stocking: 1965:61).

[13] This is shown (for example) by various comments in which Alfred Kroeber agonizes over his inability to understand the meaning or significance of Yurok Indian music as an indicator of cultural moods and attitudes. In one place (Kroeber 1925:95–96) he outlines the difficulties involved—the prejudices that we hold as a result of our own cultural conditioning and the inadequacy of western staff notations as a tool for analysis, then he goes on to express his own conviction that Yurok songs (and those of their immediate neighbors) are clearly unique in character from those of other California tribes, even though he himself remains at a loss to explain exactly how or why. He mentions "a few external traits" but basically admits that he does not have adequate musical training himself. Finally, Kroeber calls upon future music specialists to get involved, calling this a "rich and unexplored field that lies cultivable for him with sympathy, patience, and a catholic musical sense" (1925:96). Elsewhere, he is even more explicit in asserting that Yurok music reflects "a deliberate endeavor to express a mood or feeling tone" that future analysis would surely disclose (Kroeber 1936:114).

[14] As Bruno Nettl (1973:148) notes, the term was applied not only to studies that were comparative in the strict sense but rather to virtually any type of research focusing on tribal music, folk music, or art music of the non-western world. Nettl (1973:159) also suggests that the term was first employed in Germany, identifying its earliest published appearance in the title of a theoretical treatise by Robert Lach (1924) and noting its later prominence in periodicals such as the *Sammelbände für vergleichende Musikwissenschaft* and *Zeitschrift für vergleichende Musikwissenschaft*.

[15] Hickerson lists 16 monographs or other separate volumes and 101 articles published by Densmore (1961:179–201). Densmore's articles include many

titles of a popular nature and others which seem to duplicate the same subject matter; many of these are not listed in the bibliographies which follow here.

[16] See for example Densmore (1905, 1906, and 1909).

[17] Among the many fascinating subjects which Roberts comments upon in passing are multi-part vocal styles (1936:6–8), music based on simultaneous contrasting meters (1936:11), isorhythm (1936:11), the possible discrimination of distinct musical styles associated with the Hokan and Shoshonean language families (1936:32–33), and musical influences of the Mexican civilizations on northerly tribes of the Southwest, Plains, and Southeast culture areas (1936:34 and 38).

[18] For further discussion on this point see (for example) the opening chapter in Bruno Nettl's textbook on *Theory and Method in Ethnomusicology* (1964:1–26).

[19] This monograph (*North American Indian Musical Styles*) was originally produced as Nettl's doctoral dissertation (Indiana University) and was first published as a series in the *Journal of American Folklore*.

[20] One other approach that needs to be mentioned is the cantometrics system developed by Alan Lomax. Cantometrics is a comparative methodology which rates various world music styles according to 36 measures or parameters, then analyzes the results using statistical methods more elaborate than those of Nettl (1954). The major source (Lomax 1968) contains comparative findings on Native American and Arctic-Siberian music which I consider highly significant, even though Lomax's sampling procedures seem inadequate and other aspects of the methodology strike me as being overly simplistic. Generally speaking, other Indian music specialists seem to have responded even more negatively to cantometrics, presumably for similar reasons, and its impact in this particular area has been quite limited. The results of cantometrics research on Native American music are also discussed in greater detail in a dissertation by Erickson (1969).

[21] Writings by McAllester in this vein are too numerous to explore here in depth. They include various titles in the General bibliography (1977, 1980, 1984, 1988) and others listed in the Southwest bibliography (1954, 1960, 1980a, 1980b, 1980c).

[22] Charlotte Heth and Richard Keeling initiated one such project in northwestern California as early as 1978, and Keeling conducted a statewide California Indian Music Project from 1983 to 1986. The Federal Cylinder Project, conducted by various members of the staff at the American Folklife Center (Library of Congress) and the Smithsonian Institution, has involved dissemination of recordings in many different regions and communities. These projects are described in Federal Cylinder Project (1984), Gray (1989), and Keeling (1984a, 1984b).

[23] Two leaders in research on Pan-Indian music have been the late James Howard (1951, 1983) and Willam Powers (1960, 1961a, 1961b, 1961c, 1994, and other writings lisited in the Plains bibliography). Other sources include Huenemann (1978), Whitehorse (1988), and Zotigh (1991).

[24] For example, see Heth (1984), Howard (1976), Levine (1993), or Wapp (1984).

[25] For example, see Draper (1982) on Choctaw hymns or Beaudry (1992) on Christian-influenced music among Dene (Athabascan) Indians of western Canada.

[26] In the Preface, Hickerson states that the bibliography focuses on North American Indian and Eskimo music, then writes: "All works are included which minimally include a description, a discussion, an analysis or an example of the rhythm, melody, structure, vocal technique or function of Indian music, whether in general or for a specific tribe or area. Any omissions are purely unintentional" (1961: i). Besides the list of sources themselves, Hickerson provides an extensive analysis of the literature by type or genre and subject matter (1961: 50–110). He also includes a history of research (1961: 2–48) and indices by tribe and culture area (1961: 381–463).

[27] For example, Wissler (1926), Kroeber (1939), and Driver (1969).

[28] For example, I have always felt that the Yurok (of northwestern California) were best viewed as a California tribe, but Drucker (1965) and others have classified them as belonging to the Northwest Coast culture area because of the importance of wealth in Yurok society, the presence of a First Salmon ceremony, and for other reasons.

[29] For example, the Shoshones are generally recognized as a Great Basin tribe, but some Shoshone groups migrated onto the Plains as early as the sixteenth century and were among the first groups on the northern Plains to acquire the horse. Indeed, the subsequent development of prototypic Plains culture during the eighteenth and nineteenth centuries was itself a phenomenon based largely on the acquisition of the horse, which was first introduced by the Spanish during the 1500s.

NORTH AMERICAN INDIAN MUSIC

I. General or Inter-Regional

Asch, Michael I., Compiler and editor

1973   (Recording and liner notes) "An Anthology of North American Indian and Eskimo Music" (Folkways Records, FE 4541).

Currently reissued on cassette, this two-record set contains selections from previous Folkways and Asch recordings. Includes indigenous styles from various culture areas as well as Christian songs in Indian languages and other examples of post-contact and contemporary music.

Baker, Theodore

[1882]   *On the Music of the North American Indians.* Translated by Ann Buckley. Source Materials and Studies in Ethnomusicology no. 9. Buren, The Netherlands: Frits Knuf, 1976. First published as *Über die Musik der nordamerikanischen Wilden* (Leipzig).

Often called the first "serious" study of Indian music, the original was submitted as a doctoral dissertation at the University of Leipzig. Baker did the research among Senecas of New York State during the summer of 1880 and also notated 22 songs from other (mainly Plains) tribes at the Training School for Indian Youth at Carlisle, Pennsylvania. The core of the work consists of 32 annotated notations (made by the author without recording equipment), and other sections contain Baker's observations about the music and its meaning to Indians. Eleven other musical examples are quoted from earlier sources, making a total of 43. The study is marred by evolutionist thinking and a general presumption that Native American musical styles were fairly uniform in character. But on the positive side, Baker was a sharp observer and the book also includes much information from earlier sources. Baker's ideas concerning the origins and categories of Indian music are discussed in Rhodes (1952b below).

Balfour, Henry

1899   *The Natural History of the Musical Bow: A Chapter in the Developmental History of Stringed Instruments.* Oxford. Reprint. Portland, Maine: Longwood Press, 1976.

Speculates on (three) stages through which the instrument evolved, then discusses the geographical distribution of various types. The section on "America and the West Indies" (pp. 38–47) includes very little evidence of indigenous musical bows, and Balfour questions whether the instrument existed in America before the beginning of the slave trade (pp. 86–87). For more on the subject see Roberts (1936:13–16 below).

Bierhorst, John

1979   *A Cry from the Earth: Music of the North American Indians.* New York: Four Winds Press.

A useful survey describing instruments, musical styles, and uses of music in various culture areas. Many of the musical examples can also be heard on a commercial disc of the same name (Folkways Records, FC 7777). The book and the record both incorporate data from research by others. See the record review by Nettl (1980 below).

Boas, Franz

1904   Some Traits of Primitive Culture. *Journal of American Folklore* 17(64): 243–254.

Argues that mental processes in "primitive" culture are basically similar to those of modern civilization. Boas also emphasizes that various aspects of culture ("religion and science; music, poetry, and dance; myth and history; fashion and ethics") are "intrinsically interwoven" (p. 243). Contains no discussion of music as such but does include general remarks on the cultural significance of symbolism in the arts and ritual.

(1927)   Primitive Literature, Music, and Dance. Pp. 299–356 (Chapter 7) in *Primitive Art*. New York: Dover Publications, 1955. First published by H. Aschehoug for the Oslo Institute of Comparative Research in

Human Culture (Oslo, Norway). Also published by Harvard University Press in 1928. This focuses on the relationships between sung and spoken texts as found among various tribal peoples, including comments on syncopation, rhythmic repetition, symmetry, metaphor, and symbolism. Song texts and translations from various North American Indian tribes are given as examples throughout.

Boekelman, Henry J.

1936 Shell Trumpet from Arizona. *American Antiquity* 2:27–31.
  Boekelman begins by describing a specimen from a Hohokam site at Gila River (Arizona). He notes the use of a similar trumpet in a Zuni ceremony, then discusses the broad occurrence of shell trumpets in archeological sites from northern Arizona to Canada (120 separate finds).

Brown, Bill

1989 The Art of Native American Music. Pp. 32–42 in *Songs of Indian Territory: Native American Music Traditions of Oklahoma* edited by Willie Smyth. Oklahoma City: Center for the American Indian.
  Focuses on the work of contemporary artists who produce drums, flutes, Apache violins, turtle shell shackles or gourd rattles.

Brown, Donald

1989 Who Influences Whom? The Interplay of Native American and European Musical Cultures. Pp. 43–48 in *Songs of Indian Territory: Native American Music Traditions of Oklahoma* edited by Willie Smyth. Oklahoma City: Center for the American Indian.
  First discusses how contact with Euro-Americans affected Indian music, noting that the intertribalism often considered a post-contact phenomenon is actually an old tradition among Native Americans. Brown then discusses the use of Indian melodies by composers such as Edward MacDowell and Arthur Farwell. Finally, he draws conclusions as to why the influence of Indian music on Euro-American music was proportionately greater than the Euro-American influence on Indian music.

North American Indian Music

Burlin, Natalie (Curtis)

1907   *The Indians' Book: An Offering by the American
            Indians of Indian Lore, Musical and Narrative, to
            Form a Record of the Songs and Legends of Their
            Race.* New York: Harper. Expanded second edition
            published in 1923. Reprints of the second edition
            published by Dover of New York (1950 and 1968).
This contains 149 melodies and texts from various tribes, generally with translations or brief explanations of content. The author notated the songs in the field by ear and seems to have regarded recording equipment as unnecessary. This represents an early attempt to characterize Indian music in positive terms and from a native viewpoint; comparative analysis is lacking, but there is much information on myths, legends, and the cultural background of songs. Includes musical examples from the following groups: Penobscot (6), Passamaquoddy (4), Malecite (2), Dakota (18), Omaha (2), Pawnee (16), Cheyenne (20), Arapaho (9), Kiowa (9), Winnebago (17), Kwakiutl (2), Pima (3), Apache (3), Mohave-Apache (4), Yuma (1), Navajo (12), Zuni (5), San Juan Pueblo (1), Acoma (3), Laguna (3), and Hopi (9). Page references to these musical notations are given in the regional bibliographies. Several other publications by Burlin are listed in Hickerson (1961 below).

See **Burton** (1909) in the Northeast bibliography. This contains much general information on Indian music and the history of Indian music research.

Buss, Judy Epstein

1977   The Flute and Flute Music of the North American
            Indians. Master's thesis. University of Illinois at
            Urbana-Champaign.
Contains notations and analysis of flute music from recordings collected between 1905 and 1952. This information is from Wapp (1984:55 below).

Cadman, Charles W.

1915   The "Idealization" of Indian Music. *Musical
            Quarterly* 1:387–396.
Discusses the use of Indian musical materials by American composers and includes three arranged melodies based on songs collected by Frances Densmore (1 Chippewa) and by Cadman him-

self (2 Omaha). Other related writings by Cadman are listed in Hickerson (1961 below).

Cardin, Clarisse

1947   Bio-bibliographie de Marius Barbeau. *Les Archives de folklore* 2:17–26.
Also see the memorial biography by Katz (1970 below) and various writings by Barbeau listed in the Northwest and Northeast bibliographies.

Chase, Gilbert

1955   *America's Music: From the Pilgrims to the Present.* New York: McGraw-Hill.
This mainly incorporates descriptions and notations of Indian music from earlier sources, but it also includes a historical survey on the artistic use of Indian themes by American composers (pp. 383–400) and a brief discussion of contemporary musical activities ("Indian Tribal Music Today," pp. 430–432). For more information see Hickerson (1961:160–161 below).

Collaer, Paul, Editor

(1973)   *Music of the Americas: An Illustrated Music Ethnology of the Eskimo and American Indian Peoples.* New York: Praeger. Original German edition published in Leipzig (1968). English translation first published by Curzon Press (London, 1970).
The first 44 pages of this oversized volume provide an overview of New World musical practices, with an emphasis on the cultural functions of music and historical relationships. Here, Collaer also summarizes the musical styles of various culture areas in North and South America, including 23 transcriptions. The remainder of the volume (pp. 45–207) contains historical photographs of musical subjects, each with rather extensive commentary on the musical or dance events pictured. The text portions are mainly by Collaer; other contributors as listed on the title page are Willard Rhodes, Samuel Marti, Vicente T. Mendoza, Eva Lips, and Rolf Krusche.

Conlon, Paula

1983   The Flute of the Canadian Amerindian: An Analysis
            of the Vertical Whistle Flute with External Block and
            Its Music. Master's thesis. Carleton University.
        An extensive study of instrument design and construction, in-
    cluding acoustical measurements. This information is from Wapp
    (1984:55 below).˙

Curtis, Edward S.

1907–1930   *The North American Indian, Being A Series of*
            Volumes Picturing and Describing the Indians of the
            United States and Alaska. Edited by Frederick Webb
            Hodge. 20 vols. Cambridge, Mass.: University Press.
            Reprint (Landmarks in Anthropology series). New
            York: Johnson Reprint Corporation, 1970.
        A vast storehouse of information containing notations of songs
    from the following tribes: Teton (5 songs), Assiniboin (3), Dakota
    (7), Crow (16), Hidatsa (9), Mandan (2), Arikara (14), Gros Ventre
    (5), Piegan (12), Cheyenne (13), Arapaho (4), Yakima (4), Interior
    Salish (11), Kutenai (14), Klickitat (2), Nez Perce (9), Chinook (2),
    Wishram (6), Cowichan (5), Twana (2), Clallam (4), Kwakiutl
    (23), Nootka (9), Haida (5), Hopi (3), Diegueño (1), Oto (4), and
    Ponca (2). Also includes song texts and translations. More com-
    plete references (by volume and page number) are given in the re-
    gional bibliographies which follow. The songs were recorded by
    Curtis and transcribed by various associates.

Danckert, Werner

1937   Musikwissenschaft und Kulturkreislehre. *Anthropos*
            32:1–14.
        Works of the German *Kulturkreis* ("culture circle") school at-
    tempted to speculate on historical relationships by studying the ap-
    parent diffusion of cultural elements as occurring in integrated trait
    complexes or "circles."
        This article includes comparisons of North American Indian and
    Eskimo musical styles with those of other areas (pp. 8–9, and 12).

"Demonstration Collection of Erich M. von Hornbostel and the Berlin Phonogram Archive"

1963   (Recording and liner notes) Ethnomusicological Series, Archives of Folk and Primitive Music, Indiana University. Ethnic Folkways Recordings (FE 4175).
This two-record set contains early recordings from all over the world. Among them are North American Indian and Eskimo recordings collected by Christian Leden (ca. 1910 and 1911), Franz Boas (1900), Erich von Hornbostel (1906), and Otto Abraham (1906). Tribes or culture groups represented are identified as follows: Greenland Eskimo, Plains Cree, Thompson River, Pawnee, and Hopi. These and other recordings were originally deposited at the Berlin Phonogramm-Archiv during the years when Hornbostel served as its director. The album was jointly produced in cooperation with the Ethnomusicological Division of the Museum of Ethnology (Berlin). The liner notes (40 pp.) are by Kurt Reinhart and George List.

Densmore, Frances

1905   The Music of the American Indian. *Overland Monthly* (Series 2) 45:230–234.
Contains general remarks on Indian music and theoretical ideas based on the writings of John C. Fillmore. See Fillmore (1893, 1895, 1899 below).

1906   A Plea for the Indian Harmonization of All Indian Songs. *Indian School Journal* 6(4): 14–15.
Another article based largely on the writings of John C. Fillmore. Densmore discusses the "harmonic" nature of Indian songs and the best way to reproduce this harmony in notations.

1909   Scale Formation in Primitive Music. *American Anthropologist* 11:1–12.
Densmore speculates on the origin of a "basic pentatonic scale" found in the music of American Indians and other native peoples.

1917   Recent Developments in the Study of Indian Music. *Proceedings of the International Congress of Americanists at Washington* (1915). Vol. 19, pp. 298–301.

This contains a brief history of the phonograph in Native American research and describes Densmore's approach to analysis of Indian melodies.

1920   The Rhythm of Sioux and Chippewa Music. *American Anthropologist* 9:59–67.

Discusses various aspects of rhythm and explains how Densmore could produce English-language renditions of Indian songs while maintaining the original rhythms.

1926   *The American Indians and Their Music.* New York: Woman's Press. Reprint. New York: Johnson Reprint Corporation, 1970.

A general survey covering topics such as musical instruments, typology of songs, the functions of music in culture, typical scales, and various "peculiarities" or general characteristics of Indian music. Densmore also discusses the use of Indian themes by fine art composers and gives a brief history of research on Indian music. Includes musical examples from the following groups: Pawnee (1), Cocopa (1), Ute (1), Menominee (1), Chippewa (2), and Teton Sioux (2). All the notations are from earlier sources.

1927a   The Study of Indian Music in the Nineteenth Century. *American Anthropologist* 29:77–86.

An historical survey which discusses the work of Baker, Fletcher, Stumpf, Boas, Gilman, Fillmore, Troyer, and other early researchers including Densmore herself.

1927b   The Use of Music in the Treatment of the Sick by American Indians. *Musical Quarterly* 13:555–565.

Describes the use of songs in curing and related beliefs and customs in North American cultures and among the Tule Indians of Panama. Contains musical examples of healing songs from the following tribes: Chippewa (1), Sioux (1), Menominee (1), Papago (2), Yuma (1), and Makah (2). Densmore concludes that the usual intention of curing songs is to soothe and quiet the patient rather than stimulate the person (p. 561).

1929   What Intervals Do Indians Sing? *American Anthropologist* 31:271–276.

In this paper, Densmore discusses the irregularities of intonation in Indian music and concludes that it is generally not necessary for scholars to ascertain the precise pitches of Indian singing.

1930   Peculiarities in the Singing of the American Indians. *American Anthropologist* 32:651–660.

Discusses various unusual or exceptional aspects of Indian music, with sections on the following: (1) differences between Native American and Euro-American music, (2) regional differences (3) "peculiarities" in certain classes of songs (by function), and (4) personal peculiarities. The approach is fairly eclectic, but Densmore gives interesting examples such as the contrast in style between various animal songs used for curing among the Papago (pp. 658–659).

1931   Music of the American Indians at Public Gatherings. *Musical Quarterly* 17:464–479.

This is a general survey article containing musical examples reprinted from earlier publications by Densmore. Includes musical notations from the following groups: Papago (2), Dakota (1), Yaqui (2), Ute (2), Chippewa (2) and Pawnee (1).

1934   The Songs of Indian Soldiers During the World War. *Musical Quarterly* 20:419–425.

Discusses Indian soldiers' attitudes towards the war as reflected in their songs. The musical examples, all with song texts in English, are identified as Winnebago (2) and Pawnee (1). Several other song texts in English are included without notations.

1938   The Influence of Hymns on the Form of Indian Songs. *American Anthropologist* 40:175–177.

Discusses the paired-phrasing structure in songs of the Native American Church, the Ghost Dance, and handgame songs. Densmore traces its origins to hymn singing as taught to Indians by early missionaries.

1941   Native Songs of Two Hybrid Ceremonies Among American Indians. *American Anthropologist* 43:77–82.

First describes Catholic and indigenous elements in the Yaqui Deer Dance (with translations of five song texts). Densmore then discusses Christian elements in music of the Native American Church. She concludes that Euro-American influence (on words and melody) is more apparent in the peyote songs than in the Deer Dance.

1944   Traces of Foreign Influences in the Music of the American Indians. *American Anthropologist* 46: 106–112.

This is a rather unsystematic discussion of musical correspondences, but it does contain interesting data. In discussing polyphony, for example, Densmore describes women's singing a high vocal drone against another melody as a practice which exists among several tribes, including the Papago, Pawnee, Makah, and Quileute Indians (p. 108).

1947   Imitative Dances among the American Indians. *Journal of American Folklore* 60(235): 73–78.

This includes six musical examples, one each from the following tribes: Alabama, Choctaw, Maidu, Menominee, Seminole, and Winnebago.

1948   The Use of Music in Treatment of the Sick by American Indians. Pp. 25–46 in *Music and Medicine*, by Dorothy M. Schullian and Max Schoen. New York: H. Schumann.

Describes curative uses of music and related beliefs and customs among various tribes. Contains notations for songs from the Chippewa (1 song), Cheyenne (1), and Papago (1). Also includes song texts in English from various tribes.

1950a   Communication with the Dead as Practised by the American Indian. *Man* 50:40–41.

Discusses several examples of songs learned from spirits of the dead. Includes nine texts in English from various tribes.

1950b   The Words of Indian Songs as Unwritten Literature. *Journal of American Folklore* 63:450–458.

A general discussion of the meaning of words in Indian songs.

1953a   Technique in the Music of the American Indian. *Bureau of American Ethnology Bulletin* no. 151, pp. 211–216.

This contains comments on the music of various tribes, with sections on the following: (1) tone production (vocal quality), (2) use of words, (3) accuracy (and purposeful variation), (4) difference in tempo of voice and drum, and (5) change of pitch level during renditions of a song. Includes interesting and unusual examples for each, for example the use of a "peculiar" nasal voice in older love songs of the Chippewa and techniques of improvisation in animal (story) songs of the Northern Ute.

1953b   The Belief of the Indian in a Connection Between Song and the Supernatural. *Bureau of American Ethnology Bulletin* no. 151, pp. 217–223

Focuses on the connection between songs and spiritual power in various cultures. Densmore distinguishes songs received in dreams from those gotten in purposeful vision quest (fasting vigil). She then discusses animals (bear, wolf, buffalo) and natural forces (thunder, wind) which figure prominently in the imagery of the songs and visions. Related use of fetishes or symbolic ornaments is also mentioned. This includes English translations of four song texts.

Driver, Harold E.

1941   Girls' Puberty Rites in Western North America. Culture Element Distributions, no. 16. *University of California Anthropological Records* 6(2): 21–90.

A very thorough survey of the literature on girls' puberty observances among tribes of the Northwest Coast, Plateau, California, Great Basin, and Southwest culture areas. Related songs, instruments, and dances are only briefly discussed (p. 28). Driver speculates on the history of these customs (pp. 59–62), discerning several layers or complexes, the oldest of which he considers to be extremely ancient and probably brought to North America by the earliest immigrants (p. 60).

1953   The Spatial and Temporal Distribution of the Musical Rasp in the New World. *Anthropos* 48:578–592.

This is a survey based on ethnographic and archeological literature (with two maps). Driver finds the musical rasp occurring throughout much of North American but absent in South America (except where introduced in post-Columbian times) . He postulates a single origin and speculates on reasons for the development of variant forms of the instrument.

Driver, Harold E., and William C. Massey

1957   *Comparative Studies of North American Indians.* Transactions of the American Philosophical Society 47 (2). Philadelphia.

This contains much useful information for comparative research on music and ritual. For example, a section entitled "Social and Religious Aspects of Subsistence" (pp. 253–259) discusses the distribution of bear rituals, green corn ceremonies, and other ritual complexes relating to subsistence.

Driver, Harold E., and S.H. Riesenberg

1950   Hoof Rattles and Girls' Puberty Rites in North and South America. *Indiana University Publications in Anthropology and Linguistics, Memoir* 4. Bloomington.

This contains tables indicating the distribution of various hoof rattles and girls' puberty customs by region and tribe (pp. 14–22). Based on a survey of the ethnographic and archeological literature, the essay is intended to explore Nordenskiöld's assertion of an ancient connection between hoof rattles and girls' puberty observances. The authors conclude that both may be ancient, but they question whether any close affinity can be established on the basis of existing evidence (p. 14). Also see Nordenskiöld (1912 below).

Driver, Wilhelmine

1969   Music and Dance. Pp. 194–207 in *Indians of North America* edited by Harold E. Driver. Second edition. Chicago: University of Chicago Press.

An excellent overview for the anthropology-oriented nonspecialist. Based mainly on Nettl (1954 below), Roberts (1936 below), and various works of Herzog and Kurath. Also covers Mayan and Aztec music.

Erickson, Edwin E.

1969   The Song Trace: Song Styles and the Ethnohistory of Aboriginal America. Doctoral dissertation (Anthropology), Columbia University.

Using statistical analyses of codings based on cantometrics (See Lomax 1968 and 1976 below), Erickson attempts to taxonomize song performance styles in North and South America and considers the results in relation to findings from archeology, linguistics, and other fields. The opening chapters on methodology contain a section which defines various levels of historical relationship ("Models of Song and Music History," pp. 26–33) . Chapter Three considers questions such as the relation of Amerindian musical styles to those of Siberia (pp. 105–117), general characteristics of Amerindian music (pp. 117–122), and the bipolar division between North America and South America, including Mexico (pp. 123–129). Chapter Four (North America, pp. 129–267) discusses various regional styles and related ethnohistorical issues. Contains relatively few references to the writings of other specialists in the area of Native American music.

Evans, Bessie, and May G. Evans

(1931)   *American Indian Dance Steps.* New York: A. S. Barnes. Reprint. New York: Hacker Art Books, 1975.
     Contains 15 musical examples transcribed by Bessie Evans and George Herzog. All the songs are from San Ildefonso Pueblo except for one each from the Tewa and Navajo.

Farwell, Arthur

1901   *American Indian Melodies.* Newton Center, Massachusetts.
     This contains ten arranged melodies based on Omaha songs published by Fletcher and Fillmore (Plains bibliography, 1893). Farwell's introduction explains the rationale behind the arrangements.

1902   Aspects of Indian Music. *Southern Workman* 31:211–217.
     Discusses the use of Indian melodies by Western composers and outlines the "proper" method for supplying harmony to Indian melodies. Includes two examples from Farwell (1901 above).

Feder, Norman

1964   The Origin of the Oklahoma Forty-Nine Dance. *Ethnomusicology* 8(3): 290–294.
     The author discusses several different explanations concerning the origin of the Forty-Nine Dance, some quite humorous. Feder concludes that the dance originated among the Kiowa or Comanche between 1911 and 1918.

The Federal Cylinder Project: A Guide to Field Cylinder Collections in Federal Repositories, Volume 1: Introduction and Inventory

1984   Edited by Erika Brady, Maria La Vigna, Dorothy Sara Lee, and Thomas Vennum, with the assistance of Gregory Pontecorvo. Washington: American Folklife Center, Library of Congress.

This provides an inventory of cylinder collections which are more fully described in subsequent volumes of the series. It also includes indices to the recordings by tribe, region, and collector. The Introduction covers topics such as the following: (1) the mechanics of the Edison phonograph, (2) how it was used by collectors, and (3) technical and other limitations that need to be considered by researchers who use the recordings. Other cylinder catalogues in the series are listed below (Gray 1984) and in the following regional bibliographies: Northwest Coast (Gray 1988), California (Gray and Schupman 1990), Great Basin and Plateau (Gray 1988), Northeast (Gray 1985), Southeast (Lee 1985), and Mexico (Gray 1990).

Fewkes, Jesse W.

1890   On the Use of the Phonograph in the Study of the Languages of American Indians. *Science* 15 (May): 267–269.

    Discusses Fewkes's collecting of songs among the Passamaquoddy Indians in 1889 and contains one musical example (including text) transcribed by an associate (Mrs. H. E. Holt). See also Fewkes (1890) in the Northeast bibliography. These are the earliest published studies of Indian music based on recordings collected with the Edison-type phonograph.

Fillmore, John Comfort

1893   The Scale and the Natural Harmonies of the Indian Songs. *Music Review* 2 (August): 539–546. Reprinted in *Music* 4 (September 1893): 478–489.

    Fillmore postulates that there is a general tendency in primitive music to construct melodies according to certain "natural harmonic laws."

1895   What Do the Indians Mean to Do When They Sing, and How Far Do They Succeed? *Journal of American Folklore* 8:138–142.

    Discusses the innate tendency of Indian singers to produce melodies of a "harmonic" nature and describes a method for obtaining the "true" notes of a song even when the singers deviate from natural patterns.

1899   The Harmonic Structure of Indian Music. *American Anthropologist* 1:297–318.

A posthumous article describing steps in the development of music viewed as following certain "lines of least resistance." This includes 14 musical examples identified as Navajo (5), Kwakiutl (4), Omaha (2), Tewa (2), and Yaqui (1). There is an introduction by Alice Fletcher.

Fletcher, Alice Cunningham

1894   Indian Music. *Music* 6 (June): 188–199.
Discusses various aspects of Indian music, particularly the "harmonic" nature of Indian melodies as theorized by Fillmore (See writings above).

1898   Indian Songs and Music. *Journal of American Folklore* 11:85–104.
Discusses various aspects of Indian music, particularly as found among the Plains tribes. Includes nine musical examples (seven harmonized). Two of the songs are translated and one native text is given.

1900   *Indian Story and Song from North America.* Boston: Small and Maynard. Reprint. New York: AMS Press, 1970.
Contains 27 musical examples, each of which is accompanied by a story. Nearly all of the songs are harmonized by John C. Fillmore or Edwin Tracy, and the following tribes are represented: Omaha (13 songs), Ponca (2), Pawnee (6), Dakota (2), Kwakiutl (1), Tewa (1), Arapaho (1), and Oto (1).

1907   Music and Musical Instruments. Pp. 958–961 in *Handbook of American Indians North of Mexico,* edited by Frederick Webb Hodge. Vol. 1 of 2. Bureau of American Ethnology Bulletin, no. 30.
This early survey of general trends gives information on the following: contexts for music, musical form, vocal quality, ownership of songs, Eskimo song duels, musical instruments, and bibliography. Includes small photos of ten musical instruments and one photo of Kiowa peyote ceremony.

1915   *Indian Games and Dances with Native Songs; Arranged from American Indian Ceremonials and Sports.* Boston: C. C. Birchard. Reprint. New York: AMS Press, 1970.

Contains descriptions of dances and games written in a style intended for children. Includes 31 musical examples with English words.

Frisbie, Charlotte (Johnson)

1977   The Music of the American Indians. Pp. 95–105 in *Music in American Society, 1776–1976: From Puritan Hymn to Synthesizer* edited by George McCue. New Brunswick, N.J.: Transaction Books.

Frisbie discusses general aspects of style, social functions, and values of Native American music in an essay for general readers. Contrasts with Euro-American music are emphasized throughout, as are continuing historical transformations in Indian music and culture.

1980   Book Review of *Ritual of the Wind: North American Indian Ceremonies, Music, and Dances*, by Jamake Highwater (1977). *Ethnomusicology* 24(3): 589.

This is a very criticial review of a book intended for general readers. Frisbie points out that Highwater's descriptions of ceremonies are distorted and cites at least one instance of plagiarism.

1981   Film Review-Essay: Interviews with American Indian Musicians. *Ethnomusicology* 25(2): 365–381.

Describes a series of eight video cassettes containing interviews with singers and other knowledgeable persons from the following tribes: Yurok, Tolowa, San Juan Pueblo, Navajo, Creek, and Cherokee. The programs are based on three-hour interviews conducted by producer Charlotte Heth in 1976 and 1977. These were later edited into 60-minute videotapes which are available through the American Indian Studies Center at UCLA. Frisbie's review emphasizes the importance of the project and discusses the (two) Navajo programs and their implications for research and teaching.

1989   In Memorium, Helen Heffron Roberts (1888–1985). *Ethnomusicology* 33(1): 97–112.

Contains much information on the life and career of this important scholar, even touching on how she was first encouraged to enter the field of "primitive music" research by Franz Boas around 1918 (p. 99).

Galpin, Francis W.

1902–1903   Aztec Influence on American Indian Instruments. *Sammelbände der internationale Musik-Gesellschaft* 4:661–670.
Galpin speculates on the possible Aztec origin of instruments used among tribes of the Northwest Coast region.

Gilbert, Tamara B.

1982   American Indian Powwow in Los Angeles: Dancers' Perspectives. Master's thesis (Dance). University of California at Los Angeles.
This focuses on the significance of powwow dancing for the individual participants, with chapters on "Values and Symbols of Powwows" (Ch. 3) and "Dancers' Perspectives on Powwow Dance" (Ch. 4). Appendix A also contains descriptions of various dances (pp. 98–153).

Giles, Martha Mead

1977   A Synthesis of American Indian Music as Derived from Culture: Examination of Style, Performance Practices, and Aesthetics for Music Education. Doctoral dissertation (Music Education), University of Oklahoma.
This study presents an extraordinary volume of information, but the interpretation and framework remain obstinately ethnocentric throughout. Giles seeks to generalize about "the Indian" and what music represented "to him" mainly in order to incorporate the subject into a western music curriculum. Contains 18 musical examples.

Gillis, Frank J.

1967   Special Bibliography: Helen Heffron Roberts. *Ethnomusicology* 11 (May):228–233.
See also the memorial bibliography by Frisbie (1989 above).

1969   Special Bibliography: Willard Rhodes. *Ethnomusicology* 13 (May):305–308.
See also the obituary by McAllester (1993 below).

1984   The Incunabula of Instantaneous Ethnomusicological Sound Recordings, 1890–1910: A Preliminary List. Pp. 323–355 in *Problems and Solutions: Occasional*

Essays in Ethnomusicology Presented to Alice M. Moyle edited by J. Kassler and J. Stubbington. Sydney, Australia: Hale and Iremonger. This is a very useful guide to the location of early cylinder recordings in museums and archives. The focus is world wide, but American Indian recordings predominate and are listed by area and tribe (pp. 327–339).

See **Gilman** (1891) in the Southwest bibliography. This is historically important as being the first analytical study of "primitive" music based on recorded sound evidence.

Goddard, Pliny Earle

1906   A Graphic Method of Recording Songs. Pp. 137–142 in *Boas Anniversary Volume: Anthropological Papers Written in Honor of Franz Boas*. New York: Stechert and Co.
        The article describes use of a device called the kymograph for making precise measurements of pitch. This may well represent the earliest use of sound registration equipment for musical transcription. Contains one notation and graph of a Hupa Indian song.

Gray, Judith

1984   (Editor) *The Federal Cylinder Project: A Guide to Field Cylinder Collections in Federal Agencies, Volume 8: Early Anthologies*. Washington: American Folklife Center, Library of Congress.
        This lists and describes the contents of cylinder recordings in two important collections: (1) The Benjamin Ives Gilman Collection of cylinders recorded at the 1893 World's Columbian Exposition at Chicago (pp. 1–34) and (2) The Erich Moritz von Hornbostel Demonstration Collection of cylinders from the Berlin Phonogramm-Archiv (pp. 35–78). The Gilman collection includes 18 cylinders featuring "Kwakiutl or Vancouver Island Indians" (pp. 30–34). The Hornbostel collection includes items identified as follows: Polar Eskimo, Stony or Carrier Indian, Pawnee, Hopi, Huichol, and Cora.

1989   Early Ethnographic Recordings in Today's Indian Communities: Federal Agencies and the Federal Cylinder Project. Pp. 49–55 in *Songs of Indian Territory: Native American Music Traditions of*

Oklahoma edited by Willie Smyth. Oklahoma City: Center for the American Indian. This gives information on early collections of Indian music from the State of Oklahoma and also describes a project to preserve the recordings and disseminate copies in Indian communities. See also The Federal Cylinder Project (1984 above).

Guédon, Marie Françoise

1972   Canadian Indian Ethnomusicology: Selected Bibliography and Discography. *Ethnomusicology* 16(3): 465–478.

Guédon lists selected publications, recordings, and films under five regional headings: (1) Eastern Woodlands and Great Lakes, (2) Plains, (3) Mackenzie and Yukon Basin (Athapaskan), (4) Plateau (Cordillera), and (5) Northwest Coast. The listings of commercial recordings and archival collections at the National Museum of Man (Ottawa) and elsewhere are particularly valuable.

Gundlach, Ralph H.

1932   A Quantitative Analysis of Indian Music. *American Journal of Psychology* 44 (January): 133–145.

A statistical study of relationships between musical traits and other aspects of tribal culture and society. Musical elements such as intervals, rhythm, and range of melody are correlated with various functions of music in tribal life. The analysis is based on notations published by Frances Densmore (Chippewa, Teton Sioux, Mandan, Hidatsa, Northern Ute, Pagago) and by Frederick Burton (Ojibwa).

Gustaver, Bror

1923   On a Peculiar Type of Whistle Found in Ancient American Indian Graves. *American Anthropologist* 25:307–317.

This describes whistles found at several midwestern archeological sites.

Haefer, J. Richard

1974   North American Indian Musical Instruments: Some Organological Distribution Problems. *American Musical Instrument Society Journal* 1: 56–85.

The article has three main goals or research issues: (1) to summarize previous writings on musical instrument distributions, (2) to outline a methodology for coordinating data on instruments, and (3) to consider the implications of instrument-distribution analysis for research.

Hallowell, A. Irving

1926   Bear Ceremonialism in the Northern Hemisphere. *American Anthropologist* 28:1–173.
A classic study comparing aspects of bear ceremonialism in various North American culture areas and among northern Eurasian peoples. Contains scattered references to songs but is mainly important for insights on religious functions or contexts of music over a vast geographical area.

Hatton, Orin

1989   "Indians for Indians Hour" Collection: 1943–1950. Pp. 59–62 in *Songs of Indian Territory: Native American Music Traditions of Oklahoma* edited by Willie Smyth. Oklahoma City: Center for the American Indian.
This describes a radio program for Native Americans which was broadcast from Norman Oklahoma for nearly 45 years beginning in 1941.

Hawley, E.H.

1898   Distribution of the Notched Rattle. *American Anthropologist* (old series) 11: 344–346.
Hawley begins by describing the instrument and mentioning examples collected among the Ute, Hopi, and Tonkawa (of western Texas). He then discusses similar notched rattles in other parts of the world including Mexico, Brazil, Java, and Africa.

Haywood, Charles

1951   *A Bibliography of North American Folklore and Folksong, Volume 2: The American Indians North of Mexico, including the Eskimos.* New York: Greenberg (pp. 750–1301). Second revised edition. New York: Dover Publications, 1960.
This lists an impressive number of folklore titles, but references to music and dance are less extensive. Still, it was the most

comprehensive bibliography of Indian music before that of Hickerson (1961 below). The book is arranged by culture area and includes some annotations.

Herndon, Marcia

1980   *Native American Music.* Norwood, Pa.: Norwood Editions.
This is basically a textbook and the only one that exists on the subject. The author includes much information from earlier sources but consistently distinguishes the scholarly literature from the perceptions and experiences of Indian people themselves. Disparities between the two viewpoints are addressed in several chapters. The review by Nettl (1982 below) is distinctly critical.

1991   Book Review of *Women in North American Indian Music* edited by Richard Keeling (1989). *World of Music* 33(2): 104–105.
Praises the book for challenging previous assumptions of male dominance in Indian music and for departing from the "one culture/one music" paradigm that permeates much earlier research.

Herzog, George

1930   Musical Styles in North America. *Proceedings of the 23rd International Congress of Americanists at New York* (1928), pp. 455–458.
Herzog distinguishes two main styles of Indian music, mainly on the basis of vocal quality: (1) a strongly accentuated style that he considers typical of most Indian music and (2) a less emphatic type of singing heard among the Yuman tribes and others of the Southwest and southern California.

1932   On Primitive Music. *American Anthropologist* 34:546–548.
Responds to a theoretical article by Roberts (1932 below) in the same volume and clarifies Herzog's position on the analysis of tonal structures in American Indian music.

1933   The Collections of Phonograph Records in North America and Hawaii. *Zeitschrift für vergleichende Musikwissenschaft* 1:58–62.
This gives the locations for some 12,428 cylinder recordings in various museums and archives during the 1930s. It was the only guide to recordings that existed for decades, and it still remains

very useful because of its organization (by culture area and tribe), bibliography, and indication of important collections during the period it represents.

1934   Speech-Melody and Primitive Music. *Musical Quarterly* 20:452–466.
        Discusses various ways in which speech tone can influence musical melody. Discusses music associated with an African "tone-language" and then discusses speech and music relationships in Navajo songs. Includes six musical notations of songs Herzog recorded among the Navajo in 1933.

1935   The Plains Ghost Dance and Great Basin Music. *American Anthropologist* 37:403–419. Reprint. Pages 116–131 in *Readings in Ethnomusicology* edited by David McAllester. New York: Johnson Reprint Corporation, 1971.
        A classic study in which Herzog defines a prototypic Ghost Dance musical style and traces its diffusion from the Great Basin region to tribes of the Plains and elsewhere. Comparative tables are used to analyze the songs with respect to melodic range, melodic form or structure, and position of the final tone. Musical examples from the following tribes are quoted from other sources: Pawnee (2 songs), Arapaho (1), Teton Dakota (1), Southern Paiute (1), Northern Ute (1), Navajo (1), and Yanktonai Dakota (1).

1935   Special Song Types in North American Indian Music. *Zeitschrift für vergleichende Musikwissenschaft* 3:22–33.
        An important essay in which Herzog points out that repertories of Indian music are not typically homogeneous but tend to contain "foreign elements" and "survivals" as well as songs in the predominant style. He discusses four types of songs that seem to be present among many tribes: (1) Ghost Dance songs, (2) love songs, (3) songs of hiding games, and (4) songs in animal stories. Songs from animal stories are considered to represent "one of the oldest layers that survive in present day Indian music" (p. 30).

1936   *Research in Primitive and Folk Music of the United States, a Survey.* American Council of Learned Societies Bulletin no. 24. Washington: American Council of Learned Societies.
        The section on "Primitive Music: the Study and Its Problems" (pp.3–44) contains a history of research on American Indian music

and suggestions for future study. This also includes a survey of sound archives in the United States and discusses their holdings.

1938   Music in the Thinking of the American Indian. *Peabody Bulletin* 34(2): 8–12.
Begins by noting the lack of music theory as understood in Western music and a relatively greater concern with mythological significance of songs. Concepts subsequently discussed include: primal origins of music, music as a vehicle for spiritual contacts, the connection of songs with dreams and visions, how songs are obtained, power of songs to harm or heal, and ideas about musical values or aesthetics. This contains interesting quotes from Indian people of the following tribes: Pima, Navajo, Mohave, Southern Paiute, Hupa, and other groups.

1940   Review of Musical and Other Sound Producing Instruments of the South American Indians: A Comparative Ethnographic Study, by Karl Gustav Izikowitz (1935). *American Anthropologist* 42:338–341.
Basically a positive review. Herzog mentions several North American parallels for South American instruments.

1944   African Influences in North American Indian Music. *Papers Read at the International Congress of Musicology* (1939), pp. 130–143. New York.
Herzog focuses on aspects of music among the Southeastern tribes which may possibly be attributed to African-American influences. This includes musical examples from the following tribes: Cherokee (4 songs), Kwakiutl (1), Pawnee (1), Iroquois (1), Pima (1), and Diegueño (1). The hypothesis is criticized in an essay by Heth (Southeast bibliography, 1979).

1946   Some Linguistic Aspects of American Indian Poetry. *Word* 2:82–83.
Summary of a paper read before the Linguistic Circle of New York on December 21, 1945. Herzog mainly discusses the differences between the language of song texts and normal speech among the Pima and Dakota.

Heth, Charlotte

1976   (Recording and liner notes) "Songs of Earth, Water,
              Fire, and Sky: Music of the American Indian." New
              World Records (NW 246).
The album contains songs from the following tribes or areas:
San Juan Pueblo, Seneca, Arapaho, Northern Plains, Creek, Yurok,
Navajo, Cherokee, and Southern Plains. See the review by
McAllester (1977 below).

1980   (Editor) *Selected Reports in Ethnomusicology* 3(2).
              Los Angeles: Program in Ethnomusicology,
              Department of Music, UCLA.
This edition of the journal focuses on Native American music.
It contains articles listed in regional bibliographies as follows:
McAllester (Southwest), Powers (Plains), Vennum (Plains), La
Vigna (Southwest), Yeh (Southwest), Draper (Southeast), and
Herndon (Southeast). Heth has written the Introduction (pp. ix–xii)
and a Select Bibliography (pp. 193–200). See the review by
Varnum (1981 below).

1982   The Study of Indian Music: Insiders and Outsiders.
              American Indian Culture and Research Journal 6(1):
              3–6. Los Angeles: American Indian Studies Center,
              UCLA.
Discusses the advantages of the researcher's being an Indian,
even when conducting research on music of another tribe. Heth
discounts the possible objection that this leads to lack of objectivity, mainly on the basis that the bulk of our educational system is
also biased toward "white studies" (p. 4). She also discusses potential dangers facing the Indian researcher because of factionalism
and the possibility of effecting the dynamics of Indian communities in an adverse manner.

1984   Update on Indian Music: Contemporary Trends. Pp.
              89–102 in *Sharing a Heritage: American Indian Arts*
              edited by Charlotte Heth and Michael Swarm.
              Contemporary American Indian Issues Series, no. 5.
              Los Angeles: American Indian Studies Center,
              UCLA.
Heth begins by discussing the recent revitalization of aboriginal forms, then discusses these modern trends: Pan-Tribal Music,
Protestant Hymns and Gospel Music, Intertribal Choirs and Bands,
and Professional Musicians.

1989   Oklahoma's Indian Music: A Framework for Understanding. Pp. 10–17 in *Songs of Indian Territory: Native American Music Traditions of Oklahoma* edited by Willie Smyth. Oklahoma City: Center for the American Indian.

Describes the processes through which tribes from various regions came to reside in Oklahoma and other historical factors which have shaped Indian musical traditions of the area. Includes a discography.

1992   (Editor) *Native American Dance: Ceremonies and Social Traditions*. Washington: National Museum of the American Indian, Smithsonian Institution.

The volume attempts to provide an Indian person's perspective on contemporary dances and is also visually superb, containing many color photographs of dances from various areas. This contains essays listed in the regional bibliographies as follows: LaFrance (Northeast), Rosoff and Cadaval (Mexico), Ganteaume (Southwest), Sweet (Southwest), Kavanagh (Plains), Huenemann (Plains), Williams (Northwest Coast), and Jones (below). Heth's Introduction (pp. 1–18) emphasizes the diversity of contemporary performance venues, from dances on rural reservations to staged presentations in urban theatres.

1994   Traditional and Contemporary Ceremonies, Rituals, Festivals, Music, and Dance. Pages 701–713 in *The Native North American Almanac* edited by Duane Champagne. Detroit: Gale Research.

A general introduction to the subject intended mainly for nonspecialist readers. Heth summarizes music and dance of various culture areas but mainly emphasizes historical factors and the continued importance of Native American music for contemporary Indian people. Includes two musical notations.

Hickerson, Joseph Charles

1961   Annotated Bibliography of North American Indian Music North of Mexico. Master's thesis (Folklore) Indiana University.

Includes more than one thousand titles in eight languages, spanning a period of about 350 years. Besides references and annotations, Hickerson includes a history of research on North American Indian Music (pp. 2–48), a survey listing the various types of literature that exist (pp. 49–110), and indices arranged by author (pp. 381–451) and by tribe (pp. 452–464).

Highwater, Jamake

1977   *Ritual of the Wind: North American Indian Ceremonies, Music, and Dances.* New York: Viking Press.

According to the author this was written in order to help general readers understand tribal ceremonies from a native viewpoint. Part III ("The Ceremony," pp. 56–167) includes descriptions and photos of the following: the Plains Sun Dance, the Cherokee Booger Dance, the Apache Mountain Spirit Dance, the Tewa Nuhi ("Rain Power") Ceremony, the Pawnee Hako Ceremony, the Navajo Night Chant, and the Yaqui Easter Festival. Criticized for plagiarism in review by Frisbie (1980: 589 above).

Higginson, Joseph Vincent

1954   Hymnody in the American Indian Missions. *Catholic Choirmaster* 40:161–176.

An historical survey describing the methods used for teaching hymns at Indian missions in various parts of North America.

Hinton, Leanne

1986   Musical Diffusion and Linguistic Diffusion. Pp. 11–24 in *Explorations in Ethnomusicology: Essays in Honor of David P. McAllester*, edited by Charlotte Frisbie. Detroit Monographs in Musicology, no. 9. Detroit: Detroit Information Coordinators.

Discusses differences in the nature of musical and linguistic diffusion as occurring among American Indian groups. Considers various linguistic aspects of songs (for example, types of vocables, phonology, and semantic content features) which can spread between groups even when the predominant musical styles differ considerably (pp. 14–17). Hinton also comments upon the possible role of intertribal music activities in linguistic diffusion. Most of the examples relate to Havasupai music, which incorporates songs from several other tribes (including the Hopi, Paiute, Chemehuevi, Navajo, Walapai, Yavapai, and Mojave).

Hofmann, Charles

1946   Frances Densmore and the Music of the American
Indian. *Journal of American Folklore* 59:45–50.
Contains much information on Densmore's life and career.
The section on her "Early Life" (pp. 1–30) is based on autobiographical papers, while that entitled "Professional Career" (pp. 31–
66) combines autobiographical notes with material quoted from her
reports to the Bureau of American Ethnology. This volume of the
journal also includes seven of Densmore's articles and even some
unpublished poems.

1964   (Recording and liner notes) "War Whoops and
Medicine Songs." Smithsonian-Folkways Recordings
(FE 4381).
Currently reissued on cassette, this album includes songs from
the following tribes: Winnebago, Chippewa, Sioux, Zuni, and
Acoma.

1965   (Recording and liner notes) "Healing Songs of the
American Indians." Smithsonian-Folkways Recordings (FE 4251).
Currently reissued on cassette, this contains medicine and curing songs collected by Frances Densmore during the period from
1908 to 1929. This includes songs from the following tribes:
Chippewa, Sioux, Yuma, Northern Ute, Papago, Makah, and
Menominee. The liner notes by Hofmann (7 pp.) describe the genres represented and summarize the career of Densmore.

1967   *American Indians Sing: The Thought, Religion, and
Culture of Indian Nations Across the Land as
Revealed through Their Music, Dances, Song-Poetry,
and Ceremonies.* New York: The John Day
Company.
This introduction for general readers contains sections on mu-
sic and ceremonies of the following tribes or regions: Oglala
Sioux, Plains, Iroquois, Navajo, Hopi, Zuni, Yaqui, and Northwest
Coast. There are ten musical examples (from various tribes), and
the book was published along with a 7-inch disc containing selec-
tions recorded by well-known researchers such as Willard Rhodes
and William Fenton (among others).

Howard, James H.

1983   Pan-Indianism in Native American Music and Dance.
            Ethnomusicology 27(1): 71–82.
            Howard gives a definition of Pan-Indianism and discusses the
            origins of music and dance elements in the intertribal powwow.
            Also describes the typical schedule of events in a powwow pro-
            gram and gives an overview of Pan-Indian events taking place in
            different regions of the United States.

Huenemann, Lynn

1978   *Songs and Dances of Native America: A Research
            Text for Teachers and Students.* Tsaile, Arizona:
            Education House.
            Contains musical and cultural information for general class-
            room use, teacher training, and/or classes on American Indian mu-
            sic. The section on Navajo music (Part One) discusses various cer-
            emonials, including musical transcriptions, texts, translations, and
            notes for 37 songs of various types. The section on music of the
            Plains area (Part Two) discusses the powwow and other general
            topics, including musical transcriptions, texts, translations, and
            notes for 29 songs. The section on Indians of the Great Lakes re-
            gion (Part Three) gives general information and includes 10 musi-
            cal examples. Another section on music of various tribes (Part
            Four) contains 14 musical examples as follows: Yupik Eskimo (1),
            Tulalip (1), Athapaskan (1), Apache (2), Hopi (4), Pueblo (1), Taos
            (1), Caddo (1), Winnebago (1), and Cree (1). Finally, a section on
            "Resources for Teachers and Students" (Part Five) gives biblio-
            graphic information for other culture areas. The book is published
            with a set of accompanying cassette tapes.

Hultkrantz, Åke

1967   Spirit Lodge, a North American Shamanistic Séance.
            Pp. 32–68 in *Studies in Shamanism* edited by Carl-
            Martin Edsman. Stockholm: Almqvist and Wiksell.
            Hultkrantz begins by distinguishing generalized shamanism
            from the more specialized and intense practices he refers to as
            "Arctic shamanism," mainly because of their primary geographic
            distribution (p. 35). He then discusses various "shaking tent" rit-
            uals and "spirit lodge" ceremonies that resemble the more intense
            northerly practices. These are found mainly among tribes of the
            Northeast, Plains, and Plateau regions. An Arapaho Spirit Lodge

Ceremony that Hultkrantz observed in 1955 is described in some detail (pp. 37–44). The essay includes comments on the songs and on other sounds of an animal apparition (owl). The article contains extensive bibliographic references.

1977   Ritual in Native North American Religions. Pp. 135–146 in *Native Religious Traditions* edited by Earle H. Waugh and K. Dad Prithipaul. Waterloo, Ontario (Canada): Laurier University Press.

Offers a general discussion of the ritual as an expression of underlying religious concepts. Hultkrantz lists various measures or scales according to which rituals could be classified, describes the belief system of the Sun Dance, and gives a brief survey of the types of rituals found among American Indians.

1979   *The Religions of the American Indians.* Translated by Monica Setterwall. Berkeley and Los Angeles: University of California Press. Original Swedish edition published in Stockholm (1967).

The basic organization of the book is by topic rather than area, but Hultkrantz does include chapters specifically devoted to Mayan and Aztec religion. Songs are discussed in the chapters on "Totemism and Belief in Guardian Spirits" (pp. 66–83), "Medicine Men and Shamans" (pp. 84–102), and "Religion of the Aztecs" (pp. 241–286).

Isaacs, Tony

1972   American Indian Music and Dance. Pp. 12–19 in *Focus on Dance VI: Ethnic and Recreational Dance.* Edited by Jane Harris Ericson. Washington, D. C.: American Association for Health, Physical Education, and Recreation.

Isaacs begins by discussing Native American values relating to music and how they differ from Euro-American concepts. The sections which follow are entitled "The Role of Traditional Dance in American Indian Culture," "Motivations for Development of Recreational Forms," "Powwow Dances in the United States Today," and "Today and Tomorrow."

Izikowitz, Karl Gustav

1935   *Musical and Other Sound Producing Instruments of the South American Indians: A Comparative*

Ethnographical Study. Göteberg: Elanders Boktryckeri Aktiebolag.
This comprehensive study contains references to many instruments which are also found among Indians of North America. Izikowitz gives detailed descriptions of the instruments and speculates on cultural and historical relationships. Includes many photographs and drawings. Several other North American parallels are noted in the review by Herzog (1940 above).

Jenness, Diamond

1933   An Indian Method of Treating Hysteria. *Primitive Man* 6:13–20.
Describes the treatment of "dream-sickness" among Carrier Indians of British Columbia. This involves shamanistic songs and use of a tambourine type drum. Jenness gives translations for the texts of four songs and explains how the songs are used to exorcize the spirit or power which was driving the woman insane. He also compares the native explanation with a "rational explanation."

Jones, Rosalie M.

1992   Modern Native Dance: Beyond Tribe and Tradition. Pp. 169–184 in *Native American Dance: Ceremonies and Social Traditions*, edited by Charlotte Heth. Washington: National Museum of the American Indian, Smithsonian Institution.
Discusses various intersections of Native American dance with western genres such as ballet and modern dance. Jones describes Indian-inspired dances of Ted Shawn during the 1930s and also mentions the well-known Osage ballerinas, Maria Tallchief and Marjorie Tallchief. She focuses mainly on staged dances of the American Indian Dance Theatre (founded in 1987) and on other modern choreographers such as Rene Highway (1954–1990) and Daystar.

Katz, Israel J.

1970   Marius Barbeau, 1883–1969. *Ethnomusicology* 14(1): 129–142.
Barbeau is probably best known for essays on the connections between northeast Asian and North American Indian music. His publications are listed in the Northwest and Northeast bibliographies. See also the bibliography by Cardin (1947 above).

Kealiinohomoku, Joann W.

1991   Film review of *The Longest Trail* by Alan Lomax and
            Forrestine Paulay (1988). *Yearbook for Traditional
            Music* 23:166–169.
    The film is based on a methodology known as choreometrics
and shows film segments of dances from 35 Native American
tribes. Its main thesis is that Indians of North and South America
move their bodies in an "Arctic Style" which reflects hunting and
gathering activities of their ancient ancestors in Arctic Siberia. The
review praises the visual content of the film but criticizes Lomax
severely for selecting examples to fit his hypotheses and various
other faults.

Kealiinohomoku, Joann W., and Frank Gillis

1970   Special Bibliography: Gertrude Prokosch Kurath.
            Ethnomusicology 14(1): 114–128 (January).
    Many of Kurath's articles are listed below and in the
Southwest and Northeast bibliographies.

Keeling, Richard

1984   Tribal Music and Cultural Survival. Pp. 165–176 in
            Sharing a Heritage: American Indian Arts edited by
            Charlotte Heth and Michael Swarm. Contemporary
            American Indian Issues Series, no. 5. Los Angeles:
            American Indian Studies Center, UCLA.
    Discusses the importance of contemporary Indian music as a
means of demonstrating cultural survival. Describes a project to
return recordings to the Indian communities from which they were
collected.

1989   (Editor) *Women in North American Indian Music: Six
            Essays*. Special Monograph Series no. 6.
            Bloomington: Society for Ethnomusicology.
    The book as a whole challenges the widely-held notion that
males tend to dominate in Indian music and seeks to explain how
the role of women could have ended up being so poorly understood. This includes essays listed in the regional bibliographies as
follows: Vander (Great Basin and Plateau), Vennum (Northeast),
Frisbie (Southwest), Cavanagh (Arctic and Sub-Arctic), Hatton
(Plains), and Keeling (California). Keeling's Epilogue (pp. 79–87)
reviews some of the major historical factors that have affected

gender relationships and also points out the male bias in research. There is a review by Herndon (1991 above).

1992a   An Historical Approach to Native American Music and its Implications for Northern Pacific Rim Studies. Pp. 21–30 in *Proceedings of the International Symposium on Comparative Studies of the Music, Dance, and Games of Northern Peoples*, edited by Kazuyuki Tanimoto. Sapporo: Hokkaido Kyoiku Daigaku.

This article outlines a chronological framework for Native American music and focuses on an archaic type of (animal-speech) song that is found in many native repertories of North America and northeastern Asia. Keeling suggests that more research in this direction would help define the North Pacific as a culture area and might also possibly shed light on the roots of Indian music.

1992b   The Sources of Indian Music: An Introduction and Overview. Pages 3–22 in *Music and Spiritual Power among the Indians of North America* edited by Richard Keeling. *World of Music* 92(2). Berlin: International Institute for Traditional Music.

Discusses Native American musical concepts and values by contrast with Euro-American music, then discusses the shamanistic roots of Indian music and how aboriginal concepts of music and power were transformed at various points in the period since contact with Euro-Americans.

Kolinski, Mieczyslaw

1959   The Evaluation of Tempo. *Ethnomusicology* 3:45–57.
A statistical comparison of rhythmic features in American Indian music and African songs of Dahomey. More than 1,000 Indian songs are considered, mainly from the work of Densmore.

1972   An Apache Rabbit Dance Song Cycle as Sung by the Iroquois. *Ethnomusicology* 16:415–464.
This focuses on a song cycle that the Iroquois adopted from some visiting Apaches at a gathering on the Allegheny Reservation (New York) in 1963. Kolinski compares four versions of the cycle in order to show the range of variation which occurs from performance to performance.

Krader, Barbara

(1956)   George Herzog: Bibliography. *Ethnomusicology Newsletter* 1(6): 11–20 (January). For additions see *Ethnomusicology Newsletter* 1(8): 10 (September, 1956); and *Ethnomusicology* 2(3): 321 (September, 1964).

Gives a fairly complete listing of Herzog's publications. Also see McAllester (1985 below) for further information on his life and career.

Krieger, Alex D.

1945   An Inquiry into Supposed Mexican Influences on a Prehistoric "Cult" in the Southeastern United States. *American Anthropologist* 47:483–515.

Employs comparative iconography to evaluate the extent of Mesoamerican influences on Hopewellian and Mississippian cultures of the Southeast culture area. Earlier writers argued that design similarities suggested a single religious movement or ceremonial complex which spread rapidly to the north from Middle America. Krieger questions this (without denying the importance of southern influences in general) and emphasizes the likelihood that the mound builders' religion was largely indigenous (pp. 511–512).

Kurath, Gertrude Prokosch

See Kurath (1950) in Northeast bibliography. This describes a form of dance notation using a Cayuga (Seneca) song as an example.

1953   Native Choreographic Areas of North America. *American Anthropologist* 55(1): 60–73.

Without defining areas systematically, Kurath discusses the distribution of various dance complexes according to ground plan and style of movement. For example, she begins with dances based on counter-clockwise circles, finding them centered in the Eastern Woodlands but also occurring in southeastern areas and elsewhere (pp. 60–62). Other dance prototypes are treated in similar fashion. Historical transformations are also discussed, as are contrasts between the dances of agricultural and hunting peoples (p. 70) and Mexican influences on Indian dances north of the border (p. 71).

1956   Masked Clowns. *Tomorrow* 4(3):106–112. Reprint. Pp. 220–224 in *Half a Century of Dance Research:*

Essays by Gertrude Prokosch Kurath. Flagstaff,
Arizona: Cross Cultural Dance Resources (1986).
A survey of ritual clowning and reverse behavior in sacred
ceremonies, this covers instances from the following tribes: Yaqui,
Mayo, Tarahumara, Papago, Navajo, Crow, Dakota, Iroquois, and
various Pueblo groups.

See Kurath (1956) in the Northeast bibliography for a description of
Pan-Indian dances.

See Kurath (1957) in the Northeast bibliography. This discusses the history of Catholic hymns among Indians of Michigan and the relation of hymns to native songs.

See Kurath (1957) in the Northeast bibliography. This deals with Pan-
Indian elements in a tribal festival held by Indians of the Great
Lakes area.

1960   Dance, Music, and the Daily Bread. *Ethnomusicology*
            4:1–9. Reprint. Pp. 249–256 in *Half a Century of
            Dance Research: Essays by Gertrude Prokosch
            Kurath.* Flagstaff, Arizona: Cross Cultural Dance
            Resources (1986).
An interesting precursor of later writings on the relation of
music and dance to subsistence patterns, as for example by Lomax
(1968, 1976 below). This paper also deals with choreographic
symbolism, gender patterns, and various historical developments.
Most of the examples are from American Indian cultures.

1961   Dances of Frenzy. *Folklorist* 6(6): 479–482. Reprint.
            Pp. 225–229 in *Half a Century of Dance Research:
            Essays by Gertrude Prokosch Kurath.* Flagstaff,
            Arizona: Cross Cultural Dance Resources (1986).
A brief survey of shamanism and related practices, this article
contains brief accounts of the following: Eskimo and Siberian
shamans, the Midewiwin medicine society, the Iroquois Society of
Shamans and Mystic Animals, the Indian Shaker Church, the
Ghost Dance, the Sun Dance, and Peyote religion.

1962   American Indian Ritual Dances for Sustenance (in
            two parts). *Folklorist* 7(2): 41–47; and 7(3): 70–78.
            Reprint. Pp. 276–291 in *Half a Century of Dance
            Research: Essays by Gertrude Prokosch Kurath.*
            Flagstaff, Arizona: Cross Cultural Dance Resources
            (1986).

The first part contains descriptions of harvest ceremonies in the Northeast Area (Iroquois Society of Women Planters and Tutelo Four Nights Harvest Rite) and the Southwest (Papago Prayer Stick Ritual, Tewa Pueblo Basket Dance, Santa Clara Sun Basket Dance, San Juan Yellow Corn Dance, Keresan Corn Dance, Pueblo Buffalo Dances). The second part describes mimetic animal dances from both areas (Pueblo Buffalo Dances; Tewa Deer Dances; Yaqui Deer Dances; Iroquois and Chippewa Fish Dances; Iroquois Eagle Dance; and Meskwaki, Menomini, and Ottawa Swan Dances). The two parts include six musical examples identified as Cochiti Pueblo (4), San Juan Pueblo (1) and Iroquois (1).

1969   A Comparison of Plains and Pueblo Songs. *Ethnomusicology* 13(3): 512–517. Reprint. Pp. 198–203 in *Half a Century of Dance Research: Essays by Gertrude Prokosch Kurath*. Flagstaff, Arizona: Cross Cultural Dance Resources (1986).

Compares two (northern) Grass Dance songs from Manitoba (Canada) with a Basket Dance song and two Comanche Dance songs recorded at San Juan Pueblo. Though the Comanche Dance songs are known to have come to the Pueblos from (southern) Plains tribes of Oklahoma, they differ from the Grass Dance songs by having "pyramidal" melodic contours and more distinct formal divisions (p. 517). Kurath concludes by questioning the "Plains-Pueblo area" as outlined in Nettl (General bibliography, 1954).

1986   *Half a Century of Dance Research: Essays by Gertrude Prokosch Kurath*. Flagstaff, Arizona: Cross Cultural Dance Resources.

A valuable collection containing reprints of articles that might otherwise be difficult to obtain. Besides titles listed above, this contains articles listed in the Southwest, Northeast, Southeast, and Mesoamerican bibliographies.

Laubin, Reginald, and Gladys Laubin

1977   *Indian Dances of North America: Their Importance to Indian Life*. Norman: University of Oklahoma Press.

The authors are theatrical performers of Indian dance whose purpose is to write a comprehensive overview that would appeal to general readers as well as to scholars. There is a critical review by Sweet (1981 below).

Lee, Dorothy Sara

1979   *Native North American Music and Oral Data: A
            Catalogue of Sound Recordings, 1893–1976.*
            Bloomington: Indiana University Press.
   This catalogue lists nearly 500 separate accessions deposited
at the Indiana University Archives of Traditional Music, beginning
with Mooney's cylinder recordings of Plains Indian music
(collected in 1893). While Seeger and Spear (1987 below) only list
cylinder originals, this catalogue also includes recordings on disc,
wire, and tape.

Linton, Ralph

1943   Nativistic Movements. *American Anthropologist*
            45:230–243.
   A classic anthropological study concerning motivations and
historical circumstances prompting religious movements such as
the Ghost Dance and North American peyote cult.

Loeb, Edwin M.

1929   Tribal Initiations and Secret Societies. *University of
            California Publications in American Archaeology
            and Ethnology* 25:249–288.
   This world survey of initiation rituals was inspired by Loeb's
previous research on secret societies of the Pomo (California bibliography 1926). The section on North America (pp. 266–280) includes information relating to the following groups: (1) Pomo and
other tribes of northern California; (2) Luiseño and Diegueño of
southern California; (3) Zuni and other Pueblos of the Southwest;
(4) Kwakiutl and other tribes of the Northwest Coast; and (5)
Ojibwa, Menomini, and Lenape (Delaware) Indians of the
Northeast area.

Lomax, Alan

1959   Folk Song Style. *American Anthropologist* 61:927–
            954.
   An early attempt to classify world music traditions through
statistical analysis of certain measures developed by Lomax, this
contains a profile of the "Amerindian" song style (pp. 932–934).
The analysis is based mainly on Lomax's ratings of recordings collected by others.

1968   *Folk Song Style and Culture.* Publication No. 88. Washington: American Association for the Advancement of Science.
The definitive work on a methodology known as cantometrics. This system is based on the idea that every tradition of vocal music tends to symbolize certain behavior patterns that are important for cultural continuity. Each style is measured according to 36 parameters, and from these ratings Lomax develops conclusions about musical meaning and historical relationships. Lomax discusses the cantometric profiles for "South America" (pp. 82–84), "North America" (pp. 85–87), and "Arctic Asia" (pp. 102–104). He then examines American Indian musical relationships more closely (pp. 106–110). Here, Lomax distinguishes ten separate sub-styles (p. 108) and discusses the distributions of a "masculine style" and a more "feminized" style which are broader in scope (pp. 108–110). Also see Erickson (1969 above).

1976   *Cantometrics: A Method in Musical Anthropology.* Berkeley: University of California Extension Media Center.
This explication of the cantometrics methodology is particularly useful because the text is keyed to seven cassette tapes through which students and researchers can learn and practice the rating system themselves. This includes profiles for various styles of Native American music (pp. 38–39) and several other references to American Indian music (passim). See the previous entry (Lomax 1968 above).

Lowie, Robert H.

1915   Ceremonialism in North America. Pp. 229–258 in *Anthropology in North America* edited by Franz Boas et al. New York: G. E. Stechert and Co.
This early summary begins by listing the most prominent ceremonial complexes for various culture areas (pp. 229–234). Lowie then discusses thematic topics such as the relation of ritual to myth (pp. 234–238), the diffusion of ceremonials (pp. 238–245), typical patterns in ritual activity (pp. 245–249), and the purpose or object of ceremonies (pp. 249–256).

1938   The Emergence Hole and the Foot Drum. *American Anthropologist* 40:174.

In this paper Lowie postulates a single origin for the foot drum as observed among the Pueblo tribes (Zuni, Hopi, Acoma) and among the Maidu Indians of California.

Lueders, Edward

1958   Color Symbolism in Songs of the American Indian. *Western Humanities Review* 12:115–120.
Covers the music of various tribes. Includes English translations for eleven song texts.

McAllester, David Park

1949   *Peyote Music*. Viking Fund Publications in Anthropology no. 13. New York: Viking Fund.
A comprehensive study comparing various manifestations of Peyote music among American Indian peoples. Separate tribal styles are described and analyzed. McAllester then defines a general style of Peyote music and compares this with music of the Ghost Dance. The work contains 80 musical examples (with texts), from the following tribes: Comanche (30 songs), Washo (10), Dakota (9), Fox (8), Cheyenne (8), Pawnee (4), Kiowa (3), Shoshone (2), Ute (3), Tonkawa (1), Kickapoo (1), and Arapaho (1).

1953   Review of *Old World Overtones in the New World: Some Parallels with North American Indian Musical Instruments* by Theodore Seder (1952). *American Anthropologist* 55:272.
This is a highly critical review. Seder had focused on parallels without necessarily drawing interpretive conclusions, but McAllester objects to the implicit evolutionist presumptions of the book and also points up other flaws as well.

1955   American Indian Songs and Pan-Tribalism. *Midwest Folklore* 5 (Summer): 132–136.
This is actually an essay in review of several recordings produced by Canyon Records. McAllester notes the growing market for recordings of pan-Indian music among Indian people and discusses how marketing and the professionalism of the singers have affected the style of the music.

1977   A Different Drum: A Consideration of Music in the Native American Humanities. Pp. 155–183 in *The Religious Character of Native American Humanities:*

An *Interdisciplinary Congress Held April 14–16, 1977*. Tempe: Department of Humanities and Religious Studies, Arizona State University.

Begins by emphasizing the diversity of Indian musical traditions, identifying some very general trends and noting important exceptions to each of them. McAllester then discusses how Native American musical aesthetics differ from our own (Euro-American) concepts of music as an abstract artform. The importance of texts and vocables in Indian music is discussed at some length (pp. 162–173), while other aspects of musical symbolism are noted more briefly (pp. 173–175). The essay closes by describing nine types of contemporary Indian music, some of which are closely related to traditional styles while others are strikingly different and western ("Anglo") in character. This includes extended comments on a Navajo song text ("The War God's Horse Song") and how such a text should be interpreted in a course on Native American humanities.

1977   Record review of "Songs of Earth, Water, Fire, and Sky: Music of the American Indian," recording and liner notes by Charlotte Heth (1976). *Ethnomusicology* 21(3):523–524.

Basically a favorable review but does suggest that Heth might have included some contemporary music rather than focusing on "traditional" genres. For contents of recording, see Heth (1976 above).

1980   North American Native Music. Pp. 307–331 in *Musics of Many Cultures* edited by Elizabeth May. Berkeley and Los Angeles: University of California Press.

An excellent introduction to the subject for general readers. Describes various regional styles and intertribal music of the Ghost Dance, Native American Church, and modern Indian powwow. Includes nine musical examples.

1984   North America/Native America. Pp. 12–63 in *Worlds of Music: An Introduction to the Music of the World's People* edited by Jeff Todd Titon, James T. Koetting, David McAllester, David Reck, and Mark Slobin. New York: Schirmer Books.

Another fine introduction to the subject. McAllester first discusses three regional styles (Sioux Grass Dance song, Zuni lullaby, and Iroquois Quiver Dance song); he then illustrates the dynamic character of Indian music by describing several styles currently in use among one tribe, the Navajo. This includes many notations and ten recorded examples on a cassette tape which accompanies the book.

1985   In Memorium: George Herzog (1901–1984). *Ethnomusicology* 29(1): 86–87.

Brief biography describing the career, work habits, and personality of a major figure in research on Native American music.

1988   L'Enseignement des Musiques Amérindiennes des États-Unis: Éthiques at Pédagogie ("On Teaching Native American Musics: Ethics and Pedagogy"). *Recherches Amérindiennes au Québec* 18(4): 59–64.

Discusses reasons for the lack of university courses on Native American music, identifying the following factors: cultural arrogance, the inherent complexity of the vocal styles, and ethical objections to using secret and/or sacred materials. McAllester states that there are many types of songs that can indeed be taught without objection and that performance of the songs is essential to understanding. Also describes the Native American music program at Wesleyan University.

1993   Obituary: Willard Rhodes (1901–1992). *Ethnomusicology* 37(2): 251–262.

Gives a brief biography and outlines the contents of a collection of Rhodes's personal papers and recordings to be found in the Ethnomusicology Archive at the University of California, Los Angeles.

Maguire, Marsha, Pamela Feldman, and Joseph C. Hickerson

1983   *American Indian and Eskimo Music: A Selected Bibliography Through 1981.* Library of Congress Folk Archive Reference Aid No. 1. Washington: American Folklife Center, Library of Congress.

This (40-page) booklet includes nearly 400 sources from various culture areas in one alphabetical list. Contains no annotations but does provide call numbers and useful information on alternate editions and reprints.

Mason, Otis T.

1897   Geographical Distribution of the Musical Bow. *American Anthropologist* 10 (old series): 377–380.

An early survey of musical bows from various parts of the world, this mentions museum specimens from California (Tule River) and New Mexico (Pueblo) . Others from Africa, Madagascar, and various Pacific Islands are also described. Mason concludes that stringed musical instruments were probably not known in the New World before Columbus but offers little to substantiate this assertion. The subject is also discussed by Balfour (1899 above) and Roberts (1936:13–16 below).

Merriam, Alan P.

1955   The Use of Music in the Study of a Problem of Acculturation. *American Anthropologist* 57:28–41.

Examines the hypothesis that acculturation and exchange of ideas is more prevalent between cultures that are relatively similar and less likely between cultures that have less in common. Merriam compares the degree of acculturation (to Western culture) in Flathead Indian music with that of urban music in the Belgian Congo. He finds that acculturation in Flathead music is extremely slight while music in the African culture had become dramatically altered. He concludes this owes to the fact that Western and Flathead Indian styles are so different in character, while (by contrast) European and African music share important commonalities such as diatonic scales and the use of harmony.

1960   An Annotated Bibliography of Theses and Dissertations in Ethnomusicology and Folk Music Accepted at American Universities. *Ethnomusicology* 4: 21–39.

This includes entries dealing with the following groups or areas: American Indian music in general (3), Indians of Mexico (2), Mexican Indians of Oaxaca and Chiapas, Comanche, Oglalla Sioux, California Indians (in general), Papago, Paiute, Northwest Coast tribes (in general), Pima and Papago (Herzog), Arizona Indians (in general), Northern Ute (Sun Dance), Cheyenne, Jemez Pueblo, Peyote Music (McAllester), Eskimos of Alaska, Tlingit (Mark), Twana, Arapaho (Nettl), Winnebago (Radin), Navajo and Pueblo (compared), Plains Sun Dance (Spier), Navajo, Hopi (music in traditional education), and music in Sonoran Uto-Aztecan cultures.

See **Mooney** (1896) in Plains bibliography for classic study of the Ghost Dance religion and its spread from the Great Basin to the Plains area.

Myers, Helen

1986   Ethnomusicology. Pp. 58–62 in *The New Grove Dictionary of American Music*, vol. 2 (E–K). Edited by H. Wiley Hitchcock and Stanley Sadie. London: Macmillan.

This contains an informative section entitled "Studies of American Indian Music, 1890–1954" (pp. 59–60). The history of research and theory is also discussed in an earlier study by Rhodes (1952b below).

Nettl, Bruno

1953a   Observations on Meaningless Peyote Song Texts. *Journal of American Folklore* 66:161–164.

Discusses the relations between text and melody in Peyote songs from various tribes. Includes musical examples from the Arapaho, Shawnee, and Comanche (one each). The notations are from McAllester (1949 above).

1953b   Stylistic Variety in North American Indian Music. *American Musicological Society Journal* 6:160–168.

Discusses the history of research on American Indian music and tentatively defines six distinct styles by culture area. Includes previously published notations from the Makah, Modoc, Yuma, Navajo, Arapaho, and Choctaw (one each).

Also see Nettl (1953) in the Northeast bibliography. This is a comparative study which interprets the variety of styles in different types of Shawnee songs as a result of historical contacts and migrations.

1954a   *North American Indian Musical Styles*. Memoirs of the American Folklore Society, vol. 45. Philadelphia: American Folklore Society. Previously published in the *Journal of American Folklore* 67(1954): 45–56, 297–307, and 351–368.

A classic monograph which combines the approaches of comparative musicology and American culture area theory. The preface provides a survey of writings published before 1954. Nettl then summarizes the major characteristics of music of the following (six) areas: (1) Eskimo-Northwest Coast, (2) Great Basin, (3) California-Yuman, (4) Athabascan, (5) Plains-Plateau, and (6) an Eastern area. In closing, he comments on the relation of musical areas to ethnographic culture areas and to the distribution of Indian language families.

1954b   Notes on Musical Composition in Primitive Culture. *Anthropological Quarterly* 27:81–90.

Focuses on information gathered from an Arapaho singer. Includes musical examples from the Arapaho (1 song) and Shawnee (2 songs).

1955   Change in Folk and Primitive Music: A Survey of Problems and Methods. *Journal of the American Musicological Society* 8:101–109.

Summarizes the content of several earlier publications which deal with the question of stylistic change in North American Indian music.

1956   American Primitive Music North of Mexico. Pp. 105–119 in *Music in Primitive Culture*, by Bruno Nettl. Cambridge: Harvard University Press.

A survey of Indian musical style areas based on Nettl's previous work. This contains 28 musical examples, mainly from the writings of others.

1958   Historical Aspects of Ethnomusicology. *American Anthropologist* 60:518–532. Reprint. Pp. 150–166 in *Readings in Ethnomusicology*, edited by David P. McAllester. New York: Johnson Reprint Corp. (1971).

This theoretical discussion touches on the following specific subjects relating to American Indian music: (1) stylistic change in Shawnee music as a result of historical contacts; (2) transformation in Peyote music as a result of Plains influences on an Apache prototype; (3) the retention of Northern Athabascan characteristics in Navajo and Apache music; and (4) a situation labeled the "pattern phenomenon" by Helen Roberts, which refers to the process occurring when a ceremonial complex intensifies certain specialized tendencies of a musical repertory.

1958   Notes on Musical Areas. *Acta Musicologica* 30:170–177.

Discusses theoretical issues such as identification of musical areas, the relationships between areas, and the problem of stylistic integration. Focuses mainly on North American Indian music research.

1958   Transposition as a Composition Technique in Folk
              and Primitive Music. *Ethnomusicology* 2:56–65.
    Nettl examines transpositional patterns in many musical cul-
tures of the world. Includes musical examples from the Arapaho (2
songs) and Chippewa (1).

1961   Polyphony in North American Indian Music. *Musical
              Quarterly* 47:354–362.
    Nettl reviews the published literature for instances of
polyphony and finds only a few clear references, mainly among
Indians of the Northwest Coast culture area. He then speculates on
various possible reasons for its non-occurrence, suggesting that
polyphony once possibly existed and had died out or that it was a
fairly recent discovery which had not yet spread to all areas before
the invasion of whites (p. 361). Nettl also suggests also that the
dearth of polyphony may be related to the lack of melodic musical
instruments (p. 362).

1965   The American Indians. Pp. 147–168 in *Folk and
              Traditional Music of the Western Continents*, by
              Bruno Nettl. Englewood Cliffs, N.J.: Prentice-Hall.
    An overview intended for introductory classes. Includes a
summary of musical areas outlined in Nettl (1954 above) and other
topical sections on simple songs in wide distribution, uses of
Indian music, ideas about music, musical instruments, Indian music of Latin America, the words of songs, and recent historical
trends. Includes notations from earlier sources.

1966   Some Influences of Western Civilization on North
              American Indian Music. Pp. 129–137 in *Mid-
              America Conference on Literature, History, Popular
              Culture, and Folklore, Purdue University, 1965: New
              Voices in American Studies* edited by Ray Browne,
              Donald Winkelman and Allen Hayman. West
              Lafayette, Indiana: Purdue University Studies.
    Nettl begins by distinguishing the effects of direct contact
from more indirect influences of the European presence in North
America. Patterns derived from direct contact include the following: (1) use of English words with Indian melodies, (2) use of
Indian words with European melodies, (3) general impoverishment
of Indian repertories, (4) impoverishment of musical styles through
reduction of variety or complexity, (5) use of western musical instruments, (6) westernization of scales, and (7) dances introduced
as a result of Euro-American contacts. Patterns resulting from indi-

rect influences are identified as follows: (1) mixture of traditional repertories, (2) the advent of Peyotism and other messianic religions involving music, (3) influences of Christianity, and (4) development of Pan-Indian musical styles.

1969   Musical Areas Reconsidered: A Critique of North American Indian Research. Pp. 181–189 in *Essays in Musicology in Honor of Dragan Plamenac on His 70th Birthday* edited by Gustave Reese and Robert J. Snow. Pittsburgh: University of Pittsburgh Press. Reprint. New York: Da Capo Press, 1977.

Discusses the concept of musical style areas and suggests revisions in his earlier outline (1954 above). Nettl begins by discussing problems with the assumption that areas are stylistically homogeneous. He argues that musical areas may be defined either (1) by presence or absence of traits or (2) by frequencies of occurrence. Nettl then goes on to distinguish "good" areas from those which are more poorly defined. His revised scheme consists of the following areas: (1) a very large area including the East, the Plains, and the Eastern Great Basin, together with Pueblo and Eastern Apache; (2) an Eskimo area, which has similarities with (3) the Northwest Coast and Coast Salish; (4) a region including the Western Basin and Northern California; and (5) a California-Yuman area, which also includes the Navajo.

1973   Comparison and Comparative Method in Ethnomusicology. *Yearbook for Inter-American Music Research* 9:148–161.

This discusses theory and method in studies of American Indian music by Densmore, Herzog, Roberts, Kolinski, Merriam, and Nettl himself.

1980   Record review of "A Cry from the Earth: Music of the North American Indians" produced by John Bierhorst (Folkways FC 7777, 1979). *Ethnomusicology* 24(2): 341–342.

Nettl calls this the best available survey on a commercial album. The disk includes recordings made by various major researchers such as Frances Densmore, George Herzog, Gertrude Kurath, James Mooney, and Willard Rhodes. Side A contains examples from five culture areas. Side B is arranged by genre (from various areas), including children's songs, prayers or medicine songs, war songs, flute pieces, songs for the dead, and songs reflecting culture change over the last hundred years. See Bierhorst (1979 above).

1982   Review of Native American Music, by Marcia Herndon (1980). *Ethnomusicology* 26(1): 161–162.

Acknowledges the usefulness of the book as a text for teaching but criticizes the writing style and production as careless and hurried. Nettl also questions whether Herndon succeeds in her goal of expressing "the Native American perspective," arguing that in fact the book reads like any other study based on traditional (academic) ethnomusicology (p. 161).

1985   *The Western Impact on World Music: Change, Adaptation, and Survival.* New York: Schirmer Books.

This contains several chapters dealing with American Indian music. Chapter 6 discusses the influence of musical technology and the concert format, while Chapter 7 considers the impact of western harmony. Some of these concepts are personalized in Chapter 27, which deals with two Indian singers (W. Shakespear and Calvin Boy). Chapter 28 (by Victoria Lindsay Levine) compares a musical genre among the Mississippi Choctaw and in Oklahoma Choctaw communities.

Nettl, Bruno, Gertrude P. Kurath, J. Richard Haefer, Nicholas N. Smith, Doreen Binnington, and Liang Ming-Yüeh

1980   North America: Indian and Eskimo Traditions. Pp. 295–320 in *The New Grove Dictionary of Music and Musicians,* vol. 13, edited by Stanley Sadie. London: Macmillan.

A comprehensive survey of information in highly condensed form. The section on "Music" (pp. 295–307) gives a history of research, discusses general characteristics of Native American music, and then distinguishes six regional styles in the manner of Nettl (1954 above). There follows a discussion of musical instruments by type (idiophones, membranophones, chordophones, and aerophones). Historical developments (Euro-American influences on Indian music, Peyote music, the Ghost Dance, and Pan-Indian music) are also covered. The section (by Kurath) on "Dance" (pp. 307–312) is organized into four main sections as follows: (1) religious purposes and ceremonial vestiges, (2) symbolism and elements of style, (3) relation of dance to music, and (4) modern hybrids: fiesta and powwow. Finally, a section entitled

"Representative Tribes" (pp. 312–320) gives descriptions of music and dances of the following groups: Blackfoot, Chippewa, Iroquois, Kwakiutl, Paiute, Papago, Seminole, Tewa, and Wabanaki.

Nettl, Bruno, Charlotte Heth, and Gertrude P. Kurath

1986   Indians, American. Pp. 460–479 in *The New Grove Dictionary of American Music* , vol. 2 (E–K), edited by H. Wiley Hitchcock and Stanley Sadie. London: Macmillan.

Contains sections on "Music" (pp. 460–474) and "Dance" (pp. 474–479) which are basically identical with those in the earlier encyclopedic essay by Nettl et al. (1980 above). In this encyclopedia of American music, there are many separate entries discussing the music of various tribes, thus the general entry contains no section on "Representative Tribes."

Nichols, Francis S.

1954   Index to Schoolcraft's "Indian Tribes of the United States." *Bureau of American Ethnology Bulletin* no. 152.

This index to the six-volume work by Schoolcraft (1851–1857 below) includes many references to musical subjects.

Nordenskiöld, Erland

1912   Une Contribution à la connaissance de l'anthropogéographie de l'Amérique. *Journal de la Société des Américanistes de Paris* 9:19–25.

Presents a theory of marginal survivals to explain the distribution of culture traits that are present in North America (north of Mexico) and in South America but absent or unreported in the intervening areas of higher culture. Nordenskiöld argues that these traits are survivals of an older culture which had once been spread continuously over both continents.

Parsons, Elsie Clews

1929   Ritual Parallels in Pueblo and Plains Culture, with a Special Reference to the Pawnee. *American Anthropologist* 31:642–655.

This does not contain specific references to music but remains important as an early comparative study. Parsons first examines parallels connecting the Pueblos with Plains culture (generally), finding that several ritual objects and other patterns are shared despite the disparate tendencies toward individualism (Plains) versus communalism (Pueblo) in ritual. She then focuses on stronger parallels (ceremonial calendar and organization), concluding these may have come to the Pawnee from the Pueblos along with other aspects of the maize complex.

Parthun, Paul

1976   Tribal Music in North America. *Music Educators Journal* 62(5): 32–45. Music Educators National Conference. Reston, Virginia.

An introduction for music educators and general readers with some musical background. Parthun discusses general characteristics of Indian music as viewed under the following headings: rhythm, melody, form, musical instruments, song types, and vocal quality. He also discusses changing styles in recent times. This includes eight musical examples from the following groups: Ojibwe (three songs), Kwakiutl (two songs), Pueblo, Pawnee, and Apache (one each).

Powers, William K.

1960   American Indian Music, Part One: An Introduction. *American Indian Tradition* 7(1): 5–9

This is the first in a series of eight articles designed for the student who has no technical background in music but is interested in learning how to sing Indian songs. The first four parts are listed here, since they deal with aspects of inter-tribal powwow singing, while the last four are listed in the Plains bibliography. This introductory essay gives general information and offers advice on how the hobbyist can learn songs and drum patterns mainly through listening to recordings.

1961a   American Indian Music, Part Two: The Language. *American Indian Tradition* 7(2): 41–45.

Mainly discusses the use of vocables in Indian music but also gives information on song texts in Indian languages and in English. Provides historical information on these developments and includes a standardized notation system to help the student learn song texts based on vocables.

1961b   American Indian Music, Part Three: The Social Dances. *American Indian Tradition* 7(3): 97–104.

Begins by emphasizing the extent to which some Indian songs tend to circulate between tribes—especially in social dances, which are viewed as a special (intertribal) category of Indian music. Powers deals mainly with the Round Dance and Rabbit Dance as performed by tribes of the Plains and Oklahoma regions. He describes the dance steps, drumming patterns, and overall structure of the songs. The analysis focuses on text and vocable patterns, including several diagrams but no musical notations.

1961c   American Indian Music, Part Four: War Dance Songs. *American Indian Tradition* 7(4): 128–134.

Powers begins by pointing out that the form of the War Dance songs resembles that of Round Dance songs as described in Powers (1961b above), except that the drum patterns are different. In this article he defines the War Dance (and variants) as performed among tribes of the Plains and Oklahoma regions, then he describes the dance steps, drum patterns, and formal structure of the songs. The analysis focuses on text and vocable patterns, including several diagrams but no musical notations. See Powers (1961a, 1961b, 1962a, and 1962b) in the Plains bibliography for parts five through eight of this series.

1975   The Study of Native American Music. *Keystone Folklore Quarterly* 20(3): 39–56.

The article begins by discussing the field of ethnomusicology in general, then addresses the following subjects: the need for more research on Native American aesthetics, processes of composition in Indian music, Pan-Indian music, texts and vocables, Indian songs with English words, classification of musical styles by culture area, and the variety of styles in various regional repertories. The section on stylistic classification contains an interesting clarification of "incomplete repetition" as a structural or stylistic feature in Plains Indian music (pp. 45–46). This also includes a bibliography (pp. 47–53) and list of commercial and archival recordings (pp. 53–56).

See Powers (1981) in the Plains bibliography. This record review essay discusses the professionalization of powwow singers.

1994   Powwow. Pp. 476–480 in *Native America in the Twentieth Century: An Encyclopedia* edited by Mary B. Davis. New York: Garland Publishing.

A concise summary with sections on the following: (1) the origins of the powwow in earlier ceremonies of the Pawnee and

Omaha tribes; (2) the diffusion of the complex among various
tribes of the Plains and origin of terms such as "Omaha Dance" and
"Grass Dance"; (3) a description of six basic styles of dance that
are performed in modern powwows; (4) the custom of "giveaways"
through which gifts are exchanged at powwows; and (5) the practice of holding dance contests, which became a popular feature of
the powwow in the mid-1950s.

Radin, Paul

> 1948   Music and Medicine among Primitive Peoples. Pp. 3–
>   24 in *Music and Medicine* edited by Dorothy
>   Schullian and Max Schoen. New York: H.
>   Schumann.

Radin describes the use of music for curing among the Ojibwa
(p. 17), Winnebago (p. 19–20) and Eskimo (p. 21).

Rhodes, Willard

> 1943   On the Warpath, 1942. *Modern Music* 20:157–160.

Describes some influences of World War II on songs of the
Teton Sioux. Includes two musical examples, with texts and translations.

> 1949, 1953   (Recording and liner notes) "Music of the Sioux and
>   Navajo." Smithsonian-Folkways Recordings (FE
>   4401).

Currently available on cassette, this classic album features
various different styles from the two tribes. The Sioux recordings
are identified as follows: Rabbit Dance Song, Peyote Song, Love
Song, Sun Dance Song, Omaha Dance Song about World War II,
Love Song (for flute), and Honoring Song. Songs of the Navajo are
as follows: Riding Song, Song of Happiness, Spinning Dance
Songs (2), Corn Grinding Song, Squaw Dance Song, Silversmith
Song, and Night Chant (Yeibichai).

> 1952a   Acculturation in North American Indian Music. Pp.
>   127–132 in *Proceedings of the 29th International
>   Congress of Americanists in New York* (1949) edited
>   by Sol Tax. Vol. 2 (of two). New York: Cooper
>   Square Publishers.

Rhodes considers missionization and schools as the primary
vehicles for musical acculturation. He begins by discussing the
singing of Christian hymns among the Sioux, Kiowa, Choctaw,
and Hopi. Then he focuses on musical activities at Indian boarding

schools and discusses humorous social dance songs with English words (including notations of two rather famous or well-traveled examples). Rhodes concludes that the degree of acculturation in Indian music is remarkably slight compared to that which has taken place in other spheres.

1952b   North American Indian Music: A Bibliographical Survey of Anthropological Theory. *Notes of the Music Library Association* 10:33–45.

An historical survey of theoretical developments in research on American Indian music from its beginnings until 1951. Major figures whose work is discussed and evaluated include: Theodore Baker, Alice Cunningham Fletcher, Francis La Flesche, Franz Boas, Benjamin Ives Gilman, Carl Stumpf, Erich von Hornbostel, Frances Densmore, Natalie (Curtis) Burlin, Helen Roberts, George Herzog, Marius Barbeau, William Fenton, Gertrude Kurath, David McAllester, and Willard Rhodes himself.

1954   (Recording and notes) "Music of the American Indian: Indian Songs of Today Sung by Indian Young People." Library of Congress, Recorded Sound Division (AFS L36).

One of a series of recordings collected by Rhodes circa 1940–1952 and recently reissued (during the 1980s) with updated liner notes. Contains the following: Seminole Duck Dance, Creek Lullaby, Potawatomi Song, Sioux War Song, Sioux Rabbit Dance, Navajo Squaw Dances, Tewa Basket Dance, Round Dance (Picuris Pueblo), Buffalo Dance (San Juan Pueblo), Modern Love Songs (4), Kiowa Round Dance, Kiowa Buffalo Dance, Feather Dance, Two Cherokee Christian Hymns, Stomp Dance, Tlingit Paddling Song.

1960   The Christian Hymnology of North American Indians. Pp. 324–331 in *Men in Culture: Proceedings of the 5th International Congress of Anthropological and Ethnological Sciences in Philadelphia (1956)* edited by Anthony F.C. Wallace. Philadelphia: University of Pennsylvania Press.

Rhodes begins by discussing the process of missionization and the historical background of Christian hymn singing. He then describes Christian hymns as sung among the Sioux (Dakota) and Kiowa (with one musical notation of each). The article also covers music of the Indian Shaker Church (with two musical examples).

1956   Review of *North American Indian Musical Styles* by
              Bruno Nettl (1954). *Journal of the International Folk
              Music Council* 8:106–107.
Basically a positive review, though Rhodes does question
Nettl's combining Plains and Pueblo music into a single area and
also suggests that his method of classification takes too little account of song types (or variations) within the culture areas.

1958   A Study of Music Diffusion Based on the Wandering
              of the Opening Peyote Song. *Journal of the Interna-
              tional Folk Music Council* 10:42–49. Reprint. Pp.
              132–141 in *Readings in Ethnomusicology* edited by
              David McAllester. New York: Johnson Reprint Corp.
              (1971).
The opening Peyote song is one of four songs that are fixed elements in the Peyote ritual and have traveled from tribe to tribe as
an integral part of the complex. Rhodes compares many different
versions and finds that the song has maintained a surprising degree
of consistency. He also discusses how the song has passed over
into secular repertories, even mentioning a popular commercial
version. This includes musical examples from the Kiowa, Navajo,
and Zuñi (one each), along with the notation of a melody from an
advertisement for Mohawk Carpets.

1963   North American Indian Music in Transition: A Study
              of Songs with English Words as an Index of
              Acculturation. *Journal of the International Folk
              Music Council* 15:9–14.
Focuses mainly on English-language songs which are intended
to be humorous in character. Rhodes discusses the origin of the
songs, the contexts in which they are sung, and basic characteristics of the musical style. He then addresses several issues in considering whether the songs do indeed reflect processes of acculturation and secularization. Includes quotes from a San Juan Pueblo
singer and three musical examples.

1967   Special Bibliography: Helen Heffron Roberts. *Ethno-
              musicology* 11(2): 228–233 (May).

Also see Frisbie (1989 above) for biographical information.

Riemer, Mary F. (See also Riemer-Weller)

1978 Instrumental and Vocal Love Songs of the North American Indians. Master's thesis. Wesleyan University.
  Riemer's analysis focuses on the stylistic unity of music for the courting flute and vocal love songs. The information given here is from Wapp (1984:55 below).

Riemer-Weller, Mary F. (See also Mary Riemer)

1986 Courting Flute (Music). Pp. 518–519 in *The New Grove Dictionary of American Music*, vol. 1 (A–D), edited by H. Wiley Hitchcock and Stanley Sadie. London: Macmillan.
  Focuses on an instrument used by men for serenading women among tribes of the Plains, Plateau, and Southwest culture areas. Gives detailed information on construction, including one photograph and one diagram. Also briefly describes general characteristics of the musical style.

Roberts, Helen Heffron

1922 New Phases in the Study of Primitive Music. *American Anthropologist* 24:144–161.
  Begins by noting the potential importance of vocal music as a key to cultural and historical interpretations, also suggesting that the style of ceremonial and ritual songs may be more stable and meaningful than that of miscellaneous (personal) songs. Roberts then demonstrates a system of graph notation based on that used by Densmore in Teton Sioux Music (1918). This is used to distinguish the musical styles of two ceremonies connected with the Pawnee Creation Ritual (the Skull Bundle Ceremony and the White Beaver Ceremony). Roberts discusses some historical implications and argues that this should be the goal of future (comparative) research. She criticizes certain other scholars whose work has been mainly descriptive in character (Densmore, Fletcher, Gilman, Curtis) or who have relied on evolutionist presumptions about Indian music (Burton).

1926 Ancient Hawaiian Music. *Bernice Pauahi Bishop Museum Bulletin* 29.
  The section entitled "Geographical Distribution of Instruments and Music Like the Hawaiian" (pp. 322–390) includes several references to American Indian instruments.

1932   Melodic Composition and Scale Foundations in
              Primitive Music. *American Anthropologist* 34:79–
              107.
    Takes issue with those who analyze the tonal "systems" of
Indian music and argues that this represents a projection of our
(western) compositional bias. Roberts states that in the absence of
formulated music theory, these derived tonal materials are not re-
ally scales at all (in our sense of the word) and tend to be numerous
and varied in any group. Any objective understanding of melodic
development and intervallic relationships is difficult, according to
Roberts, and broad classifications such as "pentatonic" have little
value.

1933   The Pattern Phenomenon in Primitive Music.
              Zeitschrift für vergleichende Musikwissenschaft
              1:49–52.
    Discusses the tendency for songs of a given ceremonial com-
plex to develop characteristic structural patterns that are basically
independent of melodic content. Includes musical examples from
the Pawnee (4 songs), Iroquois (2), and Nootka (1).

1936   *Musical Areas in Aboriginal North America*. Yale
              University Publications in Anthropology 12. New
              Haven, Conn. Reprinted by Human Relations Area
              Files Press (New Haven, 1970).
    A synthesis of available information about Indian music at the
time it was published, this short monograph remains important because of Roberts's broad research experience and the paucity of
other general studies to have appeared since. After discussing some
"popular traditions" about Indian music and correcting them with
some generalizations of her own, Roberts gives a survey of instrumental and vocal music in various culture areas.

Rodriguez-Nieto, Catherine

1982   *Sound Recordings in Native American Languages: A
              Catalogue*. Berkeley: Language Laboratory,
              University of California.
    A catalogue of tape recordings of spoken narratives and songs
from 88 different culture (language) groups. Most are from
California but other culture areas also represented. The musical
items date from 1948 to 1980.

Sachs, Curt

1929   *Geist und Werden der Musikinstrumente.* Leipzig.
Reprinted by Frits Knuf (Hilversum, the Netherlands,
1965).
Discusses the world distribution of musical instruments in relation to a school of diffusionist theory known as *Kulturkreise*
("culture circles"). Sachs outlines five culture trait complexes
relating to instruments from Indian and Eskimo cultures (pp. 9–
71).

Sapir, Edward

See Sapir (1910) in Great Basin and Plateau bibliography. This deals
with songs depicting the speech of animals in Paiute mythology.

1916   *Time Perspective in Aboriginal American Culture: A
Study in Method.* Canadian Department of Mines.
Geological Survey Memoir 90 (13). Ottawa: Government Printing Bureau.
Sapir outlines the proper use of comparative ethnology and
linguistics to produce historical interpretations. This does not discuss musicology as such but contains useful information on related
methodologies.

Schoolcraft, Henry Rowe

1851–1857   *Historical and Statistical Information Respecting the
History, Condition, and Prospects of the Indian
Tribes of the United States.* 6 vols. Philadelphia.
Contains much ethnographic information including song texts
and translations from the following tribes: Chippewa (33 songs),
Dakota (3), Cherokee (1), and Chinook (1). Volume Three includes
a description of Chippewa song characteristics (pp. 325–330),
which Schoolcraft considered typical for Indian music in general.
For more complete references see the regional bibliographies. Also
see the index by Nichols (1954 above).

Seder, Theodore A.

1952   *Old World Overtones in the New World: Some
Parallels with North American Indian Musical
Instruments.* University Museum Bulletin 16(4).
Philadelphia: University of Pennsylvania.

This is basically a photographic essay showing several American Indian instruments with parallels in the Old World. The review by McAllester is distinctly critical (1953 above).

Seeger, Anthony, and Louise S. Spear

1987   *Early Field Recordings: A Catalogue of Cylinder Collections at the Indiana University Archives of Traditional Music.* Bloomington: Indiana University Press.

The collection includes roughly 7,000 cylinder recordings from all culture areas of North America and from elsewhere in the world. The catalogue lists 158 separate collections dating from the years 1893 to 1938. Basic documentation and other descriptive information are provided for each collection. The catalogue is organized by accession number, but there are also (four) indices which provide access to the collection by individual name, culture group, subject, and geographical region. The catalogue by Lee (1979 above) also includes more recent recordings.

Smyth, Willie, Editor

1989   *Songs of Indian Territory: Native American Music Traditions of Oklahoma.* Oklahoma City: Center for the American Indian.

This contains essays by Charlotte Heth, Gloria Young, Irving Whitebread and Howard Meridith, William Brown, Donald Brown, Judith Gray, and Orin Hatton (all listed in this general bibliography). Also contains notes by Smyth for a cassette tape accompanying the book (pp. 63–71).

Stevenson, Robert

1973a   Written Sources for Indian Music until 1882. *Ethnomusicology* 17(1): 1–40.

A survey of musical references in Spanish and French sources dating from as early as 1535. Stevenson provides quotations from many early sources and discusses the extent of acculturation which affected Native American music in the period before systematic research began. This also includes early notations of music from the following tribes: Mutsun Costanoan (5), Yokuts (1), Micmac (3), Illinois (1), Iroquois (1), Alaskan Indian (3), Eskimo (2), and one not identifiable (Example 10).

1973b   English Sources for Indian Music until 1882.
             Ethnomusicology 17(3): 399–442.
A continuation of Stevenson (1973a), this paper covers references in English-language sources. The author tends to focus on the problem of spurious references and (for example) criticizes Baker (1882 above) for including notations of songs that are not actually Indian but rather based on hymn tunes or other European composed melodies. This includes musical notations identified as follows: Alaskan Indian (1); Chippewa (4); Sioux (1); Dakota (1); Indians of Washington State, near Walla Walla (2); Indians of Utah (2); and Clallam (2).

Stumpf, Carl

1911   *Die Anfänge der Musik*. Leipzig: J. A. Barth.
A speculative work which attempts to explore the origins of music. This contains a lengthy section on North American Indian music and history of research on the subject (pp. 140–185). Includes several musical examples quoted from earlier sources.

Sweet, Jill Drayson

1981   Book review of *Indian Dances of North America* by
             Reginald   and   Gladys   Laubin   (1977).
             Ethnomusicology 25(1): 137–138.
Criticizes the book for focusing on Indian dances of the plains and eastern woodlands while giving little attention to dances of other culture areas. Sweet also notes that the book fails to relate dance to other aspects of life and lacks any sytematic analyses of music or dance.

Tiersot, Julien

1910   La Musique chez les peuples indigenes de
             l'Amerique du Nord (Etats-Unis et Canada).
             Sammelbande der internationalen Musik-gesellschaft
             11:141–231.
An early survey of Indian music and research on the subject, this includes information and notations from earlier writings by Theodore Baker, Franz Boas, Natalie (Burlin) Curtis, and John C. Fillmore.

Varnum, John

1981   Book review of *Selected Reports in Ethnomusicology* 3(2) edited by Charlotte Heth (1980). *Ethnomusicology* 25(3): 533–534.
Praises the essays by McAllester (Southwest bibliography) and Powers (Plains bibliography). Criticizes Draper's paper (Southeast bibliography) on the grounds the paper does not deal with "precontact" music as claimed.

von Ende, A.

1903   Die Musik der nordamerikanischen Indianer. *Die Musik* 2(10): 271–279.
The author attempts to delineate basic characteristics of Indian music, with discussions of formal structures, rhythms, scales, and instruments. Includes 12 musical examples quoted from earlier sources.

von Hornbostel, Erich M.

1910   U.S.A. National Music. *Zeitschrift der internationalen Musikgesellschaft* 12:64–68.
Hornbostel criticizes the use of Indian melodies by American composers and the general movement towards a "national music."

1923   Musik und Musikinstrumente: Musik der Makuschí, Taulipáng, und Yekuaná. Pp. 397–442 in *Vom Roroima zum Orinoko*, vol. 3 (of 5). Edited by Theodor Koch-Grünberg. Stuttgart.
Includes the description of a vocal performance style that Hornbostel considered typical for all Indians of the western hemisphere. This is characterized by strong accent, vocal pulsations, and melodic outlines consisting of small descending steps rendered with strong legato or glide.

1936   Fuegian Songs. *American Anthropologist* 38:357–367.
Describes what Hornbostel considered the characteristic American Indian vocal style (see previous entry) and comments on another style found among several North American Indian tribes.

Wallaschek, Richard

1893   *Primitive Music: An Inquiry into the Origin and Development of Music, Songs, Instruments, Dances, and Pantomimes of Savage Races.* London. Reprinted by Da Capo Press (New York, 1970). The chapter on the "Americas" (pp. 44–62) contains rather eclectic comments on music of the following North American groups: Nootka, Apache, Tlingit, Yaqui, Iroquois, Eskimo, and various tribes of California. Based on information from earlier publications.

Wapp, Edward, Jr.

1984   The American Indian Courting Flute: Revitalization and Change. Pp. 49–60 in *Sharing a Heritage: American Indian Arts* edited by Charlotte Heth and Michael Swarm. Contemporary American Indian Issues Series, no. 5. Los Angeles: American Indian Studies Center, UCLA.
Wapp discusses performers and others who have been influential in the revival of the courting flute and describes how the instrument has come to be used in art music and other new settings. Includes discography and bibliography. See also the record album of flute music by Gillis (Plains bibliography, 1979) and the article by Payne (Plains bibliography, 1988).

Wead, Charles Kasson

1900   The Study of Indian Music. *American Anthropologist* 2:75–79.
Discusses some of the problems involved in recording and transcribing songs using the early phonographic cylinder equipment.

1900   Recent Outlooks Upon Music. *Science* 11:206–215.
Wead criticizes the scientific accuracy and objectivity in a book on Omaha music by Fletcher and La Flesche (Plains bibliography 1893). The book relies upon theoretical assumptions of John C. Fillmore (listed above).

1902   Contributions to the History of Musical Scales. *Report of the United States National Museum* (for 1900), pp. 417–462.
Focuses on the importance of musical instruments as a major factor in the evolution of scales, with many references to Indian music.

Whitebread, Irving, and Howard Meredith

1989   Nuh-Ka-Oashun: Hasinai Turkey Dance Tradition.
            Pp. 26–31 in *Songs of Indian Territory: Native
            American Music Traditions of Oklahoma* edited by
            Willie Smyth. Oklahoma City: Center for the
            American Indian.
        Describes the dance and its importance as a vehicle for pre-
serving Hasinai (Caddo) tribal history and identity. The tribe originally inhabited parts of Arkansas and other southeastern states but
its members are now dispersed in Oklahoma, Texas, Kansas, and
other areas of the southwest. This does not contain musical
notations but does describe the textual content and sequence of the
songs.

Whitehorse, David

1988   *Pow-Wow: The Contemporary Pan-Indian Celebra-
            tion.* San Diego State University Publications in
            American Indian Studies No. 5. San Diego:
            Department of American Indian Studies, San Diego
            State University.
        This slim volume provides an excellent introduction to the
subject. Opening chapters discuss the history of the pow-wow and
the nature of the modern pow-wow experience for Indian people.
Chapter three (pp. 14–42) discusses the organization of a pow-wow
and describes the basic music and dance styles which occur. This is
followed by a final chapter (pp. 43–60) which deals with the proto-
col or sequence of events at a pow-wow. Contains many recent
photographs.

Yeh, Nora, Compiler

1982   *Musics of the World, a Selective Discography, Part
            III.* Los Angeles: Ethnomusicology Archive, UCLA.
        Pages 24–30 provide a brief listing of commercial recordings
of Indian music from various culture areas (with annotations).

Young, Gloria

1989   The Dream Dance and the Ghost Dance in Okla-
            homa. Pp. 18–25 in *Songs of Indian Territory: Native
            American Music Traditions of Oklahoma* edited by
            Willie Smyth. Oklahoma City: Center for the
            American Indian.

Describes nineteenth century religious movements which formed the basis for important music and dance traditions and also helped lay the foundation for intertribal music of the modern pow-wow.

Zotigh, Dennis

1991   *Moving History: Evolution of the Powwow.* Oklahoma City: Center for the American Indian.

This 70-page booklet is basically a typescript (without page numbers) but contains much information on the history of pow-wows in general and of various rituals, contests, dances, and other events within the powwow. Written from a Native American view-point, it contains descriptions of the the following: regalia, staff and participants, the style of powwow music, sequence of events, traditional rituals and contests, and various dances. The section on music outlines the basic structure of Northern and Southern Plains powwow songs. Includes a bibliography and discography.

II. Arctic and Sub-Arctic

Abel, Kerry

1986   Prophets, Priests, and Preachers: Dene Shamans and Christian Missions in the Nineteenth Century. Winnipeg: Canadian Historical Association. *Historical Papers* (1986): 211–224.

While previous studies viewed native revitalization movements as responses to historical traumata, this paper argues that the activities of Dene (Athapaskan) shamans and prophets were actually quite consistent with traditional cultural patterns. This contains no discussion of music but does provide information on religious developments that affected native music during the 19th century. See also Beaudry (1992 below).

Anisimov, A.F.

1963   The Shaman's Tent of the Evenks and the Origin of the Shamanistic Rite. Pp. 84–123 in *Studies in Arctic Shamanism* edited by H. N. Michael. Toronto: Arctic Institute of North America.

This classic study argues that shamanism originated from totemistic practices and gives detailed descriptions of singing and dancing which occurred during a ritual attended by Anisimov in 1931 (pp. 100–105). Deals mainly with cultures of northeastern Asia. Translated from a Russian publication dated 1952.

Arima, E.Y., and Magnús Einarsson

1976   Whence and When the "Eskimo Fiddle"? *Folk* 18:23–40. Copenhagen.

Focuses on "Eskimo fiddles" of the eastern Canadian Arctic. First describes the physical form of 12 specimens from museum collections (with 10 photographs), then explores the question of how this particular instrument came to be used among Inuits. The authors speculate that it was most likely derived from a Norse stringed instrument (the *fidla*) that was used by Orkneymen working with the Hudson's Bay Company during the late seventeenth and early eighteenth centuries.

Asch, Michael I.

1975   Social Context and the Musical Analysis of Slavey Drum Songs. *Ethnomusicology* 19(2): 245–257.

Compares five different "musical events" that take place in the larger context of the Slavey Drum Dance. Asch concludes that each was associated with a predominant musical style as distinguished by tonal range, melodic form, and rhythmic accompaniment. The events are: (1) Rabbit Dance, (2) Cree Dance, (3) Tea Dance or Round Dance, (4) "religious context" (no local term), and (5) "practice situation" (no local term).

1988   *Kinship and the Drum Dance in a Northern Dene Community*. Edmonton, Alberta: The Boreal Institute for Northern Studies.

Asch focuses on social transformations and stresses that occurred when previously nomadic bands of Canadian Slavey Indians came to be relocated in a settled community during the 1960s. The Drum Dance is viewed as an important unifier that mitigated social tensions. Includes notations and analysis for 20 songs.

Baké, Arnold A.

1952   Review of "Die Musik der Eskimo" by Zygmunt Estreicher. *Journal of the International Folk Music Council* 4:97–98.

Baké criticizes Estreicher's comparative and historical analysis of Eskimo music as a "writing desk production."

Balikci, Asen

1963   Shamanistic Behavior among the Netsilik Eskimo. *Southwestern Journal of Anthropology* 19:380–396.

Contains no discussion of music but does give useful information on the contexts of shamanistic singing. Based on data collected in 1960 and on writings of Rasmussen (listed below).

See **Barbeau** (1933) in the Northwest Coast bibliography This contains musical notations and translations of songs identified as Tahltan (Athabascan) and Carrier Indian (Athabascan).

See Barbeau (1934) in the Northwest Coast bibliography. This contains musical notations and translations of Athabascan tribes from the Nass River and Skeena River regions.

Beaudry, Nicole

1978a   Le katajjaq un jeu Inuit traditionnel ("Katajjaq: An Inuit Traditional Game"). *Études Inuit Studies* 2(1): 35–53.

Focuses on vocal games from the central Canadian Arctic region. Defines the genre in terms of formal properties and social functions, also comparing the *katajjaq* with other traditional Inuit games.

1978b   Toward Transcription and Analysis of Inuit Throat Games: Macro-structure. *Ethnomusicology* 22(2): 261–274.

Employs successive stages of transcription and analysis in order to provide more holistic understanding concerning various dimensions of the throat game as musical behavior. See also Charron (1978 below).

1980   Book review of *The Effects of Acculturation on Eskimo Music of the Cumberland Peninsula* by Maija Lutz (1978). *Ethnomusicology* 24(3): 592–594.

Commends Lutz as being the first to examine the history of musical contacts between Eskimos and whites but criticizes the lack of musical examples (except from earlier sources) and questions her concept of "acculturation" as applied to Eskimo musical life.

1988   La Danse à tambour Yupik: Une analyse de sa performance. ("The Yupik Drum Dance: An Analysis of its Performance"). *Recherches Amérindiennes au Québec* 18(4).

Begins by describing several traditional rituals in which drum dancing plays a prominent part, then outlines in detail how a single evening of drum dancing unfolds. Beaudry identifies four stages in the performance of a single dance and interprets the social function of each stage. Finally describes two dances and discusses how the performance can be modified depending on context.

1991   Rêves, chants, et prières Dènès: Une confluence de
              spiritualités ("Dene Dreams, Songs, and Prayers: A
              Confluence of Spiritual Traditions"). *Recherches
              Amérindiennes au Québec* 21(4): 23–36.

This paper examines a religious movement which occurred
among Dene people of the Mackenzie River region during the
nineteenth century. Beaudry gives a brief history of missionary activity, then describes the religious dualism that occurred as traditional beliefs were blended with ideas taught by the Catholic missionaries. She describes how the Dene sometimes use two sets of
practices (one Catholic, one native) for the same occasion.

1992   The Language of Dreams: Songs of the Dene Indians
              (Canada). Pp. 72–90 in *Music and Spiritual Power
              among the Indians of North America* edited by
              Richard Keeling. *World of Music* 92(2). Berlin:
              International Institute for Traditional Music.

Focuses on historical transformations in music and spiritual
life mainly as occurring among the northern Slavey Indians. First
describes guardian spirit songs and medicine songs characterizing
the pre-Christian era, then discusses the "prophet movement"
(which began around 1860) and the gradual development of the
contemporary Drum Dance. Based on archival sources and fieldwork conducted between 1988 and 1990. Includes three musical
examples.

Béclard-d'Harcourt, Marguerite

1928   Le Système pentaphone dans les chants des Copper-
              Eskimos ("The Pentatonic Scale Structure in Copper
              Eskimo Songs"). *Proceedings of the International
              Congress of Americanists* (Rome, 1926). Volume 22
              (2): 15–23.

Contains tonal analyses based on song transcriptions by Helen
Roberts. See Roberts and Jenness (1925) below. See also some
critical comments in Roberts (General bibliography, 1932).

Bergsland, Knut, and Moses L. Dirks, Editors

1990   *Unangam Ungiikangin Kayux Tunusangin/ Unangam
              Uniikangis ama Tunuzangis: Aleut Tales and Narra-
              tives, Collected 1909–1910 by Waldemar Jochelson.*
              Fairbanks: Alaska Native Language Center.

This mainly contains translations of spoken narratives but includes one song text from the Jochelson corpus ("Blanket-Tossing Song," p. 486–487). Appendix A also gives translations for 12 Eastern Aleut song texts first published in Russian by Ioann Veniaminov in 1840 and 1846. Cylinder recordings of (18) Aleut songs collected by Jochelson are among the holdings at the Archives of Traditional Music, Indiana University (Catalogue, 80–226-F).

See **Bierhorst** (1979) in the General bibliography. This contains information on Inuit music from the work of Diamond Jenness and Laura Boulton.

Birket-Smith, Kaj

[1959]   *The Eskimos*. Translated from the Danish by W. E. Calvert. Revised Second Edition. London: Methuen and Co. An earlier English edition was published by Dutton (New York, 1935).

A classic survey of Eskimo cultures based on earlier sources and the author's own research circa 1921–1924. This contains descriptions of drum dances and songs (pp. 148–149 and 155–157). Also touches on the use of songs in hunting (pp. 84 and 141) and describes song duels (pp. 150–151).

Boas, Franz

1887   Poetry and Music of Some American Tribes. *Science* 9:383–385.

Contains three melodies and texts (with translations) collected by Boas among Inuits of Baffin Island and another song collected by him among Indians of British Columbia. Also includes general comments on the style of native music in these areas.

1888   *The Central Eskimo*. Annual Report of the Bureau of American Ethnology (1884–1885), vol. 6, pp. 399–669. Washington: Smithsonian Institution. Reprint. Toronto: Coles Publishing Co., 1974.

This contains musical transcriptions and analyses of 25 melodies collected by Boas in 1883–1884 and four musical examples reprinted from Parry (1824 below) and other early sources. These notations are included in a general discussion of poetry and music (pp. 648–658). The work also includes sections on dance houses, drum construction, and performance techniques. The fieldwork was conducted in the Cumberland Sound and Davis Strait areas.

1894   Eskimo Tales and Songs. *Journal of American Folklore* 7:45–50.

Includes song texts and translations for six songs, five of which are also included in Boas (1888 above). Also lists and explains certain shamanic words in the songs.

1897   Eskimo Tales and Songs. *Journal of American Folklore* 10:109–115.

Contains texts and translations for twelve songs, four of which are quoted from Boas (1888 above).

Boas, Franz, and Henry Rink

1889   Eskimo Tales and Songs. *Journal of American Folklore* 2:123–131.

Provides musical notations, song texts, and translations for two songs. Also includes translations of origin myths and discusses language dialect relationships. Based on fieldwork done at Cumberland Sound in 1885.

Bogoras, Waldemar

1913   *The Eskimo of Siberia*. American Museum of Natural History, Memoir. *Jesup North Pacific Expedition* 8(3). Leiden: E. J. Brill.

The section on "Songs" (pp. 437–452) contains free and interlinear translations of 43 song texts. Various types of songs are represented, but shamanistic songs are particularly numerous (12 examples). One group of six shaman's songs (pp. 445–447) is a set of incantations connected with walrus hunting; the other six are songs performed at winter ceremonials.

Boulton, Laura

1954   (Recording and liner notes) "The Eskimos of Hudson Bay and Alaska." Smithsonian-Folkways Recordings (FE 4444).

Currently reissued on cassette. The contents are listed as follows: Johnnie Bull Song (Southampton Island), His First Hunt (Chesterfield), All Songs Have Been Exhausted (Chesterfield), Hunting for Musk Ox (Chesterfield), Hunting Seals (Chesterfield), I Sing About a Dance (Chesterfield), Before We Came to This

Religion (Southampton Island), Girls' Game (Baker Lake), Bird Imitations (Southampton Island), Walrus Imitations (Southampton Island), Animal Stories (Chesterfield), Hunting Song (Baker Lake), Dance Songs (Point Barrow), Story Songs, and Inviting-In Dance Song.

Bours, Etienne

1991   *Musiques des peuples de l'arctique: Analyse discographique* ("Music of the Arctic Peoples: A Discographic Analysis"). Bruxelles: Médiathèque de la Communauté Française de Belgique.

This highly useful discography is organized by genre and includes much information on musical styles, performance contexts, compositional practices, and instruments, as well as indicating available recordings for each type of music. Contains three main divisions: Music of the Inuits; Vocal Music of the Sammy Lapps; and Music of the Peoples of Arctic Siberia. Historical and recent musical styles are given equal coverage.

Burch, Ernest S.

1971   The Nonempirical Environment of the Arctic Alaskan Eskimos. *Southwestern Journal of Anthropology* 27(2): 148–165.

Describes earlier (nineteenth century) concepts relating to mythological beings (some quite monstrous in character) and discusses how these ideas were syncretized with Christian elements based on teachings of the early missionaries. Contains no discussion of music.

Cavanagh, Beverley (Diamond)

1972   Annotated Bibliography: Eskimo Music. *Ethnomusicology* 16(3): 479–487.

This is particularly useful because of the information it contains on foreign language sources in German, Swedish, Norwegian, Danish, French, and Italian. Includes manuscripts, journalistic articles, and other items which are not given in the present bibliography.

1973   Imagery and Structure in Eskimo Song Texts. *Canadian Folk Music Journal* 1:3–15.

Focuses on central Canadian Eskimos (Netsilik, Copper, Caribou, and Iglulik). Based mainly on material collected by

Rasmussen (circa 1920s) but also compares texts collected by Cavanagh in 1972. The section on imagery touches on the following topics: personification of animals, weather imagery, modern subjects (and resistance to change), women's medicine songs, ambiguity in songs associated with spiritual power, modesty or self-deprecation, and rivalry in dialogue songs. Cavanagh also analyzes the narrative structure and musical style of a Netsilik Eskimo song (with one musical example).

1976   Some Throat Games of Netsilik Eskimo Women. *Canadian Folk Music Journal* 4:43–47.
          Focuses on Netsilik Eskimo throat games as documented by Cavanagh at Gjoa Haven in May 1975. Cavanagh identifies ten types, then discusses the style in terms of textual content, rhythms, and musical structures.

1977   The Legato Principle in Netsilik Eskimo Music. *Studies in Music from the University of Western Ontario* 2:15–21.
          Cavanagh defines the legato style as "the musical result when one attempts to sing in as smooth and continuous a manner as possible" (p. 15). She suggests that this principle operates at many levels in Netsilik music and shows how it influences musical structure and performance practice in songs of the Drum Dance. Contains five musical examples.

1981   Record review of "Inuit Games and Songs: Chants et Jeux des Inuits" (Unesco Collection, Musical Sources, Philips 6586 036). *Ethnomusicology* 25(2): 349–352.
          Favorable review of a prize-winning album produced by researchers at the University of Montreal under the direction of Jean-Jacques Nattiez. The recordings are from various locales in the eastern Arctic area and include the following genres: throat games (48), juggling song (1), songs for children (6), individual songs (2), sung narratives (2), animal imitation (1), song for string game (1), assalalaa game song (1), shaman song (1), and excerpts of music for Jew's harp (1) and violin (1). Cavanagh praises the technical quality of the recordings, the photographs, and the liner notes.

1982   *Music of the Netsilik Eskimo: A Study of Stability and Change.* 2 vols. Canadian Ethnology Service Paper No. 82. National Museum of Man Mercury Series. Ottawa: National Museums of Canada.

Defines the traditional genres and styles of Netsilik Inuit music and examines the extent of change that has occurred as a result of contact with music of Europeans and North American Indian peoples. Volume Two contains notations, texts, translations, and commentary for 121 songs recorded from 1958 to 1972. Most are Drum Dance songs (96), but other genres such as animal songs and game songs are also included. The book was published along with a 7-inch disc recording of musical examples.

1983   Book review of *Musical Traditions of the Labrador Coast Inuit* by Maija Lutz (1982). *Ethnomusicology* 27(3): 540–542.

States that Lutz's work is important among ethnomusicological studies of the Inuit because she emphasizes the importance of non-traditional styles while others have concentrated mainly on traditional music genres. This is basically a favorable review, but Cavanagh does suggest that the author has focused too much on Moravian influences without adequately considering secular influences caused by Euro-American settlers in the region.

1986   Inuit (Music). Pp. 494–497 in *The New Grove Dictionary of American Music* , vol. 2 (E–K). Edited by H. Wiley Hitchcock and Stanley Sadie. London: Macmillan.

Focuses mainly on Eskimo groups of Alaska. The opening section on "Genres and Functions" (pp. 494–496) gives a good overview of musical activities, distinguishing ceremonial practices of the northwestern and southwestern regions. Contains descriptions of the following ceremonials: the Whale Festival, the Messenger Feast, the Bladder Festival, the Feast for the Dead, and the Inviting-In Feast. Cavanagh also discusses "power" songs used by individuals, various types of secular music, musical instruments, and general characteristics of the Alaskan Eskimo musical style.

1985   Les Mythes et la musique Naskapi ("Naskapi Myths and Music"). *Recherches Amérindiennes au Québec* 15(4): 5–18.

Analyzes the style of songs in mythic texts and also discusses the performance style of mythic narration in general. Includes ten brief musical examples and several translations of song texts.

1987   The Canadian Broadcasting Corporation and Native
                Music Records. *Yearbook for Traditional Music*
                19:161–165.
        This is a record review essay focusing on six commercial
recordings produced by the Canadian Broadcasting Corporation.
The albums discussed feature performers of the following groups:
Montagnais (3 record albums), Huron (1), Inuit (1), and Abenaki
(1).

See Cavanagh (1987) in Northeast bibliography This focuses on hymn
        singing in Canadian Indian communities.

1989   Music and Gender in the Sub-Arctic Algonkian Area.
                Pp. 55–66 in *Women in North American Indian Music*
                edited by Richard Keeling. Ann Arbor: Society for
                Ethnomusicology.
        Focuses on music and culture of the Naskapi, Montagnais, and
Eastern Cree. Cavanagh discusses musical genres in which participation is limited to males or females and also comments on other
factors through which the style or meaning of songs is influenced
by gender. She reviews the work of anthropologist Eleanor
Leacock in criticizing western images of male dominance and
notes the complementarity which seems to characterize Algonkian
ways of thinking and speaking about gender relations.

**Cavanagh, Beverley (Diamond), Sam Cronk, and Franziska von
Rosen**

1988   Vivres ses traditions: Fêtes intertribales chez les
                Amérindiens de l'est du Canada ("Living the
                Traditions: Intertribal Events in Native Communities
                of Eastern Canada"). *Recherches Amérindiennes au
                Québec* 18(4): 5–22.
        Focuses on three events: (1) the Champion of Champions
Powwow in Ontario, (2) the Mi'kmaq Summer Games in Nova
Scotia, and (3) the Innu Nikamu Festival in Québec. The authors
describe how tradition and native identity are expressed on multi-
ple levels in each one.

Charron, Claude Y.

1978a   Le tambour magique: un instrument autrefois útile
                pour le qûete d'un conjoint ("The Magical Drum: A
                Formerly Useful Instrument for Those in Search of a
                Spouse). *Études Inuit studies* 2(1): 3–28.

Charron examines three Inuit stories in order to show the significance of the drum in Inuit mythology. In each case the instrument is shown to be a symbolic tool for resolving specific contradictions or difficulties. The narratives are from Alaska, Canada, and Greenland.

1978b   Toward Transcription and Analysis of Inuit Throat Games: Micro-structure. *Ethnomusicology* 22(2): 245–260.

Focuses on the problem of analyzing this unusual genre in which neither fixed pitches nor fixed intervals occur with significant regularity. Suggests the idea of "intonational contours" to indicate relative pitch levels and then discusses the contrast or interaction between voiced and voiceless sounds in musical and acoustic terms. See also Beaudry (1978 above).

Cranz, David

1767   *The History of Greenland: Containing a Description of the Country and Its Inhabitants.* 2 vols. London. Another edition (Historie von Grönland, 3 vols.) was published at Leipzig in 1765.

Volume One contains a description of songs and dances. Includes one song text and translation (p. 176). This is probably the earliest published source with information on Eskimo music.

See **Curtis** (1907–1930) in the General bibliography. Volume Twenty contains song texts from the following Alaskan Eskimo groups: 17 Nunivak texts in English (pp. 57–58, 87, 92, 246–250); four Selawik song texts in English (pp. 233, 236, 262); three Kobuk song texts in English (p. 215); and two Kotzebue songs, native texts and translations (pp. 257, 259).

d'Anglure, Bernard Saladin

1978   Entre cri et chant: Les Katajjait, un genre musical féminin. ("Between Cry and Song: the Katajjait, a Feminine Musical Genre"). *Etudes Inuit studies* 2(1): 85–94.

Focuses on ambiguities of the *katajjait*, which can simultaneously be viewed as crying or language, singing or dance, music or game, and ritual or performance. D'Anglure also discusses how the genre can symbolize the relationship between men and women or spiritual connections of humans with nature and the supernatural.

DeNevi, Don

1969   Essays in Musical Retribalization: Hudson Bay. *Music Educators Journal* 56:66–68.
This contains some very general information on Inuit music and the history of research on the subject. Also includes translations of three song texts from Boulton (1954 above).

d'Harcourt, Marguerite Béclard

1928   Le Système pentaphone dans les chants des Copper-Eskimos ("The Pentatonic Scale in Copper Eskimo Songs"). *Proceedings of the International Congress of Americanists* (1926). 2 volumes. Volume 22, no. 2, pp. 15–23. Rome.
The author discusses scales and tonal organization of 113 songs notated in Roberts and Jenness (1925). D'Harcourt's style of analysis receives some criticism in Roberts (General bibliography, 1932).

Diamond, Beverley (See Beverley Cavanagh, above)

Estreicher, Zygmunt

1947   Zur Polyrhythmik in der Musik der Eskimos ("On Polyrhythm in Eskimo Music"). *Schweizerische Musikzeitung* 87: 411–415.
Contains notations of two drum songs collected by Jean Gabus among the Caribou Eskimos west of Hudson Bay. The paper deals with a genre called *piherk*, which Estreicher calls "the classical dance of the Canadian Eskimo." The analysis focuses mainly on rhythmic relationships between the singers, drummers, and a women's chorus.

1948a   La Musique des Esquimaux-Caribous: Collection Gabus ("Music of the Caribou Eskimos from the Gabus Collection"). *Bulletin de la Société Neuchâteloise de Géographie* 44(1):1–53.
Gives descriptions and analyses of songs collected among the Padleirmiut Eskimos (west of Hudson Bay) by Jean Gabus in 1938. The collection includes 100 disks. This contains 11 original transcriptions of Padleirmiut songs and three republished notations of Eskimo songs from other regions. Also contains ethnographic information relating to songs. Part One distinguishes two principal melodic types in Eskimo music. Part Two defines four regional

styles (Caribou, Copper, Alaskan, and Greenland) and speculates on the evolution and diffusion of Eskimo music.

1948b   La Polyphonie chez les Esquimaux ("Eskimo Polyphony"). *Journal de la Société des Americanistes* 37:259–268.

This is based on notations of three songs collected by Gabus among Caribou Eskimos west of Hudson Bay. Estreicher makes the following assertion: "a characteristic trait lies in the play of two tonalities, the principal (one) represented by the melody in the bass, and the second, which the accompanying voice effects around a second tonal center (p. 268). He also (mistakenly) suggests that Alaskan Eskimo polyphony probably developed as a result of European influences (p. 260).

1950   Die Musik der Eskimo: Eine vergleichende Studie. *Anthropos* 45:659–720.

A comparative study based mainly on songs notated in earlier sources but also including 9 songs collected by Gabus and notated by Estreicher. Contains fifty musical examples in all. The emphasis is on musical structures, and information concerning socio-cultural aspects is slight. Estreicher presumes that the music of the Padleirmiut (Caribou Eskimos) represents the purest style (*Grundstil*) and postulates a possible course of development for the styles of other regions. He concludes that there were Indian and northeast Asian influences on music of the Alaskan groups and also sees European influences in northern and southwestern Greenland. Music of eastern Greenland is considered closer to the Padleirmiut style and thought to represent an earlier stage. It should be noted that Alaskan Eskimo music was not well documented at the time and that Estreicher's comments on the subject are conjectural. There is a critical review by Baké (1952 above). See also the critical evaluation in Johnston (1975 below).

1954   Eskimo-Musik. *Die Musik in Geschichte und Gegenwart: Allgemeine Enzyklopädie der Musik.* Vol. 3, columns 1526–1533.

An overview of Eskimo music, including analysis of migratory patterns, descriptions of social customs involving music, comparative analysis of regional styles, and Estreicher's ideas about the evolution of various styles. Contains one musical example (a drum song from the Caribou Eskimo) and a bibliography.

Fredericksen, Svend

1952   Aspects of European Influence in the Poetry of
              Greenland. *Midwest Folklore* 2(4): 251–261.
      Fredericksen analyzes the texts of songs from Western
Greenland and finds various aspects of style and expression that
reflect Danish ways of thinking. Based on texts collected by
Thalbitzer circa 1905–1906.

Gabus, Jean

1947   *Iglous*. Second edition. Neuchâtel: Allinger.
      Chapter 14 contains seven song texts. There is also a descrip-
tion of Inuit singing in a diary entry for July 28, 1938. Based on research conducted in the area west of Hudson Bay.

See **Goddard**, (1914 and 1919) in the Plains bibliography. These deal
with dances of the Sarsi and Cree.

Golder, Frank A.

1905   Aleutian Stories. *Journal of American Folklore*
              18:215–222.
      Contains translations for nine song texts.

1907   The Songs and Stories of the Aleuts, with Transla-
              tions from Veniaminov. *Journal of American Folk-
              lore* 20(77): 132–142.
      This contains translations of stories only; the songs are only
described. See also Bergsland and Dirks (1990 above) for translations from Veniaminov.

Goulet, Jean-Guy

1982   Religious Dualism among Athapaskan Catholics.
              Revue Canadienne d'Anthropologie 3(1): 1–18.
      Mostly sociological analysis but contains a description of a
Dene Prophet Dance attended by the author in 1981 (pp. 11–12).

Grant, John W.

1980   Missionaries and Messiahs in the Northwest. *Sciences
              Religieuses/Studies in Religion* 9(2): 125–135.
      Discusses various incidents and processes through which
Indian prophets and visionaries appropriated Christian ideas and
imagery in ways not intended by the missionaries. Grant begins

with an account of how two evangelical hymns, translated into Cree, inspired the religious experiences of two medicine men (p. 125). Based on 19th-century historical documents.

Graves, Margaret C.

1913   An Ingalik Ceremony in Alaska. *Journal of American Folklore* 26(100): 191–192.
This is a personal letter describing "nature dances" held in large underground chambers. The Ingalik are Athabascan Indians whose culture has been greatly influenced by that of adjacent Eskimo groups.

See **Gray** (1984) in the General bibliography. This contains information on cylinder recordings collected among the Polar Eskimo of Greenland and among Carrier Indians of Canada.

See Gray (1988) in the Northwest Coast bibliography. This gives information on cylinder recordings collected among the Polar Eskimo of Greenland.

Guédon, Marie Françoise

1974   *People of Tetlin, Why Are You Singing?* Mercury Series No. 9. Ottawa: National Museum of Man.
Despite the title, this is actually a general ethnography of the Upper Tanana Indians with special focus on kinship and related aspects of social life. Chapter Six ("Social Ceremonialism") does contain a section entitled "Dancing and Singing" (pp. 219–225) and also describes a potlatch that was held at Tetlin in 1969 (pp. 226–235).

Hague, Eleanor

1915   Eskimo Songs. *Journal of American Folklore* 28:96–98.
Contains musical notations of three melodies (two with texts) collected by Captain George Comer near Cape Fullerton. The area is Caribou Eskimo, west of Hudson Bay. Comer's field recordings (made in 1901 and 1910) are available at the Archives of Traditional Music (Indiana University). See the catalogues by Lee (1979) and by Seeger and Spear (1987) in the General bibliography.

See **Hallowell** (1926) in the General bibliography. This is a classic study of bear ceremonialism among northern peoples, including descriptions of related practices in several cultures of the Arctic and Sub-Arctic areas.

Hauser, Michael

1977   Formal Structure in Polar Eskimo Drumsongs. *Ethnomusicology* 21(1): 33–54.

The Polar Eskimo are a small and isolated group located on the western coast of Greenland. Hauser begins by noting that the repertory as a whole contains songs with three types of structure. The paper gives a detailed analysis of form type I, which is the most common type and also the most complex. Hauser describes the principal parts of the (six period) structure and various stereotyped patterns which occur. In concluding remarks, Hauser compares the musical structure to linguistic structure (p. 52). This includes 18 musical examples. Form type III consists of simple songs with narrow melodic range; these occur in stories and are presumed by Hauser to be quite old (p. 34).

1978   Inuit Songs from Southwest Baffin Island in Cross-Cultural Context. *Études Inuit studies* 1(1): 55–83; and 1(2): 71–105.

In working with a large corpus of recordings from the Thule District, it was found that a special (divergent) song type was sung by descendants of some Canadian Inuits who had settled in Thule around 1875. In order to trace the origin of this form type, Hauser examines various repertories from the Central and Eastern Arctic. In the course of this comparative survey he introduces the concept of "melody spheres." Hauser concludes that the divergent form type was brought by certain migrant families from Southern Baffin Island. The argument is outlined in Part One (pp. 55–83); Part Two (pp. 71–105) contains notations and detailed analyses for 45 songs.

1992   *Traditional Greenlandic Music*. Acta ethnomusicologica Danica 7. Danish Folklore Archives Skrifter 8. Copenhagen: Forlaget Kragen; and Sisimut, Greenland: ULO. Available from the Danish Folklore Archives, Birketinget 6, DK-2300 Kobenhavn.

A detailed comparative study of Inuit music in the following five areas: (1) East Greenland, (2) South Greenland, (3) Central West Greenland, (4) Uummannaq-Upernavik, and (5) North Greenland. Except for two more acculturated areas (South

Greenland, Central West Greenland), Hauser gives fairly complete analyses of traditional music in each region, with sections on song categories, musical instruments, tonal material, melodic formulas, part-singing, formal structures, and other features. He gives complete information on previous writings and available recordings from each area. The study includes 55 musical notations of songs collected between 1901 and 1984.

Hawkes, Ernest William

1913   *The "Inviting In" Feast of the Alaskan Eskimo.* Ottawa: Canadian Department of Mines. Geological Survey Memoir 45, Anthropological Series #3.
       This describes a feast which took place at St. Michael Alaska (near the mouth of the Yukon River) in the winter of 1911–1912. Hawkes discusses religious beliefs relating to the event and describes the dance house or *kazqi.* Then he discusses songs and drumming, including descriptions of various types of dances that are performed. Contains one musical example (p. 10) and several drawings and photographs. An addendum describes some Eskimo dances that were borrowed by neighboring Athapascan Indians of the Yukon River area.

1914   *The Dance Festivals of Alaskan Eskimo.* University of Pennsylvania: The University Museum; Anthropological Publications, vol. 6, no. 2.
       Based on Hawkes's observations while living in the Bering Strait area on the Diomedes Islands (two years) and at St. Michael at the mouth of the Yukon River (one year). No dates given. An opening chapter entitled "The Dance in General" (pp. 9–12) contains descriptions of music and dancing, also discussing the participation of Eskimo women. This is followed by a description of the dance house (pp. 13–18). Hawkes then describes the following events: the Asking Festival, the Bladder Feast, the Feast of the Dead, the Annual Feast (*Ailígi*), the Great Feast (*Aithukatukhtuk*), and the Inviting-In Festival. Contains no musical notations but does provide superb historical photographs.

Herzog, George

1926   Review of *Songs of the Copper Eskimo* by Helen Roberts and Diamond Jenness (1925). *Journal of American Folklore* 39:218–225.

Herzog criticizes Roberts's approach to tonal analysis and rec-
ommends a less biased approach such as that employed by
Hornbostel.

Hofmann, Charles

1974   *Drum Dance: Legends, Ceremonies, Dances, and
            Songs of the Eskimos.* Agincourt, Ontario: Gage.
    Could not be obtained for inspection of contents. Listed in the
bibliography by Maguire et al. (General bibliography 1983:17).

Holm, Gustav Frederik

1914   Ethnological Sketch of the Ammassalik Eskimo. Pp.
            1–147 in *The Ammassalik Eskimo* (2 vols.) edited by
            William Thalbitzer. Meddelelser om Grønland, vol.
            39.
    Contains description of songs and two musical notations (pp.
125–130). The location is western Greenland.

Holtved, Erik

1967   Eskimo Shamanism. Pp. 23–31 in *Studies in
            Shamanism* edited by Carl-Martin Edsman. Stock-
            holm: Almqvist and Wiksell.
    A survey of shamanistic beliefs and practices based mainly on
earlier writings of Rasmussen, Jenness, Thalbitzer, and others.

Hughes, Charles C.

1959   Translation of I. K. Voblov's "Eskimo Ceremonies."
            Anthropological Papers of the University of Alaska
            7:71–90.
    This is translated from a Russian publication dated 1952. The
paper describes seven ceremonies of Siberian Eskimos living along
the coast of Chukotka. The ceremonies are identified as follows:
(1) *Atigak*, ritual for launching a boat at the start of a hunt; (2)
Nashkunikhkilik ("Ceremony of the Tusks"); (3) *Akhisakhmuk*
("Feeding the Dead"); (4) *Attigak* ("Whale Hunting Preparation"),
(5) *Sayak* ("All Is Open, All Is Free"), (6) *Kamygtak* ("The
Boots"), and (7) *Kaziva* ("The Winding Around").

Jenness, Diamond

1922   Eskimo Music in Northern Alaska. *Musical Quarterly*
8:377–383.
Contains four melodies transcribed by ear and harmonized by
George Young. Also includes some general remarks on music and
instruments. The area is northern Alaska from Barrow to the
Canadian border.

1932   Oratory and Drama, Music and Art. Pp. 200–215 in
              The Indians of Canada by Diamond Jenness. Nation-
              al Museum of Canada Bulletin No. 65 (Ottawa).
Contains brief descriptions of song types, instruments, and
musical styles among various groups. Includes one Eskimo melody
and text.

Jensen, Bent

1963   Notes on an Eskimo "Thanking Act." *Folk Dansk
              Etnografisk Tidsskrift* 5:187–198.
Describes a female solo dance offered as a "thanking act" to
celebrate a successful hunt. The region is Umanak district of
western Greenland.

Jetté, Julius

1911   On the Superstitions of the Ten'a Indians (Middle
              Part of the Yukon Valley, Alaska). *Anthropos* 6:95–
              108, 241–259, 602–615, and 699–723.
This focuses on the Koyukon tribe, an Athapascan group. The
section entitled "Songs" (pp.253–255) lists various types of songs
used in medicine making and includes several texts and translations. The section on "Mourning Songs" (pp. 712–716) contains
one musical example along with several more texts and translations.

Johnston, Thomas F.

1974   Eight North Alaskan Eskimo Dance Songs.
              Tennessee Folklore Society Bulletin 40(December):
              123–136.
Contains musical notations and analysis for eight songs collected by Johnston at Point Hope in 1973–1974. The author identifies (four) native categories of songs and gives detailed commentary on the song texts.

1974   A Historical Perspective on Alaskan Eskimo Music. *The Indian Historian* 7(4): 17–26.

Mainly an introductory essay for non-specialist readers, but this does contain excellent historical photographs of the Wolf Dance and other music-related subjects from the University of Alaska Archives.

1975   Eskimo Music: A Comparative Survey. *Anthropologica* 17(2): 217–232. Ottawa.

Begins with a brief history of research and describes environmental and socio-cultural factors that have affected Eskimo music of different regions. Johnston lists basic characteristics which distinguish the music of Siberian and Alaskan Eskimos from that of Eskimos in Eastern Canada and Greenland (pp. 222–224). He also discusses Estreicher's ideas on Eskimo music history (1950 above) and generalizations about Eskimo music in Nettl (General bibliography, 1954) and Roberts (General bibliography, 1936).

1975   Form and Function in Alaskan Eskimo and Indian Musics. *Northwest Anthropological Research Notes* 9(Fall): 267–280.

Focuses on the problem of stability as versus change in Eskimo music, basically arguing that musical structures and texts have changed little but that the functions of music and dance have become secularized. Concludes by outlining a plan for future research comparing current developments in different regions of Alaska.

1976   *Eskimo Music by Region: A Comparative Circumpolar Study.* Canadian Ethnology Service Paper No. 32. Ottawa: National Museums of Canada.

This actually focuses mainly on Alaskan Eskimo music. Chapters 1 and 2 describe general characteristics of Alaskan Eskimo singing and musical behavior. Chapters 3 through 17 discuss topics and genres relating to Northwest Alaskan groups only. Chapters 18 through 24 cover other Alaskan sub-areas and adjacent regions. Various musical styles of Canada and Greenland are covered in Chapters 25 through 34. Johnston includes musical notations and commentary for nine songs from Northwest Alaska (pp. 193–215). The review by Lutz (1980 below) is rather critical.

1976   Eskimo Music from King Island, Alaska. *Tennessee Folklore Society Bulletin* 42(December): 167–171.

This briefly describes some unique features of King Island music, including the Wolf Dance and instruments such as the box drum and puffin-bill gauntlet rattles. Includes six photographs of dance masks and/or instruments.

1976   The Mackenzie Delta: Meeting Ground of Different Eskimo Styles. *Anthropological Journal of Canada* 14(2): 30–33.

Briefly describes differences between Alaskan Eskimo music and that of Canadian Eskimos to the east. Johnston notes that both styles are present in the centrally located Mackenzie Delta region, an area which includes elements of ancient dance styles and recent (acculturated) dances.

1976   The Social Background of Eskimo Music in Northwest Alaska. *Journal of American Folklore* 89 (October–December): 438–448.

Discusses how the survival of musical traditions in this area has been influenced by the following "determinants": (1) subsistence resources, (2) long-term sessility, (3) geographic isolation, (4) tolerant missionization, (5) mass media impact, (6) changing government policy, (7) language, and (8) the Land Claims movement.

1977   Differential Cultural Persistence in Inuit Musical Behavior, and Its Geographical Distribution. *Études Inuit Studies* 1(2): 57–72.

Explores how contrasting historical influences and other factors have affected the retention of music among Inuit groups in the following areas: Alaska, Siberia, West Greenland, East Greenland, and Canada. Also includes separate sections discussing the effects of missionization and changes in material culture.

1978a   Eskimo Music in Southwest Alaska. *Ethnologische Zeitschrift Zürich* 1: 81–90. Bern, Frankfurt, and Las Vegas: Verlag Peter Lang.

Brief survey discussing styles and relative strength of musical traditions in various Yupik Eskimo communities. Johnston discusses the diffusion of Yupik musical elements to nearby Athabascan Indians and contrasting cultural attitudes underlying the process (Eskimo conservatism versus Indian pragmatism). He also touches on differences between Yupik Eskimo music and that of Northwest Coast Indians. Finally, there is a summary of Yupik instruments and musical characteristics, including remarks on comparative and historical relationships.

1978b   Eskimo Music in Central and Eastern Canada. *Ethnologische Zeitschrift Zürich* 1: 91–105. Bern, Frankfurt, and Las Vegas: Verlag Peter Lang.

Begins by pointing out how the music of central and eastern Eskimo groups differs from that of the Alaskans and (western) Mackenzie Delta groups. Johnston then gives brief descriptions of the following central and eastern styles: Copper Eskimo, Nesilik Eskimo, Caribou Eskimo, and Labrador Eskimo. The summaries are based mainly on earlier sources such as Jenness and Roberts (1925 above), Rasmussen (1931 below), and Estreicher (1948 and 1954 above).

1978c   Musical Characteristics Common to Different Alaskan Eskimo Areas. *Ethnologische Zeitschrift Zürich* 1:107–115. Bern, Frankfurt, and Las Vegas: Verlag Peter Lang.

Identifies traits occurring throughout Alaska but distinguishing the Alaskan styles (along with Siberian Eskimo music) from Eskimo musical styles of Canada and Greenland. Uses standard comparative terminology but contains no transcriptions.

1979   Music of the Tanaina Indians of South-Central Alaska. *Tennessee Folklore Society Bulletin* 45 (March): 12–16.

Johnston first describes older music and dance genres, drawing information from *The Ethnography of the Tanaina* (1937) by Cornelius Osgood. He then discusses the general characteristics of Tanaina music and how it differs from Eskimo or Tlingit music. Makes a broad stylistic division between fast ("happy") songs and slow ("cry") songs.

1980   Review of *The Effects of Acculturation on Eskimo Music of the Cumberland Peninsula* by Maija Lutz (1978). *Journal of American Folklore* 93(370): 478–480.

Basically a positive review, but Johnston does question Lutz's manner of describing how Christian hymns replaced earlier forms of singing as if by automatic cause and effect. He notes that (by contrast) Eskimo singers in remote whaling villages sing Western hymns and also continue to sing earlier traditional genres with no acculturation between the two styles.

1981   Alaskan Folklore. *Review of Ethnology* 7(13–15): 97–
            119. Vienna (Austria).
An overview of story songs and dance songs from different
groups. Contains the following musical examples: (1) Eskimo story
song from Barrow, (2) Eskimo dance song from Point Hope, (3)
juggling-game song from Point Hope, (4) Tlingit Indian
"woodworm song," and (5) Athabascan Indian "happy song" for
funeral potlatch.

1982   Cognitive Patterns in Eskimo Dance. *Inter-Nord* 16:
            127–135.
Examines various forms of mimetic dancing in order to determine mimetic classifications and other aspects of cognitive
patterning. The dances are analyzed on the following levels:
semantics of movement, social function, learning behavior, formal
play behavior, time concept, and aural communication. The
research was conducted circa 1973–1981.

1982   Review of *Inuit Songs from Eskimo Point* by Ramon
            Pelinski, Luke Suluk, and Lucy Amarock (1979).
            Ethnomusicology 26(1): 162–163.
Criticizes Pelinski for giving textual translations and musical
notations without adequate analysis or commentary. The review
discusses the nature of the *ajajait* songs (usually reserved for re-
counting personal adventures or life-cycle crises), the strong association of song texts with animals or subsistence activities, and use
of parallel fifths or other harmonic intervals in some of the songs.

1983   Alaskan Eskimo Music: Stylistic Features and Social
            Function. *Samus* 3:21–25.
Gives a brief overview of musical characteristics and psycho-
social functions of singing among Yupiks and Inupiaqs from various Alaskan communities.

1984   Review of *La Musique des Inuits du Caribou: Cinq
            perspectives methodologiques* by Ramon Pelinski
            (1981). *Ethnomusicology* 28(2): 336–338.
Critical review which questions the adequacy of Pelinski's
fieldwork and calls the book "a rather pretentious semiological ex-
ercise" (p. 337).

1988a   Community History and Environment as Wellspring
            of Inupiaq Eskimo Songtexts. *Anthropos* 83:161–171.
Based on research conducted in northern Alaska. Discusses the
functions of song texts as repositories of local oral histories and

other relationships between music and subsistence activities. Also discusses the functions of music for regulating deviance and fostering social cohesion. Describes the following music-related institutions: the Whaling Feast, the Inviting-In, the Masquerade Dance, and the Box Drum Dance.

1988b   Drum Rhythms of the Alaskan Eskimo. *Anthropologie* 26(1): 75–82.

Discusses the social role of the hunter-drummer among north Alaskan Eskimos in ancient culture and in contemporary traditional communities. Johnston explores various respects in which additive and asymmetrical drum rhythms seem uniquely suited to mimetic dances, local subsistence patterns, and even the arctic ecology. The paper touches on gender roles as reflected in music and compares the divergent styles of Yupik versus Inupiaq drum songs. Also includes information on drum construction and symbolism.

1988c   Film review of *Songs in Minto Life* produced and directed by Curt Madison (1986). *Ethnomusicology* 32(1): 162–163.

The film features songs by (Tanana) Athabascan elders from the village of Minto in the Alaskan Interior. It shows seasonal movements and songs appropriate to various activities. Of special interest are the mimetic songs about animals, and one elder states on camera that the songs were given to humans by animals. Highly favorable review of an outstanding film.

1989   Song Categories and Musical Style of the Yupik Eskimo. *Anthropos* 84:423–431.

Johnston suggests that vocal music is classified by the Yupik into 13 main categories and discusses the musical style of each. The categories are identified as follows: (1) dance songs, (2) shaman songs, (3) hunting songs, (4) teasing songs, (5) traveling songs, (6) berry-picking songs, (7) story songs, (8) juggling game songs, (9) jump-rope game songs, (10) ghost game songs, (11) bird identification songs, (12) fish identification songs, and (13) *inqum* ("cooing") songs.

Jones, Owen R.

1972   (Recording) "Music of the Algonkians, Woodland Indians: Cree, Montagnais, and Naskapi." Smithsonian-Folkways (FE 4253).

Currently available on cassette, this album includes liner notes (2 pp.) by Owen Jones. The songs are mainly involved with the hunting of bear, caribou, and other game. Also includes spoken monologues about hunting.

Keillor, Elaine

1985   Les Tambours des Athapascans du Nord ("Northern Athabascan Drums"). *Recherches Amérindiennes au Québec* 15(4): 43–52.

This is a comparative study of the round single-headed drum which is used widely among northern Athabascan Indians and adjacent groups. Keillor finds that the lacing system at the back varies by region and that (except for Inland Tlingit and Carrier groups) this drum will usually have snares either over or under the drumhead. Includes musical notations (with texts) for two Dogrib songs.

1986   The Role of Youth in the Continuation of Dogrib Musical Traditions. *Yearbook for Traditional Music* 18:61–75.

This describes a Ti Dance which took place after a wedding ceremony in April 1984. Keillor describes various musical events which occurred and compares her observations with those of previous researchers. She argues that children and young people were active participants in these events, contrary to earlier reports. Includes five musical examples (with texts).

1987   Hymn Singing among the Dogrib Indians. Pp. 33–44 in *Sing Out the Glad News: Hymn Tunes in Canada*, edited by John Beckwith. CanMus Documents I. Toronto: Institute for Canadian Music.

Could not be obtained for inspection of contents.

1988   Naissance d'un Genre Musical Nouveau: Fusion du Traditionnel et du "Country" ("The Emergence of a New Musical Genre: Fusion of Traditional and Country Music"). *Recherches Amérindiennes au Québec* 18(4): 65–74.

Keillor examines contemporary songs from the Montagnais (Algonkian) and Dene (Athabascan) cultures and describes how some new (syncretistic) musical styles are being developed from a mixture of American Indian and western musical elements.

1990   Record review of "Old Native and Métis Fiddling in Manitoba," volumes 1 and 2 (two discs in each), produced by Anne Lederman (Falcon Productions, 1987). *Ethnomusicology* 34(1): 192–196.

The discs contain historical and recent recordings of fiddle music performed by Saulteaux (Northern Ojibwa) Indians of Manitoba (Canada). The music is based on Euro-American traditions yet also reflects certain characteristics of traditional Ojibwa style. Keillor's review provides much information and praises an essay by Lederman ("The Old Music") in the liner notes. See also Lederman (1986 below).

Kingston, Deanna

1993   *Illuweet* (Teasing Cousin) Songs as an Expression of King Island Inupiaq Identity. Master's Thesis in Interdisciplinary Studies. Oregon State University.

Describes 11 songs taught by the author's uncle (Alex Muktoyuk) to a group of displaced Inupiaq living in Tacoma Washington. Contains no musical analysis but does discuss song texts and the stories behind them (pp. 38–48). Emphasizes the continuing importance of music as a vehicle for expressing ethnic identity in the contemporary social setting.

Kleivan, Inge

1971   Song Duels in West Greenland: Joking Relationships and Avoidance. *Folk* 13:9–36. Copenhagen.

Discusses how the song duels function to bring inter-personal and inter-group antagonisms out into the open in a formalized manner, thus making it possible to avoid more overt forms of hostility. Based mainly on historical sources, the paper incorporates references dating back to the 1700s. This does not contain musical notations but does include an early print (ca. 1741) and a drawing (ca. 1860) which depict song duels.

1976   Status and Role of Men and Women as Reflected in West Greenland Petting Songs to Infants. *Folk* 18:5–22. Copenhagen.

Gives translations and commentary for 30 song texts in order to compare the content of songs sung to male children as versus those sung to females. Kleivan shows that many of the texts tend to express gender inequalities and thus reinforce traditional role images of man as the active extravert (and procurer of food) and woman as the more passive and dependent sex. Gives translations of songs collected by earlier researchers, including examples documented during the nineteenth century.

Koranda, Lorraine

1964 Some Traditional Songs of the Alaskan Eskimo. Alaska. *University Anthropological Papers* 12(1): 17–32.

Includes musical transcriptions and analysis for the following: Messenger Feast songs (3 songs), Box Drum Song for the Wolf Dance, War Challenge Song, Juggling Song, and a Story Song (with animal mimicry). Also gives brief descriptions of the Messenger Feast and the Wolf Dance. Most of the songs were recorded in 1962 (one in 1951)

1968 Three Songs for the Bladder Festival. Alaska. *University Anthropological Papers* 14(1): 27–32.

Contains musical notations and analysis for three songs recorded in 1965. These are as follows: Wild Parsnip Song, Song to the Bladders, and Jump Dance Song. Also includes brief description of the Bladder Festival.

1972 "Alaskan Eskimo Songs and Stories" (cassette or disc recording). Seattle: University of Washington Press.

The recording contains 42 songs and stories collected in the field between 1950 and 1964. The songs are sung in Eskimo language, and the stories are told in English. The accompanying booklet (31 pages) provides native texts, translations, and musical transcriptions for each of the songs. The album includes a wide range of musical genres including songs for good weather, songs for good luck in hunting, and other songs associated with shamanism or stories.

1980 Music of the Alaskan Eskimos. Pp. 332–362 in *Musics of Many Cultures* edited by Elizabeth May. Berkeley and Los Angeles: University of California Press.

Gives an overview of song types, musical instruments, and general characteristics of the music. Koranda describes major ceremonies such as the Messenger Feast, Bladder Festival, and Feast for the Dead. She also discusses hunting songs, shamanistic (*angakok*) songs, top-spinning fortune songs, and juggling songs. Contains 14 musical examples.

Kurath, Gertrude

1966   Dogrib Choreography and Music. Pp. 12–28 in *The*
              Dogrib Hand Game by June Helm and Nancy
              Oestereich Lurie. National Museum of Canada
              Bulletin 205, Anthropological Series 71. Ottawa:
              National Museums of Canada.
       Focuses on Dogrib (Athabascan) Indians of the Northwest
Territories (Canada). The book is based on research conducted by
Helm and Lurie at various dates from 1959 to 1962. The paper by
Kurath is based on sound recordings, verbal descriptions, and
photographic slides provided by Lurie. The paper gives transcriptions and analysis for the following: Tea Dance songs (12 songs),
Drum Dance songs (4), and Hand Game songs (8). Several of the
songs have prominently triadic melodies, and Kurath mentions the
similarity in this respect to songs of the Navajo and Apache (pp.
27–28).

Lantis, Margaret

1938   The Alaskan Whale Cult and Its Affinities. *American*
              Anthropologist 40(3): 438–464.
       A broad comparative study of whale hunting ceremonialism
among cultures of northeast Asia, the American Arctic, and the
Northwest Coast. Lantis first gives an overview of regional variants by discussing the complex in terms of 32 elements (pp. 438–
447). These include musical elements such as individual ownership
of songs (p. 441) and special songs for whaling (p. 444). The next
sections (pp. 447–464) cover ceremonials in more detail and also
discuss historical relationships. The article includes a translation of
a Nootkan whale towing song which invokes the spiritual power of
the whaler's wife to draw the animal towards her (pp. 460–461).

1940   Note on the Alaskan Whale Cult and Its Affinities.
              American Anthropologist 42:366–368.
       See the previous entry (Lantis 1938 above). This paper pro-
vides additional information on Aleut ceremonial practices and
also on the role of the whaler's wife in magically influencing game
animals.

1947   *Alaskan Eskimo Ceremonialism*. Monographs of the
              American Ethnological Society, no. 11. Seattle: Uni-
              versity of Washington Press. Reprinted in 1971.
       Part One (pp. 1–84) contains descriptions of about 20 cere-
monies. Part Two (pp. 85–122) addresses more general topics such

as shamanism, dancing masks, ritual numbers, and related topics. This includes a section entitled "Song, Dance, and Musical Instruments" (pp. 98–104). The book is based mainly on secondary sources but covers the early literature quite well.

Larsen, Helge

1969   Some Examples of Bear Cult among the Eskimo and Other Northern Peoples. *Folk* 11:27–42.

Hallowell (General bibliography, 1926) had stated that bear ceremonialism was not practiced among Eskimos, but this paper discusses some examples. Larsen emphasizes the attention given by Eskimos to the head and skin of the (slain) bear. Based on secondary sources.

Leden, Christian

1911   Musik und Tänze der grönlandischen Eskimos und die Verwandtschaft der Musik der Polareskimos mit der Indianer. *Zeitschrift für Ethnologie* 43:261–270.

This contains descriptions of song duels and drum dances among the Greenland Eskimo, along with general statements about Eskimo music and comparisons with the music of North American Indians. Includes five transcriptions of Eskimo songs and three previously published examples from the Pawnee, Thompson River, and Hopi Indians. The Greenland data are from the Umanak district.

1952   *Über die Musik der Smith Sund Eskimos, Und Ihre Verwandtschaft mit Musik der Amerikanischen Indianer.* Meddelelser om Grönland, vol. 152, no. 3.

This contains transcriptions (with texts) and analyses for 31 Smith Sound Eskimo songs collected by the author in 1909. The Eskimo songs are compared with previously published examples from the Cree (4 songs), Pawnee (1), Thompson River (1), and Hopi (1).

1954   *Über die Musik der Östgrönlander.* Meddelelser om Grönland, vol. 152, no. 4.

This contains transcriptions and analyses for 70 East Greenland Eskimo songs collected by Leden in 1910 and 1926. There are texts and translations (into German) for all the songs. Leden also describes musical instruments and discusses various relationships between texts and melodies and between the dancing and music. The data comes from the Angmagssalik region and Scoresby Sound.

Lederman, Anne

1986   Old Native and Métis Fiddling in Two Manitoba Communities: Camperville and Ebb and Flow. Master's thesis, York University.
Describes a tradition of fiddle music that was first adopted from French and Scottish fur traders and subsequently modified to incorporate native (northern Ojibwa) musical characteristics. Based on historical sources and research conducted in 1985–1986. Some of this information is also found in an essay ("The Old Music") among the liner notes of Lederman's recording Old Native and Métis Fiddling in Manitoba (Falcon Productions, 1987). For more information, see the record review by Keillor (1990 above).

See the catalogue by **Lee** (1979) in the General bibliography. This lists recordings at Indiana University Archives of Traditional Music. The collection includes recordings from the following Arctic and Sub-Arctic groups: Beothuk, Cree, Dogrib, Eskimo (of various regions), Kutchin, Montagnais, Naskapi, and Slave.

Loyens, William

1964   The Koyukon Feast for the Dead. *Arctic Anthropology* 2(2): 133–148.
This describes a Koyukon mortuary feast which is known locally as the "Stick Dance." Loyens compares it with similar celebrations as practiced among neighboring Athabascan and Eskimo peoples. The article is based on fieldwork conducted circa 1962–1963 and on various earlier sources. Contains no musical notations.

Lundström, Hakan

1980   North Athabascan Story Songs and Dance Songs. Pp. 126–164 in *The Alaska Seminar* edited by Anna Birgitta Rooth. Acta Universitatus Upsaliensis, Studia Ethnologica Upsaliensis. Stockholm: Distributed by Almqvist and Wiksell International.
This focuses on 69 songs recorded by Anna B. Rooth at Minto and other locations in 1966. Lundström begins by discussing song types, musical instruments, and recent musical influences. The

main body of the paper gives transcriptions and comments for each of the songs (pp. 131–155). This is followed by musical analyses and a comparison of the Northern Athabascan vocal style with profiles for the following groups: Eskimo, Salish, (Other) Northwest Coast, and Southern Athabascan (Apache and Navajo). Lundström also discusses the stylistic differences between solo songs and dance songs within the Northern Athabascan repertory.

Lutz, Maija M.

1978   *The Effects of Acculturation on Eskimo Music of Cumberland Peninsula.* Canadian Ethnology Service Paper No. 41. National Museum of Man Mercury Series. Ottawa: National Museums of Canada.

Lutz examines contemporary musical life, then places present-day society in historical perspective by describing changes that have taken place in music and culture over the last hundred years. The study focuses on Inuit people living at Pangnirtung on the Cumberland Peninsula (Northwest Territories). This is based on earlier sources and research conducted by Lutz in 1973–1974. The book also includes two (5 inch) disc recordings. Reviewed by Beaudry (1980 above) and Johnston (1980 above).

1980   Book review of *Eskimo Music by Region: A Comparative Circumpolar Study* by Thomas Johnston (1976). *Ethnomusicology* 24(3): 590–592.

Contains several criticisms, first noting that the title is misleading because Johnston focuses mainly on musical sub-areas of Alaska and only deals with styles of the eastern regions briefly. Lutz also criticizes the book for failing to define musical areas systematically and for conjectural remarks concerning the determinants of musical style.

1982   *Musical Traditions of the Labrador Coast Inuit.* Canadian Ethnology Service Paper No. 82. National Museum of Man Mercury Series. Ottawa: National Museums of Canada.

Describes musical life among the Inuits of northern Labrador and how it was influenced by Moravian missionaries during the period since 1771. The chapter entitled "Current Musical Trends in Nain, Labrador" covers the following subjects: Moravian music, teasing songs, baby chants, children's music, contemporary songs, and dance activities. In her conclusions, Lutz compares church influences in this area with those among the Cumberland Peninsula

Inuit she previously studied (Lutz 1978 above). There is a review
by Cavanagh (1983 above).

1990   Record review of "Canada: Jeux vocaux des Inuit"
              (compact disc) produced by Jean-Jacques Nattiez
              (Ocora HM 83, 1989). *Ethnomusicology* 34(3): 511–
              513.
The recording includes examples of vocal games from the
Caribou Inuit, Netsilik Inuit, and Igloolik Inuit. Nattiez has provided extensive liner notes (40 pages) and also divides the recorded
examples into two main categories: "narrative games" and "games
by juxtaposition." The review is highly favorable.

McKennan, Robert A.

1959   *The Upper Tanana Indians.* Yale University
              Publications in Anthropology 55. New Haven.
This ethnographic monograph (223 pages) includes comments
on "Songs" (pp. 99–100) and on "Dancing" (pp. 100–101). There
is also information on songs and use of a bull-roarer in
McKennan's descriptions of shamanistic rituals he attended in
December 1929 (pp. 152–156). These accounts are given in the
style of a diary.

See **Mark** (1955) in the Northwest Coast bibliography. This discusses
the musical structure of Inland Tlingit and Tagish (Athabascan) songs recorded in the Southern Yukon.

Marsh, Gordon H.

1954   A Comparative Study of Eskimo-Aleut Religion.
              Anthropological Papers of the University of Alaska
              3(1): 21–36.
The section on "Charms" (p. 22) makes a distinction between
magical formulas and songs that have power in their own right (as
in systems of mana or magic) and those connected with animistic
belief systems. Marsh considers the latter to represent a later development.

Mason, John Alden

1946   *Notes on the Indians of the Great Slave Lake Area.*
              Yale University Publications in Anthropology 34.
              New Haven.

This contains brief remarks on "Music" (pp. 28–29) and "Dances" (p. 35). More interesting is the discussion of medicine songs and shamanism in the section on "Religious Culture" (pp. 37–40). Also includes three song texts and translations.

Mather, Elsie

1992   Alaskan Ceremonialism. Pp. 31–38 in *Proceedings of the International Symposium on Comparative Studies of the Music, Dance, and Games of Northern Peoples* edited by Kazuyuki Tanimoto. Sapporo (Japan): Hokkaido Kyoiku Daigaku.

Mather is a Yupik Eskimo, and she begins by describing her efforts to produce a publication on pre-contact ceremonials (in Yupik) for use in high school programs for bilingual education. Emphasizing the native viewpoint, she discusses her interviews with elders and then describes the Bladder Festival, the Inviting-In Feast, the Messenger Feast, and other ceremonial activities.

Merkur, Daniel

1991   *Powers Which We Do Not Know: The Gods and the Spirits of the Inuit.* Moscow, Idaho: University of Idaho Press.

A comparative study of religious and metaphysical concepts among Inuit groups from Alaska to Greenland. This contains interesting sections on the cosmology of songs, magic words, and shamanism (pp. 53–71). Based on earlier writings by Rasmussen, Jenness, and others.

Mishler, Craig

1974   (Recording) "Music of the Kutchin Indians of Alaska." Smithsonian-Folkways (FE 4384).

Currently available on cassette, this fine collection also includes liner notes by Mishler (8 pages). The contents are identified as follows: Song of the Snow Geese, Love Songs (3), Medicine Songs (3), War Song, Crow Dance Songs (2), Songs of Tribute (2), The Boy in the Moon (story song), New Year's Song, Goodbye Song, Steamboat Song, Red River Jig, Duck Dance, Rabbit Dance, Virginia Reel, Double Jig, Fox Trot, Eight Couple, Square Dance, and Four Hand Reel.

1981   Gwich'in Athabascan Music and Dance: An Ethnography and Ethnohistory. Doctoral dissertation, University of Texas at Austin.

Could not be obtained for inspection of contents nor could information be gotten from other sources.

1993   *The Crooked Stovepipe: Athapaskan Fiddle Music and Square Dancing in Northeast Alaska and Northwest Canada.* Urbana and Chicago: University of Illinois Press.

This describes music and dance traditions which originally came to the Gwich'in (also called Kutchin or Koyukon Athapaskan) around 1850 and gradually developed indigenous characteristics that were entirely distinct from other (western) styles of fiddle music. The introductory chapter questions the concept of pure culture and describes how many aspects of modern life have become "Athapaskanized" among these people. Mishler then gives an historical overview of fiddle styles that are used with various dances in different communities. This contains numerous photographs and 22 musical transcriptions (by Pamela Swing). Based on historical sources and on research conducted at various locations between 1972 and 1992.

Murdoch, John

1892   *Ethnological Results of the Point Barrow Expedition.* Annual Report of the Bureau of American Ethnology (1887–1888), vol. 9, pp. 3–441. Washington: Smithsonian Institution.

This contains descriptions of musical instruments and three song texts, along with some disparaging remarks on Eskimo music (pp. 385–389).

Nattiez, Jean-Jacques

1982   Comparison within a Culture: The Katajjaq of the Inuit. Pages 134–140 in *Cross-Cultural Perspectives on Music* edited by Robert Flack and Timothy Rice. Toronto: University of Toronto Press.

Compares vocal games or "throat games" among various Inuit groups. Nattiez considers regional differences relating to the games under three headings: (1) "creation circumstances" and related ideas, (2) performance contexts or functions, and (3) sound structures. He then employs various analytical grids in order to explain the disparities in semiotic terms and discusses historical processes through which the genre became diversified.

1983a   The *Rekkukara* of the Ainu (Japan) and the *Katajjaq* of the Inuit: A Comparison. *World of Music* 25(2): 33–44.

Nattiez attempts to demonstrate that the two genres can be viewed in general as manifestations of the same circumpolar music culture. He first notes similarities (and some differences) between the styles, then examines meanings associated with each in their respective cultures. He concludes that both function as incantations. The paper also discusses implications relating to gender complementarity (p. 40), as both genres are exclusively sung by women and also connected with the ritualization of hunting, which is otherwise a predominantly male activity.

1983b   Some Aspects of Inuit Vocal Games. *Ethnomusicology* 27(3): 457–476.

The paper summarizes earlier research and explains concepts and methodologies developed by Nattiez and other members of the Groupe de Recherches en Sémiologie Musicale (University of Montreal). Nattiez describes the cultural significance of the games as symbolic and multifunctional, explaining that they provide a sort of "host-structure" which can absorb sound sources of various origins (p. 460). He then uses "paradigmatic transcriptions" and other diagrams to delineate typical structures and progressions found in the games. In concluding, Nattiez discusses the problem of understanding compositional processes on the basis of inductive methods as versus native statements (pp. 468–470) and also explores the idea that the vocal games express a nonlinear concept of time that is typical of Inuit thought (pp. 470–472).

1988   La Danse à tambour chez les Inuit Igloolik (Nord de la Terre de Baffin). *Recherches Amérindiennes au Québec* 18(4).

This is based on data collected by Nattiez at Iglulik and Pond Inlet in 1976 and 1977. The paper does not include musical analysis but does give information on the following: composition of songs, song festivals, the unfolding of dances (order of events), the drum, the drum dance as a competition or endurance contest, song tournaments, musical aesthetics, poetic content of songs, and the link between songs and soul names.

1992   Inuit, Ainu, and Siberian Vocal Games in a Circumpolar Perspective. Pp. 39–46 in *Proceedings of the International Symposium on Comparative Studies of the Music, Dance, and Games of Northern Peoples* edited by Kazuyuki Tanimoto. Sapporo: Hokkaido Kyoiku Daigaku.

This discusses musical and cultural aspects of vocal games as practiced among Canadian Inuits and northeast Asian peoples. Nattiez defines the stylistic similarities between Inuit *katajjait* and Ainu *rekukkara* according to three basic characteristics. He then examines their symbolism, defining both as "host-structures" capable of absorbing various sound-origins and levels of meaning. In conclusion, Nattiez examines the connections between vocal games and earlier shamanistic practices.

Nelson, Edward William

1899   *The Eskimo About Bering Strait.* Annual Report of the Bureau of American Ethnology (1896–1897), vol. 18 (Part 1). Washington: Smithsonian Institution.

Contains descriptions of songs, dances, and instruments (pp. 347–357). Includes one musical example and three song texts with translations.

See **Nettl** (1954a) in the General bibliography. Discusses predominant musical characteristics of the "Eskimo-Northwest area" (pp. 50–56).

Olsen, Rovsing

1967   Intervals and Rhythm in the Music of the Eskimos of East Greenland. Pp. 54–59 in *Proceedings of the Centennial Workshop in Ethnomusicology held at the University of British Columbia, Vancouver, 1967* edited by Peter Crossley-Holland. Vancouver.

Begins by describing the isolation of East Greenland Eskimos, who had first contact with Europeans in 1884. Olsen classifies the songs into four groups: recitative songs, songs with two tones (in lullabies and stories), songs with three tones (mainly magic songs and women's songs), and songs with four or more tones. He discusses the melodic structure of a particular song and how the scale may be varied between performances while singers consider it the same. He then gives a similar account of the rhythm and acceptable rhythmic variations. Closes by describing drum duels and shamanic rituals.

1972   Acculturation in Eskimo Songs of the Greenlanders. *Yearbook of the International Folk Music Council* 4:32–37.
Focuses on surviving musical traditions in the relatively isolated communities of eastern and northern Greenland. States that indigenous and western (occidental) musics tend to be kept separated in the minds of the Eskimos but also notes that in recent recordings the relation between song rhythms and drum rhythms seems to have become more regularized as a result of occidental influence (p. 34). Also discusses how Eskimo music of the west coast has been much more acculturated, giving a transcription of a Scottish (originally) fiddle tune played by the locals. Includes 10 musical examples in all.

Osgood, Cornelius B.

1932   The Ethnography of the Great Bear Lake Indians. *National Museum of Canada Bulletin* 70:31–97.
Contains brief descriptions of song types and instruments (pp. 67–68).

1933   Tanaina Culture. *American Anthropologist* 35: 695–717.
Contains brief descriptions of song types and instruments (pp. 705–706).

1936   *Contributions to the Ethnography of the Kutchin.* Yale University Publications in Anthropology No. 14.
Includes descriptions of songs and instruments among the Peel River Kutchin (pp. 94–95) and Crow River Kutchin (p. 100). Also see pp. 103–105 for comments on Kutchin music in general.

1959   *Ingalik Mental Culture.* Yale University Publications in Anthropology, no. 56. New Haven: Yale University Press.
Based on research conducted in 1937 and in 1956. There are sections on "Drumming and Clapping" (pp. 93–94), "Dancing" (pp. 94–95), and "Singing" (pp. 95–96). A section on "Incantations" (pp. 118–125) gives information on the concept of "animal songs" and how they are used for medicine-making. Osgood describes magical functions associated with songs of 32

different animals and 10 other spiritual beings such as Moon, Fog, and Rock.

Parry, William Edward

1824	*Journal of a Second Voyage for the Discovery of a North-East Passage from the Atlantic to the Pacific.* New York.

Contains a description of singing by Eskimos of Melville Peninsula, including two musical examples (pp. 541–543). Could not be obtained. Information given here is from Hickerson (General bibliography, 1961:318).

Pelinski, Ramon

1977	Inuit *A Ja Ja* Songs: On Music Tradition and Change in Rankin Inlet. *Western Canadian Journal of Anthropology* 7(3): 1–15.

Gives a survey of contemporary musical activities, including traditional and nontraditional genres. Also discusses personal songs (*a ja ja*) which accompany the Canadian Eskimo drum dance.

1978	Système émique de substitutions intervalliques dans le chant personnel des Inuit Caribou ("Emic Analysis of Interval Substitution in Personal Songs of the Caribou Inuit"). *Études Inuit Studies* 2(1): 21–34.

This paper deals with songs recorded by Leden at Churchill (Manitoba) in 1914 and compares these with recordings of the "same" songs as collected by Pelinski at Eskimo Point (Northwest Territory). Pelinski attempts to taxonomize the variations which occur in different performances. He relies on musical analysis and on verbal statements by the singers.

1981	*La musique des Inuit du Caribou: Cinq perspectives méthodologiques.* Montréal: Presses de l'Université de Montréal.

The first chapter gives a survey of contemporary musical culture at Rankin Inlet and is based largely on Pelinski (1977 above). Succeeding chapters each employ different methodological approaches in discussing the following subjects: linguistics and polyphony (Chapter 2), interval substitution in personal songs (Chapter 3), typology of melodic contours (Chapter 4), and structure of 31 personal songs (*a ja ja*) from Eskimo Point (Chapter 5). Transcriptions of the latter songs are published in Pelinski, Suluk, and Amarook (1979 below). The review by Johnston is highly critical (1984 above).

Pelinski, Ramon, Luke Suluk, and Lucy Amarook

1979   *Inuit Songs from Eskimo Point.* Canadian Ethnology Service Paper No. 60. National Museum of Man Mercury Series. Ottawa: National Museums of Canada.

Contains native texts, translations, and musical notations for 41 songs. The following genres are represented: *ajajait* songs (35), animal songs (2), and children's game songs (3). This is presented as a "songbook" and analysis is generally minimal. Includes a 7-inch disc with sixteen minutes of recorded examples. Reviewed by Johnston (1982 above).

Preston, Richard

1985   Transformations musicales et culturelles chez les Cris de l'est ("Musical and Cultural Transformations among the Eastern Cree"). *Recherches Amérindiennes au Québec* 15(4).

Preston discusses various musical genres and the impact of historical influences and recent developments. Contains sections on the following: European fiddle tunes, Anglican hymns, Country Western music, Christian Fundamentalist hymns, Rock Music, and "Traditional" Pan-Indian music.

Rainey, Froelich G.

1947   *The Whale Hunters of Tigara.* Anthropological Papers of the American Museum of Natural History 41(2). New York.

Focuses on whaling and related ceremonialism among the Tigara (Eskimos) of the Point Hope area. The section on cosmology or "Native Theory" (pp. 267–278) gives information on shamanistic songs used by individuals and in group rituals.

Rasmussen, Knud

1930a   *Intellectual Culture of the Hudson Bay Eskimos.* Report of the Thule Expedition (1921–1924), vol. 7, no. 1.

The section "Songs and Dances, Games and Pastimes" (pp. 227–250) contains descriptions of singing with several song texts and translations.

1930b   *Observations on the Intellectual Culture of the Caribou Eskimos.* Report of the Thule Expedition (1921–1924), vol. 7, number 2.

The section "Ballads and Songs of Derision" (pp. 66–78) contains 14 song texts and translations; other texts are also given in translation only. Also includes descriptions of dancing and participation of women in songfests.

1930c   *Iglulik and Caribou Eskimo Texts.* Report of the Thule Expedition (1921–1924), vol. 7, no. 3.

Could not be obtained. According to Hickerson (1961:321) this contains 11 song texts and translations.

1931   *Netsilik Eskimos: Social Life and Spiritual Culture.* Report of the Thule Expedition (1921–1924), vol. 8, nos. 1 and 2.

Part One deals with Eskimos of the Pelly Bay area. It includes translated quotations from an Eskimo shaman (speaking about the creation of songs) and information on the following genres: derision songs, personal songs, sentiment songs, hunting songs, and travel songs. Rasmussen also gives texts, translations, and commentary for several songs (pp. 324–355). Part Two deals with Eskimos of the Black River area and also includes several song texts and translations.

1932   *Intellectual Culture of the Copper Eskimos.* Report of the Thule Expedition (1921–1924), vol. 9.

The section "Songs and Spirituals" (pp. 119–191) contains 30 song texts and translations plus eight texts in English only. The research was done at Queen Maud Gulf.

Ridington, Robin

1971   Beaver Dreaming and Singing. Pp. 115–128 in *Pilot not Commander: Essays in Memory of Diamond Jenness* edited by P. Lotz and J. Lotz. *Anthropologica*, vol. 13.

Contains no musical analysis but gives much information on the totemic and shamanistic symbolism of songs in Beaver culture. Also includes description of a Beaver ceremonial (pp. 126–128).

1978 *Swan People: A Study of the Dunne-Za Prophet Dance*. National Museum of Man Mercury Series. Canadian Ethnology Service Paper No. 38. Ottawa: National Museum of Canada.

Beliefs about songs and particularly the connection between songs and dreaming are discussed in sections identified as follows: "Medicine, Power, Dreaming, and the Vision Quest" (pp. 7–11); "Dreaming and the Prophet Tradition" (pp. 13–17); and "Prophet Dancing: Walking the trail to Heaven" (pp. 24–26). This is based on field work conducted among the Dunne-Za (Beaver Indians) from 1964 to 1971.

1979 Metaphor and Meaning: Healing in Dunne-Za Music and Dance. Western Canadian *Journal of Anthropology* 8(2): 9–17.

Could not be obtained for inspection of contents nor could information be gotten from other sources.

See **Roberts** (1936) in the General bibliography. This contains a section on general characteristics of vocal music among Eskimo groups of various regions (pp. 27–29).

Roberts, Helen Heffron, and Diamond Jenness

1925 *Songs of the Copper Eskimo*. Report of the Canadian Arctic Expedition (1913–1918), vol. 14. Ottawa: F. A. Ackland.

This contains musical notations, texts, translations, and detailed analyses for 137 songs collected on wax cylinders by Jenness between 1914 and 1916. Groups represented are the Copper Eskimo (113 songs), Mackenzie River Eskimo (12), Inland Hudson Bay Eskimo (7), and Eskimos of Point Hope, Alaska (5). Each song is analyzed separately, and various types of songs are described. The first chapter contains a comparison of various dance song styles, then also compares the basic style of the dance songs to that of weather incantations. Other discussions focus on scales and tonality, different versions of the same song, and instances of melodic borrowing. There are some criticisms in the review by Herzog (1926 above).

Saindon, J. Emile

1934 Two Cree Songs from James Bay. *Primitive Man* 7(1):6–7. January.

Contains descriptions of singing and musical notations for a lullaby and a medicine ("conjuring") song.

See the catalogue by **Seeger and Spear** (1987) in the General bibliography. This lists early cylinder recordings among the holdings at the Indiana University Archives of Traditional Music. The collection includes Arctic and Sub-Arctic recordings from the following groups: Beothuk, Cree, Eskimo (of various regions), Kutchin, and Montagnais.

Søby, Regitze

1969   The Eskimo Animal Cult. *Folk* 11:43–78.
An overview of hunting ceremonialism based on references in earlier literature. Deals with beliefs and customs relating to hunting of all sorts of land and marine animals. Discusses the animal hunting complex in terms of various elements, with sections on the following: "Hunting Amulets and Chants" (pp. 48–50), "Entertainment and Dancing" (pp. 61–62), and "Alaskan Eskimo Ceremonials in Honor of Game Animal's Souls" (pp. 69–71).

Speck, Frank Gouldsmith

1935   *Naskapi: The Savage Hunters of the Labrador Peninsula.* Norman: University of Oklahoma Press.
Chapter 7 ("Magical Practices") contains a section entitled "Invoking the Soul Spirit by Singing, Drumming, and Rattling" (pp. 174–182) and also includes sections on "Singing" (pp. 182–186), and "Dancing" (pp. 186–187). Speck describes the recording of songs in 1909, discusses the style of the songs (mainly "songs for animals" that are used in hunting), and gives texts and translations for five songs.

Stein, Robert

1902   Eskimo Music. Pp. 337–356 in *The White World: Life and Adventures Within the Arctic Circle Portrayed by Famous Living Explorers* edited by Rudolph Hersting. New York.
This contains 39 musical examples (with texts) that were notated by Stein at Cape York and Cape Sabine. The transcriptions were apparently done by ear without recording equipment. Information given here is from Hickerson (General bibliography, 1961:353).

See **Stevenson** (1973a) in the General bibliography. This discusses some early sources on native music of Alaska and other Arctic regions (pp. 23–26).

Stryker, Miriam

1966   (Recording and liner notes) "Eskimo Songs from Alaska." Smithsonian-Folkways (FE 4069).

Currently reissued on cassette, the album contains songs recorded at actual singing sessions during the early 1960s. Contents are described as follows. Side One: Drum "sing" at Tim Cologergen's home in the village of Savoonga, May 7, 1963 (10 items). Side Two: Village of Gambell; an Eskimo "sing" at the home of Thomas Apassingok, August 1961 (10 items).

Tanimoto, Kazuyuki

1992   Typology of Song and Dance among the Northern Peoples. Pages 115–119 in *Proceedings of the International Symposium on Comparative Studies of the Music, Dance, and Games of Northern Peoples* edited by Kazuyuki Tanimoto. Sapporo: Hokkaido Kyoiku Daigaku.

Compares the musical characteristics of drum dance songs among various northern peoples. Tanimoto focuses mainly on differences in the shape and playing technique of the single-headed drum which is used. He uses this and other evidence to speculate on various comparative issues, for example trying to explain the non-occurrence of vocal games among Alaskan Eskimos despite their occurrence among native peoples of northeastern Asia and Arctic regions of eastern Canada.

See **Tarasoff** (1980) in Plains bibliography for study of ceremonialism among the Plains Cree and Saulteau.

Thalbitzer, William Carl

1904   *A Phonetical Study of the Eskimo Language.* Meddelelser om Grønland, vol. 31.

The section on "Old Fashioned Songs" (pp. 289–313) contains 107 song texts and translations from northern Greenland. Another section entitled "Eskimo Music from Greenland" (pp. 372–387) includes 88 melodies (with texts) collected among Eskimos of western Greenland and one musical example from the Ammassalik Eskimo.

1923   Language and Folklore. Pp. 113–564 in *The Ammassalik Eskimo* edited by William Thalbitzer (2 vols.). Meddelelser om Grønland, vol. 40.

The section on poetry (pp. 160–179) discusses the textual form and content of songs, including 20 Ammassalik song texts. More than 200 other texts and translations are given in following pages, also with discussions on the meaning and use of songs (pp. 185–378, 496–564). The section "Melodies from the Cape Farewell District" (pp. 539–543) contains 14 musical examples transcribed by Thalbitzer from his own cylinder recordings. There is also a discussion on use of the cylinder phonograph for research (pp. 544–559).

1939   *Inuit Sange og Danse vra Grönland* ("Inuit Songs and Dances from Greenland"). Copenhagen: Einar Munksgaard.

This contains musical notations and textual translations for 65 songs arranged in three main groups: (1) Modern Music from West Greenland, 1900–1938; (2) West Greenland Music from 1750–1900; and (3) Aboriginal Eskimo songs from Greenland and Baffinland. The explanatory texts are in Danish but generally include translations or summaries in English. The song texts are translated in Danish, only the titles being given in English.

Thalbitzer, William Carl, and Hjalmar Thuren

1923   Melodies from East Greenland, with a supplement containing Melodies from North-West Greenland. Pp. 47–112 in *The Ammassalik Eskimo* edited by William Thalbitzer (2 vols.). Meddelelser om Grønland, vol. 40.

Contains 129 musical notations (including texts) of songs that Thalbitzer collected in 1905–1906. Some were notated by ear (by Thalbitzer) and others from cylinders (by Thuren). Thalbitzer also gives information concerning the cultural meaning and uses of songs.

Thuren, Hjalmar Lauritz

1923   On the Eskimo Music in Greenland. Pp. 1–45 in *The Ammassalik Eskimo* edited by William Thalbitzer (2 vols.). Meddelelser om Grønland, vol. 40.

Contains detailed discussions of Eskimo music and the history of research on the subject, including comparative analyses of music from various regions. The following (4) areas are considered: East Greenland, Smith Sound, Northwest Greenland, and Southwest Greenland. Includes several musical examples quoted from previous sources.

Thuren, Hjalmar Lauritz and Thalbitzer, William Carl

1911   *The Eskimo Music*. Copenhagen.
Includes reprinted versions of Thalbitzer and Thuren (1923 above) and Thuren (1923 above). Information given here is from Hickerson (General bibliography, 1961:363).

Victor, Anne-Marie

1992   Pathfinders of the Universe: Inupiak and Siberian Yupik Dance. Pp. 65–76 in *Proceedings of the International Symposium on Comparative Studies of the Music, Dance, and Games of Northern Peoples* edited by Kazuyuki Tanimoto. Sapporo: Hokkaido Kyoiku Daigaku.
Discusses whale ceremonialism among various groups and includes much information from manuscript collections of Otto Geist (ca. 1927–1929) and Froelich Rainey (ca. 1940–1941), both of which are housed at the University of Alaska, Fairbanks. Includes descriptions of magical songs used by hunters and shamans in rituals for whale hunting.

Whidden, Lynn

1984   How Can You Dance to Beethoven?: Native People and Country Music. *Canadian University Music Review* 5:87–103.

1985   Les Hymnes, une anomalie parmie les chants traditionnels des Cris du nord ("Christian Hymns as an Anomalous Element in Traditional Songs of the Northern Cree"). *Recherches Amérindiennes au Québec* 15(4): 29–36.
Whidden examines the juxtaposition of traditional Cree songs and Christian hymns as a means of illustrating the degree to which native and non-native belief systems have become intermingled. The paper includes an interesting section on the occurrence of hymn elements in hunting songs. Includes seven musical examples.

Whitbread, Donald H.

1953   The Eskimo Violin. *Canadian Forum* 33(390): 82–
              83.
       An interesting introduction to the subject for general readers.
       Also contains comments on the use of concertinas and harmonicas.
       Focuses on native communities on the east coast of Hudson's Bay.

Williams, Maria

1992   Contemporary Alaska Native Dance: The Spirit of
              Tradition. Pp. 149–168 in *Native American Dance:
              Ceremonies and Social Traditions* edited by Charlotte
              Heth. Washington: National Museum of the
              American Indian, Smithsonian Institution.
       Describes the revitalization of native dances since the mid-
       1970s and adaptation of the dances to modern social conditions.
       Focuses on dances of the following groups: the Alutiiq/Aleut of
       Kodiak Island, various Tlingit dance groups, the Inupiat of King
       Island, and Yupik dancers of Hooper Bay. Contains excellent color
       photographs.

III. Northwest Coast

Amoss, Pamela

1978   *Coast Salish Spirit Dancing: The Survival of an Ancient Religion.* Seattle: University of Washington Press.

An historical and ethnographic study of the revival of Spirit Dances mainly among the Nooksack of northwestern Washington. Discusses how native beliefs have been combined with Pentecostal and Shaker concepts. Also gives detailed descriptions concerning the initiation and training of Spirit Dance participants, including the teaching and rehearsal of songs and dances. See Jilek (1974 below) and the review by Halpern (1980 below).

Angulo, Jaime de

1929   A Tfalati Dance Song in Parts. *American Anthropologist* 31:496–498.

The Tfalati are a division of the Kalapuya Indians formerly located near Portland, Oregon. The article describes a song performed in four parts as explained to Angulo by one Kalapuya man (Louis Kennoyer). Two women sang closely-related versions of a principal melody, while two men sang variations of an ostinato accompaniment in lower range. The multipart texture is illustrated with a form of graph notation, and Angulo also describes movements of a dance that goes with the song.

See **Abraham and Hornbostel** (1906) in the Great Basin and Plateau bibliography. This contains transcriptions and analyses of 43 songs collected among the nearby Thompson River Indians by Franz Boas.

Barbeau, C. Marius

1933   Songs of the Northwest. *Musical Quarterly* 19:101–111.

Contains 8 musical notations and translations of songs from a total collection of 300 songs recorded by Barbeau in 1920 and years following. The transcriptions (by Barbeau and Ernest MacMillan) seem excellent, but tribal and linguistic identifications are not always clear. The songs were collected along the Nass River and the Skeena River, in an area belonging equally to the Northwest Coast and Sub-Arctic culture areas. Tribal groups identified include the Tahltan (Athabascan), Carrier (Athabascan), Gitskan (Penutian), and Tsimshian (Penutian). An Asiatic origin for the songs is asserted but not systematically demonstrated.

1934   Asiatic Survivals in Indian Songs. *Musical Quarterly* 20:107–116.

A continuation of topics touched on in Barbeau (1933 above), this includes five musical examples from the Nass and Skeena River regions in northern British Columbia. The relationship of these songs to musical traditions of Siberia, Japan, and China is argued mainly on the basis of subjective impressions shared by Barbeau and a Chinese scholar.

1951   Tsimshian Songs. Pp. 94–280 in *The Tsimshian: Their Arts and Music* by Viola E. Garfield, Paul S. Wingert and Marius Barbeau. Publications of the American Ethnological Society, vol. 18. New edition by University of Washington Press (Seattle, 1966).

This contains musical transcriptions, analyses, texts, and translations for 75 songs collected by James Teit in 1915 and by Barbeau (ca. 1920–1929). The transcriptions are by Barbeau and Ernest MacMillan, while musical analyses are by Marguerite Béclard d'Harcourt. Analysis and musical examples are edited by George Herzog. The cultural background of the music is discussed, and there is a general comparison between musical styles of the coastal and interior regions. Also see Garfield (1951).

1957a   Indian Songs of the Northwest. *Canadian Music Journal* 2(Autumn): 16–25.

Could not be obtained for inspection of contents nor could information be gotten from other sources.

1957b   Review of *Songs of the Nootka Indians of Western Vancouver Island* by Helen Roberts and Morris

Swadesh (1955). *Ethnomusicology Newsletter* 9 (September): 30–32.
Bascially a positive review but criticizes Roberts's musical notations as being overly detailed.

1962   Buddhist Dirges on the North Pacific Coast. *Journal of the International Folk Music Council* 14(January): 16–21.
Seeks to demonstrate a connection between the style of Japanese melodies (generally) and songs recorded by Barbeau among Indians of the Nass and Skeena River region (in Alaska and northern British Columbia). The main musical parallel cited by Barbeau is a type of descending melodic pattern, which leaps to a high note then gradually descends by wide intervals to the bottom, where it ends in a "leisurely drone" (p. 16). Includes six musical examples.

See Katz (1970 below) for biography of Barbeau (1883–1969) and a more comprehensive list of his writings.

See **Baker** (1882) in the General bibliography. Pages 132–137 contain 24 fragments of Twana and Clallam songs previously published in Eels (1879 below).

Barnett, Homer G.

1937a   Culture Element Distributions, VII: Oregon Coast. *University of California Anthropological Records* 1(3): 155–204.
Contains information on the presence or absence of various traits in tabular form. Includes elements relating to musical instruments (p. 174) and various ritual activities (pp. 188–192).

1937b   Culture Element Distributions, IX: Gulf of Georgia Salish. *University of California Anthropological Records* 1(5): 221–295.
Contains information on the presence or absence of various traits in tabular form. Includes elements relating to musical instruments (pp. 251) and various ritual activities (pp. 257–258 and 271–276).

1941   Review of *Nootka and Quileute Music* by Frances Densmore (1939). *Journal of American Folklore* 54:225–226.

Summarizes the contents and criticizes the manner in which the texts are transcribed.

1957   *Indian Shakers: A Messianic Cult of the Pacific Northwest.* Carbondale: Southern Illinois University Press.
Classic study of a nativistic movement which began in Washington during the 1870s and spread widely during the 1920s. Contains no musical notations or analysis but does include descriptions of the (syncretistic) singing and ringing of bells. See also Gunther (1949 below).

Boas, Franz

See Boas (1987) in Arctic and Sub-Arctic bibliography. This contains one musical notation (with text and translation) of a song collected by Boas among Indians of British Columbia.

1888a   On Certain Songs and Dances of the Kwakiutl of British Columbia. *Journal of American Folklore* 1(1): 49–64.
Includes four melodies and texts (with translations) collected by Boas in 1886 and 1887. Two other song texts are also translated.

1888b   Chinook Songs. *Journal of American Folklore* 1(3): 220–226.
Contains 39 song texts and translations (one Tlingit example included), three of which are transcribed in staff notations. The research was conducted in 1886.

1891   Second General Report of the Indians of British Columbia. Pp. 562–715 in *Report of the Meeting of the British Association for the Advancement of Science (in 1890)*, vol. 90.
Includes one melody and text (p. 581) identified as Lku'ngen (Songish), 15 melodies and texts (mostly translated) from the Nootka (pp. 588–603), and 20 Kwakiutl song texts and translations (pp. 625–632). All the material was collected by Boas in 1889.

1894a   *Chinook Texts.* Bureau of American Ethnology Bulletin no. 20.
Contains 12 song texts (and translations) with rhythmic notations for each. (See pp. 116–118, 144, 146, 150–151, 192, and 234–235.)

1896   *Songs of the Kwakiutl Indians.* Internationales Archiv
        für Ethnographie 9 (supplement):1–9. Leiden: E. J.
        Brill.
    Contains notations of five melodies and texts (with transla-
    tions) of songs that Boas transcribed by ear and from phonographic
    recordings collected by John C. Fillmore. Six other song texts are
    given without notations.

1897   *The Social Organization and the Secret Societies of
        the Kwakiutl Indians.* Pp. 311–738 in *Report of the
        United States National Museum for 1895.* Reprint.
        Johnson Reprint Corporation (1975).
    A comprehensive study based on information collected by
    Boas and his collaborator George Hunt (Tlingit). A chapter on the
    potlatch (pp. 341–358) gives translations of 20 songs and many
    historical photographs. Other chapters deal with clan legends (pp.
    366–392) and spiritual entities (pp. 393–417) which are important
    for understanding the native ceremonials. The main chapter on
    winter ceremonial activities (pp. 431–499) gives detailed informa-
    tion on songs and dances of the *hamatsa* (cannibal) dance and
    about 50 related initiatory dances (listed on pp. 498–499). Song
    texts, translations, and extraordinary illustrations are provided
    throughout. Musical transcriptions, song texts, and translations are
    mainly given in an Appendix (pp. 665–738). This contains 36 mu-
    sical notations transcribed from cylinders collected by Boas and
    John C. Fillmore in 1893 and 1895.

1898–1900   *The Mythology of the Bella Coola Indians.* Pp. 25–
            127 in *Jesup North Pacific Expedition* 1. Memoirs of
            the American Museum of the Natural History. Leiden
            and New York. Reprinted by AMS Press (New York,
            1975).
    Includes notations of four songs, three with texts (pp. 71, 82,
    93, and 94). Many other song texts and translations are also given
    (*passim*).

    See **Teit** (1900) in the Basin and Plateau bibliography. This
    includes a section by Boas on music of Thompson River Indians.

1901   *Kathlamet Texts.* Bureau of American Ethnology
        Bulletin no. 26.
    This contains texts and translations for four songs. One is tran-
    scribed in staff notation and two of the others are illustrated in
    rhythmic notation only (pp. 21, 24, 65, and 154).

1902   *Tsimshian Texts.* Bureau of American Ethnology
            Bulletin no. 27.
Contains texts and translations of eight songs, three of which
are also transcribed in staff notation and two with rhythmic notation only (pp. 11, 63, 222, 224, 228, 231, 232, and 233).

1912   *Tsimshian Texts, New Series.* Publications of the
            American Ethnological Society, vol. 3, pp. 65–284.
            Leiden: E. J. Brill.
Contains texts and translations for six spoken narratives collected by Boas' collaborator Henry Tate, who is identified as "a
full blood Indian of Port Simpson, British Columbia" (p. 67). This
includes texts and translations for five songs (pp. 92–93, 174–175,
232–233, and 238–239). One of the songs (sung by a group of
geese in the story) is given in staff notation (p. 174).

1916   *Tsimshian Mythology* (Based on Texts Recorded by
            Henry W. Tate). 31st Annual Report of the Bureau of
            American Ethnology (1909–1910), pp. 29–1037.
Contains translations of myths and tales recorded by Henry
Tate (Tsimshian) over a period of twelve years. The free transla-
tions by Boas are based on interlinear translations by Tate (p. 30).
Many of the texts contain embedded songs. Musical examples are
found on pages 109, 112, 133, 264, 265, and 269.

1944   Dance and Music in the Life of the Northwest Coast
            Indians of North America (Kwakiutl). Pp. 7–16 in
            *The Function of Dance in Human Society: First
            Seminar, Primitive Society* edited by Franziska Boas.
            New York.
Contains general comments on music and translations of four
song texts.

Boas, Franz, and George Hunt

(1902–1905) *Kwakiutl Texts.* Publications of the Jesup North
            Pacific Expedition 3. Memoir of the American Muse-
            um of Natural History 5. Leiden: E. J. Brill.
Part III (1905) contains a section on "Songs" (pp. 475–491).
This gives interlinear translations of 32 song texts, including texts
for 20 Cannibal Dance (Hamatsa) songs and various others. There
is also a description of a winter ceremonial (pp. 484–491).

Bose, Fritz

1956   Book review of *Songs of the Nootka Indians of Western Vancouver Island*, by Helen H. Roberts and Morris Swadesh. *Journal of the International Folk Music Council* 8:106.
Basically a highly favorable review. However, Bose does feel that the shift in pitch level of some songs (upward pitch drift) might have been indicated in a simpler manner (instead of using detailed chromatic signs).

See **Burlin** (1907) in the General bibliography. This contains notations, texts, and translations for two Kwakiutl songs (See pp. 302–307 and 550).

Bursill-Hall, G. L.

1964   The Linguistic Analysis of North American Indian Songs. *Canadian Linguistic Journal* 10:15–36.
Examines certain relationships between the musical structure and the textual structure of two Haida songs.

See **Curtis** (1907–1930) in the General bibliography. *Volume Eight* contains notations for two Chinook melodies (pp. 96–98 and 100). *Volume Nine* contains the following: five Cowichan melodies, one with text and translation, one with English translation only (pp. 73 and 176–178); two Twana melodies (pp. 98 and 111); and four Clallam melodies (pp. 179–180). *Volume Ten* contains 23 Kwakiutl melodies, 22 with texts and translations, one in English only (pp. 187–191, 195–196, 200, 223–224, 244–245, and 311–326). *Volume Eleven* contains the following: 9 Nootka melodies, three with texts and translations, five in English only (pp. 13, 37–38, 41, 48, 52–53, 61, 66–67, 81–82, and 92–93); and five Haida melodies, one with text and translation, four in English only (pp. 123–124, 140–141, 147, and 191–193).

Davis, Carol Berry

1939   *Songs of the Totem*. Juneau, Alaska: Empire Printing.
Contains musical notations for 25 Tlingit melodies and native texts for each, some with translations. Also includes general information on Tlingit music. Could not be obtained. Information given here is from Hickerson (General bibliography, 1961:177).

Davis, Philip W.

1966   Bella Coola Songs and Tales. 77-page manuscript,
            typewritten. Ottawa: National Museums of Canada,
            National Museum of Man Archives.
     Could not be obtained. Listed in a bibliography of Canadian
Indian music by Guédon (General bibliography 1972:475).

de Laguna, Frederica

1972   *Under Mount Saint Elias: The History and Culture of
            the Yakutat Tlingit.* 3 volumes. Washington: Smithso-
            nian Institution.
     The section on "Music" (vol. 2, pp. 560–579) discusses the
following subjects: eighteenth century singing (in references by
explorers and others), recording Yakutat songs, the style of Tlingit
songs, the relation of songs to dance, native categories of songs,
poetic imagery in song texts, and the process of acquiring or composing songs. The Appendix provides more detailed descriptions of
songs from a total corpus of 138 items recorded by the author in
1952 and 1954 (vol. 3, pp. 1149–1374). The author provides song
texts, translations, and other background information. There are
also 120 musical transcriptions by David McAllester. The following categories of songs are distinguished: (1) Sib Potlatch Songs;
(2) Walking, Resting, Sitting Down, and Dancing Songs; (3) Peace
Songs; (4) Funny Songs about Raven; (5) Songs for Children; (6)
Shaman's Songs; (7) Haida Mouth Songs; and (8) Foreign or
Miscellaneous Songs.

Deans, James

1891   A Weird Mourning Song of the Haidas. *American
            Antiquarian* 13:52–54.
     Description of a song heard by the author around 1870.

Densmore, Frances

1939   *Nootka and Quileute Music.* Bureau of American
            Ethnology Bulletin no. 74.
     This contains musical notations for 211 songs collected by
Densmore in 1923 and 1926. Some texts are given in English but
native texts are lacking. The following groups are identified:
Makah (138 songs), Clayoquot (52), Quileute (11), unspecified of
Vancouver Island (7), Nootka (1), Quinault (1), and Yakima (1).
Ethnographic background on the songs is also provided, and the

collection is compared with 1,553 songs from other tribes using tables indicating melodic and rhythmic characteristics. See the critical review by Barnett (1941 above).

1943   *Music of the Indians of British Columbia.* Bureau of American Ethnology Bulletin no. 136, Anthropological Papers no. 27.

Contains musical notations of 98 songs from various tribes. Each song is analyzed and described. The collection is compared with others the author has made using a (quantitative) tabular approach. The following categories of songs are identified: songs for treatment of the sick, war songs, potlatch songs, dance songs, social songs, game songs, canoe songs, story songs, songs for children, love songs, divorce songs, and miscellaneous.

1952   (Recording and liner notes) "Songs of the Nootka and Quileute." Library of Congress, Music Division, Recorded Sound Section (AAFS L 32).

The contents are identified as follows: Potlatch Songs (5), Songs for Contest of Strength at Potlatch (2), Klokali Songs (5), Social Dance Songs (2), Song of Social Gatherings (1), Song of Social Custom (1), Game Songs (2), Dream Songs (2), Song for Treatment of the Sick (1), Songs Connected with Stories (2), Songs for Children (3), and Miscellaneous (2).

Dixon, George

1789   *A Voyage Around the World: But More Particularly to the North-West Coast of America.* London.

Contains a description of singing by Tlingit Indians at Norfolk Sound in August 1787. Includes one musical notation, with text (pp. 242–243). This is evidently the earliest published source containing information on music of the Northwest Coast area. Could not be obtained. The information given here is from Hickerson (General bibliography, 1961:202).

Drucker, Philip

1940   Kwakiutl Dancing Societies. *University of California Anthropological Records* 2(6): 201–230. Berkeley.

Describes secret societies and initiatory rituals among various divisions of the Kwakiutl that are not dealt with in Boas (1897). Related rituals of the Bella Coola, Tsimshian, Haida, Tlingit, and Nootka are also summarized more briefly for comparative purposes. Drucker describes general features of these rituals and speculates on the history of the secret society complex (pp. 227–230). This is based on information collected during the winter of 1936–1937, when most of the dances were no longer being performed.

1950   Culture Element Distributions, XXVI: Northwest
            Coast. *University of California Anthropological
            Records* 9(3): 157–294.
Contains information on the presence or absence of various traits in tabular form. Includes data on musical instruments (pp. 197–199) and various ritual activities involving songs (pp. 222–231).

1965   *Cultures of the North Pacific Coast*. San Francisco:
            Chandler Publishing Co.
This contains an overview of Indian ceremonials in the Northwest area (pp. 94–102). Drucker also describes whaling rituals and dance societies of the Nootka (pp. 156–160) and Kwakiutl dancing societies (pp. 161–167).

Eels, Myron

1879   Indian Music. *American Antiquarian* 1:249–253.
Describes music and instruments as observed by the author in 1875. Includes 24 melodic notations transcribed by ear, from the following tribes: Clallam (10), Twana (12), and unspecified (2).

Fillmore, John Comfort

1893   A Woman's Song of the Kwakiutl Indians. *Journal of
            American Folklore* 6:285–290.
Contains a transcription and harmonization for one song in the context of a general discussion of primitive music and its "natural harmonic laws." Also see writings of Fillmore in the General bibliography.

Frachtenberg, Leo J.

1921   The Ceremonial Societies of the Quileute Indians.
            American Anthropologist 23(3): 320–352.
Frachtenberg begins by discussing the Kwakiutl origin of Quileute winter ceremonials, then describes the following initiatory rituals: (1) Wolf Ritual (*Tlokwali*), (2) Fish Ritual (*Tsayeq*), (3) Hunter Society Ritual, (4) Whale Hunter Society Ritual, and (5) Ritual of the Weather Society. This does not include musical nota-

tions, but songs and other musical activities (for example, the use of whistles in ceremonies) are described throughout.

Galpin, Frances W.

1903   The Whistles and Reed Instruments of the American Indians of the Northwest Coast. *Proceedings of the Musical Association* (1902–1903) vol. 29, pp. 115–138. London.

Contains a classification and description of instruments for various tribes with notations of the scales produced by nine flutes.

Galphin (1903) in the General bibliography. This discusses possible Aztec influences on Indian music of the Northwest Coast and other areas.

Garfield, Viola Edmundson

1951   The Tsimshian and Their Neighbors. Pp. 1–70 in *The Tsimshian: Their Arts and Music*, by Viola E. Garfield, Paul S. Wingert and Marius Barbeau. Publications of the American Ethnological Society, vol. 18. New edition by University of Washington Press (Seattle, 1966).

The section "Drama, Dancing, and Music" (pp. 56–58) describes various types of songs and also discusses song contests.

George, Graham

1962   Songs of the Salish Indians of British Columbia. *International Folk Music Journal* 14:22–29.

Gives transcriptions and analysis for 15 songs from a total corpus of 60 that were recorded by Marius Barbeau in 1912. The analysis focuses on the following elements: (1) phrase structure, (2) scale structure, (3) interval structure, (4) pattern of percussion accompaniment, and (5) presence of exclamations or "extraneous cries" at the beginning or end of songs.

Goodman, Linda

1977   *Music and Dance in Northwest Coast Indian Life.* Tsaile, Arizona: Navajo Community College Press.

This slim volume (38 pp.) focuses mainly on music and dance of the Nootka and Kwakiutl but also covers music of the Makah Indians. Does not contain musical notations but gives general information on ceremonies, medicine-making, types of songs, musical instruments, song texts, and the basic characteristics of Indian music of the Northwest Coast area.

1978   This Is My Song: The Role of Song as a Symbol in Makah Life. Doctoral dissertation, Washington State University.

Examines the character of the song as personally owned property which also functions to symbolize personal identity. Goodman proposes a binary concept of the song as a symbol, with "internal" meanings derived from spiritual experiences and "external" meanings relating to personal status. She also explores how these concepts have been affected by modern social changes. In traditional society the song symbols functioned within a hierarchical status system, but conflicts relating to the use of songs have developed in today's more egalitarian social setting. This includes thirteen musical examples.

1981   Record review of "Nootka: Indian Music of the Pacific Northwest Coast," recording and notes by Ida Halpern (Folkways FE 4524). *Ethnomusicology* 25(1): 162–166.

The recording features various genres including songs from the *Klukwala* (Wolf Ritual) and *Hamatsa* (Cannibal Dance) ceremonies. Also included are war songs, animal songs, canoe songs, and social dance songs. Several cuts provide examples of two-part singing in thirds and fourths (mainly augmented fourths). The recordings were made circa 1947–1953 and 1965–1972. Goodman criticizes the technical quality of the recordings and also the liner notes. She allows that the musical transcriptions and analyses are fairly reliable but raises several questions concerning the ethnographic information. There is a response by Halpern (1981b below).

1986   Nootka (Music). Pp. 380–381 in *The New Grove Dictionary of American Music*, vol. 3 (L–Q). Edited by H. Wiley Hitchcock and Stanley Sadie. London: Macmillan.

Focuses on the Nootka Indians whose territory lies in the United States (in northwestern Washington), also known as the Makah. Discusses the importance of hierarchical social organization in ceremonial life and the importance of songs as symbols of power and prestige. Lists various types of ceremonies that existed in earlier times, describing the potlatch as the principal ceremony that still exists today. Discusses musical instruments and outlines basic characteristics of the musical style.

1991   Traditional Music in Makah Life. Pp. 223–233 in *A Time of Gathering: Native Heritage in Washington State* edited by Robin K. Wright. Seattle: Burke Museum and University of Washington Press.

An overview of songs and dances currently being performed on the reservation at Neah Bay and other ceremonies which are now extinct. Includes brief descriptions of musical instruments and summarizes some basic characteristics of Makah Indian music.

1992   Aspects of Spiritual and Political Power in Chiefs' Songs of the Makah Indians. Pp. 23–42 in *Music and Spiritual Power among the Indians of North America* edited by Richard Keeling. *World of Music* 92(2). Berlin: International Institute for Traditional Music.

Distinguishes "internal" (spiritual) and "external" (political) levels of meaning in the songs and how these were affected by social and historical factors during the period between 1880 and 1930. Goodman concludes that concepts underlying internal meanings have diminished in this century but may be still be revitalized through the resurgence of the personal vision quest.

Gray, Judith A.

See Gray (1984) in the General bibliography. This contains a list of early wax cylinder recordings featuring "Kwakiutl or Vancouver Island Indians."

1988   (Editor) Northwest Coast/Arctic Indian Catalog. Pages 79–288 in *The Federal Cylinder Project: A Guide to Field Cylinder Collections in Federal Agencies, Volume 3: Great Basin/Plateau Indian Catalog and Northwest Coast/Arctic Indian Catalog.* Washington: American Folklife Center, Library of Congress.

This lists and describes the contents of cylinder recordings in 20 separate collections. The annotated listing for each is preceded by an introduction which gives background information on the recordings themselves and on sources for transcriptions, translations, and other documentation. Tribes represented are identified as follows: Carrier Indian, Clackamas Chinook, Clayoquot, Comox (Mainland), Eskimo (Polar), Halkomelen, Ingalik Indian,

Kalapuya, Kwakiutl, Makah, Nitinat, Nootka, Quileute, Shasta,
Squamish, Tlingit, Tsimshian, Tututni, and Upper Umpqua.

Gunther, Erna

1949   The Shaker Religion of the Northwest. Pp. 37–76 in
            Indians of the Urban Northwest edited by Marian W.
            Smith. New York: Columbia University Press.
        Focuses on a nativistic religion which involves the singing of
hymns in a syncretistic style. See also Barnett (1957).

See **Hallowell** (1926) in the General bibliography. This contains
    descriptions of bear ceremonialism among tribes of the North-
    west Coast and other northern areas.

Halpern, Ida

1967   (Recording and liner notes) "Indian Music of the
            Pacific Northwest Coast." Smithsonian-Folkways
            Records (FE 4523).
        The two discs include songs from the Kwakiutl, Nootka, and
Tlingit. The notes (26 pp.) begin with biographical profiles of the
(8) performers and then provide information on the musical style.
This includes analytical comments for all items and six complete
transcriptions. The contents are identified as follows: Wolf Songs
(2), Grizzley Bear Songs (2), Raven Songs (3), Potlatch Songs (2),
Headdress Song, Finishing Song, Hamatsa Songs (2), Mourning
Song, Ghost Songs (2), Love Song, War Song for Marriage, Song
to Pay for Daughter, Cradle Song, Baby Song, Cedar Bark Dance
Song, and Gambling Song. The recordings are currently being issued on cassettes.

1968   Music of the British Columbia Northwest Coast
            Indians. Pp. 23–42 in *Centennial Workshop on Eth-
            nomusicology, University of British Columbia* (1967),
            edited by Peter Crossley-Holland. Vancouver:
            Government of the Province of British Columbia.
        Emphasizes the artistry of Kwakiutl music, describing
Kwakiutl and Haida music as the most "artistically important"
traditions in the Pacific Northwest Coast area (p. 24). Halpern begins by discussing musical values and ownership of songs. She
then discusses characteristics such as scales, use of polyphony,
complex structures, microtonality, mixture of recitative and
melody, polyrhythm (between vocal part and accompaniment), and

the symbolic aspect of vocables. Several examples are analyzed and one song (Raven Song) is completely notated.

1974   (Recording and liner notes) "Nootka: Indian Music of the Northwest Coast." Smithsonian-Folkways Recordings (FE 4524).

Currently available on cassettes, this classic two-record set contains recordings originally collected circa 1947–1953 and 1965–1972. The singers are mostly Nootka, but some items are identified as Kwakiutl. Contents are listed as follows: Canoe Paddle Songs (2), Quiquatla Dance Songs (3), Medicine Man Song, Whale Song, Farewell Songs (2), Welcome Song, Warrior Song, Wolf Song, Sisiutl Song, Robin Song, Grizzley Bear Song, Victory Song, Quiquatla Dance Hamatsa Song, Potlatch Song, and others. The liner notes (16 pp.) contain much information on songs and singers.

1976   On the Interpretation of "Meaningless-Nonsensical Syllables" in the Music of the Pacific Northwest Indians. *Ethnomusicology* 20(2): 253–272.

Explores various levels of meaning in song vocables mainly among the Nootka, Kwakiutl, and Salish. Also notes frequent occurrence of vocables at the end of phrases or longer sections. Distinguishes three main types: (1) syllables with specific meaning based on abbreviated words, (2) syllables which refer to totemic names of animals, and (3) syllables which imitate animal sounds (p. 270). Includes six musical examples with commentary.

1980   Review of *Coast Salish Spirit Dancing* by Pamela Amoss (1978). *Ethnomusicology* 24(2): 287–290.

A favorable review which discusses several related issues and sources. Halpern notes the lack of musical analysis and also suggests that Amoss should have addressed the connection between modern Spirit Dances and earlier forms of the Guardian Spirit ceremonial as practiced among many tribes of the Northwest Coast (p. 288).

1981a   (Recording and liner notes) "Kwakiutl: Indian Music of the Pacific Northwest." (Folkways Records, FE 4122).

The contents of this two-record set are described in the review by Herndon (1985 below).

1981b   Nootka Music: Reply to Goodman. *Ethnomusicology* 25(2): 294–297.

Halpern responds with indignation to criticisms in a record review by Goodman (1981 above). She focuses primarily on the alleged inaccuracies in the notes, emphasizing her closeness to the informants and arguing that Goodman's review contains "innuendos and contradictions based on secondary sources" (p. 297).

1986   (Recording and liner notes) "Haida: Indian Music of the Northwest Coast." Smithsonian-Folkways Recordings (FE 4119).

Currently available on cassettes, this two-record set contains songs and spoken dialogues between Halpern and the Indian singers. The songs are identified as follows: Play Songs, Love Songs, War Song, Drinking Songs, Paddle Song, Hummingbird Song, King Song, Tsimshian Song, Celebration Songs, Lullaby Songs, Marriage Songs, Pride Songs, Welcome Dance Songs for Edenshaw's Potlatch.

Hawley, E.H.

1899   An Inverted Double Reed. *American Anthropologist* 1:587–588.

Describes several specimens from various tribes of British Columbia.

Herndon, Marcia

1985   Record review of "Kwakiutl: Indian Music of the Pacific Northwest," recording and notes by Ida Halpern (1981). Two 12-inch 33 1/3 rpm discs. Ethnic Folkways FE 4122. *Ethnomusicology* 29(3): 540.

The four sides contain the following genres: (1) Raven song and two examples of both Hagok songs and mountain goat songs by two different singers; (2) Different versions of Hamatsa songs by three different singers; (3) longer songs; and (4) dance songs, love song, whale song, and four potlatch songs. Herndon stresses the value of having several Hamatsa songs and potlatch songs for comparative study; she also feels that the notes and musical transcriptions actually constitute a "mini-monograph." Very positive review.

Herzog, George

1934   Appendix: Songs. Pp. 422–430 in *Folk-Tales of the Coast Salish* by Thelma Adamson. Memoirs of the American Folklore Society, vol. 27.
This contains detailed musical notations for 19 songs, including native texts for each and translations for some.

1949   Salish Music. Pp. 93–109 in *Indians of the Urban Northwest* edited by Marian W. Smith. New York: Columbia University Press.
This is a fairly detailed discussion of musical style among various Salishan tribes such as the Snohomish, Chehalis, Bella Coola, Squamish, Chilliwack, and Thompson River groups. Contains no notations, but Herzog considers various style features as shown in previously published sources. Basic characteristics of Salish music are listed and discussed (pp. 96–100). Herzog then considers stylistic differentiations by genre (pp. 101–103) and the relation of Salish musical style to that of other Northwest Coast cultures (pp.103–108). The opening pages contain information on the work of pioneer researchers such as Stumpf, Boas, and Hornbostel (pp. 93–95).

Hymes, Dell

1971   Masset Mourning Songs. *Alcheringa* 2:53–63 (Summer).
This contains retranslations and commentary for 12 song texts originally published in Swanton (1912 below). "Masset" is the name Swanton gave to the northern dialect of Haida. Mourning songs constitute one of 14 categories of Haida songs that were distinguished by Swanton (1905 below).

Jacobs, Melville

1959   *The Content and Style of an Oral Literature: Clackamas Chinook Myths and Tales*. Viking Fund Publications in Anthropology 26. Also published by University of Chicago Press.
Chapter Fifteen ("Songs") contains 28 translations for texts of songs that appear in myths and tales (pp. 200–208). Duplicate recordings of the songs are available from the Melville Jacobs Collection at the University of Washington (Seattle). See the catalogue by Seaburg (1982 below).

Jilek, Wolfgang G.

1974   *Salish Indian Mental Health and Culture Change: Psychohygienic and Therapeutic Aspects of the Guardian Spirit Ceremonial.* Toronto and Montreal: Holt, Rinehart, and Winston of Canada.

The author is a physician and psychiatrist who worked among the Coast Salish of Washington State for six years (1966–1971). The book describes the revival of Guardian Spirit dancing and argues that (besides its complex traditional functions) the ritual complex provides therapeutic benefits that are uniquely suited to psychological and social disorders that have become prevalent in modern Indian communities as a result of historical trauma. Songs and their functions in the spirit quest are discussed throughout, and the book contains interesting quotations from native speakers.

Johnston, Thomas F.

1975   A Historical Perspective on Tlingit Music. *Indian Historian* 8(1): 3–10.

Mentions several contemporary dance groups and then describes earlier music and dance traditions of the pre-contact period. Johnston discusses the general characteristics of Tlingit music (pp. 6–9) and also provides (nine) superb historical photographs from the University of Alaska Archives.

1977   Tlingit Indian Music and Dance. *Viltis* 36 (Sept.– Nov.): 5–13.

An introductory essay focusing mainly on contemporary musical activities. This contains a listing of song-types and also describes general characteristics of Tlingit music (pp. 6–10). Includes three musical notations and several song texts translated into English.

1992   The Socio-Mythic Contexts of Music in Tlingit Shamanism and Potlatch Ceremonials. Pp. 43–71 in *Music and Spiritual Power among the Indians of North America* edited by Richard Keeling. *World of Music* 92(2). Berlin: International Institute for Traditional Music.

This paper provides an overview of pre-contact shamanistic practices and discusses the extent to which shamanistic elements have survived in modern potlatch ceremonies viewed by Johnston circa 1975–1980. The author also lists and discusses the general characteristics of Tlingit music (pp. 62–70). Includes historical photographs and some of David McAllester's transcriptions of shamanic songs as published in de Laguna (1972 above).

Katz, Israel

1970   Marius Barbeau, 1883–1969. *Ethnomusicology* 14(1): 129–142.

Summarizes the career of this renowned Canadian folklorist and gives a bibliography of his ethnomusicological publications.

Kiefer, Thomas M.

1969   Continuous Geographical Distributions of Musical Patterns: A Test Case from the Northwest Coast. *American Anthropologist* 71(August): 701–706.

This gives a statistical analysis of melodic interval patterns (sequences) in transcribed songs from ten nearly contiguous native cultures of the Northwest Coast and Arctic regions. The paper attempts to view the degree of statistical similarity or difference as a function of geographical distance. The paper seems flawed in several respects, but particularly because Kiefer equates degree of historical relationship with geographic distance in an overly simplistic manner.

Koller, James

1971   Wolf Songs and Others of the Tlingit. *Alcheringa* 2:31–34 (Summer).

This contains free translations of ten song texts that were originally published in Swanton (1909 below).

Kolstee, Anton F.

1982   *Bella Coola Indian Music: A Study of the Interaction Between Northwest Coast Indian Structures and Their Functional Context.* Canadian Ethnology Service Paper No. 83. National Museum of Man Mercury Series. Ottawa: National Museums of Canada.

Kolstee examines various genres of Bella Coola music in relation to performance context and concludes that it is possible to define a hierarchy of musical complexity as determined by social function. Kolstee provides musical transcriptions and commentary for 73 songs, including some from archival recordings made during the 1920s. The study considers various types of ceremonial songs and other non-ceremonial types such as animal songs, love songs, and gambling songs. In a section discussing implications of the work (pp. 109–113) Kolstee questions the assumptions and methods in Bruno Nettl's outline of musical style areas (General bibliography 1954).

1986   Tlingit (Music). Pp. 397–398 in *The New Grove Dictionary of American Music*, vol. 4 (R–Z). Edited by H. Wiley Hitchcock and Stanley Sadie. London: Macmillan.
Focuses mainly on music of the Yakutat (Tlingit) group as described by de Laguna (1972 above). Kolstee emphasizes the heterogenous character of Tlingit musical repertories, as songs from neighboring peoples are freely imitated or borrowed. He describes sib songs and "song contests" which take place at potlatches and other ceremonies, emphasizing the central importance of moiety social divisions in organizing these events. Kolstee also lists other musical genres and describes basic characteristics of the Tlingit musical style.

Krause, Aurel

[1885]   *The Tlingit Indians: Results of a Trip to the Northwest Coast of America and the Bering Straits.* Translated from the original German edition by Erna Gunther. Seattle: University of Washington Press,1956.
This contains one musical transcription and a description of musical instruments (pp. 166–167).

Kurath, Gertrude Prokosch

1957   Book review of *Songs of the Nootka Indians of Western Vancouver Island* by Helen H. Roberts and Morris Swadesh. *Midwest Folklore* 7:134–135.
A highly favorable review, but one which also suggests that the analyses by Roberts might be overly detailed. Kurath allows that this approach brings out certain subtleties and irregularities that give the music its special character (especially the prevalence of small intervals), but she questions whether Roberts has adequately considered factors such as mechanical deviations in the recording equipment, natural deviations in the human voice, or rhythmic flexibility in performance.

See the catalogue by **Lee** (1979) in the General bibliography. This lists historical and recent recordings at the Indiana University Archives of Traditional Music. The holdings include collections from the following Northwest Coast groups: Chinook, Clackamas, Clayoquot, Cowichan, Klallam, Klikitat, Lummi, Makah, Nitinat, Nootka, Nootsak, Quileute, Quinault, Salish, Skagit, Snohomish, Snoqualmie, Tlingit, Toqualit, and Tsaiyak.

Lieberman, Frederic

1987   In Memorium, Ida Halpern (1910–1987). *Ethnomusicology* 31(3): 537–538.
        Summarizes Professor Halpern's career and discusses her theoretical contributions to the study of Indian music of the Northwest Coast region.

McAllester, David Park

1957a   (Record) Review of "Music of the American Indian: Northwest (Puget Sound)," recorded and edited by Willard Rhodes. *Midwest Folklore* 7(1): 55–57.
        A highly favorable review. McAllester discusses the rationale behind Rhodes's decision to include syncretistic styles such as Indian Shaker Church Songs and hymns in Chinook Jargon. He also notes that the album provides good examples of upward pitch drift and drone polyphony, both often cited as prominent traits in Indian music of the Northwest Coast.

1957b   Book review of *Songs of the Nootka Indians of Western Vancouver Island by Helen H. Roberts and Morris Swadesh. Journal of the American Musicological Society* 10:44–47.
        Basically a highly favorable review. McAllester begins by discussing the difficulties of transcribing and analyzing American Indian music; then he describes some of the basic characteristics of Nootka music as revealed in the book. These include upward pitch drift, irregular rhythms, and a melodic tendency that Roberts calls "vertical augmentation."

McIlwraith, Thomas Forsyth

1948   *The Bella Coola Indians.* 2 vols. Toronto.
        Volume Two contains a section on "Songs" (pp. 267–337) which includes descriptions of singing and 110 song texts and

translations that were collected by the author between 1922 and 1924. Could not be obtained. Information here is from Hickerson (General bibliography, 1961:293).

Mark, Lindy Li

1955   The Structure of Inland Tlingit Music. Master's thesis (Anthropology), University of Alaska at Fairbanks. 133 pages.

This contains analyses of Inland Tlingit and Tagish Indian songs which were recorded in the Southern Yukon region by Catherine McClellan between 1949 and 1951.

Morrison, Dorothy

1988   A Descriptive Analysis of Yakutat Tlingit Musical Style. Master's thesis (Music), University of Alaska at Fairbanks.

Focuses on ninety-nine songs which were transcribed by David McAllester in the general ethnography by de Laguna (1972 above). Morrison explores the stylistic differences between various song types or genres. She concludes that there are clear stylistic differences between the two largest categories: traditional Sib Potlatch Songs and Haida Mouth Songs (which were composed more recently). Other categories also showed distinctive features but their styles could not be conclusively defined.

Mulder, Jean

1994   Structural Organization in Coast Tsimshian Music. *Ethnomusicology* 38(1): 81–125.

This contains musical and linguistic analyses for 20 songs, mainly collected by the author circa 1979–1981 but also including examples from Boas (1902 and 1916 above). Mulder focuses mainly on three features: (1) relations between text and music, (2) patterns of repetition and variation, and (3) the function of vocables. He concludes (among other things) that vocables are more prominent in dance songs than in children's songs or legend songs (p. 101).

Myers, Helen

1986   Salish (Music). Pp. 122–124 in *The New Grove Dictionary of American Music*, vol. 4 (R–Z). Edited by H. Wiley Hitchcock and Stanley Sadie. London: Macmillan. This focuses on musical life among numerous Coast Salish tribes of Washington State. Myers first discusses social, religious, and musical aspects of the Guardian Spirit Dance and the Potlatch. She then describes songs connected with the Indian Shaker Religion and a gambling game called *slahal* (also called Bone Game or Stick Game). She outlines basic characteristics of the Coast Salish musical style and compares the style of (secular) *slahal* songs with that of the spirit songs. Includes (one) musical transcription of a Guardian Spirit Dance song (with text and translation).

See **Nettl** (1954a) in the General bibliography. Discusses predominant musical characteristics of the "Eskimo-Northwest area" (pp. 8–14).

Rhodes, Willard

1954   (Recording and notes) "Music of the American Indian: Northwest (Puget Sound)." Library of Congress, Recorded Sound Division (AFS L34).
One of a series of recordings collected by Rhodes circa 1940–1952 and recently reissued with updated liner notes. This contains items identified as follows: Skagit Guardian Spirit Song, Lummi Paddling Song, Story of the Rock and Little Crabs (Lummi), Chinook Jargon Songs, Shaker Church Songs, Love Songs (Clallam and Quinault), Quinault Lullaby, Tsaiyak Society Songs, and Makah Bone Game Songs. Recorded in 1950.

1974   Music of the North American Indian Shaker Religion. Pp. 180–184 in *Festschrift to Ernst Emsheimer on the Occasion of his 70th Birthday* edited by Gustaf Hilleström. Studia Instrumentorum Musicae Popularis, vol. 3. Stockholm: Nordiska Musikförlaget.
Rhodes begins by listing Christian and native elements in the syncretistic Shaker religion. He then covers the following topics: (1) how songs are "received" through spiritual revelation, (2) individual ownership of songs, and (3) how and when songs are used in Shaker services. The resemblance of the texts to those of Gospel hymns is noted (p. 182) and general characteristics of the music are defined (pp. 182–183). Includes five musical transcriptions of Shaker songs which are also heard on a commercial album produced by Rhodes (1954 above).

See **Roberts** (1936) in the General bibliography. This discusses musical instruments (p. 20) and general characteristics of Indian music in the Northwest Coast and Plateau regions (pp. 29–30).

Roberts, Helen Heffron, and Herman K. Haeberlin

1918   Some Songs of the Puget Sound Salish. *Journal of American Folklore* 331:496–520.

This contains notations, texts, translations, and analysis for 11 songs identified as Snohomish (10) and Snoqualmie (1). The songs were collected by Haeberlin in 1916. The transcriptions and analyses are by Roberts, who also outlines general characteristics of the music.

Roberts, Helen Heffron, and Morris Swadesh

1955   Songs of the Nootka Indians of Western Vancouver Island. *Transactions of the American Philosophical Society* 45(3): 199–327.

Contains notations and detailed analyses for 99 Nootka songs recorded by Edward Sapir in 1910, 1913, and 1914. The sections on music are by Roberts, while Swadesh writes on ethnography and linguistics. The reviews by Bose (1956 above), Kurath (1957 above) and McAllester (1957b above) contain much information and critical discussion of methods used by Roberts.

Sapir, Edward

1907   Religious Ideas of the Takelma Indians of Southwestern Oregon. *Journal of American Folklore* 20:33–49.

Includes one musical example plus two song texts and translations.

1909   *Takelma Texts*. University of Pennsylvania: the University Museum; Anthropological Publications, vol. 2. no. 1.

This includes 14 song texts and translations (pp. 14, 15, 46, 62, 102–107, and 164–167). Four of these are also given in staff notation, and nine are given with rhythmic notation only.

1919   A Flood Legend of the Nootka Indians of Vancouver Island. *Journal of American Folklore* 32:351–355.

The text includes two incidents in which the protagonist (a character whose name is translated "Has-His-Place-Full-of-Whale-

Oil") learns songs from supernatural experiences and passes ownership of the songs and related ceremonies to his descendants.
Sapir gives texts and translations for both of the songs (p. 353 and
354). He does not include staff notations but does note that at least
one of the songs was recorded. The recording is presumably among
the holdings at the Indiana University Archives of Traditional
Music. See the catalogues by Lee (1979) and by Seeger and Spear
(1987) in the General bibliography.

1939   Songs for a Comox Dancing Mask. *Ethnos* 4:49–55.
Based on research conducted among the Nootka in 1913. The
paper focuses on a "Grizzly-Bear Dance" that came to the Nootka
from the Comox Indians. This contains a native explanation of the
legend on which the dance is based. It also includes musical notations for three songs, with song texts and translations. The transcriptions are by George Herzog.

Sapir, Edward, and Morris Swadesh

1955   Native Accounts of Nootka Ethnography. *Interna-
          tional Journal of American Linguistics* 21(4).
The monograph contains three fairly long texts and translations concerning the Nootka Wolf Ritual (pp. 57–128). Another
text is entitled "Highabove Dreams Marriage Songs" (pp. 228–
229), and there are some others relating to the Potlatch (pp. 230–
266).

See **Schoolcraft** (1851–1857) in the General bibliography. Volume Six
contains one Chinook song text in English (p. 621).

Seaburg, William R.

1982   *Guide to Pacific Northwest Native American
          Materials in the Melville Jacobs Collection and in
          Other Archival Collections in the University of
          Washington Libraries.* Seattle: University of Wash-
          ington Libraries.
A useful guide to recordings and manuscripts collected among
various tribes of the Pacific Northwest and adjacent culture areas.
The recordings (of songs and narratives) were collected by Jacobs
and others between 1929 and 1962.

See the catalogue by **Seeger and Spear** (1987) in the General bibliography. This lists early cylinder recordings in the Indiana

University Archives of Traditional Music. The collection in-
cludes recordings from the following Northwest Coast groups:
Chinook, Clackamas, Clayoquot, Cowichan, Klallam, Klikitat,
Makah, Nitinat, Nootsak, Quileute, Quinault, Salish,
Snohomish, Snoqualmie, and Tlingit.

See **Spier** (1935) in the Great Basin and Plateau bibliography. This describes nativistic religious movements in the Pacific Northwest
region during the nineteenth and early twentieth centuries.

See **Stevenson** (1973b) in the General bibliography. This discusses
some early written sources on Indian music of the Northwest
Coast area, including one notation for a polyphonic song first
published in 1789 (pp. 408–409).

Stuart, Wendy B.

1972   *Gambling Music of the Coast Salish Indians.*
            Mercury Series, Ethnology Division Paper, no. 3.
            Ottawa: Ethnology Division, National Museum of
            Man, National Museums of Canada.
      Describes regional variations in the *slahal* game and the music
that accompanies it. Focuses on Salish tribes of British Columbia
(Canada) and Washington State.

1974   Coast Salish Gambling Music. *Canadian Folk Music
            Journal* 2:3–12.
      Brief encapsulation of the material in the previous entry
(Stuart 1972). This describes the bone game (*slahal*) and general
characteristics of the songs. Includes nine musical examples.

Stumpf, Carl

1886   Leider der Bellakula-Indianer. *Vierteljahrsschrift für
            Musikwissenschaft* 2:405–426. Reprint. Pp. 87–103 in
            *Adhandlungen zur Vergleichenden Musikwissen-
            schaft.* Vol. 1 of *Sämmelbande für Vergleichende
            Musikwissenschaft* edited by Carl Stumpf and Erich
            M. von Hornbostel. Munich, 1922.
      Based on observations made by the author concerning the visit
of some Bella Coola Indians to Germany in 1885. This essay marks
the beginning of German comparative scholarship involving Native
American music. It contains musical notations and detailed analyses for nine songs from the following tribes: Bella Coola (6 songs),

Haida (2), and Kwakiutl (1). The transcriptions were done by ear without recording equipment.

Suttles, Wayne

1957   The Plateau Prophet Dance among the Coast Salish. *Southwestern Journal of Anthropology* 13(4): 352–396.
Begins with descriptive and historical information on the Prophet Dance among tribes of the Plateau and Northwest Coast areas (pp. 353–375). Suttles then lists the basic elements of the Prophet Dance religious complex (pp. 375–387). He also includes an "historical reconstruction" which traces the origin, development, and spread of the movement.

Swan, James Gilchrist

1857   *The Northwest Coast; Or, Three Years' Residence in Washington Territory.* New York: Harper and Brothers.
Contains comments on singing among Chinook and/or Chehalis Indians of the Shoal Water Bay area (near the mouth of the Columbia River). This also includes musical notations for seven songs (pp. 200–202).

1870   *The Indians of Cape Flattery, at the Strait of Fuca, Washington Territory.* Smithsonian Institution Contributions to Knowledge, vol. 16, no. 8.
An early description of Makah culture by one who lived among the tribe while serving as a teacher and dispenser of medicines for the United States Government during the 1860s. Contains description of the following: religious festivals (pp. 13–14), songs (p. 49), winter ceremonies (pp. 62–64), shamanistic ceremonies (pp. 73–75), and funeral ceremonies (pp. 85–86).

Swanton, John R.

1905   *Contributions to the Ethnology of the Haida.* Jesup North Pacific Expedition 5. Memoirs of the American Museum of Natural History, vol. 8, part 1. Leiden/New York. Reprint. New York: AMS Press, 1975.
This contains a listing of song types and general description of songs among the Haida (p. 212). See also Swanton (1912 below).

1909   *Tlingit Myths and Texts.* Bureau of American Ethnol-
            ogy Bulletin no. 39. Washington.
Could not be obtained for inspection of contents but probably
contains information on songs embedded in texts.

1912   *Haida Songs.* Publications of the American Ethnolog-
            ical Society 3:1–63.
This gives texts and translations for 106 songs collected by
Swanton in research sponsored by the Jesup North Pacific
Expedition (1900–1901). The songs are classified into three
groups: Cradle Songs (88 songs), Mourning Songs (12 songs), and
Miscellaneous Songs (6 songs). The style is discussed in Swanton
(1905 above).

See **Williams** (1992) in the Arctic and Sub-Arctic bibliography. This
contains information on contemporary Tlingit dances.

IV. California

Aginsky, Burt W.

1943   Culture Element Distributions, XXIV: Central Sierra. *University of California Anthropological Records* 8(4): 393–468.

This gives information on the presence or absence of various traits in tabular form. Includes data on musical instruments (p. 425) and various ritual activities (pp. 437–443).

Angulo, Jaime de

1931   The Background of Religious Feeling in a Primitive Tribe. *American Anthropologist* 28:352–360.

Contains information on gambling, shamanism, and several types of medicine-making which involve songs. The style is sometimes anecdotal and subjective. See also de Angulo and d'Harcourt (1931).

Angulo, Jaime de, and Marguerite Béclard d'Harcourt

1931   La Musique des indiens de la Californie du nord. *Journal de la Société des Americanistes de Paris* 23(1): 189–228.

The writing is by de Angulo and the (28) musical notations by d'Harcourt are transcribed from de Angulo's vocal renditions of Indian songs rather than from recordings. Despite the limitations, this remains an invaluable source on several groups whose music is otherwise not well known. The essay begins with a section on musical instruments and how they are played (flute, musical bow, clapstick, and log drum). De Angulo then describes distinctive styles of vocal music in the following regions: Northeastern (Achumawi, Atsugewi, Paiute), Central (Pomo, Miwok), and Northwestern (Yurok, Hupa, Karok). The genres discussed here in-

clude shaman songs, gambling songs, puberty songs, hunting
songs, war songs, animal songs, love songs, and dance songs. In
each case there are interesting comments on musical style and native ideas about singing. There is a translation by Garland (1988
below).

Azbill, Henry

1967   Native Dances: A Basic Part of Culture, Tradition,
              Religion. *The Indian Historian* 1(1): 16–17, 20.
      Azbill was a Concow Maidu elder who died in 1973. In this
paper he describes traditional dances at Chico and on the
Grindstone Reservation.

Baca, Lorenzo

1986   Songs, Dances, and Traditions of the Tuolumne Band
              of California Miwoks. Master's thesis (American
              Indian Studies), University of California at Los
              Angeles.
      This focuses on contemporary musical activities as described
by Miwok elder and dance leader Brown Tadd. Baca also produced
a videotape as part of the thesis project.

Barrett, Samuel A.

1917a   Ceremonies of the Pomo Indians. *University of
              California Publications in American Archaeology
              and Ethnology* 12(10): 397–441.
      This begins by describing some general features of Pomo cer-
emonies. Barrett then gives detailed accounts of the Ghost or Devil
Ceremony (in which dancers impersonate spirits of the dead) and
of the Kuksu Ceremony (in which Kuksu and other deities are im-
personated). This also includes information on the "Messiah cult"
(also called Dream cult or Bole-Maru), which came to this area
during the latter part of the nineteenth century. The data were gathered from Northern, Central, and Eastern Pomo speakers circa
1903–1904. Recordings by Barrett are available at the Hearst
Museum of Anthropology and are listed in Keeling (1991 below).
See also the posthumous study by Halpern (1988).

1917b   Pomo Bear Doctors. *University of California Publi-
              cations in American Archaeology and Ethnology*
              12(11): 443–465.

This describes Pomo beliefs and customs concerning certain persons who were able to transform themselves into grizzly bears. Use of songs to invoke supernatural powers is described (pp. 458–461).

1919   The Wintun Hesi Ceremony. *University of California Publications in American Archaeology and Ethnology* 14(4): 437–488.

This describes a four-day event held in Cortina Valley (Colusa County) in May 1906. Does not contain musical transcriptions, but musical style, dance movements, and other ritual activities are described throughout. Nine song texts (with translations) are given, and there are photos of the dance costumes (Moki and Bighead) and the roundhouse. The songs and speeches recorded by Barrett (38 items) are available at Phoebe Hearst Museum. See the catalogue by Keeling (1991 below).

1963   The Hupa Jump Dance at Hupa, 1962. *Kroeber Anthropological Society Papers* 28: 73–85. Berkeley.

This is the most complete account of the Jump Dance in the literature. Barrett begins by describing the preparation of the dancing area and various rituals preceding the public dance itself. The costumes, dance movements, and various events that took place during a dance held in October 1962 are then described in some detail.

Barrows, David P.

1895   Some Coahuia Songs and Dances. *Land of Sunshine* 14:38–41.

This contains five melodies and texts collected by the author in 1891. The melodies are harmonized by John C. Fillmore. See Fillmore (1893, 1895, and 1899) in the General bibliography.

Beals, Ralph L.

1933   The Ethnography of the Nisenan. *University of California Publications in American Archaeology and Ethnology* 31(6): 335–414.

The section on "Ceremonials" (pp. 395–405) describes several different ceremonies and discusses the historical sequence of ceremonies postulated for the Southern Maidu (Nisenan) by Gifford (1927 below). Beals also discusses musical instruments and regalia (pp. 397–398).

Blackburn, Thomas C.

1975   *December's Child: A Book of Chumash Oral Narratives.* Berkeley and Los Angeles: University of California Press.
This contains free translations of 111 narratives that were collected by John P. Harrington from various persons between 1912 and 1928. Many of the stories involve songs (sung by Coyote and other mythic characters), and translations of (one or more) song texts are given in the following narratives: #16, #21, #23, #43, #48, #53, #54, #57, #57, #60, and #66. Narrative #89 (pp. 287–288) concerns an actual person who had love medicine songs that were used to make a woman's man return to her. Recordings of the songs may exist in collections at the Library of Congress and the Santa Barbara Museum of Natural History. See the catalogues by Gray and Schupman (1990 below) and Tegler (1979 below).

Boscana, Geronimo

[1846]   Chinigchinich: A Historical Account of the Origin, Customs, and Traditions of the Indians at the Missionary Establishment of St. Juan Capistrano, Alta California; Called the Acagchemem Nation. Translated by Alfred Robinson. Pp. 230–341 in *Life in California* by Alfred Robinson. New York: Wiley and Putnam. Reprinted by Da Capo Press (New York, 1969).
Ethnocentric in tone but highly valuable for information on early Juaneño culture. The original was written by the Franciscan missionary Boscana between 1814 and 1826. Dances and rituals are described in the chapter entitled "Of Their Principal Feasts and Dances" (pp. 289–295).

Cason, Georgie Rees

1937   An Introduction to a Study of California Indian Music. Master's thesis (Music), University of California (Berkeley).
This considers three main aspects of the subject: (1) references to music or ceremonies in earlier works, (2) musical instruments, and (3) analysis of songs collected by others. The information given here is drawn entirely from Merriam (General bibliography, 1960).

Coyote Man (Robert Rathbun)

1975   (Recording and liner notes) "Songs of the California Indians, vol. 1: Concow, Nisenan, Mountain Maidu." Folsom, California: Pacific Western Traders.
This is an excellent collection with informative liner notes (11 pages). It contains 60 brief items that are identified as follows by genre: animal songs, ancient ceremonial songs, songs from stories, songs with deer hoof rattle, courting songs, shamans' songs, gambling songs, flute song (1 only), and miscellaneous. There are five versions of "Dick Harry's (Gambling) Song," giving a good illustration of the extent to which individual performances of a given song can vary.

Cummins, Marjorie W.

1978   *The Tache-Yokuts, Indians of the San Joaquin Valley: Their Lives, Songs, and Stories.* Fresno: Pioneer Publishing Co.
The author is a teacher and long-time resident in the area. The book was published with a cassette containing ten songs that were recorded by Cummins in 1940. Several musical instruments are pictured and described, and each of the songs that Cummins recorded is notated and discussed. There is a summary (pp. 122–125) covering the following subjects: ideas about how songs are conceived, norms or values in relation to songs, formal structure, scales, melodic contour, rhythm, and texture. The author also discusses recordings collected by Kroeber (in 1903) and by Harrington (various dates between 1916 and 1931).

See **Curtis** (1907–1930) in the General bibliography. *Volume Fifteen* contains one Diegueño song text and translation (p. 46).

Demetrocopoulou, Dorothy

1935   Wintu Songs. *Anthropos* 30:483–494.
This contains translations and commentary for 49 song texts collected by the author circa 1929–1931. The following genres are identified: dream songs, girls' puberty songs, bear hunting songs, love songs, and songs from forgotten myths.

1940   Wintu War Dance: A Textual Account. Pp. 141–143 in volume 4 of *Proceedings of the 6th Pacific Congress at Toronto, 1939.* Berkeley and Los Angeles: University of California Press.

Could not be obtained for inspection of contents nor could information be gotten from other sources.

Densmore, Frances

1958   *Music of the Maidu Indians of California.* Los Angeles: Southwest Museum.
This contains notations and analysis for 53 songs collected by Densmore in 1937. Densmore gives information on the context or purpose of each song, and several different song types are represented. There is also a discussion of musical instruments (pp. 10–15). The musical style of the corpus as a whole is compared with that of other collections studied by the author (pp. 64–66). Densmore concludes that the style of the dance songs is fairly distinctive but that other types of songs are more variable (p. 65).

Devereux, George

1957   Dream Learning and Individual Ritual Differences in Mohave Shamanism. *American Anthropologist* 59(6): 1036–1045.
Examines the dynamics through which shamanistic songs and other song-cycles are learned or composed. Ideally (according to Mohave belief) myths and songs are supposed to be learned in dreams. Devereux argues that shamans and singers actually learn them in waking life, then have dreams which condense or allude to them (p. 1044).

Dixon, Roland B.

1901   The Musical Bow in California. *Science* 13:274–275.
Dixon describes a Maidu instrument and associated playing techniques . He concludes that it was probably an indigenous instrument because of its sacred character (being used only by shamans or medicine men).

1905   The Northern Maidu. *Bulletin of the American Museum of Natural History* 17(3): 119–346.
This contains descriptions of musical instruments (pp. 221–223) and considerable information on ritual life and dances. Dixon also recorded Northern Maidu songs (23 cylinders) for the American Museum of Natural History in 1899, and the recordings are available at the Indiana Archives of Traditional Music. See the catalogues by Lee (1979) and Seeger and Spear (1987) in the General bibliography.

1907   The Shasta. *Bulletin of the American Museum of Natural History* 17(5): 381–498.
This contains information on musical instruments (pp. 449–450), the War Dance (pp. 439–440), the Girls' Puberty Dance (pp. 457–461), and use of songs in personal medicine rituals for acquiring luck (pp. 489–490).

Driver, Harold E.

1937   Culture Element Distributions, VI: Southern Sierra Nevada. *University of California Anthropological Records* 1(2): 53–154.
Contains information on the presence or absence of various traits in tabular form. Includes elements relating to musical instruments (p. 85) and various ritual activities (pp. 97–106).

1939   Culture Element Distributions, X: Northwest California. *University of California Anthropological Records* 1(6): 297–433.
Contains information on the presence or absence of various traits in tabular form. Includes elements relating to musical instruments (p. 337) and various ritual activities (pp. 360–367).

Drucker, Philip

1936   A Karuk World-Renewal Ceremony at Panaminik. *University of California Publications in American Archaeology and Ethnology* 35(3): 23–28.
Gives two explanations of the *Pikia'vish* ("to make again") ceremony as described by Louis Johnny and Peter Tom (both Karuk Indians of Orleans, California). Drucker compares this local ritual with other world renewal ceremonies of the Yurok and Hupa. See Kroeber and Gifford (1949 below).

1937a   Culture Element Distributions, V: Southern California. *University of California Anthropological Records* 1(1): 1–52. Berkeley.
Contains information on the presence or absence of various traits in tabular form. Includes elements relating to musical instruments (p. 25) and several native ceremonies (pp. 32–41).

1937   The Tolowa and Their Southwest Oregon Kin. *University of California Publications in American Archaeology and Ethnology* 36(4): 221–300.

This contains sections on the following: the gambling game (p. 239), rituals in general (pp. 256–257), the girls' puberty dance (pp. 262–264), a "wealth display" dance (p. 264), the War Dance (pp. 265–266), and the custom of "training" for good luck (p. 266).

See Drucker (1941) in Southwest bibliography. This is a culture element distribution study focusing on various Yuman and Piman groups.

Dubois, Constance

1904   The Story of Chaup: a Myth of the Diegueños. *Journal of American Folklore* 17: 217–242.
This contains translations of about 60 brief texts which comprise the song cycle as a whole.

1905   Religious Ceremonies and Myths of the Mission Indians. *American Anthropologist* 7:620–629.
This contains brief descriptions of Diegueño and Luiseño ceremonies identified as follows: (1) the *toloache* fiesta, for the initiation of boys at puberty; (2) the puberty ceremony for girls; and (3) the fiesta of Images of the Dead, which includes the eagle-killing ceremony. Songs are mentioned throughout and a mythic account concerning the origin of songs and ceremonies is also given (pp. 627–628).

1906   Two Types or Styles of Diegueño Dancing. *Proceedings of the 15th International Congress of Americanists.* Vol. 2, pp. 135–138.
This deals with a Bird Dance which is called "Ee-sha" or "Ah-sha" in native dialects and is accompanied by the singing of song cycles. Dubois describes how the dance style at Mesa Grande differs from that of the Campo-Manzanita area, and she suggests that the more theatrical Mesa Grande style was influenced by (Chinigchinich) ceremonies of tribes from the coast. She also describes a song with falsetto accompaniment added by women (p. 136).

1908a   Ceremonies and Traditions of the Diegueño Indians. *Journal of American Folklore* 21:228–239.
This contains sections on "A Dance Song from Manzanita" (pp. 228–231) and "Awikunchi, a Fair-Weather-Making Ceremony" (pp. 231–232). Both of these accounts describe song cycles, giving texts and translations for many songs (each of which is quite brief). Dubois also describes two Songs of Creation (p.

234). Recordings of the songs are available at Hearst Museum of Anthropology (Berkeley). See the catalogue by Keeling (1991 below).

1908b   The Religion of the Luiseño Indians of Southern California. *University of California Publications in American Archaeology and Ethnology* 8(3): 69–186.

This contains descriptions of native rituals as divided into two main categories: Initiation Ceremonies (pp. 77–99) and Mourning Ceremonies (pp. 100–104). There follows a discussion of ceremonial songs (pp. 105–127). This begins with a listing of song cycles, then provides translations and commentary for 53 songs collected by the author in 1906. Four of these are also transcribed in staff notations. 23 of the recordings are available at Phoebe Hearst Museum (UC Berkeley), and these are listed in the catalogue by Keeling (1991 below). Others are found at Indiana University Archives of Traditional Music (Bloomington). For the latter, see the catalogue by Lee (1979) or Seeger and Spear (1987) in the General bibliography.

DuBois, Cora

1935   Wintu Ethnography. *University of California Publications in American Archaeology and Ethnology* 36(1): 1–148.

This contains descriptions of ceremonies (pp. 40–43). Also see sections on shamanism (pp. 88–117), modern cults of the late 1800s (pp. 118–120), and musical instruments (p. 123). Includes photographs of shaman and singer with split-stick rattle (p. 148).

1939   The 1870 Ghost Dance. *University of California Anthropological Records* 3(1): 1–150. Berkeley.

A detailed study describing the earliest Ghost Dance movement among Indians of northern California and adjacent areas of Oregon and Nevada. DuBois discusses the responses among various tribes of the region and includes many interesting quotes from people DuBois interviewed circa 1932–1934. This also deals with the Big Head Cult, a related development that originated among the Pomo (pp. 117–146). Contains illustrations of dance patterns (pp. 52, 68, 70, and 121) and photographs of ceremonialists and costumes (pp. 146–148). Also see Gayton (1930b below).

Erikson, Erik H.

1943   Observations on the Yurok: Childhood and World
            Image. *University of California Publications in
            American Archaeology and Ethnology* 35(10): 257–
            302.
     A psychoanalytic interpretation of Yurok culture, this views
various aspects of the spiritual life as regressive responses to distinctively Yurok child-rearing practices. Contains detailed information from interviews with a Yurok shaman (pp. 260–267).

Essene, Frank

1942   Culture Element Distributions, XXI: Round Valley.
            University of California Anthropological Records
            8(1): 1–97.
     Contains information on the presence or absence of various
traits in tabular form. Includes elements relating to musical instruments (p. 23), girls' puberty rites (p. 33–34), and other ritual activities (pp. 41–47).

Foster, George M.

1944   A Summary of Yuki Culture. *University of California
            Anthropological Records* 5(3): 155–244. Berkeley.
     An excellent ethnography based on information collected in
1937. Music-related contents include descriptions of the following:
(1) musical instruments (pp. 171–172); (2) girls' puberty dances
(pp. 182–184); (3) social dances (pp. 182–184); (4) the Acorn
Sing, with several (vocable) song texts (pp. 192–193); (5) initiation
ceremonies (pp. 209–212); and (6) relatively recent religious developments such as the Ghost Dance and the Pentecostal movement (pp. 219–222). Includes descriptions of singing at Pentecostal
meetings and gives (English) texts for four Pentecostal hymns (p.
222).

See **Frisbie** (1981) in the General bibliography for review of video-
tapes containing interviews with Yurok and Tolowa singers.

Garland, Peter

1988   *Jaime de Angulo: The Music of the Indians of
            Northern California.* Berkeley and Santa Fe:
            Soundings Press.

This contains a translation of de Angulo and d'Harcourt (1931 above) and an index to musical contents in a set of tapes that were broadcast on the radio in a series entitled "Old Time Stories." The radio programs feature de Angulo narrating Indian stories and performing the songs himself. Also contains 36 pages showing a notational system developed by de Angulo.

Gatschet, Albert S.

1894   Songs of the Modoc Indians. *American Anthropologist* 7:26–31.
This contains general comments on Modoc Indian singing and texts and translations for three songs.

Gayton, Anna H.

1930a   Yokuts-Mono Chiefs and Shamans. *University of California Publications in American Archaeology and Ethnology* 24(8): 361–420.
Gayton discusses the political status of chiefs and shamans respectively. She also describes ceremonies and the processes through which they are authorized (pp. 379–380). Contains information on the dream song of a chief who was also known as a "poisoner" (pp. 404–405).

1930b   The Ghost Dance of 1870 in South-Central California. *University of California Publications in American Archaeology and Ethnology* 28(3): 57–82.
Traces the spread of the movement from the Western Mono of North Fork to various Yokuts groups of the San Joaquin Valley and possibly to Miwok and Costanoan groups of the Pleasanton area. Songs accompanied by elderwood clappers are described on page 71. See DuBois (1939 above).

1948   Yokuts and Western Mono Ethnography. *University of California Anthropological Records* 10(1–2): 1–302. Berkeley.
A fine ethnographic survey of various related groups based on data collected between 1925 and 1930. Part One (pp. 1–142) deals with various Yokuts divisions of the Tulare Lake, Southern (San Joaquin) Valley, and Central Foothill regions. Part Two (pp. 143–302) focuses on the Northern Foothills Yokuts and Western Mono. Gayton describes public ceremonies, dances, and shamanistic practices for every local group. The book also gives interlinear translations for about 20 songs of various types (pp. 34, 40, 42, 45,

48, 92, 99, 117, 118, 121, 157, 158, 202, and 242). Includes drawings of ceremonial costumes (p. 68).

Gifford, Edward

1926   Miwok Cults. *University of California Publications
              in American Archaeology and Ethnology* 18(3): 391–
              408. Berkeley.
     Views Northern Sierra Miwok religion as a blending of two
influences: the Kuksu (God-impersonating) religion to the north
and a Bird Cult that the Miwok share with tribes to the south.
Gifford suggests that Miwok cult dances can be divided into three
historical strata. No discussion of songs.

1927   Southern Maidu Religious Ceremonies. *American
              Anthropologist* 29(3): 214–257.
     This describes Kuksu ceremonials and shamanistic practices
among the Southern Maidu (or Nisenan) Indians. Gifford postulates three distinct "strata" of religious dances (pp. 220–238): (1)
revivalistic dances introduced around 1872 (after the Ghost dance)
from areas to the south, (2) an earlier stratum of god-impersonating
dances introduced from the north, and (3) certain god-impersonating dances that are not documented elsewhere and are presumably
indigenous. This hypothetical sequence of ceremonies is discussed
in Beals (1933 above).

1931   *The Kamia of Imperial Valley.* Bureau of American
              Ethnology Bulletin 97.
     Contains a survey of musical instruments (pp. 43–44) and a
description and listing of song cycles (pp. 62–64). The designation
"Kamia" refers to peoples also called "Southern Diegueño" in earlier literature and "Tipai" or "Ipai-Tipai" in sources after 1950.

1955   Central Miwok Ceremonies. *University of California
              Anthropological Records* 14(4): 261–318.
     Contains detailed descriptions of twenty dances connected
with the Kuksu or god-impersonating cult based on data obtained
during the 1910s and 1920s (pp. 266–295). Also covers mourning
observances (pp. 295–303) and social dances (pp. 303–309). Does
not include notations or analysis but gives the author's verbal descriptions of music and interesting quotes on various subjects from
native speakers. The cylinder recordings collected by Gifford are
listed in Keeling (1991 below).

Goddard, Pliny Earle

1903–1904   Life and Culture of the Hupa. *University of California Publications in American Archaeology and Ethnology* 1(1): 1–88. Berkeley.

This contains excellent early descriptions of the girls' puberty ceremony (pp. 53–54), the gambling game (pp. 60–61), the doctor dance for shamans (pp. 65–66), the Brush Dance (pp. 67–69), the Winter Dance (p. 82), the Deerskin Dance (pp. 82–85), and the Jump Dance (pp. 85–87). No musical notations. Based on Goddard's residence in Hoopa Valley from 1897 to 1900.

Goldschmidt, Walter, and Harold Driver

1940   The Hupa White Deerskin Dance. *University of California Publications in American Archaeology and Ethnology* 35:103–142. Berkeley.

Focuses on sociological aspects of the ritual (which lasts several days), particularly noting the significance of the regalia as wealth objects. Gives descriptions of dances observed in 1935 and 1937, with diagrams of dance movements and two musical examples. One notation shows a Boat Dance song in two parts (p. 111); another illustrates the multi-part texture of Deerskin Dance songs in general (p. 112). Contains a rare photo of the Boat Dance (p. 135) and other photographs.

Gray, Judith, and Edwin Schupman, Editors

1990   California Indian Catalogue. Pp. 1–328 in *The Federal Cylinder Project, Volume 5: California Indian Catalogue, Middle and South American Catalogue, Southwestern Catalogue.* Edited by Judith Gray and Edwin Schupman. Washington: American Folklife Center, Library of Congress.

The editors list and describe the contents of early cylinder recordings in 34 collections, most notably those of John Peabody Harrington and Helen Heffron Roberts. The catalogue for each collection is preceded by an introduction giving background information on the recordings and the circumstances under which they were collected. Documentation in published sources and manuscripts is cited throughout. The volume includes recordings from the following tribes: Cahuilla, Chumash, Costanoan, Diegueño, Gabrielino, Hupa, Karuk, Kitanemuk, Klamath, Konkow, Konomihu, Luiseño, Miwok (Central Sierra), Mono,

Nomlaki, Pomo (Northeastern, Southeastern, Eastern, Central, and Northern groups), Salinan, Serrano, Wailaki, Yokuts (Southern Valley), Yuki, and Yurok.

See **Hall and Nettl** (1955) in Great Basin and Plateau bibliography. This contains general information on Modoc songs (with notations).

Halpern, Abraham M.

1988   *Southeastern Pomo Ceremonials: The Kuksu Cult and Its Successors*. University of California Anthropological Records 29. Berkeley: University of California Press.

A posthumous publication based on notes collected from five Pomo speakers of the Clear Lake area in 1936–1937. No musical analysis but does contain detailed information on dances of the Kuksu (god-impersonating) cult and provides an excellent history of more recent religious activities occurring in the period from 1850 to 1937. These include the Ghost Dance movement, the Bole-Maru (dreamer) religion, Power-Doctoring, and Pentacostal worship. The article incorporates lengthy quotations from the five main informants Halpern interviewed. See also Barrett (1917 above) for descriptions of related Pomo ceremonies.

Harrington, John P.

1942   Culture Element Distributions, XIX: Central California Coast. *University of California Anthropological Records* 7(1): 1–44.

This contains information on the presence or absence of various traits in tabular form. Includes elements relating to musical instruments (p. 28) and ritual activities (pp. 36–41).

Hatch, James

1958   Tachi Yokuts Music. *Kroeber Anthropological Society Papers* 19:47–66. Berkeley.

This comparative study of Tachi Yokuts music examines recordings collected by Alfred Kroeber (circa 1904) and Margaret Cummins (1940), as well as those collected by the author in 1957. Hatch's explanation of the text of Dawis Sapagay's power song provides a good illustration of the depth of hidden meaning in songs with relatively few words. Twelve songs are notated with scalar and formal analyses.

Heidsick, Ralph G.

1966   Music of the Luiseño Indians of Southern California:
            A Study of Music in Indian Culture with Relation to a
            Program in Indian Music. Doctoral dissertation
            (Music), University of California, Los Angeles.
        Discusses various aspects of Luiseño music and how the sub-
ject could be presented in a program of general music education.
The main discussions on Luiseño music are in Part II (pp. 125–
314); this includes descriptions from earlier sources (pp. 125–145)
and transcriptions and analyses for 15 songs (pp. 146–251). The
songs are identified as belonging to the Cook Collection at
Southwest Museum (Los Angeles) and were recorded between
1934 and 1937. Also includes sections on "Dances" (pp. 252–279)
and on musical instruments (pp. 280–314).

Heizer, Robert F.

1955   Two Chumash Legends. *Journal of American
            Folklore* 68(267): 34, 56, 72.
        This contains two texts that were originally collected by
Lorenzo Yates of Santa Barbara in 1887. Notes from Yates indicate that "the legends appear to be explanatory of the dances in
which the various incidents are dramatically recorded" (p. 34). The
narratives are entitled "Coyote and Bat" (p. 56) and "Coyote and
the Tortoise" (pp. 56 and 72). Both contain songs (sung by Coyote)
and translations of the texts are given.

Heizer, Robert F., and G.W. Hewes

1940   Animal Ceremonialism in Central California in the
            Light of Archeology. *American Anthropologist* 42(4):
            587–603.
        This discusses archeological and ethnographic evidence for
ritual interment of animals among Indians of the Central California
area. The authors list sites with burials of raptorial birds (eagle,
condor, falcon) and various other animals. The article also includes
photos of bear and badger burial excavations (facing p. 588).
Heizer and Hewes conclude that the archeological evidence indicates a generic "ceremonial attitude" toward animals but that this
can not be definitely connected to the Bird Cult or Kuksu ceremonials as documented in ethnographic sources.

Herzog, George

1928   The Yuman Musical Style. *Journal of American Folklore* 41(160): 183–231.

This contains detailed transcriptions (with texts but no translations) and analyses for 39 songs which were collected by Herzog in 1927. Tribes represented include the Mohave (10 songs), Yuma (12), Diegueño (12), Maricopa (1), and Mohave-Yavapai (4). There is much information on Yuman song-cycles and related ethnographic subjects. Musical analysis covers the following elements: manner of singing, tonality and melody, rhythm, accompaniment, and form (structure). Musical instruments are also discussed, as are the relationships between Yuman music and other styles in Arizona and California. Of particular interest in this regard are Rabbit Songs which the Mohave evidently borrowed from the Yavapai or "Mohave-Apache" (pp. 198–199 and 225–227).

1934   Review of *Form in Primitive Music* by Helen H. Roberts (1933). *American Anthropologist* 36:476–478.

This includes comments comparing the Southern California styles studied by Roberts and the music of the Yuman tribes as described in Herzog (Southwest bibliography, 1928).

Hinton, Leanne

1986   Diegueño (Music). Page 623 in *The New Grove Dictionary of American Music*, vol. 1 (A–D). Edited by H. Wiley Hitchcock and Stanley Sadie. London: Macmillan.

Summarizes basic elements of the Diegueño musical style and describes the organization of songs into lengthy song cycles which take several days to perform. Hinton also discusses musical instruments and gives an overview of song types in the repertory.

1986   Mojave (Music). Pp. 254–255 in *The New Grove Dictionary of American Music*, vol. 3 (L–Q). Edited by H. Wiley Hitchcock and Stanley Sadie. London: Macmillan.

Hinton begins by discussing musical interactions between the Mojave and other tribes of southern California and Arizona. She then lists various contexts or functions of songs in earlier Mojave life, also discussing the native belief that songs originate in dreams. She describes the musical style and the organization of songs into lengthy cycles based on myths.

1988   Song: Overcoming the Language Barrier. *News from Native California* 2(5): 3–4.

This describes musical communication between Indians speaking entirely different languages. The author and a group of Ipai (Diegueño) Indians from San Diego visited among the Kiliwas of northern Baja California. Some of the latter spoke Spanish, but none of the Ipais spoke Spanish, nor did the Kiliwas speak English. Despite the language barrier they had no problem singing Bird Songs in the same style. This edition of *News from Native California* also includes other music-related articles such as "How I Learned to Sing" (pp. 7–8) by Bernice Torres (Kashaya Pomo).

1992   Songs Without Words. *News from Native California* 6(3): 33–36.

Hinton discusses the use of vocables and words of unknown meaning in songs of various tribes. This edition of *News from Native California* also includes other articles on contemporary dance groups from various localities in California.

See **Hinton and Watahomigie** (1984) in Southwest bibliography. This includes information on songs and stories from Yuman tribes of California.

Holt, Catherine

1946   Shasta Ethnography. *University of California Anthropological Records* 3(4): 299–349

This contains information on ceremonials and personal medicine making (pp. 335–338). The study is based mainly on data collected from an individual named Sargent Sambo in 1937 but also includes information from Dixon (1907 above).

Hooper, Lucille

1920   The Cahuilla Indians. *University of California Publications in American Archaeology and Ethnology* 16(6): 315–380.

Hooper provides translated texts of five enemy songs (pp. 344–345) and also describes songs used in various ceremonies (pp. 345–348). Copies of her recordings are available at the Hearst Museum of Anthropology. See Keeling (1991 below). The research was conducted in 1918.

Hudson, Travis, Editor

1979   *Breath of the Sun: Life in Early California as Told by
            a Chumash Indian, Fernando Librado, to John P.
            Harrington.* Banning, Ca.: Malki Museum Press.
Based on manuscript notes of interviews conducted by
Harrington between 1912 and 1915. Hudson has edited the notes
into thematic chapters and also altered the pronoun patterns (from
third to first person) so that the material is again worded as Librado
spoke it. The chapter on "Music and Ceremonies" (pp. 129–136)
includes brief comments on playing the musical bow (p. 129) and
information on how Chumash ceremonies are organized.

**Hudson, Travis, Thomas Blackburn, Rosario Curletti, and Janice
Timbrook**

1977   *The Eye of the Flute: Chumash Traditional History
            and Ritual as Told by Fernando Librado (Kitsepawit)
            to John P. Harrington.* Santa Barbara: Santa Barbara
            Museum of Natural History.
This contains narrative texts and other chapters reconstructed
from Harrington's unpublished notes of interviews conducted with
Librado between 1912 and 1915 (the year of Librado's death). Part
Two (pp. 33–96) contains the following chapters: "Cosmology: the
Ritual Universe" (Ch. 10), "Siliyak: the Ritual Setting" (Ch. 11),
"Hutash: the Harvest Festival" (Ch. 12), "Kakunupmawa: the Sun
Festival" (Ch. 13), "Dances of the Islanders" (Ch. 15), and
"Dances of the Mainlanders" (Ch. 16). The book includes texts and
translations for 22 songs and many descriptions of songs and
dances. Harrington's recordings of Chumash singers (including
Librado) are found at the Library of Congress and at the Santa
Barbara Museum of Natural History. See the catalogues by Gray
and Schupman (1990 above) and Tegler (1979 below).

Keeling, Richard H.

1982   Songs of the Brush Dance and Their Basis in Oral-
            Expressive Magic: Music and Culture of the Yurok,
            Hupa, and Karok Indians of Northwestern California.
            Doctoral dissertation (Music). University of
            California, Los Angeles.
Keeling describes the Brush Dance and its music in the larger
context of local Indian religion and medicine making. This contains more detailed information on the dance itself than Keeling

(1992a below) and uses sound registrations produced by a melograph to analyze melodic intonation and "special effects" in the singing. The author concludes that intonation is rather inconsistent even when focused (clearly sung) pitches are involved and describes tonal structures in terms of "scale tone areas" rather than scale tones as such (pp. 220–228). Contains extensive transcriptions and musical analyses (pp. 371–593). Based largely on research conducted in the lower Klamath River area from 1978 to 1980.

1985   Contrast of Song Performance Style as a Function of Sex Role Polarity in the Hupa Brush Dance. *Ethnomusicology* 29(2): 185–212.

Keeling describes an improvisatory and ecstatic style performed by men and contrasts this with the more restrained and symmetrical style expected of young girls in this particular performance context. Offers explanations in terms of cultural ideals relating to gender roles and other factors such as the social functions of the Brush Dance. Includes seven musical examples.

1986a   Maidu (Music). Page 161 in *The New Grove Dictionary of American Music*, vol. 3 (L–Q). Edited by H. Wiley Hitchcock and Stanley Sadie. London: Macmillan.

This focuses on Kuksu ceremonials as the most important context for ritual singing. Keeling describes the musical style of songs heard in Kuksu ceremonials and discusses use of musical instruments such as the log drum and whistles made from legbones of the crane or other birds. Also mentions the female puberty ritual and the hand game, both of which involve special songs.

1986b   Pomo (Music). Pp. 585–586 in *The New Grove Dictionary of American Music*, vol. 3 (L–Q). Edited by H. Wiley Hitchcock and Stanley Sadie. London: Macmillan.

This begins by discussing historical transformations that occurred as the indigenous Kuksu religion was influenced by the Ghost Dance of the 1870s and the subsequent origin of the Bole-Maru (Dream Dance) cult. Keeling identifies different types of songs and describes the musical style from a comparative perspective. Includes one transcription of a Pomo dance song.

1986c   Shasta (Music). Page 209 in *The New Grove Dictionary of American Music*, vol. 4 (R–Z). Edited by H. Wiley Hitchcock and Stanley Sadie. London: Macmillan.

Identifies the Girls' Puberty Ceremony as the most important public ritual in Shasta culture and describes basic elements of the musical style. This includes one musical transcription of a puberty dance song quoted from de Angulo and d'Harcourt (1931 above).

1986d   Wintun (Music). Page 544 in *The New Grove Dictionary of American Music*, vol. 4 (R–Z). Edited by H. Wiley Hitchcock and Stanley Sadie. London: Macmillan.

This describes how the indigenous ceremonial life was altered by the Ghost Dance movement of the 1870s and the subsequent development of what anthropologists call the Bole-Maru (Dream Dance) cult. The author also discusses the nature of song texts and outlines basic elements of the musical style among the Wintun, Nomlaki, and Patwin tribes.

1986e   Yurok (Music). Pp. 585–586 in *The New Grove Dictionary of American Music*, vol. 4 (R–Z). Edited by H. Wiley Hitchcock and Stanley Sadie. London: Macmillan.

Keeling begins by emphasizing the close relationship between Yurok culture and that of the neighboring Hupa and Karok Indians. He identifies major dances involving music (Deerskin Dance, Jump Dance, Brush Dance, War Dance, and Kick Dance) and discusses the use of personal medicine songs for hunting, wealth, and other practical functions. Also describes basic elements of the musical style from a comparative perspective.

1989   Musical Evidence of Female Spiritual Life among the Yurok. Pages 67–79 in *Women in North American Indian Music* edited by Richard Keeling. Ann Arbor: Society for Ethnomusicology.

Points out the gender bias in earlier research on Yurok ethnography and criticizes the impression given by Kroeber (1925 below) and others that women were largely excluded from spiritual activities. Keeling focuses on early recordings and narratives which show that Yurok women had a separate spiritual life, parallel to that of the men, which has never been adequately documented. Includes four musical examples.

1991   *A Guide to Early Field Recordings (1900–1949) at
            the Lowie Museum of Anthropology.* Berkeley and
            Los Angeles: University of California Press.
An annotated catalogue of songs and spoken narratives on
2,713 cylinder recordings collected mainly in California as part of
a continuing research survey initiated by Alfred Kroeber in 1900.
References to musical transcriptions, textual translations, or other
available ethnographic data concerning the recordings are cited
throughout. The introduction gives a history of ethnographic research in California and identifies the locations of other archives
containing early recordings of California Indian music. The museum's holdings of more recent recordings on disc, wire, and tape are
summarized in two appendices. The institution became known as
the Phoebe Hearst Museum of Anthropology in 1992.

1992a   *Cry for Luck: Sacred Song and Speech among the
             Yurok, Hupa, and Karok Indians of Northwestern
             California.* Berkeley and Los Angeles: University of
             California Press.
This book interprets ritual singing against the larger background of medicine making as documented by Kroeber and other
early researchers in the area. The introductory chapters (1–4)
summarize beliefs and practices of the precontact period. Chapters
5 and 6 describe the major public rituals and their music, with
comparison of recent examples and recordings that were made
shortly after 1900. The following chapters (7,8, and 9) describe
medicine songs and spoken formulas for various purposes, considering 216 examples in all. Chapter 10 takes a comparative approach and attempts to relate various strands of the musical tradition to the prehistory of the area. In chapter 11 Keeling discusses
the meaning or symbolism of the music, focusing mainly on the
"sobbing" vocal quality and exploring its mythic significance.
Contains 70 musical examples.

1992b   Music and Culture History among the Yurok and
             Neighboring Tribes of Northwestern California. *Jour-
             nal of Anthropological Research* 48(1): 25–48.
An elaboration of the historical interpretations in chapter 10 of
Keeling (1992a above). Keeling speculates on the historical development of various local music styles and attempts to interpret their
significance in the larger context of North American Indian music
and culture history.

1992c   Music and Culture Areas of Native California. *Journal of California and Great Basin Anthropology* 14(2): 146–158.

This outlines the predominant styles of vocal music in the following areas: (1) Northwestern California, (2) Northeastern California, (3) North-Central California, (4) San Joaquin Valley and Adjacent Foothills, (5) Southern California, and (6) the Central Coast. Keeling also describes certain "animal-speech songs" as an older genre occurring throughout California and summarizes general features that distinguish this particular region in the overall sphere of Native American music.

See **Kelly** (1932 and 1964) in Great Basin and Plateau bibliography. These deal with music and dance among the Southern Paiutes and closely-related Chemehuevis.

Klimek, Stanislaus

1935   Culture Element Distributions, I: The Structure of California Indian Culture. *University of California Publications in American Archaeology and Ethnology* 37(1): 1–70.

This outlines a methodology for statistical analysis of trait distributions. The system includes elements relating to musical instruments (p. 25) and various dances or rituals including music (pp. 28–29).

Kroeber, Alfred

1922   Elements of Culture in Native California. *University of California Publications in American Archaeology and Ethnology* 13(8): 259–328.

This includes descriptions of musical instruments (pp. 277–278) and information about other aspects of culture involving music (passim).

1925   *Handbook of the Indians of California.* Bureau of American Ethnology Bulletin 78. Washington, D.C. Reprinted by Dover Publications (New York, 1976).

A comprehensive overview of California Indian ethnography. This contains no musical notations, but it does provide information on the cultural contexts and functions of Indian music in all areas of the state. The coverage of Mohave song-cycles (pp. 755–774) is particularly detailed, but Kroeber also gives translations of song texts and other information relating to music of the following tribes: Yurok (pp. 95–97), Yuki (p. 194), Modoc (p. 321), Wintun (p. 385), Costanoan (pp. 471–472), Yokuts (pp. 506 and 514–515), Chemehuevi (p. 599), Juaneño (pp. 641–642), Luiseño (pp. 657–660), and Diegueño (p. 713).

1936   Culture Element Distributions, III: Area and Climax. *University of California Publications in American Archaeology and Ethnology* 37(3): 101–116.
A sophisticated discussion of culture areas in California. This indicates four musical sub-areas (pp. 109 and 113–114) and also shows the geographic and cultural distribution of major religious systems (pp. 110–112).

1948   Seven Mohave Myths. *University of California Anthropological Records* 11(1).
This contains translations of texts collected between 1900 and 1910 but not previously published except as summarized in Kroeber (1925 above). Kroeber gives full translations and commentary for each of the texts. This does not include musical notations, but it does indicate the places in myths where songs occur and gives native texts and translations for many of the songs. The style of the singing is also discussed in the commentary which precedes each of the texts. Kroeber's recordings are available at the Hearst Museum of Anthropology. See the catalogue by Keeling (1991 above).

Kroeber, Alfred L., and Edward W. Gifford

1949   World Renewal: A Cult System of Native Northwest California. *University of California Anthropological Records* 21(1): 1–210. Berkeley.
This focuses on a ceremonial complex shared equally by the Yurok, Hupa, and Karok tribes of northwestern California. The authors describe dances and other rituals conducted at various locations, often including explanations by native informants. This includes musical notations for seven songs identified as follows: songs for the ritual at Kepel Creek fish dam (4 songs), Deerskin Dance songs (2), and Jump Dance song (1). Recordings of the songs are available at the Hearst Museum of Anthropology. See the catalogue by Keeling (1991 above).

See **Laird** (1974 and 1976) in the Great Basin bibliography. These focus on music and culture of the Chemehuevi Indians.

Latta, Frank

1949   *Handbook of Yokuts Indians.* Bakersfield: Kern
        County Museum.
        The author was not a professional anthropologist but an educa-
tor who was born in the San Joaquin Valley and studied Indians of
the region most of his life. Chapter seven ("Stories and
Ceremonies," pp. 197–216) contains descriptions of the Boys'
Initiation Ceremony, the Rainmaking Ceremony, and the
Rattlesnake Dance. Chapter Eight ("Indian Statements," pp. 217–
286) gives information as spoken by an elderly woman named
Yoimut (Tulare Lake Yokuts) during the 1920s. This includes descriptions of various types of songs and translations of several song
texts.

See **Lee** (1979) in the General bibliography. This catalogue of record-
        ings at Indiana University lists some important collections
        such as de Angulo's recordings of Achomawi songs (circa
        1925), Dixon's recordings among the Maidu (1910), Herzog's
        recordings among the Diegueño (1927), and Herzog's record-
        ings of Hupa songs (1927). Other California Indian recordings
        are identified as follows: Diegueño, Mohave, Patwin, Pomo,
        Round Valley, Santa Catalina, Yuki, and Yurok.

Loeb, Edwin M.

1926   Pomo Folkways. *University of California Publica-
        tions in American Archaeology and Ethnology* 19 (2):
        149–405.
        Loeb distinguishes Pomo cult observances into two strata, an
earlier Ghost Cult and a later Kuksu (God-impersonating cult).
This contains many descriptions of music, including song texts and
translations. Also gives data on musical instruments (pp. 188–190).

1932   The Western Kuksu Cult. *University of California
        Publications in American Archaeology and
        Ethnology* 33(1): 1–137.
        A detailed study of initiatory ceremonies and spirit impersona-
tions as practiced among various Pomo divisions and other groups
including the Kato, Huchnom, Yuki, Wailaki, Wappo, Coast
Miwok, and Lake Miwok. Loeb also describes other secular and religious dances. This is based mainly on fieldwork conducted in
1930. Contains no musical notations, but songs are mentioned
throughout. See also Loeb (1933 below).

1933   The Eastern Kuksu Cult. *University of California Publications in American Archaeology and Ethnology* 33(2): 139–232.
This is a detailed account of ceremonies practiced among various divisions of the Maidu and Patwin tribes. Besides the Kuksu ceremonies Loeb also describes other rituals such as the Acorn Dance, Bear Dance, and Mourning Ceremony. This is based mainly on interviews conducted in 1931 but includes information from earlier sources such as Dixon (1905 above) and Powers (1877 below).

Loether, Christopher

1993   Niimina Ahubiya: Western Mono Song Genres. *Journal of California and Great Basin Anthropology* 15(1): 48–57.
Loether distinguishes eleven categories of songs (with sub-divisions) and describes seven types of songs that are still being performed. This includes informative comments on the styles but no musical examples. Based on earlier sources (which are carefully summarized) and research conducted at Northfork (California) at various periods from 1980 to 1985.

See **Lowie** (1938) in General bibliography. Deals with foot drum as used among California Indians.

Mason, J. Alden

1912   The Ethnology of Salinan Indians. *University of California Publications in American Archaeology and Ethnology* 10(4): 97–240.
This contains information on musical instruments (pp. 156–159) and on various dances (pp.177–179). Includes texts and translations for a Bear Dance song and an Owl Dance song.

Meighan, Clement, and Francis Riddell

1972   *The Maru Cult of the Pomo Indians.* Southwest Museum Papers no. 23. Los Angeles.
This contains descriptions of Eastern Pomo dances held at Big Valley Rancheria (Lake County) between 1948 and 1953. It covers the origins of the Maru religion as influenced by the Ghost Dance movement of 1870 and describes various aspects of the Bighead Dance, including dance patterns (pp. 49–56). The authors also dis-

cuss two secular dances, identified as the Hindl Dance and the Ball Dance (pp. 62–68). Tape recordings dated 1949 are available at the Hearst Museum of Anthropology and are listed in Appendix II of the catalogue by Keeling (1991 above).

Merriam, Alan P., and Robert F.G. Spier

1959   Chukchansi Yokuts Songs. Pp. 611–638 in *Proceedings of the 33rd International Congress of Americanists held at San José, Costa Rica*. San José: Editorial Lehmann.
    Spier collected the songs and ethnographic data in 1950, and the paper consists mainly of notations and detailed analyses by Merriam. Most of the 32 songs are handgame songs by women, but also included are shamanistic songs, totemic animal songs, and mourning songs. Merriam's most striking conclusion is that "the rise," which Nettl had presumed to be a hallmark of California-Yuman singing (General bibliography 1954:18–19) is not apparent in these songs. Merriam is at a loss to account for this, but readers should also note that this is an area in which California and Great Basin styles overlap and that the repertory as a whole may have included other types of songs besides these.

Mills, Elaine, and Ann Brickfield

1986   *The Papers of John Peabody Harrington in the Smithsonian Institution (1907–1957)* . 7 vols. White Plains, N.Y.: Kraus International Publications.
    Harrington (1884–1961) was an anthropological linguist who collected recordings and ethnographic data from various tribes of California and adjacent areas mainly during the 1910s, 1920s, and 1930s. Relatively little of this information has been published; thus the Harrington manuscripts are very important as a resource for future research on Indian music and other aspects of culture. California tribes he studied include the following: Cahuilla, Chumash, Costanoan (Chochenyo), Gabrielino, Karok, Luiseño, Salinan, Serrano, Tachi Yokuts, and Tubatalabal.

Nettl, Bruno

See Nettl (1954a) in the General bibliography. This includes a general description of the "California-Yuman" musical style (pp. 18–19).

1965   The Songs of Ishi: Musical Style of the Yahi Indians. *Musical Quarterly* 51(3): 460–477.
Ishi became famous as a "wild" Yahi Indian who had virtually no contact with whites before he wandered into the town of Oroville in 1911. This study of 60 recordings collected by Waterman and Kroeber between 1911 and 1914 touches on some interesting questions such as the difficulty of generalizing about a native musical style from the repertory of a single person. The recordings are available at Hearst Museum and are listed in the catalogue by Keeling (1991 above). Little has been published on music from this (northeastern) part of the state, but see also Hall and Nettl (1955) and de Angulo and d'Harcourt (1929).

Park, Susan

1986   *Samson Grant, Atsuge Shaman.* Occasional Papers of the Redding Museum no. 3. Redding, California: Redding Museum and Art Center.
This is a recent publication of data collected by Park circa 1931–1933. It mainly contains myths and stories as related by Samson Grant but also includes a description of the girls' puberty ceremony (pp. 15–20) and an account of how the shaman obtained his powers (pp. 13–15 and 21–25). There are superb historical photographs of local Indian subjects.

Pietroforte, Alfred

1965   *Songs of the Yokuts and Paiutes.* Healdsburg, California: Naturegraph Publishers.
This slim volume provides comments and notations for 25 songs from the following groups: Tachi Yokuts (12), Wukchamni Yokuts (2), Paiute (9), and Western Mono (2). The transcriptions seem quite good, and the author provides background information on the singers and recording sessions, but there is not much musical analysis. For more information on Tachi Yokuts music see Hatch (1958).

Powers, Stephen

[1877]   *Tribes of California.* Contributions to North American Ethnology 3. Washington: U. S. Geographical and Geological Survey of the Rocky Mountain Region. Reprinted by University of California Press (Berkeley and Los Angeles, 1976).

Based on the author's travels through northern California in 1871–1872, this contains valuable descriptions of Indian cultures in transition during the period of early encounters with white settlers. There are musical notations (with texts) for songs of the Karok (1 song), Concow Maidu (1), Huchnom (2), and Pomo (2). Other information relating to music or dance is given for the following groups: Karok (pp. 25–26, 29, 30–31), Yurok (pp. 56–57), Hupa (pp. 78–79, 85), Wiyot (p. 105), Pomo (pp. 159–160, 171, 179–180, 211–213), Wintun (p. 236), Nomlaki (p. 237), Maidu (pp. 285–288, 296), Concow Maidu (pp. 306–309), and Nisenan (pp. 333–336).

Rathbun, Robert. See Coyote Man (above).

Roberts, Helen H.

1932   The First Salmon Ceremony of the Karuk Indians. *American Anthropologist* 34(3): 426–440.

This general description of the ritual includes two musical examples, with song texts (pp. 433 and 438). Based on research conducted in 1926. While working among the Karok (or alternatively, Karuk), Roberts also collected recordings and extensive information on music and dance in the form of unpublished field notes (typed, including musical transcriptions). These are available at the Library of Congress and are described in Gray and Schupman (1990 above).

1933   *Form in Primitive Music: An Analytical and Comparative Study of the Melodic Form of Some Ancient Southern Californian Indian Songs.* New York: W. W. Norton.

This contains transcriptions (with texts and translations) and analyses of songs from the following tribes: Luiseño (14 songs), Gabrielino (5), and Catalineño (5). The analysis is primarily based on structure or form, with tonal material also considered. See the reviews by Herzog (1934 above) and von Hornbostel (1934 below).

See Roberts (1936) in the General bibliography. This contains a section on the general characteristics of vocal music among the Indians of California (pp. 30–32).

Robins, R.H., and McLeod, Norma

1956   Five Yurok Songs: A Musical and Textual Analysis. *Bulletin of the School of Oriental and African Studies* 18:592–609.
The authors discuss musical and linguistic aspects of five Yurok songs collected by Robins in 1951. The analyses are detailed, but information on cultural contexts of the song types represented is lacking.

Rust, Horatio N.

1906   A Puberty Ceremony of the Mission Indians. *American Anthropologist* 8(1): 28–32.
This focuses on a girls' puberty ceremony which the author witnessed at Campo (San Diego County) in 1889. He notes that the ritual was sometimes called "roasting of girls" (p. 28). Ritual activities are described, but songs are only mentioned in passing. The tribal identification is presumably Ipai or northern Diegueño.

See the catalogue by **Seeger and Spear** (1987). This lists and describes cylinder recordings at the Indiana University Archives of Traditional Music. The collection includes recordings from the following California tribes: Achomawi, Diegueño, Hupa, Maidu, Mohave, Pomo, Yuki, and Yurok.

Siva, Ernest H.

1986   Cahuilla (Music). Pp. 342–343 in *The New Grove Dictionary of American Music*, vol. 1 (A–D). Edited by H. Wiley Hitchcock and Stanley Sadie. London: Macmillan.
Siva begins by discussing the functions of songs and the specialized role of certain ceremonial singers (*hauiniktam*) whose position is determined by inheritance. He then gives a general description of the musical style, with three musical examples (partial transcriptions, not complete songs).

Sparkman, Philip Stedman

1908   The Culture of the Luiseño Indians. *University of California Publications in American Archaeology and Ethnology* 8(4): 187–234.

This contains descriptions of the puberty ceremonies and mourning ceremonies (pp. 221–227). The information is less detailed than that provided in the study by Dubois (1908b above).

Spier, Leslie

1923   Southern Diegueño Customs. *University of California Publications in American Archaeology and Ethnology* 20(16): 295–358.
This contains descriptions of ceremonies (pp. 316–326) and a list of song cycles (p. 327). It provides a useful complement to the studies of northern Diegueño groups by Dubois (1905, 1906, 1908a, and 1908b above) and Waterman (1910 below).

Spott, Robert, and Alfred L. Kroeber

1942   Yurok Narratives. *University of California Publications in American Archaeology and Ethnology* 35(9): 143–256.
Spott was Kroeber's principal informant on Yurok spiritual practices. This volume contains narratives dictated by him along with commentaries by Kroeber. Gives information on the following subjects: doctoring songs (pp 153–156 and 158–162), the First Salmon Ceremony (pp. 171–179), a Wiyot dance (pp. 179–180), a Tolowa Dance (pp. 180–182), songs gotten from animals (pp. 235–238), the White Deerskin Dance (pp. 244–249), and a story about dentalia (shells) and their songs (pp. 249–250).

Sterling, Clarence

1988   Chumash Wind Instruments. *News from Native California*, vol. 2, no. 2. (May–June), pp. 4–6. Berkeley: Heyday Books.
This describes whistles, flutes, bull-roarers, and musical bows. It provides information on native terminology, playing techniques, and mythological associations of the instruments. Based on unpublished notes of John P. Harrington. See Mills and Brickfield (1986 above).

See **Stevenson** (1973a) in the General bibliography. This discusses early written sources on Indian music of the California region (pp. 4–13).

It contains musical notations for six Costanoan songs that were orginally transcribed by Fray Felipe Arroyo de la Cuesta at Mission San Juan Bautista between 1810 and 1823.

See **Steward** (1933) in the Great Basin and Plateau bibliography. This contains information on music of the Owens Valley Paiute.

Tegler, Gary

1979   An Index of Harrington's Chumash Recordings. *UCLA Institute of Archeology Occasional Papers* 3:22–48.
An annotated catalogue of 74 cylinder recordings which were collected by John P. Harrington from 1912 to 1916. This gives the following types of data from Harrington's notes: biographical information on the performers, index of songs grouped by language, index of songs by type or genre, native texts as transcribed by Harrington, and other information on the meaning or use of songs. The recordings are also available at the Library of Congress and are described in Gray and Schupman (1990 above).

1986   Chumash (Music). Page 429 in *The New Grove Dictionary of American Music*, vol. 1 (A–D). Edited by H. Wiley Hitchcock and Stanley Sadie. London: Macmillan.
A brief summary of available information on music of a tribe that is not well documented in published sources. Tegler lists the musical genres and discusses the functions of Chumash music. He also discusses instruments and describes general characteristics of the music. This is based mainly on cylinder recordings and field-notes of the ethnologist John P. Harrington.

Treganza, Adam E., Edith S. Taylor, and William J. Wallace

1947   The Hindil, a Pomo Indian Dance in 1946. *Masterkey* 21:119–125.
This includes references to music and instruments but contains no musical examples or other detailed information.

Valory, Dale

1966   The Focus of Indian Shaker Healing. *Kroeber Anthropological Society Papers* 35:67–112.
Valory describes Shaker services which took place at Smith River California in 1966. See pp. 85–88 for information on the

music and an interesting explanation of how a new curing song is "received" and rehearsed prior to being used in services.

Vennum, Thomas, Jr.

1979   Record review of "Songs of Love, Luck, Animals, and Magic: Music of the Yurok and Tolowa Indians." Produced by Charlotte Heth (New World Records NW 297). *Ethnomusicology* 23(2) 349–352.
A very favorable review. Vennum notes that this is the only commercial recording of Indian singing from northwestern California and describes various unusual aspects of the style. The review also contains references to earlier sources in the anthropological literature and indicates areas for further research.

Voegelin, Erminie (Wheeler)

1942   Culture Element Distributions, XX: Northeast California. *University of California Anthropological Records* 7(2): 47–251.
This contains information on the presence or absence of various traits in tabular form. There is data on musical instruments (pp. 93–94), social dances (pp. 102–104), girls' puberty ceremony (pp. 122–128), boys' puberty observances (p. 128), and other ritual activities (pp. 150–162).

von Hornbostel, Erich M.

1934   Review of *Form in Primitive Music* by Helen H. Roberts (1933). *Zeitschrift für vergleichende Musikwissenschaft* 2:2–3, 60–64.
A favorable review. This contrasts the southern California material discussed by Roberts with what Hornbostel presumes to be the basic style of American Indian music. Includes nine musical examples quoted from Roberts (1933 above).

Wallace, William J.

1978   Music and Musical Instruments. Pp. 642–648 in *Handbook of North American Indians, Volume Eight: California*, edited by Robert F. Heizer. Washington: Smithsonian Institution.
This describes general characteristics of California Indian music from a non-technical perspective. Wallace begins by discussing vocal music, emphasizing the functions of music and character

of the song texts, then describes musical instruments (including drawings and photographs).

Waterman, Thomas T.

1908   Diegueño Identification of Color with the Cardinal Points. *Journal of American Folklore* 21:40–42.
This includes one song text and translation.

1908   Native Musical Instruments of California and Some Others. *Outwest* 28:276–286.
This contains non-technical descriptions of rattles, clappers, whistles, and flutes among the holdings at Phoebe Hearst Museum of Anthropology (University of California, Berkeley).

1910   The Religious Practices of the Diegueño Indians. *University of California Publications in American Archaeology and Ethnology* 8(6): 271–358.
Waterman describes several different ceremonies as listed under two headings: "Customs Concerning Birth and Adolescence" (pp. 284–304) and "Mourning Ceremonies" (pp. 305–327). This also includes numerous song texts, some with translations. Waterman also collected cylinder recordings that are available at the Hearst Museum of Anthropology. See the catalogue by Keeling (1992 above).

Woodruff, Charles E.

1892   Dances of the Hupa Indians. *American Anthropologist* 5(1): 53–61.
This describes ceremonies known today as the Jump Dance, Deerskin Dance, Brush Dance, and Flower Dance. The essay is ethnocentric in tone, but valuable for capturing glimpses of Hupa culture during an early period of transition. For example, this includes comments on the younger Indians' reticence to admit that they believe in "old customs and superstitions" and yet also describes the continuing belief in "bad Indians (who) can kill their distant enemies by simply poisoning the air" (pp. 60–61).

V. Great Basin and Plateau

Abraham, Otto, and Erich M. von Hornbostel

1906   Phonographierte Indianermelodien aus Britisch-Columbia. Pp. 447–474 in *Boas Anniversary Volume: Anthropological Papers written in Honor of Franz Boas.* New York: Stechert and Co. Translated by Bruno Nettl in *Hornbostel Opera Omnia*, vol. 1, edited by Klaus Wachsmann et al. The Hague: Martinus Nijhoff, 1975.

This contains transcriptions and analyses of 43 Thompson River Indian songs that were recorded by Franz Boas and sent by him to Erich M. von Hornbostel of the Phonogramm Archiv of the University of Berlin. The precise tonal analyses (in cents) are intended to show that deviations from Western intonation are not accidental but purposeful and stylistic. Thus, the essay is historically important as being among the first to extend the anthropological concept of cultural relativity to native music research. The fine transcriptions, quantitative analyses, and relatively slight information on cultural contexts of the music make this a prime example of comparative methodology as practiced by the so-called "Berlin School."

Adams, Charles

1976   Melodic Contour Typology. *Ethnomusicology* 20(2): 179–215.

Adams outlines a statistical method for analysis and uses the system to compare melodic contours in songs of the Flathead and Southern Paiute. This is based on 138 notations of Flathead songs in Merriam (1967 below) and 197 Southern Paiute songs that were collected by Sapir in 1910 and notated by his father, Jacob Sapir. The Southern Paiute notations were from manuscript collections at

the Archives of Traditional Music, Indiana University. They were
later published in Sapir (1994 below).

Barber, Edwin A.

1877   Gaming Among the Utah Indians. *American
              Naturalist* 11:351–355.
      This describes hand game gambling as played among the
Yampa Ute and includes one musical transcription (with text).

See **Baker** (1882) in the General bibliography. This contains three
      melodies and texts that were collected among the Walla Walla
      and were originally published in Wilkes (1845 below).

See **Boas** (1987) in the Arctic and Sub-Arctic bibliography. This con-
      tains one musical notation (with text and translation) of a song
      collected by Boas among Indians of British Columbia.

Boas, Franz

1900   See under Teit (1900 below).

Bunte, Pamela

[1994]   See under Sapir (1994 below).

Cartwright, Willena D.

1953   A Washo Girl's Puberty Ceremony. Pp. 136–142 in
              *Proceedings of the 30th International Congress of
              Americanists, Cambridge, 1952.* London: Royal
              Anthropological Institute.
      This describes a "Fire Dance" that took place near
Gardnerville Nevada in December, 1929. The songs are not discussed, but Cartwright does give information on the dance preparations and other aspects of the ceremony. Also includes comparative
data on girls' puberty dances among other tribes of California and
Nevada.

Chamberlain, Alexander F.

1901   Kootenay "Medicine-Men." *Journal of American
              Folklore* 14:95–99.
      This gives a brief description of Kutenai shamanism in the so-
called "blanket ritual." Includes one translation of a song text (pp.
95–96).

Coale, George L.

1958   Notes on the Guardian Spirit Concept among the Nez Perce. *International Archives of Ethnography* 48(2): 135–148.

Coale discusses the acquisition of songs by vision quest and subsequent performance of these songs in winter spirit dances (pp. 138–139 and 140).

Crum, Beverly

1980   Newe Hupia: Shoshoni Poetry Songs. *Journal of California and Great Basin Anthropology, Papers in Linguistics* 2:3–23.

The author is Shoshoni herself and describes four "poetry songs" as traditionally performed at social dances. There are musical transcriptions for each of the songs (with texts and translations), and Crum's commentary focuses on metaphors and other poetic devices in the songs.

See **Curtis** (1907–1930) in the General bibliography. *Volume Seven* contains the following: four Yakima melodies (pp. 8,11, and 13–14); eleven Interior Salish melodies, one with text and translation, one with text only (pp. 74, 82, 84, 88–89, and 90–95); 14 Kutenai melodies, two with texts and translations (pp. 121–126, 132–133, 138–139, 141–145, and 168–172); and two Klickitat melodies (pp. 161–162). *Volume Eight* contains the following: nine Nez Perce melodies, seven with texts and translations (pp. 50, 54–59, 75–76, and 183–185); two Nez Perce song texts and translations (p. 60); and six Wishram melodies (pp.176–179 and 185–191). *Volume Fifteen* contains one Paviotso (Northern Paiute) song text and translation (p. 136).

d'Azevedo, Warren L.

1972   (Recording) "Washo Peyote Songs: Songs of the American Indian Native Church-Peyotist." Smithsonian-Folkways (FE 4384).

Currently available on cassette, this album features five peyote song cycles recorded by d'Azevedo during the early 1950s. The liner notes give extensive background information and even incorporate a reprint of the study by Merriam and d'Azevedo (1957 below).

1978   *Straight with the Medicine: Narratives of the Washoe Followers of the Tipi Way.* Reno, Nev.: Black Rock Press. Reprinted by Heyday Books (Berkeley, 1985).
This book is based on texts that d'Azevedo collected (on tape recorder) from various Washoe peyotists during the 1950s. The section on "Songs" (pp. 14–19) contains some beautifully-worded quotations on concepts of music and musical performance practices in the peyote service.

Dellenbaugh, Frederick S.

1908   *A Canyon Voyage: The Narrative of the Second Powell Expedition Down the Green-Colorado River from Wyoming, and the Explorations by Land, in the Years 1871 and 1872.* New York: G. P. Putnam's Sons.
This contains a brief and distinctly ethnocentric account of a Paiute "New Year's Dance," with translations of two song texts (pp. 177–179).

Densmore, Frances

1922   *Northern Ute Music.* Bureau of American Ethnology Bulletin no. 75.
This contains musical notations (with English translations only) for 114 Northern Ute songs that were collected by Densmore in 1914 and 1916. Densmore analyzes each song and also gives stylistic profiles for each genre or song type (the cultural functions of which are also discussed). The Ute songs are compared with Teton Sioux and Chippewa songs that were previously collected by Densmore, and for this she uses a form of tabular analysis which shows the relative frequency of intervals, rhythmic units, and other stylistic elements. The relation of these styles to Slovak melodies is also indicated using the tabular (quantitative) method.
See Densmore (1951b) in Plains bibliography. This is a record album containing Pawnee and Northern Ute songs.

Fowler, Catherine S.

1986   The Hunchback Dance of the Northern Paiute and Other Clown Performances in the Great Basin. In *Anthropology in the Desert West: Essays in Honor of Jesse D. Jennings* edited by Don D. Fowler and Carol J. Condie. Salt Lake City: University of Utah Press.

This contains some references to music but is mainly useful for its comparative and functional analyses of clowning in Native American rituals. Fowler begins by describing the Hunchback Dance and its limited distribution (only in the central part of Northern Paiute territory). She then explores certain parallels with dances of California Indian groups and discusses similar clowning traditions in the Pueblo Southwest and among the Plains Cree. Toward the end, she considers functional, psychological, structural, and symbolic explanations of ritual clowning.

Fowler, Don D., and Catherine S. Fowler

1970   Stephen Powers' "Life and Culture of the Washo and Paiutes." *Ethnohistory* 17(3–4): 117–149.
This is an annotated edition of an unpublished manuscript describing Powers' travels among the Washo and Paiute Indians (of western Nevada) in 1875. It contains descriptions of dances (pp. 121, 127, and 129) and a curing ceremony (p. 131).

Franklin, Robert

[1994]   See under Sapir (1994 below).

Freed, Stanley A., and Ruth S. Freed

1963   The Persistence of Aboriginal Ceremonies among the Washo Indians. Pp. 25–40 in *The Washo Indians of California and Nevada* edited by Warren d'Azevedo. University of Utah Anthropological Papers 67. Salt Lake City.
The authors describe five types of Washo ceremonies which survived into the 1950s: (1) birth ceremonies, (2) the girls' puberty dance, (3) death ceremonies, (4) shamanistic curing rituals, and (5) the Pinenut Dance. They consider various reasons why the first three seem to be capable of future survival while the curing rituals and the Pinenut Dance are on the point of disappearance. Based on research conducted in the early 1950s.

Gatschet, Albert S.

1894   Songs of the Modoc Indians. *American Anthropologist* 7:26–31.
Gatschet gives textual translations and commentary for three Modoc songs: (1) Song of the "Roll-Head" Owl, (2) Song of the Robin Redbreast (a lullaby), and (3) a satirical dance song.

Contains no staff notations but does indicate the rhythmic pattern of each song.

Gray, Judith A. (Editor)

1988   Great Basin/Plateau Catalog. Pages 1–78 in *The Federal Cylinder Project: A Guide to Field Cylinder Collections in Federal Agencies, Volume 3: Great Basin/Plateau Indian Catalog and Northwest Coast/Arctic Indian Catalog.* Washington: American Folklife Center, Library of Congress.

An annotated guide to early cylinder recordings in seven collections, the largest being the Northern Ute songs recorded by Densmore in 1914 and 1916. The list for each group is preceded by an introduction providing background information on the recordings and the sources from which translations or other information have been obtained. Includes recordings collected among the following tribes: Flathead, Nez Perce, Thompson (Okanagon), Northern Ute, and Yakima.

Haefer, J. Richard

1986   Paiute (Music). Page 463 in *The New Grove Dictionary of American Music*, vol. 3 (L–Q). Edited by H. Wiley Hitchcock and Stanley Sadie. London: Macmillan.

Haefer describes two basic genres of Paiute songs: (1) songs with a structure based on paired phrases, typified by Ghost Dance songs; and (2) a type of "song recitative" that depicts the speech or singing of animals in myths. The latter is more fully described in Sapir (1910 below). Haefer also mentions musical influences from Yuman tribes to the south.

Hall, Jody C., and Nettl, Bruno

1955   Musical Style of the Modoc. *Southwestern Journal of Anthropology* 11: 58–66.

This contains 17 transcriptions (without texts) of Modoc songs collected by Leslie Spier in 1934. The musical analysis focuses on manner of performance, melodic material, and rhythmic patterns. The authors distinguish two basic styles in Modoc music, one with narrower range and fewer scale tones than the other. They describe the musical style generally as being more simple than that of Northwest Coast or Central California and also suggest that the closest affinity is with Great Basin songs (pp. 65–66). Information on the functions of the songs is generally lacking.

Hoebel, E. Adamson

1935   The Sun Dance of the Hekandika Shoshone. *American Anthropologist* 37(4): 570–581.

Hoebel describes singing (by men and women) and blowing of whistles during the ritual (pp. 573–575). He also discusses the mythic origin of the ceremony and particularly of four songs that were originally given by a buffalo in a vision (p. 579).

Jeancon, Jean Allard

1927   Music of the Indians of Colorado. *Lookout* 1:69–74. Published by the Denver Public Library. Denver: Carson Press.

This deals mainly with music of the Arapaho, Cheyenne, and Ute tribes. The author was a museum curator and amateur composer who sought to preserve Indian melodies by using them in art music compositions. This article describes "primitive" music as related to the Sun Dance, the (Ute) Bear Dance, and the courting flute.

Jorgenson, Joseph G.

1972   *The Sun Dance Religion: Power for the Powerless.* Chicago: University of Chicago Press.

A political, economic, and psychological analysis of the Sun Dance as practiced among the Shoshones and the Northern Utes. The chapter on "The Modern Sun Dance Ritual" (pp. 177–205) gives a generalized account with frequent references to songs and singers. Another section entitled "The Dancers" (pp. 244–264) focuses on motivations for participating in the Sun Dance and gives various statistics relating to participation.

1986   Ghost Dance, Bear Dance, and Sun Dance. Pp. 660–672 in *Handbook of North American Indians, Volume 11: Great Basin* edited by Warren L. d'Azevedo. Washington: Smithsonian Institution.

This contains descriptions and historical information relating to the following: the Ghost Dance of 1869, the Ghost Dance of 1889, the Bear Dance, the Mourning Ceremony, the Sun Dance Religion, and the (recent) Traditional Unity Movement.

See **Keeling** (1991) in the California bibliography for a catalogue of cylinder recordings at Hearst Museum of Anthropology (UC Berkeley). The collection includes recordings from the following tribes of the Great Basin and Plateau areas: Bannock, Klamath Lake, Modoc, Northern Paiute, Owens Valley Paiute, Shoshone, Uintah Ute, and Washo.

Kelly, Isabel T.

1932   Ethnography of the Surprise Valley Paiute. *University of California Publications in American Archaeology and Ethnology* 31(3): 67–210.
      This contains brief descriptions of musical instruments (pp. 146–147).

1936   Chemehuevi Shamanism. Pp. 129–142 in *Essays in Anthropology Presented to A. L. Kroeber in Celebration of His 60th Birthday* edited by Robert H. Lowie. Berkeley and Los Angeles: University of California Press.
      Kelly discusses the use of songs by shamans (p. 131), sorcerers (p. 133), and others who specialize in treating snake bites or injuries (pp. 137–138).

1939   Southern Paiute Shamanism. *University of California Anthropological Records* 2(4): 151–167.
      This describes the work of "sucking doctors" and other shamans among various Southern Paiute groups. Songs are repeatedly mentioned in relation to acquisition of shamanic power and curing rituals themselves. The data were collected between 1932 and 1934.

1964   *Southern Paiute Ethnography.* Glen Canyon Series 21. University of Utah Anthropological Papers 69. Salt Lake City.
      This is a revised version of a manuscript Kelly originally wrote circa 1933–1934 and contains information based on fieldwork conducted in 1932. There are brief descriptions and drawings of musical instruments (p. 85). Kelly also describes various dances (pp. 103–122), including a Circle Dance ("Squaw Dance") which the author considers to be indigenous and others (the Ghost Dance and the Bear dance) that were introduced more recently. The "Cry" or mourning ceremony is also briefly discussed (pp. 103 and 104).

Laird, Carobeth

1974   Chemehuevi Religious Beliefs and Practices. *Journal of California Anthropology* 1(1): 19–25.
Laird discusses "Deer Songs" and "Mountain Sheep Songs" which both have hereditary (even totemistic) implications and describes how they were sung at night before hunting (p. 23). She also discusses the Ghost Dance and songs of the mourning ceremony, particularly a special "talking song" that is sung toward the end.

1976   *The Chemehuevis.* Banning, California: Malki Museum Press.
Chapter One ("Identity, Distribution, and Organization") contains sections on the following: "Mountain Sheep Song" (pp. 11–14), "Deer Song" (pp. 14–16), "Salt Song" (pp. 16–18), and "Other Songs" (pp. 18–21). Chapter Six ("Mythology") includes several narratives with embedded songs, and Laird gives translations for the song texts. There is also much information on the mourning ceremony or "Cry" (pp. 25–26, 41–43, 78, 91, and 245–246).

See the catalogue by **Lee** (1979) in the General bibliography. This lists historical and recent recordings at the Indiana University Archives of Traditional Music. The collection includes recordings from the following tribes of the Great Basin and Plateau areas: Bannock, Flathead, Klamath, Kutenai, Modoc, Nez Perce, Paiute (Northern and Southern), Sahaptin, Shoshone, Simnasho, Skoahchinuh, Thompson, Umatilla, Ute (various sub-groups), Washo, Wishram, and Yakima.

Lenmon, Norman H.

1954   An Okanagan Winter Dance. Pp. 35–36 in *Anthropology in British Columbia, 1953–1954*, vol. 4. Victoria.
This describes the singing of guardian spirit songs by shamans and other activities (such as gambling) which took place during a winter ceremonial held at Riverside, Washington, in February 1954.

See **Loether** (1994) in the California bibliography. This contains descriptions of song genres among the Western Mono of Northfork (California).

Lowie, Robert H.

1909   The Northern Shoshone. *Anthropological Papers of the American Museum of Natural History* 2(2): 165–307.

The section on "Music" (pp. 206–207) gives brief descriptions of instruments (drums, whistles, and a courting flute). The section on "Dances" (pp. 216–223) begins by discussing the fairly recent introduction of the Sun Dance, then describes other dances practiced in earlier times. These included a dance to ensure abundance (*nuakin*), a First Salmon ceremony (*tama-gai*), and others. Lowie gives text and translation for a *nuakin* song, commenting on the resemblance of the style to that of Ghost Dance songs but emphasizing that it belongs to an earlier tradition. Lowie (p. 218) supports Mooney's argument (See Plains bibliography, 1896) that the Ghost Dance was actually a revival of an earlier indigenous dance.

1915   Dances and Societies of the Plains Shoshone. *Anthropological Papers of the American Museum of Natural History* 11(1): 803–835.

This deals with dances and societies of the Comanche (pp. 809–812), the Ute (pp. 823–835), and the Wind River Shoshone (pp. 813–822). Lowie gives brief descriptions of several dances without discussing the music in detail.

1919   The Sun Dance of the Shoshone, Ute, and Hidatsa. *Anthropological Papers of the American Museum of Natural History* 16(5): 387–431. New York.

Could not be obtained for inspection of contents nor could information be gotten from other sources.

1939   Ethnographic Notes on the Washo. *University of California Publications in American Archaeology and Ethnology* 36:301–352. Berkeley.

This contains information on the use of songs in the girls' puberty ceremony (pp. 305–308). Lowie also mentions two other dances borrowed from the Pit River (Achomawi) Indians and from the Paviotso or Northern Paiute (pp. 314–315).

McAllester, David Park

See McAllester (1949) in the General bibliography. This describes Peyote songs as used among various tribes including the Washo, Shoshone, and Ute.

1970   Review of *Ethnomusicology of the Flathead Indians* by Alan P. Merriam (1967). *Journal of American Folklore* 83(330): 481–482.

This is basically a favorable review, but McAllester does criticize Merriam for not including song texts in his transcriptions and for not attempting to explain the stylistic differences between various categories of songs that are distinguished in chapter Nine.

1986   Flathead (Music). Pp. 138–139 in *The New Grove Dictionary of American Music*, vol. 2 (E–K). Edited by H. Wiley Hitchcock and Stanley Sadie. London: Macmillan.

McAllester begins by noting how the Salishan-speaking Flathead adopted musical styles and other cultural patterns from Plains tribes to the east. He emphasizes the distinction made between "real" songs obtained through visions and "make-up" music created by known composers or borrowed from other tribes. The entry describes basic elements of the (Plains-influenced) musical style and discusses historical developments such as Christian hymn singing and other Euro-American styles.

McLeod, Norma

1971   The Semantic Parameter in Music: the Blanket Rite of the Lower Kutenai. Pp. 83–101 in *Inter-American Institute for Musical Research Yearbook*, vol. 7. Austin: Department of Music and Institute of Latin American Studies, University of Texas.

The Blanket Rite is a ceremony in which a shaman (situated behind a blanket with hands and feet tied) becomes possessed and communicates with various guardian spirits of the community. Songs occur throughout the ceremony, and each is associated with a particular spirit. The paper explores how various aspects of the music symbolize these guardian spirit identities. McLeod finds that the musical structures are very diverse, validating the native belief that "each spirit has its own song" (p. 89). This includes transcriptions and analysis for nine songs. The data was collected in northern Idaho and southern Alberta (Canada) in 1964 and 1965.

Merriam, Alan P.

1951   Flathead Indian Instruments and Their Music. *Musical Quarterly* 37:368–375.

This mainly describes the flageolet (block flute) and drum as used among Flathead Indians. Merriam also discusses the musical style in general and gives musical notations for two flute melodies.

1953   (Recording) "Songs and Dances of the Flathead Indians." Smithsonian-Folkways Recordings (FE 4445).

Currently available on cassette, this album includes excellent liner notes by Merriam. The contents are identified as follows: War Dance Songs (2), Wake-Up Song, Love Songs (3), Snake Dance Song, Sweathouse Song, Canvas Dance Song, Stick Game Song, Lullaby, Life Song, Scalp Dance Songs (2), Gift Dance Song, Jump Dance Song, and Harmonica Song.

1965   The Importance of Song in the Flathead Indian Vision Quest. *Ethnomusicology* 9(2): 91–99.

This contains much information (including interesting quotations) relating to Flathead spiritual beliefs and practices. Merriam interprets the creation of vision quest songs as a result of cultural conditioning (p. 96). Based on historical sources and data collected in 1950.

1967   *Ethnomusicology of the Flathead Indians.* Viking Fund Publications in Anthropology, no. 44. Chicago: Aldine Publishing Co.

A comprehensive study of Flathead Indian music as viewed in its own cultural context and from comparative perspectives. Chapter titles are as follows: (1) Sources of Music, (2) Ideas on Music and Musicianship, (3) Sound Instruments, (4) Uses of Music, (5), Acculturation and Change, (6) Problems of Interpretation, (7) The Sample, (8) Analysis, and (9) Conclusions and Further Problems. The chapter on analysis includes 138 notations of songs belonging to thirty different categories (by function). The final chapter (Conclusions) points out problems such as that of defining Flathead style in general (as versus various sub-styles) and the difficulty of determining the relation of the Flathead musical styles to those of Salish groups to the west and Plains tribes to the east. There is a review by McAllester (1970 above).

1967b   Music and the Origin of the Flathead Indians: A Problem in Culture History. Pp. 129–138 in *Music in the Americas* edited by George List and Juan Orrego-Salas. Inter-American Music Monograph Series, no.

1. Bloomington: Indiana University Research Center in Anthropology, Folklore, and Linguistics.
This is a revised version of chapter Six in Merriam (1967a). The paper seeks to explain the fact that the Flathead speak a Salishan language (which tends to suggest western origins) while their music and related aspects of culture suggest Plains affinities. Merriam considers sources describing early population movements and concludes that tribes of the eastern Plateau and Plains culture areas are more closely connected than previously thought.

Merriam, Alan P. , and Warren L. d'Azevedo

1957   Washo Peyote Songs. *American Anthropologist* 59(4): 615–641.
This contains much information on the musical style and the social history of peyotism among the Washo. Merriam outlines the basic style of Washo peyote songs (including five musical notations) and compares that with the general style of peyote music as summarized by McAllester (General bibliography, 1949). Other topics covered here are musical values, ideas about how songs are obtained, and musical instruments.

Merriam, Alan P., and Barbara W. Merriam

1950   *Flathead Indian Music: Report on Field Research, Summer 1950.* Evanston, Illinois.
This discusses preliminary research problems identified by the authors and provides a descriptive index of their field recordings. There is also other information on ethnography, informants, and musical instruments. Could not be obtained. Information given here is from Hickerson (General bibliography, 1961:301).

See **Nettl** (1954a) in General bibliography. This contains a general description of musical style among tribes of the Great Basin area (pp. 14–18).

Opler, Marvin H.

1941   A Colorado Ute Indian Bear Dance. *Southwestern Lore* 7(2): 21–30.
This contains many descriptions of songs and dancing. It also includes a mythic narrative describing how the dance was originally taught to a Ute man by a bear who had just emerged from hi-

bernation (p. 325). Based on fieldwork conducted in 1936 and 1937.

Pantaleoni, Hewitt

1983   On Rhythmic "Dissociation" in a Salish Gift-Dance Song. *Progress Reports in Ethnomusicology* 1(1): 1–24.

This focuses on a Flathead (Interior Salishan) song which can be heard on a commercial album produced by Alan Merriam (1953 above). The song is remarkable for its complex rhythm, particularly because the tempo of the vocal melody differs from that of the (hand) drum accompaniment. Pantaleoni attempts to show that the parts are deliberately coordinated and not "dissociated" as Merriam suggests in the liner notes. Includes one melodic transcription and several other diagrams.

Park, Willard

1941   Cultural Succession in the Great Basin. Pp. 180–203 in *Language, Culture, and Personality: Essays in Memory of Edward Sapir*. Edited by Leslie Spier, A. Irving Hallowell, and Stanley Newman. Menasha: Sapir Memorial Publication Fund.

Park traces historical relationships by analyzing the distribution of several dance patterns. He focuses mainly on the Round Dance (which is the most widely distributed and presumed to be the oldest dance in the area) and on the Bear Dance (which has apparently spread into the western and central Basin more recently). Park also discusses the Rain Dance and the Hump or Masquerade Dance but without drawing conclusions about their histories. Also see Fowler for historical analysis of the Hunchback Dance (1986 above).

See **Pietroforte** (1959) in the California bibliography. This discusses songs of the (Northern) Paiute and Western Mono.

Randle, Martha C.

1953   A Shoshone Hand Game Gambling Song. *Journal of American Folklore* 66(260): 155–159.

This contains musical notations for five songs that were collected by the author in 1949.

Ray, Vernon F.

1942   Culture Element Distributions, XXII: Plateau. *University of California Anthropological Records* 8(2): 99–257.
This contains information on the presence or absence of various traits in tabular form. Includes data on musical instruments (pp. 185–187) and on dances and other ritual activities (pp. 234–255).

Reed, Verner Z.

1896   The Ute Bear Dance. *American Anthropologist* 9(4): 237–244.
This describes a Southern Ute dance that was attended by the author in March 1893. Reed discusses mythic beliefs through which the Indians identify themselves with bears, then gives a verbal description of events which took place during the four-day ceremony. Contains descriptions of singing but no musical notations.

Rhodes, Willard

1954   (Recording and notes) "Music of the American Indian: Great Basin: Paiute, Washo, Ute, Bannock, Shoshone." Library of Congress, Recorded Sound Division (AFS L38).
This is one of a series of recordings that were originally collected by Rhodes between 1940 and 1952 and have recently been reissued on cassette with updated liner notes (during the 1980s). The collection includes items from various tribes, and the following types of songs are identified: Coyote Song, Mountain Sheep Song, Round Dance Song, Hand Game Songs, Legend Song, Lullaby, Stick Game Songs, Girls' Puberty Song, (Ute) Bear Dance Song, Peyote Songs, (Ute) Turkey Dance Song, Warrior's Dance Songs, Ghost Dance Songs, and Sun Dance Songs.

See **Roberts** (1936) in the General bibliography. This contains comments on the general characteristics of vocal music among tribes of the Great Basin and Plateau areas (pp. 29, 32, and 36).

Sapir, Edward

1909   *Wishram Texts*. Publications of the American Ethnological Society, vol. 2.

This contains musical transcriptions for three songs embedded in texts, two with song texts and translations (pp. 58, 68–71, and 90–91). Sapir also gives texts and translations for seven other songs which are transcribed in rhythmic notation only (pp. 94–97, 134–135, 142–143, and 150–151).

1910   Song Recitative in Paiute Mythology. *Journal of American Folklore* 23(89): 455–472.

This contains musical notations, texts, translations, and comments relating to eleven songs which depict conversational passages in Paiute mythology. Each mythic character has his own distinctive style, even carrying over into different narratives. Sapir also notes that the songs have the following general characteristics : (1) fairly repetitive rhythmic structure, (2) words not fixed but improvised, (3) use of vocables or other "padders," (4) a distinctive melody identified with each mythic character, and (5) certain phonological transformations which distinguish the song language from ordinary speech (pp. 457–460).

1912   The Mourning Ceremony of the Southern Paiutes. *American Anthropologist* 14(1): 168–169.

Sapir distinguishes four types of songs which occur in the ceremony: Roan Songs, Bird Songs, Coyote Songs, and Mountain Sheep Songs. He notes that the texts are rarely in Paiute and that there is reason to believe that the songs and the ceremony as a whole may have been borrowed from nearby Yuman tribes (p. 169).

1930   Texts of the Kaibab Paiute and Uintah Utes. *Proceedings of the American Academy of Arts and Sciences* 65: 297–535.

This contains musical notations, texts, translations, and commentary for fifteen Paiute songs (pp. 414, 426–429, 432, 434, 436, 440, and 478–482). It also includes one transcription of a Uintah Ute song (p. 508). Texts and translations only are given for several other songs.

[1992a]   Texts of the Kaibab Paiutes and Uintah Utes. Pp. 315–555 in *The Collected Works of Edward Sapir, Volume 4: Ethnology*. Edited by William Bright. Berlin and New York: Mouton de Gruyter.

This is a posthumous work based on manuscripts from Sapir's research circa 1909–1910. It contains translated texts concerning the mythic origins of the Mourning Ceremony (pp. 365–367) and the Bear Dance (pp. 368–371). Another mythic text about the Round Dance gives musical notations for (3) songs that were performed by Rat, Deer, and Mountain Sheep (pp. 446–449). There is also another section on recitative songs in Paiute myths, with notations for six songs performed by animal characters (pp. 499–503).

[1992b]   Kaibab Paiute Ethnographic Notes. Pp. 785–865 in *The Collected Works of Edward Sapir, Volume 4: Ethnology.* Edited by William Bright. Berlin and New York: Mouton de Gruyter.

A posthumous work based on information Sapir collected from Tony Tillohash (Southern Paiute) in 1910. This contains sections concerning the Mourning Ceremony (pp. 834–842), the Ghost Dance (p. 843), Paiute names for various types of songs (pp. 847–848), the Bear dance (pp. 848–851), and the Round Dance (pp. 851–852).

[1994]   Southern Paiute Song Texts. Edited by Robert Franklin and Pamela Bunte. With a Note on Musical Transcriptions by Thomas Vennum, Jr. Pp. 589–708 in *The Collected Works of Edward Sapir, Volume 4: Ethnology.* Edited by Regna Darnell and Judith Irvine. Berlin and New York: Mouton de Gruyter.

A posthumous work containing musical notations, song texts, and notes (including many with translations) for 209 songs that Sapir collected from Tony Tillohash (Southern Paiute) in 1910. The editors provide descriptions of the musical genres represented, with sections on: (1) Cry or Mourning Songs, (2) Round Dance Songs, (3) Ghost Dance Songs, (4) Bear Dance Songs, and (5) Medicine Songs and Others. The musical notations were produced by Jacob Sapir, the collector's father. The recordings are available at the Archives of Traditional Music at Indiana University. See the catalogue by Lee (1984) or Seeger and Spear (1987).

See **Seeger and Spear** (1987) in the General bibliography for a list of cylinder recordings at the Archives of Traditional Music (Indiana University). The collection includes early recordings from the following Great Basin and Plateau area tribes: Flathead, Klamath, Kutenai, Nez Perce, Paiute (Northern and Southern), Sahaptin, Shoshone, Thompson River, Ute (various sub-groups), Wishram, and Yakima.

Shimkin, Demitri B.

1942   Dynamics of Recent Wind River Shoshone History.
              American Anthropologist 44:451–462.
      This examines various adaptations of Wind River Shoshone
culture in response to pressures from white civilization, beginning
from the earliest direct contacts circa 1801. Shimkin argues that
there was a deliberate quest for new religious values, describing
the introduction of the Sun Dance, Ghost Dance, Peyotism, and
various other cults or dances adapted from other tribes. Some
lesser known ones mentioned here include the Wolf Dance
(adapted from the Crow Hot Dance), the Women's Dance (from
the Gros Ventre), and the Cree Dance (from the Cree).

1953   *The Wind River Shoshone Sun Dance.* Bureau of
              American Ethnology Bulletin no. 151, pp. 399–491.
      This is a classic study based on historical sources and field-
work conducted in Wyoming circa 1937–1938. Shimkin begins by
giving comparative and historical information on an older Sun
Dance complex of the mid-nineteenth century (pp. 403–434). He
then describes modern forms of the Sun Dance (with marked
Christian influences) as it took shape among the Wind River
Shoshone by 1905 (pp. 435–471). Translations of songs and
prayers are given throughout, and there are excellent historical
photographs of the dancers (following p. 484).

Spier, Leslie

1930   *Klamath Ethnography.* University of California
              Publications in American Archaeology and
              Ethnology 30.
      This contains information on musical instruments (pp. 88–90)
and texts and translations for eleven songs (pp. 88, 131–138). 130
other song texts are given in English only, and there is a description of shamanistic singing.

1935   *The Prophet Dance of the Northwest and its Deriv-
              atives: The Source of the Ghost Dance.* American
              Anthropological Association General Series in
              Anthropology 1. Menasha, Wisconsin: George Banta
              Publishing Co. 74 pages.
      This gives background information on nativistic religious
movements that transformed Indian cultures of the Plateau and adjacent areas during the nineteenth and early twentieth centuries.
Not much information on music.

Also see Spier (1921) in Plains bibliography. This discusses the diffusion of the Sun Dance among tribes of the Great Basin and Plateau areas.

Spinden, Herbert J.

1907–1915   *The Nez Percé Indians.* Memoirs of the American Anthropological Association, vol. 2 (part 3), pp. 65–274.

This contains information on musical instruments (pp. 230–231). Songs are discussed in a section on "Acquisition of Guardian Spirits" (pp. 247–250), and the section entitled "Ceremonies" (pp. 261–267) contains descriptions of the Guardian Spirit Dance, the War Dance, and the Scalp Dance.

Steward, Julian H.

1932   A Uintah Ute Bear Dance, March 1931. *American Anthropologist* 34(2): 121–130.

Steward describes the dance as performed during the 1930s and also gives information on earlier versions of the dance as described by Ute persons he interviewed. There is a description of songs which are accompanied by the playing of wooden rasps (pp. 266–267).

1933   Ethnography of the Owens Valley Paiute. *University of California Publications in American Archaeology and Ethnology* 33(3): 231–350.

This gives brief descriptions of instruments (pp. 277–278) followed by musical transcriptions (with texts, translations, and commentary) for 18 songs (pp. 278–285). Steward later describes the dances in which the songs were used (pp. 320–323). Based on research conducted in 1927 and 1928. Recordings of the songs are available at Hearst Museum. See the catalogue by Keeling (California bibliography, 1992).

1941   Culture Element Distributions, XIII: Nevada Shoshone. *University of California Anthropological Records* 4(2): 209–358.

This contains information on the presence or absence of various traits in tabular form. It includes data on musical instruments (pp. 251) and various dance rituals (pp. 255–256 and 265–266).

1943   Culture Element Distributions, XXIII: Northern and
                Gosiute Shoshoni. *University of California*
                Anthropological Records 8(3): 263–392.
    This contains brief descriptions of dances (pp. 287–290) iden-
tified as follows: Circle Dance, Back-and-Forth Dance or Bear
Dance, Rabbit Dance, Scalp Dances, Sun Dance, War Dance, and
Kwapakin. Also includes data on musical instruments (p. 278) and
the girls' puberty ceremony (p. 280).

Stewart, Omer C.

1941   Culture Element Distributions, XIV: Northern Paiute.
                University of California Anthropological Records
                4(3): 361–446
    This contains information on the presence or absence of vari-
ous traits in tabular form. It includes data on musical instruments
(p. 403) and various ritual activities (pp. 410–418).

1942   Culture Element Distributions, XVIII: Ute-Southern
                Paiute. *University of California Anthropological*
                Records 6(4): 231–356.
    Contains information on the presence or absence of various
traits in tabular form. It includes data on musical instruments (pp.
294) and various dances (pp. 321–324). There are also photos of
peyote tipi interior and exterior (following p. 356).

See **Suttles** (1957) in Northwest Coast bibliography. This discusses the
    spread of the Plateau Prophet Dance among the Coast Salish.

Teit, James Alexander

1900   *The Thompson Indians of British Columbia*. Pp. 163–
                392 in Jesup North Pacific Expedition 1. Memoirs of
                the American Museum of the Natural History, vol. 2.
                Leiden/New York. Reprinted by AMS Press (New
                York, 1975).
    The chapter entitled "Art" (pp. 376–386) is written by Franz
Boas, and this contains a section which lists various types of songs
and describes musical instruments (pp. 383–385).

1930   *The Salishan Tribes of the Western Plateaus*. Annual
                Report of the Bureau of American Ethnology (1927–
                1928) 45:23–396. Washington: Smithsonian
                Institution.

This contains brief descriptions of musical instruments among the Coeur d'Alêne (pp. 164–165) and Okanagon (p. 278).

Turney-High, Harry H.

1941   *Ethnography of Kutenai.* Memoirs of the American Anthropological Association, vol. 56. 202 pages.
The section on "Music" (pp. 102–110) contains nine musical examples transcribed by an associate (Gladys Pierson) and comments on general characteristics of the music.

Vander, Judith

1982   The Song Repertoire of Four Shoshone Women: A Reflection of Cultural Movements and Sex Roles. *Ethnomusicology* 26(1): 73–84.
This is possibly the first article to expressly address the fact that women were generally neglected in published writings on American Indian music. Vander discusses the song repertory of each woman in relation to her life experience, religious beliefs, traditional values, and ideas about music. As the women represent a gamut of different ages (23, 43, 53, and 71), the essay gives interesting insights on recent culture history.

1986   Shoshone (Music). Pp. 221–222 in *The New Grove Dictionary of American Music*, vol. 4 (R–Z). Edited by H. Wiley Hitchcock and Stanley Sadie. London: Macmillan.
This focuses mainly on regional variations in Shoshone music and culture. The eastern (Wind River) Shoshone are characterized as having a basically northern Plains musical style. Western Shoshone music (typified by songs of the Ghost Dance) is described as being more indigenous to the Great Basin area. Northern groups also share the basic Great Basin style but with influences from the Plains and Plateau. Finally, according to Vander, the southern Shoshone (Comanche) are described as having a southern Plains musical repertory.

1986   *Ghost Dance Songs and Religion of a Wind River Shoshone Woman.* Monograph Series in Ethnomusicology, no. 4. Los Angeles: Program in Ethnomusicology, Department of Music, University of California, Los Angeles.
This contains detailed analyses of 17 Ghost Dance songs performed by Emily Hill during the late 1970s. Chapter 2 ("The

Naraya," pp. 7–14) argues that the 1890 Ghost Dance was based on an earlier dance that was ancient among the Shoshone. In her musical analysis, Vander focuses on subtle variations in the paired phrase structure considered to be a distinctive characteristic of Ghost Dance songs by Herzog (General bibliography, 1935). This also contains translations and detailed analyses of the texts based on comments by Emily Hill (pp. 37–62).

1988   *Songprints: The Musical Experience of Five Shoshone Women.* Urbana: University of Illinois Press.

The title expresses Vander's idea that each woman's song repertory reflects her life experiences and personality in a unique manner. The five women represent different generations, and thus the book provides much historical information on music as related to cultural developments such as the Ghost Dance, the Native American Church, and the modern powwow movement. Vander provides notations and analysis for 77 songs, 26 of which can be heard on an accompanying cassette tape which is also available from the publishers.

1989   From the Musical Experience of Five Shoshone Women. Pp. 5–12 in *Women in North American Indian Music* edited by Richard Keeling. Ann Arbor: Society for Ethnomusicology.

Vander begins by discussing beliefs concerning menstruation as a factor limiting the musical activities of women in the Ghost Dance and the Sun Dance. She then describes the complementary relationship between male and female singers in the Sun Dance and the "unisex" singing of Handgame songs. Finally, she mentions the recent emergence of female drum groups performing the War Dance since the 1950s.

Vennum, Thomas, Jr.

1986   Music. Pp. 682–704 in *Handbook of the North American Indians, Volume 11: Great Basin.* Edited by Warren d'Azevedo. Washington: Smithsonian Institution.

An excellent study which summarizes previous literature and gives Vennum's own conclusions based on analysis of historical recordings and other sources. Vennum states that the Great Basin contains at least three musical sub-areas: (1) northeastern, (2) western, and (3) southwestern. He then describes each of the musical styles in comparative terms, providing 16 musical examples and commentary. The essay also includes separate discussions on instruments and musical styles of the Ghost Dance, Bear Dance, and Peyote religion.

[1994]   See under Sapir (1994 above).

Wilkes, Charles

1845   Narrative of the United States Exploring Expedition, during the Years 1838–1842. 5 vols. Philadelphia.
     Volume four (p.400) contains transcriptions for three songs (with texts) from the Walla Walla Indians of Washington State. Could not be obtained. The musical examples are quoted in Baker (General bibliography, 1882:138).

VI. Southwest

Aberle, David F.

1967   The Navaho Singer's Fee: Payment or Prestation? Pp. 15–32 in *Studies in Southwestern Ethnolinguistics: Meaning and History in Languages of the American Southwest* edited by Dell Hymes and William Bittle. The Hague: Mouton and Co.

Focuses on the Navajo belief that a curing ceremony will not be effective unless the ceremonialist is paid. The author notes that ritual offerings to the supernaturals and compensation in material goods to a Navajo singer are known by the same term in the Navajo language. He then discusses reciprocal relationships in other (economic and political) spheres of Navajo life, concluding that "an unbroken chain of reciprocity binds the supernatural figure, the singer, and the patient together" (p. 27).

Bahr, Donald M.

1980   Four Papago Rattlesnake Songs. Pp. 118–126 in *Speaking, Singing, and Teaching: A Multidisciplinary Approach to Language Variation: Proceedings of the Eighth Annual Southwestern Language and Linguistics Workshop* edited by Florence Barkin and Elizabeth Brant. Anthropological Research Papers, no. 20. Tempe: Arizona State University.

Analyzes the texts of a cycle of songs for curing rattlesmake sickness. Bahr provides the native texts and interlinear translations in an Appendix (pp. 124–125). The main body of the paper discusses some major themes that connect or unify the texts of the four songs. These mainly involve the movements, sounds, and emotions of the rattlesnake.

1983   Pima and Papago Medicine and Philosophy. Pp. 193–
200 in *Handbook of North American Indians, Volume
10: Southwest* edited by Alfonso Ortiz. Washington:
Smithsonian Institution.
  The section on "Ritual Cures" (p. 197) describes use of songs,
with translations of two texts quoted from Underhill (1946 below).
This also includes a photograph of a Papago man singing curing
songs in front of a sand painting (p. 198).

Bahr, Donald M., Juan Gregorio, David Lopez, and Albert Alvarez

1974   *Piman Shamanism and Staying Sickness.* Tucson:
University of Arizona Press.
  Could not be obtained for inspection of contents nor could in-
formation be gotten from other sources.

Bahr, Donald M., Joseph Giff, and Manuel Havier

1979   Piman Songs on Hunting. *Ethnomusicology* 23(2):
245–296.
  Examines three song cycles based on themes involving hunting or herding cattle. These are curing songs as described in Bahr
and Haefer (1978 below). The authors mainly consider how the cycles function as literature, analyzing narrative mode and other aspects of textual content. Contains no musical examples but
rhythmic analyses are given along with the free and interlinear
translations of texts. The pattern of references to night and day in
songs leads Bahr to conclude that singing and hunting are part of
the same phenomenon in Piman thought (p. 268). Based on data
from Giff (Papago) and Havier (Pima).

Bahr, Donald M., Joseph Giff, and J. Richard Haefer

1978   Song in Piman Curing. *Ethnomusicology* 22(1): 89–
122.
  This study focuses on a set of "blowing" songs that were
recorded in the context of an actual curing session. The authors begin by discussing native concepts of sickness, the Piman nomencla-
ture for curing songs, and the use of songs in a curing session. This
is followed by free and interlinear translations of a cycle of songs
concerning jimsonweed (pp. 94–98). Finally there are analyses of
the texts, rhythms, melodic structures, and musical forms. The paper contains no melodic transcriptions, as the authors feel many
Pimans might object if the songs were made accessible (p. 92).

Bahti, Tom

1970   *Southwestern Indian Ceremonials.* Las Vegas, Nevada: K. C. Publications. Revised in 1982 by Mark Bahti.
This is an oversized book (64 pp.) with abundant painted illustrations and photographs. It is a sort of classic for non-specialist readers and has gone through numerous printings. It contains information on myths and ceremonies for each of the following groups: Navajo, Rio Grande Pueblos, Zuni, Hopi Pueblos, Apache, Tohono O'odham (Papago), and Yaqui. There is also a calendar of southwestern Indian ceremonial events (pp. 62–63).

Bailey, Florence M.

1924   Some Plays and Dances of the Taos Indians. *Natural History* 24: 85–95.
Bailey describes a "Foot-Racing Dance" and an amusing event in which clowns climbed a pole to obtain prizes at the top. She also includes comments on the Buffalo Dance and Deer Dance. This contains superb historical photographs. No musical notations.

Bakkegard, B.M., and E.A. Morris

1961   Seventh Century Flutes from Arizona. *Ethnomusicology* 5(3): 184–186.
This describes four instruments which were excavated from a cave site in northeastern Arizona in 1931. The authors analyze the scales or tunings (which were nearly the same for each of the instruments) and speculate on how the flutes were used.

Ballinger, Franchot

1978   The Responsible Center: Man and Nature in Pueblo and Navaho Songs and Prayers. *American Quarterly* 30(Spring): 90–107.
Ballinger argues against the common view that Native American cosmologies are based on (passive) identification with nature while Europeans view man's role as being manipulative and separate from nature. He examines several ritual songs and prayers in order to show how Pueblo and Navajo Indians attempt to control the natural and supernatural worlds, exerting "creative control of the universe" (p. 91). This includes free translations of 14 songs and prayers (all quoted from earlier studies).

Barker, George C.

1957   Some Aspects of Penitential Processions in Spain and
            the American Southwest. *Journal of American
            Folklore* 70:137–142.
      This first describes Holy Week processions as observed by the
author in Spain in 1954, then describes analogous processions in
isolated Spanish communities of northern New Mexico and among
the Yaqui Indians of Arizona. Barker attempts to explain the differences between these ceremonies in concluding remarks.

Bartoli, Jane F.

1955   The Apache "Devil Dance." *Musical Courier* 152(8):
            8–10.
      A description of the Mescalero *Gahan* Dance intended mainly
for general readers. Bartoli does discuss basic characteristics of the
music, noting the prominence of major triads and wide intervals
and commenting on the uniqueness of the style in the overall
sphere of Indian music (p. 10).

Baxter, R.H.

1895   The Moqui Snake Dance. *American Antiquarian (and
            Oriental Journal)* 17:205–207.
      This is one of many early writings which describe the ritual in
sensationalistic terms and from a western ethnocentric perspective.
See also Bourke (1884 below).

See **Beatty** (1974) in the Plains bibliography for study of Kiowa-
      Apache music.

Benedict, Ruth

1959   They Dance for Rain in Zuni. Pp. 222–225 in *An
            Anthropologist at Work* edited by Margaret Mead.
            Boston: Houghton Mifflin Co.
      A short paper originally written during the 1920s. Benedict fo-
cuses on the purpose of summertime rituals to compel the forces of
nature, giving general descriptions of the songs and dances.

Black, Robert A.

1964   A Content-Analysis of Eighty-One Hopi Indian
            Chants. Doctoral dissertation, Indiana University.

These chants are announcements made by adult males from rooftops in the Hopi village. There are two categories: (1) religious chants addressed to the deities, and (2) secular chants which are addressed to the inhabitants of the village and deal with community issues. This study examines the textual structure of chants for various purposes and how they differ in style from other forms of verbal behavior. Based on fieldwork conducted in 1960.

1966   Hopi Rabbit-Hunt Chants: A Ritualized Language. Pp. 7–11 in *Essays on the Verbal and Visual Arts* edited by June Helm. American Ethnological Society Proceedings. Distributed by the University of Washington Press (1967).

Based on information from the general study by Black (1964 above). This paper examines the special characteristics of chants used to announce or call people to participate in a hunt. Unlike some other types of secular chants, these have religious connotations and in the past were only made by members of the bear and badger clans. Black discusses these practices and analyzes the content of the chants. The paper mentions a female deity who is viewed as the mother of animals or controller of game animals. Also discusses special words used in reference to animals or locations and other stereotyped language.

1967   Hopi Grievance Chants: A Mechanism of Social Control. Pp. 33–53 in *Studies in Southwestern Ethnolinguistics: Meaning and History in Languages of the American Southwest* edited by Dell Hymes and William Bittle. The Hague: Mouton and Co.

Based on information from the general study by Black (1964 above). The paper deals with chants for redressing grievances and maintaining intra-village harmony. These serve as restraints on socially unacceptable behavior such as damage to orchards or corn fields by either humans or animals. This includes three sample texts and translations.

See **Boekelman** (1936) in the General bibliography. This discusses a prehistoric shell trumpet found in Arizona.

"Borderlands from Conjunto to Chicken Scratch" (Sound Recording)

1993   (Compact Disc) Produced by Texas Folklife Resources. Smithsonian/Folkways (SF CD40418).
"Chicken scratch" (also called *waila* in Papago) is a form of Hispanic-derived social dance music popular among Indians of southern Arizona. Several different groups are featured on this compact disc, issued with liner notes by James Griffith. For more information on the genre, see also Griffith (1979 below).

Boulton, Laura

1957   (Recording and liner notes) "Indian Music of the Southwest." Smithsonian-Folkways (FE 8850).
Currently reissued on cassette, this album contains a wide sampling of different musical styles from the following tribes: Apache (Mescalero), Apache (San Carlos), Hopi, Mohave, Navajo, Papago, Pima, San Ildefonso, Santa Ana, Taos, and Zuni.

Bourke, J.G.

1884   *The Snake-Dance of the Moqui of Arizona.* New York: Charles Scribner's Sons.
This is the earliest of many writings which describe snake handling and other aspects of the ceremony in sensational and ethnocentric terms. Despite its limitations, this large book (371 pp.) contains much interesting information. There is (for example) a description of Hopi Indians chanting the Catholic rosary in a native musical style (p. 16). The book also contains three chapters (18, 19, and 20) summarizing earlier sources on serpent worship in other cultures, including that of the Aztecs (see pp. 221–224).

1885   The Urine Dance of the Zunis. *Proceedings of American Association for Advancement of Science* 34:400–404.
Describes a dance observed by the author and Frank Cushing in November 1881. The performance involved much clowning and mockery, including a parody of Mexican Catholics. At one point the dancers were served a mock "feast" at which they drank large quantities of urine.

1895   The Snake Ceremonials at Walpi. *American Anthropologist* 8:192–196.

This is yet another of many accounts which characterized the ceremony as "weird" (p. 192). In this paper Bourke also comments on similar customs among the Mohave, Apache, and Aztecs (p. 194).

Brady, Margaret K.

1981   Book review of *Language and Art in the Navajo Universe* by Gary Witherspoon (1977). *Ethnomusicology* 25(1):136–37.

An enthusiastic review which comments on Witherspoon's analysis of Navajo song texts to illustrate his central thesis that mental and physical phenomena are inseparable in Navajo cosmology.

Brown, Donald N.

1961   The Development of Taos Dance. *Ethnomusicology* 5(7): 33–41.

This paper focuses mainly on the influences of culture contact and acculturation on public dances. See also the reply by Pilling (1962 below).

1967   The Distribution of Sound Instruments in the Prehistoric Southwestern United States. *Ethnomusicology* 11(1): 71–90.

In this paper Brown plots the distribution of idiophones and aerophones as identified through bibliographic and museum research. He concludes that two basic chronological strata can be distinguished: (1) instruments dated prior to 1000 AD (including lesser divisions pre-600 and post-600) and (2) instruments dated later (with sub-divisions before and after 1300). The latter period (after 1000 AD) is characterized by greater variety of instruments.

1971   Ethnomusicology and Prehistoric Southwest. *Ethnomusicology* (15)3: 363–378.

Basically a further discussion of topics raised in Brown (1967 above). This paper gives more information on idiophones and aerophones from archeological inventories (membranophones and chordophones both being absent) and also speculates on the dances or other contexts in which these were possibly used. Brown attempts to speculate on the character of prehistoric Hohokam dances through analysis of iconography on ceramic pieces from archeological sites (pp. 371–372).

1974   Evidence for Dance from Prehistoric Southwest.
            Congress on Research in Dance (CORD). *Dance*
            Research Annual 6:263–284.
    Analyzes representations on painted pottery and references in
the ethnographic literature in order to speculate on the character of
native dances during various prehistoric periods. Brown discusses
evidence relating to the Hohokam, Mogollon, and Anasazi cultures
(pp. 264–271).

1980   Dance as Experience: The Deer Dance of Picuris
            Pueblo. In *Southwestern Indian Ritual Drama* edited
            by Charlotte Frisbie. Albuquerque: University of
            New Mexico Press.
    Describes the Deer Dance and analyzes the symbols and
"feelings" which characterize local Indian concepts of the ritual.

1986   Taos (Music). Page 350 in *The New Grove*
            Dictionary of American Music, vol. 4 (R–Z). Edited
            by H. Wiley Hitchcock and Stanley Sadie. London:
            Macmillan.
    This brief survey emphasizes the eclectic character of the Taos
musical repertory. Brown first describes basic characteristics of the
indigenous (Taos) musical style. He then discusses influences from
the Plains region (through contacts with the Kiowa), from other
Pueblos, and from the Spanish. Spanish influence is particularly
significant in music for the matachines dance, which is performed
by Spanish-American musicians.

1986   Book review of *The Matachines Dance of the Upper*
            Rio Grande by Flavia Waters Champe (1983).
            Ethnomusicology 30(2): 362–365.
    Basically a favorable review, but Brown does question
Champe's use of theatrical concepts in analyzing the course of performance events. He also discusses the unusual relationship between the Pueblo Indian dancers and the Spanish-American musicians who accompany the dance by playing the violin and guitar.

Brown, Herbert

1906   A Pima-Maricopa Ceremony. *American Anthropol-*
            ogist 8:689–690.
    Describes a ceremony in which male dancers wear phallic or-
naments and imitate humans and animals in copulation. Songs are
mentioned, but the music is not described in much detail. Includes
no transcriptions.

Bunzel, Ruth L.

1932a   *Introduction to Zuñi Ceremonialism.* Bureau of American Ethnology, Annual Report (1929–1930) 47:467–544.
The section on "Singing and Dancing" (pp. 494–498) contains a list of songs and general description of singing.

1932b   *Zuñi Katcinas: An Analytical Study.* Bureau of American Ethnology, Annual Report (1929–1930) 47:837–1086.

A comprehensive study which considers religious concepts relating to the Katcinas, masks and costumes, organization of the Katcina society, and preparations for the dances. The section on "Patterns of Singing and Dancing" discusses rhythmic elements and the structure of Zuñi music.

See **Burlin** (1907) in the General bibliography. This contains the following musical notations (with texts, translations, and commentary): three Pima songs (pp. 316–320 and 551), three Apache songs (pp. 324–328 and 551), four Mohave-Apache songs (pp. 329–338), one Yuma song (p. 340–343 and 551), 12 Navajo songs (pp. 352–421 and 551–556), 5 Zuni songs (pp. 430–444 and 556–557), one San Juan Pueblo song (pp. 449–450), three Acoma songs (pp. 447 and 451–457), three Laguna songs (pp. 462–470 and 558), and nine Hopi songs (pp. 479–532 and 558–560).

Champe, Flavia Waters

1983   *The Matachines Dance of the Upper Rio Grande: History, Music, and Choreography.* Lincoln: University of Nebraska Press.

Begins by discussing the European origins of the dance, how it became transformed in Native American versions, and how it was introduced to Rio Grande Pueblo communities. Champe focuses mainly on the Matachines Dance at San Ildefonso, providing detailed choreographic analyses and musical transcriptions. This also includes musical examples on a 7-inch disc. Champe concludes that the performance symbolizes Montezuma's struggle to accept Christianity and that it was introduced into the Rio Grande area by Spanish colonists during the reconquest of 1692 (pp. 84–85). She makes interesting comments on the participation of Spanish-American musicians who "were uncertain of any sequence or names for the melodies" (p. 20). There is a review by Brown (1986 above).

Charters, Samuel B.

1957   (Recording and liner notes) "Yaqui Dances: the Pascola Music of the Yaqui Indians of Northern Mexico." Ethnic Folkways Recordings (FE 6957).
        This contains music recorded in Sonora (Mexico) in July 1956. Various selections feature harp and violin playing together with gourd rattles and other indigenous instruments. The contents are listed as follows: Heragua Loque, Paloma, Papusa, Mundo, Aguedada, Paloma, and Maria Loreta.

Clark, LaVerne H.

1966   *They Sang for Horses: The Impact of the Horse on Navajo and Apache Folklore.* Tucson: University of Arizona Press.
        Includes translations for 17 songs, mainly in the chapters entitled "Magic and Ritual of the Raid for Horses" (pp. 85–122) and "The Horse's Role in Other Ceremonies" (pp. 190–208). Based primarily on classic studies by Haile, Matthews, Opler, Reichard, and others.

See **Curtis** (1907–1930) in the General bibliography. *Volume Twelve* contains the following: three Hopi melodies with texts and translations (pp. 239–242); and three Hopi song texts, two translated (pp. 43, 151, and 153). *Volume Seventeen* contains six Tewa song texts and translations (pp. 14, 48, 68, 69, and 77) and eight songs in translation only (pp. 49, 52, 56, 77, and 79).

Davis, Edward H.

1920   The Papago Ceremony of Víkita. *Heye Foundation, Indian Notes and Monographs* 3:155–177.
        Based on the author's observations in northern Sonora (Mexico) and southern Arizona in the summer of 1920. Davis begins by describing the myth on which the ceremony is based (pp. 155–165). This involves a local culture hero called "Montezuma" who kills a monster and takes his heart. The name does not refer to the Aztec Montezuma but is presumed to be adopted as a result of Spanish contacts. There is then a verbal description of the cere-

mony, which involves drinking of a liquor made from saguaro cactus (pp. 165–177). This contains much information on dances, musical instruments, and song cycles. Also includes photographs of the dancing.

Densmore, Frances

1929   *Papago Music.* Bureau of American Ethnology Bulletin no. 90.
Contains musical notations for 167 songs (some with native texts and most with English translations) collected by Densmore in 1920 and 1921. There is musical analysis and cultural commentary for each song, and the entire corpus is compared with 820 songs analyzed in previous research by Densmore.

1932a   A Resemblance Between Yuman and Pueblo Songs. *American Anthropologist* 34:694–700.
This focuses on certain rhythmic patterns which Densmore considers typical in Indian music from the Southwest.

1932b   *Yuman and Yaqui Music.* Bureau of American Ethnology Bulletin no. 110.
Contains musical notations for 130 songs collected by Densmore in 1922. English words are given for some of the songs, but native texts are lacking. The tribes represented include the Yuma (80 songs), Cocopa (30), Mohave (4), Yaqui (15), and Mayo (1). There is musical analysis for each song, and the local styles are compared. The entire corpus is then compared with 1,343 songs from other tribes the author had previously studied. There is a review by Herzog (1933 below). Densmore's manner of translating Yaqui songs is also criticized by Evers and Molina (1987:25–27 below).

1938   *Music of Santo Domingo Pueblo.* Southwest Museum Papers, no. 12.
This includes musical notations for 103 songs which were obtained from a single informant. There is commentary on each of the songs, and the whole corpus is compared with 1,553 other songs the author previously studied using a (quantitative) tabular method.

See Densmore (1941) in the General bibliography for information on Yaqui songs.

1951   (Recording and liner notes) "Songs of the Yuma,
              Cocopa, and Yaqui." Library of Congress, Music
              Division, Recorded Sound Section (AAFS L 24).
      The contents are identified as follows: Yuma Deer Dance
Songs (7), Yaqui Deer Dance Songs (3), Cocopa Bird Dance Songs
(5), Cocopa *Tcumanpa 'Xwa* Dance Song, Yuma Lightning Dance
Songs (2), Yuma Songs Used in the Treatment of the Sick (2),
Yuman Song with Creation Legend, and Cocopa Songs with
Creation Legend (5).

1952   (Recording and liner notes) "Songs of the Papago."
              Library of Congress, Music Division, Recorded
              Sound Section (AAFS L 31).
      The contents are identified as follows: Songs Connected with
Legends (8), Songs Connected with Ceremonies (8), Songs
Connected with Expeditions to Obtain Salt, Songs Connected with
Treatment of the Sick (4), Dream Songs (2), War Songs, (3), Songs
of the Kicking Ball Race, and Unidentified (1).

1957   *Music of Acoma, Isleta, Cochiti, and Zuni Pueblos.*
              Bureau of American Ethnology Bulletin no. 165.
      Contains musical notations and analysis for 82 songs collected
by Densmore among the Acoma (40), Isleta (18), Cochiti (9), and
Zuñi (15) in 1928, 1930, and 1940. There is background information for each song, and various genres or song types are discussed.
The whole corpus is compared with previous collections studied by
the author. See the critical reviews by Kurath (1958) and Nettl
(1959).

Dorsey, George Amos, and Henry R. Voth

1901   *The Oraibi Soyal Ceremony.* Field Columbian Muse-
              um Publications, no. 55. Anthropological Series vol.
              3, no. 1.
      This describes a nine-day winter solstice ceremonial as ob-
served on various occasions between 1893 and 1900. The authors
focus on ritual activities (particularly the social organization of ritual societies) but also give verbal descriptions of songs (pp. 24–25
and passim). Includes rare historical photographs and drawings.

1902   *The Mishongnovi Ceremonies of the Snake and
              Antelope Fraternities.* Field Columbian Museum
              Publications, no. 66. Anthropological Series vol. 3,
              no. 3, pp. 161–261.

Describes secret society ceremonials as practiced in a Hopi village between 1893 and 1900. The rituals occur in August and last ten days. Contains descriptions of singing (pp. 214–216, 221–222, and 229) and historical photographs.

Dozier, Edward P.

1957   Rio Grande Pueblo Ceremonial Patterns. *New Mexico Quarterly Review* (Summer).
Could not be obtained for inspection of contents nor could information be gotten from other sources.

1958   Cultural Matrix of Singing and Chanting in Tewa Pueblos. *International Journal of American Linguistics* 24:68–72.
A brief but substantive paper which gives an overview of contexts for songs and dances among the Rio Grande Tewa and then compares this with analogous data for the Arizona Tewa groups. Dozier concludes with general comments on chants and speech-making.

1958   Spanish-Catholic Influences in Rio Grande Pueblo Religion. *American Anthropologist* 60:441–448.
This focuses on patterns of acculturation in ceremonies and particularly the manner in which the Indians were able to conceal important aspects of the native ceremonial system while openly celebrating Spanish-Catholic observances. Dozier classifies indigenous ceremonies as belonging to four categories in a continuum from sacred to secular. No musical examples.

Drucker, Philip

1941   Culture Element Distributions, XVII: Yuman-Piman. *University of California Anthropological Records* 6(3): 91–228.
This contains information on the presence or absence of various traits in tabular form. Includes data relating to musical instruments (p. 124) and various dances and other rituals (pp. 141, 145, and 148–162).

Evers, Larry, and Felipe S. Molina

1987   *Yaqui Deer Songs, Maso Bwikam: A Native American Poetry*. Tucson: University of Arizona Press.

The book is a collaboration between a professional scholar (Evers) and a younger Yaqui man who is himself a deer singer. The two of them provide translations and comments on songs they collected in Arizona and Sonora (Mexico) between 1979 and 1983. Four song sequences are presented in their entirety, and several other individual songs are also translated. The authors stress the narrative element and mainly seek to demonstrate the significance of the song cycles as a genre of native literature. Musical analysis is lacking, but the book contains a chapter ("One Night of Songs") describing the contexts of the singing. There is also an accompanying cassette tape containing nine songs performed by Molina (with Timothy Cruz). Reviewed by Keeling (1988 below).

Farrer, Claire

1980   Singing for Life: The Mescalero Apache Girls' Puberty Ceremony. Pp. 125–160 in *Southwestern Indian Ritual Drama* edited by Charlotte Frisbie. Albuquerque: University of New Mexico Press.
        Examines the ritual as an expression of Mescalero identity and discusses how it expresses certain cultural values such as generosity. Farrer suggests that the event should be understood as a "rite of confirmation" rather than a rite of passage.

Fewkes, Jesse Walter

1890   On the Use of the Phonograph among Zuni Indians. *American Naturalist* 24:687–691.
        Describes the collecting of Zuni songs by Fewkes in 1890.

1891a   A Suggestion as to the Meaning of the Moki Snake Dance. *Journal of American Folklore* 4:129–138.
        Fewkes characterizes the Snake Dance as an elaboration of an earlier ritual known as *Lay-la-tuk* and explains that the snake tends to symbolize water, being regarded as the guardian of springs in Moki thought.

1893   A Central American Ceremony Which Suggests the Snake Dance of the Tusayan Villagers. *American Anthropologist* (old series) 6:285–306.
        This describes an Aztec ceremony that was documented during the sixteenth century by Bernardino de Sahagún and points out parallels between this and the Snake Dance as practiced at Hopi pueblos. This includes translations of segments from a manuscript

in Nahuatl and of Sahagún's comments on the ritual. Also see writings of Sahagún in the Mexico bibliography.

1894a   Snake Ceremonials at Walpi. *Journal of American Ethnology and Archaeology* 4(1): 1–126.
The section on "Melodies of the Snake Dance" (pp. 98–101) describes songs performed in this Hopi ceremony. Some of the song texts are translated, but the paper includes no musical transcriptions.

1894b   The Walpi Flute Observance. *Journal of American Folklore* 7:265–287.
Fewkes discusses the social organization of the Flute fraternity, then describes biannual rituals performed in winter and summer. This contains several references to songs but no musical transcriptions or song texts.

1895a   The Oraibi Flute Altar. *Journal of American Folklore* 8:265–282.
This contains several references to music, including a description of flutes being played "in harmony with the songs" (p. 270). Does not include musical examples.

1895b   Provisional List of Annual Ceremonies at Walpi. *Internationales Archiv für Ethnographie* 8:215–238.
Could not be obtained for inspection of contents nor could information be gotten from other sources.

1895c   A Comparison of Sia and Tusayan Snake Ceremonials. *American Anthropologist* (old series) 8:118–141.
The comparison yields many parallels, from which Fewkes concludes that the eastern and western pueblos share a culture that is basically the same (p. 141). Contains no references to music.

1899   Hopi Basket Dances. *Journal of American Folklore* 12:81–96.
The Basket Dance is a public event which marks the end of an esoteric nine-day ritual (called *Lalakonti*). Fewkes compares the Basket Dances at five different pueblos, as observed in October 1898. Songs are frequently mentioned. The author's concluding remarks focus on the history of the ritual, noting that it contains "survivals of an early totemism which are not understood by present priests" (p. 95).

1900   The New Fire Ceremony at Walpi. *American Anthropologist* 2:80–138.

This describes a ceremony observed by Fewkes in November 1898. Songs are often mentioned in connection with ritual activities but not discussed in depth.

1901   The Lesser New Fire Ceremony at Walpi. *American Anthropologist* 3: 438–453.
Describes another New Fire ceremonial which is somewhat less complex than one discussed previously (Fewkes 1900 above). Fewkes also speculates on its origins.

1902   Minor Hopi Festivals. *American Anthropologist* 4:482–511.
Describes several ceremonials and dances. The section on prayer-stick making includes a discussion on "Songs and Prayers" (pp. 503–505), but this does not include musical notations or song texts.

1964   (Recording) "Hopi Katchina Songs and Six Others by Hopi Chanters." Smithsonian-Folkways Recordings (FE 4394).
Currently available on cassette, this posthumous release contains recordings collected by Fewkes in 1924. The following types of songs are represented: Bean Harvest Song, Buffalo Dance Song, Bear Dance Song, Mud-Head or Clown Songs (2), Rain Dance Song, Rabbit Hut Song, Duck Song, Rain Songs (3), Mud-Head Katchina Song, Butterfly Dance Song, Hoop Dance Song, Buffalo Dance Song, Eagle Dance Song, and Snake Dance Song. The album includes liner notes by Charles Hoffman.

Fewkes, Jesse W., and J.G. Owens

1892   The *La-la-Kon-ta*: A Tusayan Dance. *American Anthropologist* (old series) 5: 105–129.
This describes a nine-day women's ceremonial that was observed by the authors at Walpi Pueblo in September 1891. It contains several references to songs, particularly during a secret nightlong ceremony (pp. 116–120).

Fewkes, Jesse W., and A.M. Stephen

1892   The *Mam-Zrau'-ti*: A Tusayan Ceremony. *American Anthropologist* (old series) 5: 217–245.
This describes another esoteric ceremonial performed by women at Walpi Pueblo (See also Fewkes and Owens [1892]

above). Songs are frequently mentioned in connection with ritual activities.

Fillmore, John C.

1893–1894   Review of "The Zuni Music, as Translated by Mr. Benjamin Ives Gilman" (1891). *Music* 5:39–46.
Fillmore criticizes Gilman's transcriptions and particularly his failure to understand the "harmonic" nature of Indian melodies. He gives retranscribed versions of three songs notated by Gilman. Also see other writings of Fillmore in the General bibliography.

1894   Professor Stumpf on Mr. Gilman's Transcription of the Zuni Songs. *Music* 5:649–652.
This focuses on a review of Gilman (1891 below) by Stumpf (1892 below). Fillmore spuriously interprets Stumpf's remarks as largely agreeing with his own ideas, then reasserts the harmonic character of primitive melodies, of which Stumpf was apparently "unaware."

1896   Songs of the Navajoes. *Land of Sunshine* 5:238–241.
Based on cylinder recordings collected by Washington Matthews. Here again Fillmore asserts his theory that Indians and other primitive singers were guided by a subconscious sense of harmony which had not yet fully evolved into harmony in the western sense.

Frigout, Arlene

1979   Hopi Ceremonial Organization. Pp. 564–576 in *Handbook of the North American Indians, Volume 9: Southwest*. Edited by William Sturtevant. Washington: Smithsonian Institution.
An excellent summary which gives information on the following: the religious purpose of ceremonies, the ceremonial cycle or calendar, general characteristics of the ceremonies (pp. 567–570), the kachinas, ceremonial societies (Snake, Antelope, Flute), women's ceremonials, initiation into the societies, winter solstice (Soyal) rituals, and the social organization of ceremonial activities.

Frisbie, Charlotte (Johnson). Also see **Johnson** (1964) below.

1967   *Kinaaldá: A Study of the Navaho Girl's Puberty Ceremony*. Middletown, Conn.: Wesleyan University Press.

A comprehensive study containing chapters on the mythological basis of the ceremony, the schedule of events taking place in actual ceremonies, and the meanings and social functions of the Kinaaldá. The chapter on the music (pp. 89–346) is very extensive, including complete transcriptions for 31 songs, some quite lengthy, and numerous texts and translations. In a section entitled "Summary" (pp. 344–346), Frisbie declines to generalize on the repertory because the songs are so diverse in character.

1970   The Navajo House Blessing Ceremonial: A Study of Cultural Change. University of New Mexico. Doctoral dissertation (Anthropology), University of New Mexico.

Frisbie distinguishes two versions of the ceremony: (1) the original private version, mainly meaningful to the older generation of Navajos; and (2) a more public version which has developed since 1900 and seems to be increasing in popularity. According to Frisbie the latter represents a new ceremonial within the Blessingway Ceremonial Complex. This is based on fieldwork conducted during the mid-1960s and historical sources.

1977   *Music and Dance Research of Southwestern United States Indians: Past Trends, Present Activities, and Suggestions for Future Research.* Detroit: Information Coordinators.

This provides a history of research since the 1880s (pp. 9–50) and an extensive bibliography (pp. 67–109). The section on future research (pp.45–49) points up the need for comparative studies but also suggests a more humanistic approach that would place more emphasis on matters such as the meaning of the music for Indians themselves, persistence and change in native music, and ethical issues involved in research. Archival recordings in various collections are also listed (pp. 52–66).

1977   Record review of "Navajo Corn Grinding and Shoe Game Songs." Recording and notes by Tony Isaacs (Indian House IH 1507). *Ethnomusicology* 21(2): 355–356.

Includes favorable comments on the recording quality and liner notes, which include song translations. Frisbie describes both genres and notes that the first four corn grinding songs actually have vocable texts rather than words. Also gives additional bibliography and discography for both types of songs.

1977   Record review of "The Klagetoh Swingers: Navajo
            Songs about Love," vols. 1 and 2 (1976). Recordings
            and notes by Tony Isaacs (Indian House IH 1509 and
            1510). *Ethnomusicology* 21(3): 524–525.
This is basically a favorable review, but Frisbie does criticize
the liner notes as being anecdotal in character rather than systematic. She also notes that these social dance songs are known to
many as "Squaw Dance songs." While most of the texts deal hu-
morously with love and courtship, others focus on other subjects
such as jet planes, a jug of wine, the Navajo Nation, and Iwo Jima.

See **Mitchell** (1978 below). This is Mitchell's autobiography,
edited by Frisbie and David P. McAllester.

1980a   An Approach to the Ethnography of Navajo
            Ceremonial Performance. Pp. 75–104 in *Ethnography
            of Musical Performance* edited by Marcia Herndon
            and Norma McLeod. Norwood, Pennsylvania:
            Norwood Editions.
Frisbie suggests a model for descriptive analysis of Navajo
ceremonials based on the following topics (given as section headings): (1) Initial Idea of Performance, (2) Planning (for example,
choice of singer and location), (3) Preliminary Preparations, (4)
Actual Performance, (5) Assessment by Natives, and (6)
Assessment by the Ethnographer.

1980b   Record reviews of three albums: (1) "Klagetoh
            Maiden Singers" (Indian House IH 1508, 1975); (2)
            "The Klagetoh Swingers: Navajo Songs about Love,"
            vol. 3 (Indian House IH 1511, 1978), and (3) "The
            Klagetoh Swingers: Navajo Songs about Love," vol.
            4 (Indian House IH 1512, 1978). *Ethnomusicology*
            24(3): 628–630.
Basically a favorable review stating that the technical quality
is fine but that the notes could be more detailed. The first recording
features a female group singing social dance songs as heard during
evenings of the public part of the Enemyway ceremonial. The other
two albums feature a group whose name derives from a joke concerning their many songs about girls from different places. Frisbie
has described their songs in another review (1977 above). This review contains more information and raises questions for further research on "popular" repertories like these.

1980c   Ritual Drama in the Navajo House Blessing Ceremo-
             ny. Pp. 161–198 in *Southwestern Indian Ritual
             Drama* edited by Charlotte Frisbie. Albuquerque:
             University of New Mexico Press.
   Documents the historical development of a public version of
the domestic ritual surrounding occupation of a new hogan or other
dwelling. This is distinguished from an earlier type of private ritual
for the same purpose. Frisbie describes the songs and prayers associated with each version and concludes that the public ceremony is
being secularized and standardized as it is extended from hogans
and sweathouses to schools and other public buildings. Based on
her doctoral dissertation (1970 above).

1980d   (Editor) *Southwestern Indian Ritual Drama.*
             Albuquerque: University of New Mexico Press.
   This contains articles by the following authors (with tribe of
subject indicated in parentheses): Donald Brown (Picuris Pueblo),
Claire Farrer (Mescalero Apache), Charlotte Frisbie (Navajo),
Richard Haefer (Papago), Leanne Hinton (Havasupai), Joann
Kealiinohomoku (Hopi), Gertrude Kurath (Tewa), David
McAllester (Navajo), Don Roberts (Eastern Pueblo), and Barbara
Tedlock (Zuni). See the individual listings above and below. The
volume as a whole is reviewed by Kroskrity (1983 below).

1980e   Vocables in Navajo Ceremonial Music. *Ethnomusi-
             cology* 24(3): 347–392.
   Part I considers the origin and typology of Navajo vocables,
arranging them into four categories: (1) those which symbolize
sounds made by deities, animals, or birds, (2) archaic words, (3)
foreign words, and (4) vocables as poetic devices. Literally scores
of examples of symbolic vocables are cited (pp. 355–363). Part II
focuses on the musical characteristics, functions, and construction
of Navajo vocables (pp. 372–381). This also includes a bibliography of sources on the use of vocables in Navajo music, American
Indian music, and world music generally.

See Frisbie (1981) in the General bibliography for review of videotapes
   containing interviews with Navajo and (San Juan) Pueblo
   singers.

1986   Navajo Ceremonialists in the Pre-1970 Political
             World. Pp. 79–96 in *Explorations in Ethnomusicol-
             ogy: Essays in Honor of David P. McAllester* edited
             by Charlotte Frisbie. Detroit Monographs in

Musicology, no. 9. Detroit: Detroit Information Coordinators.
This study assesses the political stature of Navajo ceremonialists at various periods in the development of Navajo sociopolitical organization from foraging band stage to nation. Earlier evidence is not conclusive but tends to indicate that before the incarceration at Fort Sumner (1864–1868) ritual expertise was a prerequisite for leadership roles. Frisbie concludes that this expectation has eroded in recent times, particularly at the higher levels of tribal government, but continues at the community level, possibly influencing the selection of council delegates and chapter officers.

1989   Gender and Navajo Music: Unanswered Questions. Pages 22–38 in *Women in North American Indian Music* edited by Richard Keeling. Ann Arbor: Society for Ethnomusicology.
Frisbie discusses Navajo concepts relating to gender as based on mythic texts and ethnographic research, then classifies various genres of Navajo music according to gender participation. She criticizes Washington Matthews (see writings below) for creating the impression that Navajo women were songless and argues that there is no apparent division between male and female music-making in daily life (p. 26). She concludes by saying that further research is needed to understand emic concepts limiting the participation of women in traditional ceremonies.

Frisbie, Charlotte, and David P. McAllester, Editors

1978   *Navajo Blessingway Singer: Frank Mitchell, 1881–1967.* Tucson: University of Arizona Press.
Frank Mitchell was a distinguished ceremonial singer with whom the editors had worked as researchers for many years, and the book is among the earliest modern works to deal with Indian music in non-analytical fashion and from an Indian perspective. The lengthy autobiography is narrated in the first person and covers various aspects of Mitchell's life from his childhood until his death. The review by Merriam (1978 below) lists other autobiographies of noted Indian figures and raises some interesting questions.

Ganteaume, Cécile R.

1992   White Mountain Apache Dance: Expressions of Spirituality. Pp. 65–82 in *Native American Dance: Ceremonies and Social Traditions* edited by Charlotte

Heth. Washington: National Museum of the American Indian, Smithsonian Institution. This describes contemporary dances from an Indian perspective, with special emphasis on the Sunrise Ceremonial (a girls' puberty ceremony) and the Crown Dance or Mountain Spirit Dance. The author also discusses the revival of the War Dance (inspired by the 1991 Persian Gulf Conflict) and the Hoop Dance. This contains excellent color photographs and an explanation of the Crown Dance by dance-leader Edgar Perry.

Garcia, Antonio, and Carlos Garcia

1968   Ritual Preludes to Tewa Dances. *Ethnomusicology* 12(1): 239–244.
Describes various types of preparation necessary for dances performed at San Juan Pueblo. The following topics are covered: (1) announcements and summonses, (2) song preparations (composition), (3) song and dance rehearsals, (4) paraphernalia, (5) preparations on the eve of performance, and (6) preparations on the day of the plaza performance.

Garcia, Antonio, Juanito Trujillo, and Gregorita Trujillo

1966   Tanoan Gestures of Invocation. *Ethnomusicology* 10(2): 206–207.
The authors are Indians from San Juan Pueblo. The article is comprised of comments they made during a demonstration of ceremonial gestures which took place at the University of New Mexico on November 12, 1965. Typical movements from various dances are discussed. Basically, the gestures are classified into three categories: (1) mimetic; (2) symbolic, with hidden meanings; and (3) abstract in character. The paper was edited by Gertrude Kurath.

Gifford, Edward W.

1932   The Southeastern Yavapai. *University of California Publications in American Archaeology and Ethnology* 29:177–252.
This contains a brief description of musical instruments (pp. 230–232), and songs are mentioned in the description of a "Spring Dance" (pp. 238).

Gill, Sam D.

1979   *Songs of Life: An Introduction to Navajo Religious Culture*. Leiden: Brill.

The monograph has 31 pages of text followed by unnumbered pages containing 48 excellent photographs of rituals and other subjects. The text begins by providing basic information on Navajo culture and religion. Then there are sections on the following: "Blessingway" (pp. 12–14), "Holyway" (pp. 14–18), "Uglyway" (pp. 18–20), and "Modern Trends in Navajo Religion" (p. 21). The photos were taken by David Peri in 1963.

Gilman, Benjamin Ives

1891   Zuni Melodies. *Journal of American Ethnology and Archaeology* 1:65–91. Reprinted by AMS Press (New York, 1977).

Examines Zuni songs collected on Edison-type phonographic cylinders by Jesse Walter Fewkes as part of the Hemenway Archeological Expedition in 1890. The opening pages discuss technical aspects of the recordings and notations (pp. 65–70). The next section contains nine notations of Zuni melodies, without texts or translations (pp. 71–88), and the author then comments on musical characteristics such as intonation, scales, vocal quality, and melodic form (pp. 89–91). Gilman's remarks concerning the lack of musical scales in the European sense are considered fairly advanced for the time by Rhodes (General bibliography, 1952:35–36). The reviews by Fillmore (1893–1894 above) and Stumpf (1892 below) are rather critical.

1908   Hopi Songs. *Journal of American Ethnology and Archaeology* 5:1–226. Reprinted by AMS Press (New York, 1977).

This contains transcriptions of 19 Hopi melodies in staff notations and also in more detailed graph notations. The songs were transcribed from cylinders recorded by Jess Walter Fewkes in 1891. Includes commentary and analyses which stress that the music is not based on formed scales and fixed intervals as known in western music. These ideas are discussed by Rhodes (General bibliography, 1952:36).

See also Gilman (1909) in General bibliography. This discussion of "primitive" music focuses on songs of the Pueblo tribes.

Goodwin, Grenville

1942   *The Social Organization of the Western Apache.*
            Chicago.
            This contains descriptions of singing and nine song texts along
with translations (pp. 244, 299–302, 436–437, and 445–446).
Could not be obtained. Information here is from Hickerson
(General bibliography, 1961:235).

Griffith, Jim

1979   Waila—The Social Dance Music of the Indians of
            Southern Arizona: An Introduction and Discography.
            John Edwards Memorial Foundation Quarterly
            15(Winter): 192–204.
            Describes a type of Hispanic-derived social dance music per-
formed by Indians of southern Arizona. The ensemble typically
includes accordion, saxophone, guitar, bass guitar, and drums. The
Papago word *waila* derives from the Spanish *baile* ("social
dance"), but the music is also occasionally referred to as "chicken
scratch." Griffith gives a history of the genre and a fairly extensive
discography. Also includes photographs of three groups.

Gray, Judith A.

See Gray (1984) in the General bibliography. This gives information on
    early cylinder recordings collected among the Hopi.

1990   (Editor) Southwestern Indian Catalogue. pp. 383–528
            in *The Federal Cylinder Project, Volume 5:
            California Indian Catalogue, Middle and South
            American Catalogue, Southwestern Catalogue.*
            Edited by Judith Gray and Edwin Schupman.
            Washington: American Folklife Center, Library of
            Congress.
            This lists and describes the contents of cylinder recordings
from eleven collections including those of Frances Densmore,
Charles Fletcher Lummis, and Alfred Kroeber. The listing for each
collection is preceded by an introduction providing background information on the recordings and the circumstances under which
they were collected. Available documentation in published sources
and manuscripts is cited throughout. The following tribal groups
are represented: Apache (Chiricahua and Mescalero), Cocopa,
Maricopa, Mohave, Papago (Tohono O'odham), Pima, Quechuan,
and Yaqui.

Haefer, J. Richard

1977   *Papago Music and Dance.* Occasional Papers, Navajo Community College Press, vol. 3. Tsaile, Arizona: Navajo Community College Press.

A slim (35-page) volume intended for general readers. This contains chapters on "Music and Dance" (pp. 11–17), "Musical Thought" (pp. 18–23), and "Song Types" (pp. 24–32). The latter includes separate sections on earlier genres and contemporary songs. There are two musical notations and several photographs.

1980   O'odham Celkona: The Papago Skipping Dance. Pp. 239–273 in *Southwestern Indian Ritual Drama* edited by Charlotte Frisbie. Albuquerque: University of New Mexico Press.

Haefer examines the structure and history of a Papago ritual which once functioned to promote intervillage cooperation. The ritual has recently been revived after a long period of disuse.

1980   Songs of a Papago Celkona Cycle. Pp. 140–147 in *Speaking, Singing, and Teaching: A Multidisciplinary Approach to Language Variation: Proceedings of the Eighth Annual Southwestern Language and Linguistics Workshop.* Edited by Florence Barkin and Elizabeth Brant. Anthropological Research Papers, no. 20. Tempe: Arizona State University.

This gives translations of texts for eight songs in a Papago Celkona song cycle. Haefer analyzes the textual form (basically AABC) and discusses how textual patterns shape the rhythmic and metric organization of the music. Does not include musical notations or information on the recordings.

1986   Papago (Music). Pp. 468–469 in *The New Grove Dictionary of American Music*, vol. 3 (L–Q). Edited by H. Wiley Hitchcock and Stanley Sadie. London: Macmillan.

This gives a general description of musical style characteristics and lists various song types and musical events. Discusses the following traditional genres: Round Dance, Skipping Dance, healing songs, and songs for the Saguaro Wine Ceremony. Haefer also mentions a modern powwow which includes local Indian events (held since 1983) and a Papago Old Time Fiddle contest (held since 1984).

1986   Pima (Music). Page 569 in *The New Grove
                Dictionary of American Music*, vol. 3 (L–Q). Edited
                by H. Wiley Hitchcock and Stanley Sadie. London:
                Macmillan.
Haefer begins by noting that the Piman musical style is basically similar to that of the Papago. He lists eight categories of
songs which previously existed, also noting that only the social and
Round Dance songs are now widely performed. The mythic content and style of lengthy song cycles are briefly discussed. Also
mentions that various traditional song and dance genres were rein-
troduced during the 1960s and 1970s.

Haile, Father Berard

1938   Navaho Chantways and Ceremonials. *American An-
                thropologist* 40:639–652.
This provides a detailed examination of Navajo language terminology for various types of ritual activities.

1943   *Origin Legend of the Navajo Flintway: Text and
                Translation*. Chicago: University of Chicago Press.
The volume gives texts and interlinear translations for 39 song
cycles which are sung (along with numerous other prayers and
narratives) in the course of the ceremonial. Based on fieldwork
conducted during the winter months of 1929–1930 and 1930–1931.

1943   Soul Concepts of the Navajo. *Annali Lateranensi*
                7:61–94.
A classic study of Navajo ontological concepts, this contains
interesting comments on the status of ceremonial singers as the
principal bearers of esoteric knowledge (pp. 64–65).

1946a   *Navaho Fire Dance or Corral Dance: A Brief
                Account of Its Practice and Meaning*. Saint Michaels,
                Arizona: Saint Michaels Mission Press.
Focuses on a ceremonial that is also called Mountainway or
Mountain-topway. Haile discusses the mythological significance of
the dance and describes the order of events, with many comments
on songs and dances. This is a slim volume (57 pages) with no
musical examples.

1946b   *The Navaho War Dance*. Saint Michaels, Arizona:
                Saint Michaels Mission Press.
This 50-page monograph begins by describing the purpose of
the ceremony, which is performed to cure a person who is troubled

by the ghosts of enemies slain in war. Haile describes the sequence of events in the ritual and gives mythological explanations for various features. Songs and dances are mentioned throughout, and there are descriptions of the water drum (pp. 10–12) and stick rattle (pp. 12–21). No musical examples.

1947   *Navaho Sacrificial Figurines*. Chicago: University of Chicago Press.
This focuses on the ritual preparation of (mainly animal) figurines used in minor (private) curing ceremonials. Certain sets of songs are sung as the objects are being prepared, and Haile gives texts and translations for several of these. See especially the following sections: "Songs for Bear Figurines" (pp. 48–52), "Dog Songs" (pp. 73–75), and "(Songs for) Blue Lizard" (pp. 89–92).

Harrington, John Peabody

1908   Yuma Account of Origins. *Journal of American Folklore* 21:324–348.
Contains a description of song cycles and their place in Yuman religion (pp. 326–328). The main subject of the paper is Harrington's translation of an origin myth as collected from Joe Homer. This includes translations for eight texts of songs that figure in the narrative.

1912a   The Tewa Indian Game of "Cañute." *American Anthropologist* 14:243–286.
Gives a detailed description of the game, with photographs. The section on "Singing" (pp. 261–264) contains a musical transcription for one of the songs by Frances Densmore.

Harrington, John Peabody, and Helen H. Roberts

1928   *Picurís Children's Stories with Texts and Songs*. Bureau of American Ethnology, Annual Report (1925–1926) 43:289–447.
This contains Helen Roberts's transcriptions of 11 songs in 32 renditions (pp. 399–447). Texts are given for all of the songs and translations for some. Also includes an analysis of the music by Roberts, who mainly focuses on scales and melodic structure.

Harrington, M.R.

1912b   The Devil Dance of the Apaches. *University of Pennsylvania, University Museum Journal*, no. 3, pp. 6–10.

A particularly ethnocentric and insensitive description of the girls' puberty ceremony as practiced among Apaches who had been removed from their native territory to a reservation at Fort Sill, Oklahoma. Includes two photographs and descriptions of songs and dances.

Herzog, George

See Herzog (1928) in the California bibliography. This deals with music of Yuman tribes (Mohave, Yuma) which might have been classified in either culture area.

See Evans and Evans (1931) in the General bibliography. This contains musical transcriptions of four Pueblo songs by George Herzog (pp. 54–56 and 65–67).

1933a   Maricopa Music. Pages 271–279 in *Yuman Tribes of the Gila River* by Leslie Spier. Chicago: University of Chicago Press.

Contains transcriptions (with texts) and analysis for seven songs collected by Leslie Spier. Herzog also distinguishes this from the similar style of the Yuman tribes (p. 271). This is preceded by another section ("The Songs and Song Cycles") in which Spier discusses cultural and religious aspects of the music (pp. 254–270).

1933b   Book review of *Yuman and Yaqui Music* by Frances Densmore (1932). *Zeitschrift für vergleichende Musikwissenschaft* 1:91–93.

Basically a positive review, but Herzog does criticize the use of western musical concepts in Densmore's tabular comparative analyses. He also compares the findings with those of Herzog (1928 above), particularly as regards the relative frequency of a structural feature called "the rise." Herzog describes "the rise" as occurring in various Indian repertories, including transcriptions of a Yuki song (collected by Alfred Kroeber), a Klallam song (collected by Erna Gunther), and a Yuman song reprinted from the book under review.

See Herzog (1934) in the General bibliography. This discusses the relationship between speech tonality and singing, with several Navajo examples.

1936   A Comparison of Pueblo and Pima Musical Styles. *Journal of American Folklore* 49:283–417.
This detailed comparative study reveals some complex relationships. Thus (for example), while the Pueblo and Pima musical systems are clearly distinguished, Herzog finds that corn-grinding songs of the Pueblo women are distinctly Piman in style. The characterizations of the Pueblo style (pp. 288–300) and the Pima style (pp. 301–308) are outlined under five headings: (1) manner of singing or vocal technique; (2) melodic style and tonality; (3) rhythm and accompaniment; (4) structure or form; and (5) presence of sub-styles, genres, or variations. The study includes transcriptions (with texts) and analyses for 57 songs from the following tribes: San Juan Pueblo (7 songs), Cochiti Pueblo (5), Taos Pueblo (5), Zuñi Pueblo (6), Acoma Pueblo (4), Hopi (1), San Ildefonso Pueblo (1), Laguna Pueblo (7), and Pima (21). The data were collected in 1927.

Hinton, Leanne

1980   Vocables in Havasupai Song. Pp. 275–305 in *Southwestern Indian Ritual Drama* edited by Charlotte Frisbie. Albuquerque: University of New Mexico Press.
Examines Havasupai vocables in relation to their communicative and aesthetic functions. Hinton offers two hypotheses concerning the manner in which preferred vocal quality and singing style relate to the presence in vocables of high/low vowels, nasals, glides, stops, and affricates. She also postulates (as a general principle) that musical events stressing solidarity or spirituality tend to minimize the use of intelligible words through use of vocables, foreign languages, or much textual repetition.

1986   Havasupai (Music). Pp. 346–347 in *The New Grove Dictionary of American Music*, vol. 2 (E–K). Edited by H. Wiley Hitchcock and Stanley Sadie. London: Macmillan.
Discusses the basic characteristics of Havasupai music and lists the indigenous song types (curing songs, weather songs, and hunting songs). Hinton then discusses various types of songs that have been borrowed from other tribes, including the Hopi (kachina

songs), Navajo (riding songs and Circle Dance songs), Southern
Paiute (sweathouse songs), and Mohave or Chemehuevi (bird
songs and salt songs). In closing, she mentions popular new styles
such as Christian hymns (some in Havasupai), rock and roll, country western, and even reggae.

1984   *Havasupai Songs: A Linguistic Perspective.* Ars
            Linguistica, Commentationes Analyticae et Criticae.
            Tubingen: Gunter Narr Verlag.
    Hinton focuses on the contrasts between sung and spoken lan-
guage in terms of phonology, syntax, and semantics. Chapter Two
gives a survey of vocal art genres as viewed in a continuum from
intoned formal speech to relatively elaborate songs. Part II contains
musical transcriptions and analysis for 48 songs. This is a revised
version of Hinton's doctoral thesis (University of California at San
Diego, 1977) and is based on research conducted at Supai between
1964 and 1977.

1990   Song-Metrics. *Proceedings of the 16th Annual
            Meeting of the Berkeley Linguistics Society* (2 vol-
            umes). Pp. 51–60 in volume entitled *Special Session
            on General Topics in American Indian Linguistics.*
            Edited by David J. Costa.
    Compares metric structures in language with metric structures
in music with reference to a Havasupai song (Sweathouse Origin
Song) quoted from Hinton (1985 above). The song is narrative in
character and (as typical of Havasupai narrative songs) partially
improvised. Hinton concludes that linguistic metrics may prede-
termine musical metrics. Includes two notations of the song and a
portion of the text.

Hinton, Leanne, and Lucille J. Watahomigie, Editors

1984   *Spirit Mountain: An Anthology of Yuman Story and
            Song.* Tucson: Sun Tracks and University of Arizona
            Press.
    This contains texts and translations from the following tribes:
Hualapai, Havasupai, Yavapai, Paipai, Diegueño, Maricopa,
Mohave, and Quechan. The Havasupai section contains a discussion of "Havasupai Music" (pp. 106–107). This is followed by
texts, translations, and musical notations for nine Havasupai songs
(pp. 108–154). The section on Quechan texts gives texts and translations for six songs. Also contains translation of a (Lightning

Song) song cycle transcribed (without recording) by Abraham Halpern in 1938.

Hodge, Frederick Webb

1896   Pueblo Snake Ceremonials. *American Anthropologist* 9:133–136.

Previous studies suggested that snake ceremonials were performed only among the Hopi (Moki) and among the Sia of Jemez Valley (New Mexico). Hodge discusses historical evidence of related practices at other pueblos, particularly at Laguna and San Ildefonso.

See **Huenemann** (1978) in the General bibliography for general information on Navajo music (including musical transcriptions for 37 Navajo songs).

Humphreys, Paul

1982   The Tradition of Song Renewal among the Pueblo Indians of North America. *American Indian Culture and Research Journal* 6(1): 9–24. Los Angeles: American Indian Studies Center, UCLA.

Focuses on the processes through which "newly composed" songs come to incorporate elements of earlier songs. Shows how a Buffalo Dance song composed by the researcher Humphreys was changed into an Arrow Dance song by his Jemez Pueblo informant. Gives notations for the songs, both in standard notations and in a graph notation developed by Humphreys.

1984   The Tradition of Song Renewal among the Pueblo Indians, Part Two. Pp. 25–37 in *Sharing a Heritage: American Indian Arts*, edited by Charlotte Heth and Michael Swarm. Contemporary American Indian Issues Series, no. 5. Los Angeles: American Indian Studies Center, UCLA.

Based mainly on recent research at Jemez and Laguna Pueblos. The paper describes three aspects or procedures connected with song renewal: (1) borrowing and adaptation of songs, (2) composing of new songs, and (3) review and revision of new songs by experienced members of the chorus group. Contains five musical examples in a form of graph notation developed by Humphreys.

1989   Form as Cosmology: An Interpretation of Structure in
                the Ceremonial Songs of the Pueblo Indians. *Pacific
                Review of Ethnomusicology* 5:61–88. Los Angeles:
                Ethnomusicology Program, UCLA.

Humphreys discusses how the form of katcina-style songs reflects concepts relating to the four cardinal directions and concen-
tric layers relating temporal and spiritual domains in Tewa cosmology.

Johnson, Charlotte I. (Also see writings under surname Frisbie, listed
above)

1964   Navaho Corn Grinding Songs. *Ethnomusicology* 8(2):
                101–120.

This contains musical notations, analysis, and commentary for
26 songs. Fourteen of them were recorded by the author in 1963,
and the other songs were collected earlier by David McAllester and
Willard Rhodes (one only). Johnson discusses the origins and social functions of the genre and gives a general description of the
musical style.

Johnson, Jean Bassett

1940   The Piman Foot Drum and Fertility Rites. *El Mexico
                Antiqua* 5:140–141.

Discusses possible origins of the foot drum as found among
tribes of the southwestern United States and Mexico. For a related
study see Lowie (General bibliography, 1938)

Kealiinohomoku, Joann W.

1967   Hopi and Polynesian Dance: A Study in Cross-
                Cultural Comparisons. *Ethnomusicology* 11(3):343–
                358.

The comparison mainly reveals contrasts rather than similarities in the style and cultural functions of dance. The following aspects are considered: gestures and dance, performers (including
gender, values, status, etc.), ground plan and choreography, and
performance style.

1980   The Drama of the Hopi Ogres. In *Southwestern
                Indian Ritual Drama* edited by Charlotte Frisbie.
                Albuquerque: University of New Mexico Press.

Describes a ritual in which ogres come to capture misbehaving Hopi children and offers an interpretation concerning the "medicinal" value of this frightening (for children) event.

Keeling, Richard H.

1988   Book review of *Yaqui Deer Songs, Maso Bwikam: A Native American Poetry* by Larry Evers and Felipe Molina (1987). *Ethnomusicology* 32(3): 464–466.

Praises the book for giving an insider's perspective on Indian culture but also notes the lack of musical analysis and failure to comment on the broader distribution of similar song cycles among other tribes of the Southwest and adjacent areas.

1994   Book review of *Stability and Variation in Hopi Song* by George List (1993). *Quarterly Journal of the Music Library Association* (September): 208–209.

Commends the book for detailed analyses of the music and song texts but questions the author's "contour hypothesis" and the relative lack of concern with the issue of etic versus emic understandings.

Keim, Betty

1975   A Comparative Study of the Music of the Indians and the Spanish in Arizona and New Mexico: A Selective Bibliography. *Current Musicology* 19:117–121. New York: Music Department, Columbia University.

The bibliography lists about 70 books or articles from musicology and other disciplines. Includes entries on the following topics: comparison of musical styles, language influences, musical influences, and historical or cultural information pertinent to comparative studies of music.

Klah, Hasteen

1942   *Navajo Creation Myth: The Story of the Emergence.* Santa Fe: Museum of Navajo Ceremonial Art. Navajo Religion Series, vol. 1.

The section on "Navajo Ceremonial Songs" (pp. 127–162) contains texts for 30 songs performed by Hasteen Klah. These were recorded and translated by Harry Hoijer. The volume was edited by George Herzog.

Klett, Francis

1879   The Cachina: A Dance at the Pueblo of Zuni. *Report Upon U.S. Geographic Surveys: West of the 100th Meridian* 7:332–336.

An early description of singing and instruments used in a Zuñi dance. Could not be obtained for inspection of contents. Information here is from Hickerson (General bibliography, 1961:265).

Kluckhohn, Clyde

1933   The Great Chants of the Navajo. *Theatre Arts Monthly* 17:639–645.

This contains five song texts and translations as quoted from writings by Washington Matthews.

1938   Participation in Ceremonials in a Navaho Community. *American Anthropologist* 40(3): 359–369.

Focuses on ceremonial activities among about 400 Navajo people living between Ramah and Atarque (New Mexico) as interviewed in 1936 and 1937. This includes information on the number of ceremonials that were known by Kluckhohn's informants, number of ceremonial practitioners, number of ceremonies held during a specific period of time, and related subjects.

1938   Navaho Women's Knowledge of Their Song Ceremonials. *El Palacio* 45:87–92.

In a previous study (1938a above) Kluckhohn had interviewed only men, and in this follow-up he reports on interviews conducted with 60 women and girls of the same (Ramah) community. Kluckhohn concludes that the females had less knowledge of ceremonials and did not participate as singers or curers in this particular community (p. 91). In a later study of gender in Navajo music, Frisbie (1989 above, page 28) warns against general interpretations based on Kluckhohn's findings.

Kluckhohn, Clyde, and Leland C. Wyman

1940   *An Introduction to Navaho Chant Practice, With an Account of Behaviors Observed in Four Chants.* Memoirs of the American Anthropological Association, no. 53.

Part One ("Generalized Account of Navajo Chant Practice," pp. 13–110) touches on various topics related to music, but see especially the section on "Songs" (pp. 64–66). Other sections describe the following chants: Navajo Wind Way (Part Two), Chiricahua Wind Way (Part Three), Female Shooting Holy Way (Part Four), and Hand Trembling Evil Way (Part Five). Contains no musical examples but gives much information on contexts of singing.

Also see **Kolinski** (1972) in General bibliography for discussion of Apache Rabbit Dance songs.

Kroeber, Alfred Louis, Editor

1935   *Walapai Ethnography*. Memoirs of the American Anthropological Association, no. 42.
        Contains brief sections on "Music" (pp. 121–123) and "Salt Song Series" (with translations of 60 short song texts, pp. 195–198) by a writer identified as R. McKennan. Also includes sections on the "Ghost Dance" (pp. 198–202) and the "Rain Dance" (pp. 202–203), by S. Mekeel and G. MacGregor, respectively.

Kroskrity, Paul V.

1983   Book review of *Southwestern Indian Ritual Drama* edited by Charlotte Frisbie (1980). *Ethnomusicology* 27(2): 373–375.
        Basically quite favorable. Kroskrity commends the book for providing detailed explanations of ritual events as understood in their own cultural context, but he also comments on the lack of musical analysis and comparative or cross-cultural perspectives.

Kurath, Gertrude Prokosch

1957   Dance Styles of the Rio Grande Pueblo Indians. *The Folklorist* 4(3):89.
        This brief overview focuses on contrasts between the native (Pueblo) dances and those dances which have been modified as a result of influences from the Plains tribes. Includes one musical example (Buffalo Dance Song).

1957   Notation of a Pueblo Indian Corn Dance. *Dance Notation Record* 8(4): 9–10. (Winter edition).
        This contains one musical example (with text) and a form of notation showing the dance movements.

1957   The Origin of the Pueblo Indian Matachines. *El Palacio* 64:259–264.

Discusses European origins of the dance and the Pueblo legend that it was brought from Mexico by Montezuma. Describes the
blending of indigenous and Catholic elements in various forms of
the Matachines as practiced in the Southwest and Mesoamerican
culture areas.

1958a   Plaza Circuits of Tewa Indian Dancers. *El Palacio*
            65(1–2):16–28.

The outdoor ceremonial dances of Rio Grande Pueblo Indians
each follow a prescribed circuit, theoretically always counter-
clockwise and oriented in accordance with the four cardinal directions. This paper describes variations which occur in actual practice and suggests a basic Tewa prototype (pp. 23–24). Contains
four diagrams and various tables.

1958a   Book review of *Music of the Acoma, Isleta, Cochiti,
            and Zuñi Pueblos*, by Frances Densmore (1957).
            Midwest Folklore 8:61–62.

This contains several criticisms of Densmore's research techniques and methods of musical analysis.

1958b   Two Line Dances of San Juan Pueblo, New Mexico.
            Midwest Folklore 8:155–158.

Contains descriptions of the Deer Dance and the Yellow Corn
Dance, both of which are performed in February. Includes two
musical examples and commentary on the song texts.

1958c   Game Animal Dances of the Rio Grande Pueblos.
            Southwestern Journal of Anthropology 14(4): 438–
            448.

Unlike the secret masked Kachina dances, various game animal dances are partially public and spectacular to watch.
Nonetheless, they are sacred, compulsive rituals. This paper divides the dances into four categories and describes the order of
events in each. According to Kurath, the first type is native Pueblo
in origin while the others show influences from the Plains tribes (p.
447). Contains numerous diagrams.

1958d   Buffalo Dance at Cochiti Pueblo, New Mexico. *The
            Folklorist* 4(5): 149–150.

This contains interesting information on the composition of
new songs and rehearsals that are conducted before the dance.

1959   Cochiti Choreographies and Songs. Pp. 539–556 in
            Cochiti by C. H. Lange. Austin: University of Texas
            Press.
   Describes the coordination of music and dance in two rituals:
(1) the Buffalo or Game Animal Dance (pp. 539–545) and (2) the
Tablita or Corn Dance (pp. 545–553). Kurath then discusses the
similarities and differences between them (pp. 553–556). This includes six musical examples and three dance diagrams.

1960a   Calling the Rain Gods. *Journal of American Folklore*
            73(290): 312–316.
   A brief but excellent account of rain gods and ceremonials
among various Pueblo groups. The author discusses invocations
which are made in secret masked rituals and also describes public
dances, with special emphasis on song texts and mimetic gestures
in the dance. This includes free and interlinear translations of two
song texts (from Cochiti Pueblo). Also contains interesting comments on the similarity between Pueblo and Aztec rain gods (p.
315).

1965   Tewa Choreographic Music. Pages 4–19 in *Studies in
            Ethnomusicology* (Volume Two). Edited by
            Mieczyslaw Kolinski. New York: Oak Publications.
   Kurath uses musical and choreographic symbols to illustrate
the intrinsic connection between music and dance. The essay begins with notations of six basic examples of Tewa choreographic
music: (1) Rain Cloud Dance song , (2) Yellow Corn Dance song,
(3) Tablita (Corn or Harvest) Fast Dance song, (4) Deer Dance
songs (three songs), (5) Buffalo Dance songs (one set), and (6)
Pangshare Social Dance song. Kurath then discusses the connection between dance steps and musical beats (pp. 14–17), melodic
and dance structures (p. 17), song texts (pp. 17–18) and other related issues.

1966   The Kinetic Ecology of Yaqui Dance Instrumenta-
            tion. *Ethnomusicology* 10(1): 28–42.
   Contains a description of the Yaqui Deer and Pascola Dances
based on the author's fieldwork in Sonora (Mexico) in 1946 and
published sources. Kurath uses gesture graphs or "kinemes" to
show instrumental playing techniques. Also discusses nature symbolism of the song texts (p. 38) and the possible Aztec origin of the
Pascola bells or coyoles (p. 39).

See Kurath 1967 in Mexican bibliography. This compares matachines dances among the Pueblo Indians with those of Yaqui Indians of Sonora (Mexico) and various Mexican mestizo groups.

1980   Motion Pictures of Tewa Ritual Dances. Pages 93–102 in *Southwestern Indian Ritual Drama* edited by Charlotte Frisbie. Albuquerque: University of New Mexico Press.
Mainly a discussion of technical procedures and research methods.

1987   Book review of *Dances of the Tewa Indians*, by Jill Sweet (1985). *Ethnomusicology* 31(2): 358–359.
A fairly critical review which points out the lack of musical or dance analysis and calls this a book which "mingles the mystical idea of seeking life through dance with practical information for tourists" (p. 358).

Kurath, Gertrude, with Antonio Garcia

1970   *Music and Dance of the Tewa Pueblos*. Santa Fe: Museum of New Mexico Press.
A comprehensive study based on research conducted between 1957 and 1965. The assistance of Antonia Garcia (San Juan Pueblo) is cited on the title page. There are three main parts: (1) "Ceremonial Ecology" (pp. 13–46) contains chapters on Tewa religion and society; (2) "Choreographic and Musical Patterns" (pp. 47–114) gives analytical information; and (3) "Symbolic Pageantry" (pp. 115–288) contains chapters describing various particular dances in detail. The book includes 115 musical notations and/or dance diagrams. Appendix 4 contains a paper on Tewa Pueblo Round Dances by Don Roberts (1970 below).

Lamphere, Louise

1969   Symbolic Elements in Navaho Ritual. *Southwestern Journal of Anthropology* 25:279–305.
Explores various ways in which ritual chants reflect Navajo cosmological concepts. Focusing on the Male Shooting Way ritual, Lamphere identifies connections between the song sets performed and specific incidents in Navajo mythology (pp. 285–286). She also describes the sequence of events (including songs) in the ceremony (pp. 297–301).

1983   Southwestern Ceremonialism. Pp. 743–763 in *Handbook of North American Indians, Volume 10: Southwest*. Edited by Alfonso Ortiz. Washington: Smithsonian Institution.

An overview of major cosmological themes and ritual practices among the following tribes or groups: Yumans, Apaches, Navajos, Pueblos, and Pima-Papago. Lamphere gives profiles for each, then makes a comparative analysis to indicate relationships (pp. 762–763).

Laski, Vera

1958   *Seeking Life.* Memoirs of the American Folklore Society, no. 50.

Part One (pp. 1–94) contains an ethnography of the Raingod Ceremony as practiced at San Juan and other Tewa-speaking pueblos in northern New Mexico. This includes descriptions of dances and English translations of speeches and prayers. Part Two (pp. 95–168) deals with shamanism and curing. Various healing ceremonies are described (pp. 112–117), and there is an interesting chapter on "The History of San Juan Shamanism" (Chapter four, pp. 118–130). Contains no specific information on music.

La Vigna, Maria

1980   Okushare, Music for a Winter Ceremony: The Turtle Dance Songs of San Juan Pueblo. *Selected Reports in Ethnomusicology* 3(2): 77–100. Los Angeles: Program in Ethnomusicology, Department of Music, UCLA.

Examines the process of composing new songs for sacred ceremonies and the degree to which the songs fit a preconceived mold. Compares several songs for the Okushare ceremony and attempts to illustrate the archetypal song form in an analytical diagram (following p. 98). The study is based on recordings made by La Vigna in 1976 and earlier recordings from various collectors (dated 1954, 1961, 1969, 1971, and 1974).

1981   Record reviews of "Turtle Dance Songs of San Juan Pueblo" (Indian House IH 1101) and "Cloud Dance Songs of San Juan Pueblo "(Indian House IH 1102). *Ethnomusicology* 25(1): 166–168.

These recordings feature ceremonial songs composed for the 1971 Turtle Dance and the 1972 Cloud Dance at San Juan Pueblo.

For the most part, the ceremonial repertory is fixed and presumably has remained unchanged for generations. New songs and texts are composed for only three ceremonies: (1) the Turtle dance, (2) the Cloud Dance, and (3) the Basket Dance. La Vigna notes that this is the first commercial album to provide complete songs sets from the newly composed category. She provides important information on rehearsal practices and performance standards.

See the catalogue by **Lee** (1979) in the General bibliography. This lists historical and recent recordings at the Indiana University Archives of Traditional Music. The holdings include collections from the following groups: Apache (of various divisions), Cochiti, Cocopa, Hopi, Maricopa, Mohave, Navajo, Papago, Pima, Pueblo (various Pueblo tribes), Quechan, Walapai, Yaqui, Yuman, and Zuni.

List, George

1962   Songs in Hopi Culture, Past and Present. *Journal of the International Folk Music Council* 14:30–35.
        Begins by discussing the responses of List's informants (circa 1960) on listening to archival recordings collected by others in 1903 and 1926. List then discusses various recent development in Hopi music, particularly the appearance of love songs with English words. Closes with a very poignant song text predicting the end of the Hopi way of life.

1963   The Boundaries of Speech and Song. *Ethnomusicology* 7:1–16. Reprint. Pages 253–268 in *Readings in Ethnomusicology* edited by David P. McAllester. New York: Johnson Reprint Corp.
        Three musical examples (pp. 256–257) illustrate the contrast in Hopi music between a chant-like style used for "announcements" and another style with more defined or highly developed scalar structures.

1968   Hopi as Composer and Poet. Pp. 43–53 in *Proceedings of the Centennial Workshop on Ethnomusicology, University of British Columbia, Vancouver, June 19–23, 1967.* Edited by Peter Crossley-Holland. Vancouver: Government of the Province of British Columbia.
        A detailed discussion of compositional practices as related to kachina dance songs. Describes the prototypic form of kachina

songs composed at First Mesa and analyzes the differences between two Heyheya (Farmer) kachina dance songs as occurring within the basic structure. List also deals with the poetry of the songs (including translations of three texts) and the process through which newly composed songs are edited and revised by committee.

1985   Hopi Melodic Concepts. *Journal of the American Musicological Society* 38:143–152.

Advances the hypothesis that the Hopi conceive their melodies as a series of contours rather than as a series of discrete pitches.

1987   Stability and Variation in a Hopi Lullaby. *Ethnomusicology* 31(1): 18–34.

Compares 11 performances of a certain ("black bug") lullaby that were recorded between 1903 and 1960. Includes detailed analyses of the texts and music, the latter relying on the "contour hypothesis" outlined in a previous study (List 1985 above). List concludes by distinguishing three levels of stability or variation as manifest in various musical and textual elements.

1993   *Stability and Variation in Hopi Song.* Memoirs of the American Philosophical Society, Volume 204. Philadelphia: American Philosophical Society.

Attempts to define the stylistic parameters of a given song in Hopi culture. Compares 8 recordings of a particular kachina dance song and 11 versions of a lullaby. Contains extensive notations and detailed analyses of music and texts but employs a type of "pitch band notation" in which each note represents a whole tone in width. List concludes that the text and melody of a Hopi song are less stable than a song in western culture and that "Hopi music is not based on a fixed scale derived from the playing of musical instruments" (p. 99). Includes material from List (1987 above). Reviewed by Keeling (1994 above).

See **Lowie** (1938) in General bibliography. The discusses the foot drum as used among various Pueblo tribes.

Luckert, Karl W., and Johnny C. Cooke

1979   *Coyoteway: A Navajo Holyway Healing Ceremonial.* Tucson: University of Arizona Press.

A comprehensive study based mainly on research conducted during the early 1970s. Part One ("The Ceremonial and Its Priests," pp. 3–24) gives background on the singer ("Man with Palomino

Horse") and discusses mythic and historical origins of the
Coyoteway Ritual. Part Two ("Coyoteway Performed," pp. 25–
190) contains six chapters describing the nine-day ceremonial, with
many translations of song texts and excellent photographs. This includes the musical transcription of a First Coyote Song (p. 36)
which clearly shows the relationship of the musical form and the
text. Part Three ("Early records of Coyoteway," pp. 191–234)
gives additional information from various earlier sources. Luckert
is a scholar at Northern Arizona University, and his collaborator
(Cooke) is a Navajo who served as interpretor and translator.

McAllester, David Park

Also see McAllester (1949) in the General bibliography. This is a general survey of peyote music in which McAllester suggests that
the basic style probably originated among the Apache and
Navajo.

1954   *Enemyway Music: A Study of Social and Esthetic
            Values as Seen in Navajo Music.* Papers of the
            Peabody Museum of American Archaeology and
            Ethnology, Harvard University, vol. 41, no. 3.
        The first part focuses on the public portion of this curing cer-
emony, which is held to remove bad effects caused by foreign
ghosts. This includes notations (with texts and translations) for 75
songs that were recorded by McAllester in 1950. The second part
discusses how Enemyway music reflects basic Navajo cultural values.

1956   An Apache Fiddle. *Society for Ethnomusicology
            Newsletter* 8:1–5.
        Briefly describes the construction of the instrument and how it
is played. Includes one musical example.

1960   The Role of Music in Western Apache Culture. Pp.
            468–472 in *Men and Cultures: Selected Papers of the
            Fifth International Congress of Anthropological and
            Ethnological Sciences, September 1–9 (1956).* Edited
            by Anthony F.C. Wallace. Philadelphia: University of
            Pennsylvania Press.
        Examines musical concepts and the cultural functions of music
among the White Mountain Apache. McAllester focuses primarily
on the role of music in curing ceremonies, listing several differences between the way music is used among the Apache and in our
own (Euro-American) culture.

1961   *Indian Music in the Southwest.* Colorado Springs: Taylor Museum of the Colorado Springs Fine Art Center. Reprint. Pp. 215–226 in *Readings in Ethnomusicology,* edited by David McAllester. New York: Johnson Reprint Corporation, 1971.

This slim booklet (15 pp.) begins by discussing general characteristics of music among the southwestern tribes, then gives separate descriptions of music among the Pueblo tribes, the Apache, and the Navajo. Contains no musical notations but does include translations of four song texts.

See Mitchell (1978 below). This is an autobiography edited by McAllester and Charlotte Frisbie.

1980   The First Snake Song. Pp. 1–27 in *Theory and Practice: Essays Presented to Gene Weltfish* edited by Stanley Diamond. The Hague: Mouton Publishers.

Analyzes a Navajo song and text in order to show how it reveals aspects of the cognitive matrix from which the song arises. This is the first song of the Shootingway ceremonial, and McAllester begins with a summary of the mythic story on which it is based. He then provides transcriptions of the music, the sung text, and the spoken text along with interlinear and free translations into English. Noting the prominence of "double phrases" in the music, McAllester goes on to discuss the importance of repetition in various spheres of Navajo life (pp. 6–8). He then focuses on "extra" beats which interrupt the flow of the basically duple meter and compares this to Navajo speech patterns (pp. 9–11). Other aspects of the song are treated in similar manner. The data was collected by McAllester in 1957.

1980a   Shootingway: An Epic Drama of the Navajos. Pp. 199–237 in *Southwestern Indian Ritual Drama* edited by Charlotte Frisbie. Albuquerque: University of New Mexico Press.

Examines the mythological basis and structure of a complex ritual drama designed to restore normal life to those who have experienced disharmony. McAllester details the sequence of activities in this (nine-day) event and analyzes the texts of various songs. His interpretations tend to challenge conventional understandings relating to the use of "compulsive" prayers and songs for manipulating the supernatural.

1980b   The War God's Horse Song: An Exegesis in Native
             American Humanities. *Selected Reports in
             Ethnomusicology* 3(2): 1–22. Los Angeles: Program
             in Ethnomusicology, Department of Music,
             University of California, Los Angeles.
    Begins by noting that poeticized translations of the song have
been published by many western writers without adequate explication of its meaning in Navajo culture. McAllester then discusses
the significance of the song (in relation to the Blessingway ceremony) and gives suggestions as to how a song like this should be
studied in a course on Native American humanities. The paper includes free and interlinear translations of a version recorded by
McAllester in 1968.

1986a   Apache (Music). Pp. 58–59 in *The New Grove
             Dictionary of American Music*, vol. 1 (A–D). Edited
             by H. Wiley Hitchcock and Stanley Sadie. London:
             Macmillan.
    Gives a brief summary of musical characteristics and descrip-
tions of major ceremonies (girls' puberty ritual and curing ceremonies). Also discusses musical instruments (including the Apache
Fiddle) and modern trends such as musical innovations of Philip
Cassadore and A. Paul Ortega.

1986b   Navajo (Music). Pp. 327–328 in *The New Grove
             Dictionary of American Music*, vol. 3 (L–Q). Edited
             by H. Wiley Hitchcock and Stanley Sadie. London:
             Macmillan.
    Emphasizes the importance of traditional ceremonies or
"chants" which re-enact the creation story and are performed in order to restore harmony between the universe and individuals who
have become ill. Describes the musical form and the style of songs
in these chantways (of which there are between 25 and 30) and
then discusses the Blessingway in particular. Also touches on traditional popular music (for the Skip Dance, Circle Dance, and
Yeibichai Dance) and mentions various modern trends such as
Christian hymns, rock, and country music performed by Navajos.

McAllester, David P., and Susan McAllester

1980   *Hogans: Navajo Houses and House Songs*. Middle-
             town, Connecticut: Wesleyan University Press.
    Provides translations and commentary on the texts of 19 house
songs. These songs are part of ceremonies performed in order to

seek blessings and prevent illness or danger when occupying a new home. The texts describe Navajo deities in the process of building and moving into their own primordial houses. The photographs by Susan McAllester provide many images of traditional hogans and modern Navajo houses.

McAllester, David P., and Douglas F. Mitchell

1979   Navajo Music. Pp. 605–623 in *Handbook of North American Indians, Volume 9: Southwest*, edited by Alfonso Ortiz. Washington: Smithsonian Institution.

This excellent summary begins by discussing Navajo song categories and then provides separate sections on "Traditional Musics" (pp. 605–610) and "New Musics" (pp. 610–614). McAllester lists (7) general characteristics which distinguish Navajo music from other North American styles (p. 606). This includes 13 musical examples (pp. 615–623).

MacLeish, Kenneth

1941   A Few Hopi Songs from Moenkopi. *Masterkey* 15:178–184.

This contains notations for six songs (including texts and translations) and general comments on Hopi musical style. The songs were transcribed (by ear) by David McAllester in 1938. This information is from Hickerson (General bibliography, 1961:293–294).

Mason, John Alden

1920   The Papago Harvest Festival. *American Anthropologist* 22:13–25.

Includes texts and translations for eight songs.

Matthews, Washington

1887   *The Mountain Chant: A Navajo Ceremony.* Bureau of American Ethnology, Annual Report (1883–1884) 5:379–467.

Includes 18 song texts and translations (pp. 455–467). Also describes the use of songs in the ceremony. Could not be obtained. This information is from Hickerson (General bibliography, 1961:297).

1889   Navaho Gambling Songs. *American Anthropologist*
            (Old Series) 2:1–19
This contains texts and translations for 21 gambling songs
along with a description of the game and how songs are used in it.
Could not be obtained. Information here is from Hickerson
(General bibliography, 1961:297).

1894   The Basket Drum. *American Anthropologist* (Old
            Series) 7:202–208.
Matthews explains that this is the only type of basketry made
by the Navajo and that its main function is as a drum in ancient
ceremonies. Regular drums (membranophones) are never used.
Describes construction techniques, then discusses ritual and
fetishistic aspects of the basket drum as used in a Night Chant ceremony.

1894   Songs of Sequence of the Navajos. *Journal of
            American Folklore* 7:185–194.
Matthews discusses the order of songs in Navajo ceremonies
and how the singers remember the sequence. Includes translations
of 12 song texts.

1902   *The Night Chant, a Navajo Ceremony.* Memoirs of
            American Museum of Natural History, no. 6.
            Publication of the Hyde Southwestern Expedition.
            New York.
Contains detailed descriptions of ritual events, dance movements, costumes, musical instruments, and other aspects of the ceremony. Includes texts and translations for four songs.

Merriam, Alan P.

1978   Book review of *The Autobiography of Frank Mitchell
            1881–1967, Navajo Blessingway Singer*, edited by
            Charlotte Frisbie and David P. McAllester (1978).
            Ethnomusicology 22(3): 523–526.
A favorable review but one which also criticizes the editors'
decision not to include analysis or commentary on several issues.
The book is narrated in first person throughout; thus (according to
Merriam) it remains unclear why Mitchell decided to become a
ceremonial singer or in what respects he was typical or extraordinary as a Navajo person. Merriam also discusses other major autobiographies of Indian persons. See Mitchell (1978 below).

Mitchell, Frank

1978   *Navajo Blessingway Singer: The Autobiography of Frank Mitchell, 1881–1967.* Edited by Charlotte Frisbie and David McAllester. Tucson: University of Arizona Press.

The editors produced this extensive autobiography of Frank Mitchell (1881–1967) from interviews and have also included other information from tribal documents and other historical sources. Interviews with Mitchell began as early as 1957 and continued until his death, after which the editors continued working with other family members until 1975. The main body of the book (pp. 1–341) contains the ceremonialist's life story as narrated in first person. Reviewed by Merriam (1978 above).

Morris, Elizabeth Ann

1959   Basketmaker Flutes from the Prayer Rock District, Arizona. *American Antiquity* 24(April): 406–411.

Describes seven flutes excavated in northeastern Arizona in 1930 and 1931. Morris analyzes wear patterns to speculate on playing techniques and also gives tonal measurements. She considers these flutes to be fairly uniform in character (except for decorations) and suggests that the music played on them was sophisticated. Possible connections with later (ethnographic) flute rituals are also discussed (p. 410). Includes photographs and maps.

Nettl, Bruno

See Nettl (1954a) in the General bibliography. This discusses the general characteristics of music as recorded in an "Athabascan Area" (pp. 21–24) and in a "Plains-Pueblo Area" (pp. 24–33).

1959   Book review of *Music of Acoma, Isleta, Cochiti, and Zuni Pueblos* by Frances Densmore (1957). *Ethnomusicology* 3(1): 34–35.

Nettl begins by describing Densmore's monumental contributions to the field, then gives reasons for being disappointed with this posthumous publication. According to him, this book lacks the massive scale and a certain closeness to the subject matter which characterize Densmore's earlier works. Even more important (in his view) is the extent to which Densmore remained out of touch with the work of other major scholars. Her failure to consider Herzog's important study of Pima and Pueblo music (1936 above) is particularly unfortunate in the reviewer's opinion.

Nicholas, Dan

1939   Mescalero Apache Girls' Puberty Ceremony. *El
            Palacio* 46(9): 193–204. September.
    The author is a Mescalero Apache. He declines to expose sa-
cred aspects of the ceremony in this paper but does give information on teepee raising songs and on the Mountain Spirit Dance.

Opler, Morris E.

1941a   *An Apache Life-Way: The Economic, Social, and
            Religious Institutions of the Chiricahua Indians.*
            Chicago: University of Chicago Press.
    Song texts, translations, and descriptions of singing are found
in the following sections: "The Girls' Puberty Rite" (pp. 82–133),
"The Generalized Curing Rite" (pp. 257–267), "Ceremonialism in
Action: Obtaining and Using Power" (pp. 267–313), "War for
Vengeance" (pp. 336–354), and "Parties, Dancing, and Story-
Telling" (pp. 436–441). No musical examples.

1941b   A Jicarilla Apache Expedition and Scalp Dance.
            Journal of American Folklore 54:10–23.
    This is Opler's rendition of a text narrated by a Jicarilla
Apache man (Alasco Tisnando). The story describes a legendary
battle against other Indians of various Plains tribes. This contains a
good description of the Scalp Dance that followed on the Apache
victory (pp. 19–23). Includes no musical notations but does give
descriptions of songs and dances.

Parmentier, Richard J.

1979   The Mythological Triangle: Poseyemu, Montezuma,
            and Jesus in the Pueblos. Pp. 609–622 in *Handbook
            of the North American Indians, Volume 9: Southwest.*
            Edited by William Sturtevant. Washington:
            Smithsonian Institution.
    Focuses on the Pueblo culture hero Poseyemu and the identifi-
cation of Poseyemu with the Mexican figure Montezuma and the
Christian deity Jesus Christ. Discusses the mythological foundations of indigenous Pueblo dances (Turtle, Buffalo) and of the
Spanish-derived Matachine (pp. 612–613).

Parsons, Elsie Clews

1918   Pueblo Indian Folk-Tales, Probably of Spanish
            Provenience. *Journal of American Folklore* 31:216–
            255.
Includes song texts and translations from the Zuñi (4 texts),
Acoma (3), and Laguna (2) Pueblos.

1921   Note on the Night Chant at Tuwelchedu. *American
            Anthropologist* 23:240–243.
This contains comments by Tewa and Hopi persons on the
character of Navajo dance, which strikes them as being rather dis-
organized.

1922   Winter and Summer Dance Series in Zuni. *University
            of California Publications in American Archaeology
            and Ethnology* 17(3): 171–216.
This gives detailed descriptions of masked kachina dances as
observed in 1918. Includes dance diagrams (pp. 173 and 196) and
many references to songs. No musical notations.

1924   The Scalp Ceremonial of Zuni. *Memoirs of the Amer-
            ican Anthropological Association*, no. 31, pp. 1–42.
Describes the ceremonial as observed by the author in
September 1921. Gives verbal descriptions of songs and dances.

1938   The Humpbacked Flute Player of the Southwest.
            American Anthropologist 40:337–338.
Deals with a figure which is often seen in southwestern pictographs and pottery decorations. Parsons suggests that the humpbacked figure represents an insect and discusses the symbolic importance of the locust in Hopi flute societies. This includes a translation for the text of a song which is sung by locusts in a Hopi
folktale.

Parsons, Elsie Clews, and Ralph L. Beals

1934   The Sacred Clowns of the Pueblo and Mayo-Yaqui
            Indians. *American Anthropologist* 36(4): 491–514.
A comparative study of ceremonial clowns in the Southwest
and in Mesoamerica. The authors both conclude that there is little
doubt of an historical connection between these manifestations,
then address other questions such as the origin of clowns and other
masked figures. Spanish influences and earlier indigenous (Aztec)
practices are both discussed.

Payne, Richard W.

1989   Indian Flutes of the Southwest. *Journal of the American Musical Instrument Society* 15:5–31.
This contains descriptions and tone measurements of instruments from various museum collections. The survey encompasses ethnographic and archeological specimens, not only from the Southwest proper but also from adjacent culture areas. The section on End-blown Flutes (pp. 8–20) begins with instruments from the Basketmaker III period (AD 400–700) and then discusses specimens from the following tribes: Hopi, Yuma, Pomo, and Mohave. The section on Duct Flutes (pp. 21–31) focuses on instruments from the following groups: Papago, Pima, Maricopa, Zuni, Yaqui, and Tarahumara. Includes 23 photographs.

1991   Bone Flutes of the Anasazi. *Kiva* 56(2): 165–177.
Gives tone measurements and other acoustical analyses of bone flutes and whistles recovered from various archeological sites. Payne argues that examination of the instruments gives insights into early musical practices and that ancient cultures of the Southwest seem to have had some concept of "natural scales" based on simple harmonic ratios. In his words, "a high degree of sophistication is evident in their fashioning of sound generating mechanisms" (p. 175). He also discusses the unusual material (bone, most commonly from turkeys but also from other birds and small mammals) and the lack of ceramic instruments as so prevalent in Mexico. Includes eight photographs showing 42 bone flutes and whistles.

1993   *The Hopi Flute Ceremony: With Observations by Reverend Heinrich R. Voth.* Oklahoma City: Toubat Trails Publishing Co.
The Hopi Flute Ceremony (a ritual appeal for late summer rain) was traditionally held in alternate years to the better known Snake Ceremony. This 68-page monograph includes a description of the ritual as practiced at Oraibi circa 1895–1901 and documented in the writings and unpublished fieldnotes of Heinrich Voth (pp. 16–45). There is also an account of the Flute Ceremony at Mishongnovi as observed by Payne in 1978 (pp. 45–46) and other information on Hopi flutes and flute societies. Includes more than forty historical photographs and one musical notation quoted from Burlin (General bibliography 1907). Also see Voth (1912c below).

Peabody, Charles

1917   A Prehistoric Wind-Instrument from Pecos, New Mexico. *American Anthropologist* 19:30–33.
Gives a brief description of the instrument with physical measurements and a photograph. The author speculates on whether it was blown in a vertical or transverse manner, leaning towards the latter interpretation (which would make it a rare type in indigenous North American music).

Pilling, Arnold

1962   Some Questions on Taos Dancing. *Ethnomusicology* 6(2): 88–92.
This was written in reply to an article by Donald Brown (1961 above). Pilling mainly questions Brown's data concerning the date at which Taos dances began being performed for tourists.

Reagan, Albert

1906   Dances of the Jemez Pueblo Indians. *Transactions of the Kansas Academy of Science* 23:241–272.
Based on Reagan's observations as United States Indian Farmer (administrator) in 1899 and 1900. This contains descriptions of dances and other events in the following sections: "The Masked Dance" (pp. 243–252), "Open-Plaza Column Dances" (pp. 252–254), "Ceremonies of the Dead" (pp. 254–256), "The Animal Dance" (pp. 256–257), "The Medicine Dances" (p. 257), "The Bow and Arrow Dance" (pp. 257–259), "The August Dance" (pp. 259–260), "The Buffalo Dance" (p. 260), "The Bear Dance" (pp. 260–266), "The Corn Dance" (pp. 266–268), and "The Snake Dance" (pp. 268–272). Includes (one) musical notation entitled "Song to the Gods" (p. 269).

1914   *Don Diego; or, The Pueblo Uprising of 1680.* New York: Harriman.
An historical novel based on earlier sources and information gotten by Reagan after he became a government administrator at Jemez Pueblo in 1899. This contains musical notations (with texts) of songs from the following groups: Jemez (2 songs; pp. 2–3), Hopi (4 songs; pp. 166–167), and Apache (32 songs; pp. 209, 214, 219, 254, 268, 275, 283, and 345).

1929   Fourth of July Summer Solstice Ceremony of the Navajos. *Southern Workman* 58:310–313.

Describes a curing ceremony involving a series of songs being sung over a sand painting (p. 311). Reagan also comments on other songs and dancing which took place outside the medicine lodge (pp. 312–313).

Reichard, Gladys A.

1950   *Navaho Religion: A Study of Symbolism.* 2 vols. New York: Bollingen Foundation. Second edition by Pantheon (New York, 1963).
Volume one contains a section on "Songs" (pp. 279–300), and this discusses the origins, types, functions, textual content, and structure of Navajo ceremonial songs. Also includes many other references to songs and uses of music (passim).

Rhodes, Robert W.

1973   Selected Hopi Secular Music: Transcription and Analysis. Doctoral dissertation (Education). Arizona State University.
Could not be obtained for inspection of contents nor could information be gotten from other sources.

1977   *Hopi Music and Dance.* Occasional Papers of Navajo Community College, vol 3. Music and Dance Series, no. 2. Tsaile, Ariz.: Navajo Community College.
A brief (30 pp.) introduction for non-specialist readers. This gives basic information on kachina dances, musical composition practices, and Hopi beliefs about music. Also includes notations for five children's songs.

1986   Hopi (Music). Pp. 418–419 in *The New Grove Dictionary of American Music*, vol. 2 (E–K). Edited by H. Wiley Hitchcock and Stanley Sadie. London: Macmillan.
Discusses the process through which ceremonial songs are composed by individuals, then rehearsed and possibly revised by the performing group. Rhodes also describes basic characteristics of the Hopi musical style and historical changes in the tradition.

Rhodes, Willard

1951   (Recording and notes) "American Indians of the Southwest." Ethnic Folkways Recordings (FE 4420).

This contains various types of songs collected among the following tribes: Taos Pueblo, San Ildefonso Pueblo, Zuni, Hopi, Navajo, Yuma, Papago, Walapai, and Havasupai.

1954a   (Recording and notes) "Music of the American Indian: Navaho." Library of Congress, Recorded Sound Division (AFS L41).

One of a series of recordings collected by Rhodes between 1940 and 1952 and recently reissued (during the 1980s) with updated liner notes. Contents are described as follows: Yeibichai Songs, Chant from the Blessingway, Chant for Success in Racing, Silversmith's Song, Corn Grinding Songs, Moccasin Game Songs, Women's Song, Tuning Up Song, Farewell Love Song, Social Dance Song, Song Commemorating Flag Raising at Iwo Jima, Peyote Song, Chant from the Enemy Way, Circle Dance Songs, Spinning Dance Songs, and Squaw Dance Song.

1954b   (Recording and notes) "Music of the American Indian: Apache." Library of Congress, Recorded Sound Division (AFS L42).

From the same series as the previous item. Contains the following: Crown Dance Songs, Sunrise Dance Songs, Apache Violin, Love Songs, Fire Dance Song, Moccasin Game Song, and Songs from Girls' Puberty Ritual.

1954c   (Recording and notes) "Music of the American Indian: Pueblo: Taos, San Ildefonso, Zuni, and Hopi." Library of Congress, Recorded Sound Division (AFS L43).

From the same series as the previous two items. Contains the following: Taos Horse Stealing Song, Taos War Dance, Forty-Nine Song, San Ildefonso Peace Dance, San Ildefonso Buffalo Dance, San Ildefonso Eagle Dance, Zuni Comanche Dance, Zuni Rain Dance, Zuni Lullaby, Long-Haired Kachina Dance, Hopi Version of "Dixie," Hopi Lullaby, and Hopi Butterfly Dance.

Robb, John D.

1961   The Matachines Dance: A Ritual Folk Dance. *Western Folklore* 20(2): 87–101.

Reviews previous literature on the origins of the dance and gives eight reasons for believing it is derived from European prototypes (pp. 87–92). Robb then focuses on general features of the matachines and other, related ritual dances as practiced among peoples of the American Southwest and Mexico (pp. 92–101). Includes 13 musical examples (pp. 97–100).

1964   Rhythmic Patterns of the Santo Domingo Corn Dance. *Ethnomusicology* 8(2): 154–160.

Gives a fairly detailed account of music and dances observed at Santa Domingo Pueblo on August 4, 1946. It was prohibited to make recordings or take notes, so Robb attempts to reconstruct the event from memory. Since it was impossible to remember all the melodic phrases, he focuses on the rhythmic patterns and their relationship to the dances. Includes two musical examples and several dance diagrams.

Roberts, Don L.

1970   Tewa Pueblo Round Dances. Pp. 292–302 (Appendix 4) in *Music and Dance of the Tewa Pueblos*, by Gertrude Kurath and Antonio Garcia. Santa Fe: Museum of New Mexico Press.

Roberts begins by discussing the origins of the Tewa Round Dance (also called the Taos Dance by locals), then gives notations and analysis for six of the songs. These include classics such as "(I Don't Care If You're Married) Sixteen Times" and "One-Eyed Ford."

1972   The Ethnomusicology of the Eastern Pueblos. Pp. 243–255 in *New Perspectives on the Pueblos* edited by Alfonso Ortiz. Albuquerque: University of New Mexico Press.

This contains three main sections: (1) a review of previous publications, (2) a survey of music and dance as currently being performed, and (3) suggestions for future research. The bibliographic essay (pp. 243–249) gives information on music-related contents in documents from the early Spanish explorers. The section on contemporary music (pp. 249–254) discusses general characteristics of the music and describes six basic categories of dances: (1) kachina dances, (2) maskless kachina dances, (3) animal dances, (4) corn dances, (5) borrowed dances, and (6) social dances. Roberts also suggests the following areas for future research: comparison of styles from different Pueblos; studies of compositional practices, native aesthetics, and musical norms; and research on borrowing of songs from other Pueblos or non-Pueblo tribes.

1980   A Calendar of Eastern Pueblo Ritual Dramas. Pp. 103–124 in *Southwestern Indian Ritual Drama* edited by Charlotte Frisbie. Albuquerque: University of New Mexico Press.

This is basically a straightforward listing of the rituals that are performed in various Pueblos from month to month.

1986   Pueblo, eastern (Music). Pp. 654–655 in *The New Grove Dictionary of American Music*, vol. 3 (L–Q). Edited by H. Wiley Hitchcock and Stanley Sadie. London: Macmillan.

Focuses on music and dance among the Keresan-speaking groups who live along the Rio Grande and its tributaries in New Mexico. Outlines basic characteristics of the music and lists six categories or types of songs. Much of the information is also given in Roberts (1980 above), but the typical form or structure of the songs is described here with a useful diagram.

Roberts, Helen Heffron

1923   Chakwena Songs of Zuni and Laguna. *Journal of American Folklore* 36:177–184.

Contains transcriptions and comparative analysis for three versions of a Pueblo song, two versions as sung at Laguna and one from Zuñi.

1927   Indian Music from the Southwest. *Natural History* 27(3): 257–265.

Gives a brief history of research and also includes notations of songs from the Apache (2), Zuñi Pueblo (2), Picurís Pueblo (2), and Tewa (1).

1927   Variation in Melodic Renditions as an Indicator of Emotion. *Psychological Review* 34:463–71.

Compares 34 renditions of 11 Picurís Pueblo songs as performed by one person. Roberts suggests that emotional factors were possibly involved in producing melodic variations.

See Roberts (1936) in the General bibliography. This contains a section on the general characteristics of vocal music among tribes of the Southwest culture area (pp. 32–34).

Russell, Frank

1898   An Apache Medicine Dance. *American Anthropologist* (Old Series) 11:367–372.

Could not be obtained for inspection of contents nor could information be gotten from other sources.

1908   *The Pima Indians*. Annual Report of the Bureau of
             American Ethnology (1904–1905) 26:3–389.
     This contains a section on "Musical Instruments" (pp. 166–170) with descriptions and illustrations. The section on "Songs" (pp. 270–338) includes texts and translations for 62 songs.

Sands, Kathleen, and Emory Sekaquaptewa

1978   Four Hopi Lullabies: A Study in Method and
             Meaning. *American Indian Quarterly* 4(3): 195–210.
     Gives literal and free translations for the song texts, also discussing how they reflect Hopi beliefs and values. The titles (in English) are as follows: The Beetle Song, The Owl, The Prairie Dog, and The Soyok Maiden. No musical notations.

See the catalogue by **Seeger and Spear** (1987). This contains a listing of cylinder recordings at Indiana University Archives of Traditional Music. The collection includes recordings from the following southwestern tribes: Apache (various groups), Maricopa, Mohave, Navajo, Papago, Pima, Pueblo (various groups), Walapai, and Yuman.

Sekaquaptewa, Emory

1976   Hopi Indian Ceremonies. Pp. 35–43 in *Seeing with a
             Native Eye*, edited by W. H. Capps. New York:
             Harper and Row.
     The subject is native identity experience and the approach is basically autobiographical. Sekaquaptewa begins by discussing his childhood impressions of the kachina as real beings and symbols of good behavior. He then describes the thoughts and feelings of a Hopi person participating in kachina ceremonies and also discusses issues relating to communication between Indians and non-Indians. Does not contain information on music or dance as such.

Spier, Leslie

1928   Havasupai Ethnography. *Anthropological Papers of
             the American Museum of Natural History* 29(3): 81–392.
     Contains 12 song texts and translations (pp. 142, 265, 283, 338, and 342).

1933   *Yuman Tribes of the Gila River*. Chicago: University of Chicago Press.
The section on "Songs and Song-Cycles" (pp. 254–270) gives information on the following subjects relating to Maricopa songs: connection of songs to dreams, structure of cycles, differences from Mohave concepts, songs in spoken stories, fluctuation in the repertories due to diffusion and death of singers, overt and hidden meanings in various songs and song cycles, and the relationship between Maricopa songs and Mohave songs as documented by Kroeber. Also included are three tables showing the uses of songs, and texts and translations for six songs. The section described here is followed by George Herzog's analysis of Maricopa music (1933 above).

Spinden, Herbert J.

1933   *Songs of the Tewa, Preceded by an Essay on American Indian Poetry*. New York: The Exposition of Indian Tribal Arts, Inc.
The essay on Indian poetry contains translations of about 60 song texts from various tribes, and the discussion of Tewa songs includes translations for 50 song texts. The section "Notes on Tewa Songs" (pp. 112–125) discusses the meanings and uses or functions of songs. Information given here is from Hickerson (General bibliography, 1961:352).

Stricklen, E.G.

1923   Notes on Eight Papago Songs. *University of California Publications in American Archaeology and Ethnology* 20(17): 361–366.
Contains musical notations for eight songs with analyses of scales, rhythm, and melodic form.

Stumpf, Carl

1892   Phonographierte Indianermelodien. *Vierteljahrsschrift für Musikwissenschaft* 8:127–144.
A critical review of Gilman on Zuni melodies (1891 above). Stumpf gives alternate analyses for each of the nine songs considered by Gilman. He also discusses the cylinder phonograph and the problems involved with deriving very precise notations based on phonographic recordings. See also the discussion by Fillmore (1894 above).

Sweet, Jill Drayson

1983   Ritual and Theatre in Tewa Ceremonial Performan-
             ces. *Ethnomusicology* 27(2): 253–270.
    Discusses adjustments that are made by Tewa persons when
participating in commercial ceremonials during the tourist season.
From the researcher's point of view these adjustments transport the
Tewa from the (original) ritual to the theatrical side of the rit-
ual/theatre continuum. Based on observations made from 1973 to
1980 and historical sources.

1985   *Dances of the Tewa Indians: Expressions of New
             Life*. Santa Fe: School of American Research Press.
    Based on the author's doctoral thesis, this brief study (99
pages) gives historical information and discusses the meaning of
traditional dances for contemporary Tewa participants. Contains
verbal descriptions of dances and excellent photographs but no
analysis of music or dance. The review by Kurath (1987 above) is
rather critical.

1992   The Beauty, Humor, and Power of Tewa Pueblo
             Dance. Pp. 83–104 in *Native American Dance: Cere-
             monies and Social Traditions* edited by Charlotte
             Heth. Washington: National Museum of the Ameri-
             can Indian, Smithsonian Institution.
    Describes contemporary dances and their significance for
Tewa people. Contains excellent color photographs of dances and
an account of dances held at San Ildefonso Pueblo in 1974.

Tedlock, Barbara J.

1980   Songs of the Zuni Kachina Society: Composition,
             Rehearsal, and Performance. Pp. 7–35 in *Southwest-
             ern Indian Ritual Drama* edited by Charlotte Frisbie.
             Albuquerque: University of New Mexico Press.
    Examines Zuni compositional practices and social organiza-
tion, particularly the process of "group editing" and rehearsal of
songs. Tedlock also proposes a general model or methodology for
discovering native musical categories and compositional principles.

Troyer, Carlos

1913   *The Zuni Indians and Their Music*. Philadelphia:
             Theodore Presser Co.

Contains melodies arranged with harmonies for concert use after the fashion of John C. Fillmore (See above and in the General bibliography).

Underhill, Ruth Murray

1938   *Singing for Power: The Song Magic of the Papago Indians of Southern Arizona.* Berkeley: University of California Press. Reprint. Berkeley and Los Angeles: University of California Press, 1976.

Contains extensive but non-technical information on Papago songs, particularly relating to the function and meaning of songs. Includes many song texts in English (passim).

1946   *Papago Indian Religion.* Columbia University Contributions to Anthropology No. 33. Reprint. New York: AMS Press, 1969.

Contains several song texts in English (passim). Also includes a section on "Song Cycles" (pp. 35–37).

Voegelin, Carl F., and R.C. Euler

1957   Introduction to Hopi Chants. *Journal of American Folklore* 70:115–136.

Provides content and discourse analysis focusing on secular chants. This includes information on the occasions for secular chanting and on the differences between various individual styles.

Vogt, Evon Z.

1955   A Study of the Southwestern Fiesta System as Exemplified by the Laguna Fiesta. *American Anthropologist* 57:820–839.

Emphasizes the need to study entire cultural situations rather than focusing only on dance-related aspects. Vogt examines social and economic interactions between seven tribal groups and historical changes that have occurred in the years from 1919 to 1952. Also discusses Indian stereotypes of other Indians and non-Indians.

Voth, Henry R.

1901   Oraibi Powamu Ceremony. *Field Columbian Museum Publications, Anthropological Series* 3(2): 67–158.

The section entitled "Powamu Songs" (pp. 126–155) gives texts and translations for 17 lengthy songs.

1903a   Oraibi Oaqol Ceremony. *Field Columbian Museum Publications, Anthropological Series* 6(1):1–46.

Describes a nine-day ceremonial performed by women, with numerous photographs. Includes texts and translations for 12 songs.

1903b   Oraibi Summer Snake Ceremonies. *Field Columbian Museum Publications, Anthropological Series* 3(4): 267–358.

Describes various aspects of the nine-day ceremonial, with more than 70 superb photographs. Songs are frequently mentioned in connection with ritual activities (passim).

1905   *The Traditions of the Hopi.* Field Museum, Anthropological Series, vol. 8.

Gives translations of 110 myths and other texts recorded circa 1903–1905. Songs of mythic animals and kachina deities are prominent in many of the narratives, but the monograph does not include musical transcriptions. Some of the texts seem to indicate a connection between crying and singing in Hopi folklore (pp. 182, 195, and 211).

1912a   The Oraibi Marau Ceremony. *Field Columbian Museum Publications, Anthropological Series* 11(1): 1–88.

Describes a nine-day ceremony conducted by a women's fraternity, with about 40 photographs. The section "Songs Chanted in the Altar Ceremonies" (pp. 69–88) gives texts, translations, and commentary for 13 lengthy songs.

1912b   Oraibi New Year Ceremony. *Field Columbian Museum, Anthropological Series* 11(2): 111–119.

A brief description (with photographs and drawings) of the ritual which marks the beginning of the Hopi ceremonial calendar. Songs are frequently mentioned, but no musical examples or texts are included.

1912c   Tewa Bahalawu of the Oraibi Flute Societies. *Field Columbian Museum, Anthropological Series* 11(2): 121–136.

Describes prayer offerings to the sun as practiced in Hopi flute societies, focusing on ceremonies observed in 1898 and 1901. It seems clear from the descriptions that songs are sung together with the playing of flutes, but the musical texture of the ensemble is difficult to assess. This volume of the series (Miscellaneous Ceremonies of the Hopi Indians) also contains an interesting article by Voth on eagle-killing rituals. Also see Payne (1993 above)

Wallis, Wilson D., Minerva Pepinsky, Abe Pipinsky, and Elsie Clews Parsons

1936   Folk Tales from Shumopovi, Second Mesa. *Journal of American Folklore* 49(191): 1–68.
Contains five musical notations of songs collected in 1912 (pp. 34, 48–49).

Walton, Eda Lou

1930   Navajo Song Patterning. *Journal of American Folklore* 43:105–118.
Discusses textual parallelism, sequencing, and other organizational principles, including several translations of the texts into English. Based on data from various writings of Washington Matthews (listed above).

Ware, Naomi

1970   Survival and Change in Pima Indian Music. *Ethnomusicology* 14(1): 100–113.
Focuses on contemporary music among the Salt River Pima as observed by the author in 1965 and 1966. Ware describes two existing genres of traditional music (social dance songs and curing songs) and other forms of music in which the Indians have become involved more recently. The latter include marching band music, rock and roll, and a type of Hispanic-influenced music called "chicken scratch." The absence of Pan-Indian musical forms is noted (p. 105). Also includes information on earlier indigenous musical genres, based on historical sources (pp. 106–110).

Weinman, Janice

1970   The Influence of Pueblo World View on the Construction of its Vocal Music. *Ethnomusicology* 14(2): 313–315.
Focuses on songs of the Pueblo Corn Dance as observed by the author in 1969. Weinman comments briefly on various respects

in which the music seems to reflect Pueblo attitudes towards nature and human society.

Wilder, Carleton Stafford

1963   *The Yaqui Deer Dance: A Study in Cultural Change.* Bureau of American Ethnology Bulletin no. 186:145–210.

An interesting study of contemporary practices as observed in Pascua (Arizona) circa 1939–1940 and the persistence of indigenous elements in the dance. The section entitled "Musical Instruments" (pp. 167–169) also gives information on songs, including a chart which shows the relation of musical forms to dance movements. There follows a description of a dance given in February 1940 (pp. 169–175). A section entitled "The Deer Songs" (pp. 176–205) gives translations of 20 songs. Concluding remarks focus on changing patterns of symbolism in the texts, particularly noting the importance of the flower as a sacred symbol (p. 205).

Woolley, Doriane

1939   Book review of *Singing for Power*, by Ruth Underhill (1938). *Journal of American Folklore* 52(205–206): 330–331.

Basically a positive review, but Woolley does note that the book "suffers from limitations of the popular form" (p. 331). She feels that the song texts might have been more fully annotated and that Underhill sometimes fails to make clear distinctions between native theory and (actual) practice.

Wyman, Leland C.

1970   *Blessingway.* Tucson: University of Arizona Press.

A comprehensive study containing three different versions or accounts of the ceremony and its mythology as explained by ceremonialists interviewed in 1932. The information is from manuscripts collected and translated by Father Berard Haile (See writings listed above). Each of the explanations gives translations of song texts and other information on music. No musical notations.

Wyman, Leland, and Clyde Kluckhohn

1938   Navaho Classification of their Song Ceremonials. *Memoirs of the American Anthropological Association*, no. 50, pp. 1–38.

Contains detailed listing and discussion of the order of songs in Navajo ceremonials. Could not be obtained. Information above is from Hickerson (General bibliography, 1961:379).

Yeh, Nora

1980   The Pogonshare Ceremony of the Tewa of San Juan, New Mexico. *Selected Reports in Ethnomusicology* 3(2): 101–146. Los Angeles: Program in Ethnomusicology, Department of Music, UCLA.

A detailed account based mainly on observations made by the author in 1977. The author discusses the cosmological significance of music and dance patterns and particularly notes the importance of the four cardinal directions. Includes diagrams of dance formations and musical analyses. Yeh's notations show the relation of song melodies to drum rhythms and foot-lifting patterns.

VII. Plains

Around Him, John

1983   *Lakota Ceremonial Songs.* Rosebud: Sinte Gleska College.
Could not be obtained for inspection of contents nor could information be gotten from other sources.

Bahr, Donald

1988   Book review of *Sacred Language: The Nature of Supernatural Discourse in Lakota* by William Powers (1986). *Ethnomusicology* 32(3): 460–462.
The book under review employs lexical and syntactic analysis of texts in order to demonstrate Powers's thesis that Oglala songs represent a form of special language for sacred communications. Bahr questions the success of this method, arguing that literary and contextual approaches would better help to understand hidden allusions in the song texts. In other respects a positive review which commends the intellectual substance of the work.

See **Baker** (1882) in the General bibliography. This contains musical notations of songs identified as Dakota (9 examples), Iowa (7), Kiowa (2), Cheyenne (2), Pawnee (1), Comanche (2), and Ponca (3).

Beatty, John

1968, 1969   (Recording and liner notes) "Music of the Plains Apache." Smithsonian-Folkways Recordings (AHM 4252).
The contents of the recording are identified as follows: Children's Songs (4), Lullaby (1), Peyote Songs (4), Church Songs

(2), Dance Songs (2), and Handgame Songs (4). Includes liner
notes (4 pp.) by Beatty.

1974   *Kiowa-Apache Music and Dance.* Greeley:
            University of Northern Colorado, Museum of
            Anthropology. Occasional Publications in
            Anthropology, Ethnology Series no. 31.
Describes the complex musical culture of an Apachean group
which assimilated to a Plains lifestyle about 300–400 years ago.
Beatty examines several different genres or varieties of Kiowa-
Apache music in order to determine the principal "music area" af-
filiation of the group. In a core Chapter Six ("Classes of Kiowa-
Apache Music," pp. 24–56) Beatty describes various types of
songs and their regional affinities (by comparison with basic styles
of the Plains, Athabascan, or Basin areas). His conclusions are
summarized in Chapter Seven (pp. 57–60). Contains seventeen
complete musical transcriptions (Appendix A) and numerous
shorter examples throughout (passim). Based on research conducted in Oklahoma in 1965.

Beloff, Sandra

1974   Record Review of "Ponca Peyote Songs," vols. 1–3,
            produced by Tony Isaacs (Indian House IH 2005,
            2006, and 2007). *Ethnomusicology* 18(1): 178–180.
Very favorable review. Praises the choice of performers and
technical quality, also noting the excellence of the notes by Tony
Isaacs. Beloff gives information on the usual performance context
and alterations made for the purposes of recording. She also describes the general style of the music and differences in personal
styles of the singers heard on the recording.

Benedict, Ruth F.

1922   The Vision in Plains Culture. *American Anthropolo-
            gist* 24(1): 1–23.
It seems worth noting that this well-known article contains
virtually no mention of songs as related to the vision quest. It does
include comments on the importance of crying when seeking to establish spiritual contacts. This is also discussed at greater length in
Hatton (1988 and 1990 below) and in Keeling (California bibliography, 1992).

Black Bear, Ben Sr., and R. D. Theisz

1976   *Songs and Dances of the Lakota*. Rosebud: Sinta
         Gleska College.
The Introduction by Theisz (pp. 9–24) gives information on
song and dance categories and general characteristics of the music.
The sections which follow are written in Lakota and in English.
These include titles such as "Ben Black Bear on the Role of Music
in Lakota Life" (pp. 25–30), "The Omaha Tradition" (pp. 31–80),
and "Social Dances" (pp. 81–102). This does not include musical
notations and is mainly written to express local Indian perspectives
on the music.

Boas, Franz

1894   Review of *A Study of Omaha Music* by Alice C.
         Fletcher and John C. Fillmore (1893). *Journal of
         American Folklore* 7:169–171.
A very positive review which praises the book for making
readers more aware of the importance of music in various spheres
of Indian life. Most interestingly, Boas seems to support Fillmore's
ethnocentric notion that the melodies of Indian songs are guided by
"natural harmonies" of which the Indians themselves are unaware
(and unable to perform correctly). For more information see the
writings of Fillmore in the General bibliography.

1925   Review of *Teton Sioux Music* by Frances Dens-
         more(1918). *Journal of American Folklore* 38:319–
         325.
Boas criticizes the rhythmic aspects of Densmore's musical
notation and even retranscribes 10 of the songs.

Boley, Raymond

1975   (Recording) "Songs from the Battleford Powwow."
         Canyon Records (No. 6142).
This contains excellent recordings of War Dance songs and
others recorded at Battleford, Saskatchewan (Canada), in August
1975.

Boyd, Maurice

1981   *Kiowa Voices: Ceremonial Dance, Religion, and
         Song*. Vol. 1. Fort Worth: Texas Christian University
         Press.

Based on oral histories and songs collected from Kiowa elders since 1975 and on manuscript collections of the Kiowa Historical and Research Society. The book includes chapters on the following: Sun Dance, Buffalo Dance (Kiowa War Dance), Wind Songs, Scalp Dance, Warriors Dance, Black Legs Dance, Rabbit Dance, Ghost Dance, Kiowa Christian Songs (the Jesus Road and the Peyote Road), and Kiowa Gourd Dance. The final chapter describes various non-ceremonial dances and includes five musical transcriptions.

See **Burlin** (1907) in the General bibliography. This contains the following musical examples (including texts and translations): 18 Dakota songs (pp. 47–90 and 536–541), two Omaha songs (pp. 55–56 and 80–81), 16 Pawnee songs (pp. 105–143 and 541–544), 20 Cheyenne songs (pp. 151–193 and 544–545), nine Arapaho songs (pp. 198–217 and 545–546), and nine Kiowa songs (pp. 224–240 and 546–548).

Cadman, Charles Wakefield

1909   The Decadence of the Indian Powwow: Tribal Music and Something About It. *Musical Courier* 49(23): 59–60.
        Contains a brief description of Dakota (Sioux) singing. Listed in Hickerson (General bibliography, 1961:158).

Callahan, Alice Anne

1990   *The Osage Ceremonial Dance I'n-Lon-Schka.* Norman: University of Oklahoma Press.
        Detailed study of a contemporary ceremonial (with long history) based on research conducted in Oklahoma during the 1970s and 1980s. Contains chapters on "History of the I'n-Lon-Schka" (pp. 19–32), "The I'n-Lon-Schka Music" (pp. 73–96), and "The I'n-Lon-Schka Dance" (pp. 97–107). Includes 12 musical examples and many other illustrations (maps, photos, drawings). The author is part-Osage.

Catlin, George

(1867)   *O-Kee-Pa: A Religious Ceremony and Other Customs of the Mandan.* Revised edition with Introduction by John C. Ewers. Lincoln: University of Nebraska Press, 1967.

Powers calls this the earliest serious ethnography of the Sun Dance (1982:164 below). Based on events observed in 1832, this includes classic paintings depicting various aspects of the ceremony. The Introduction by Ewers discusses the history of the ritual and other related topics.

Clifton, James

1969   Sociocultural Dynamics of the Prairie Potawatomi Drum Cult. *Plains Anthropologist* 14(May): 85–93.

The Drum Cult was a revitalization movement which was originally founded by a Santee Dakota prophetess named Wananikwe in 1872. The movement spread to the Prairie Potawatomie of Kansas around 1880. This paper deals with recent forms of the Drum Cult as observed in Kansas in 1963. The paper contains a diagram showing the layout of activities on the ceremonial grounds (p. 88).

Colby, Leonard Wright

1895   *Wanagi Olowan Kin* (The Ghost Dance of the Dakotas). *Nebraska Historical Society: Proceedings and Collections (2nd series)* 1: 131–150.

An early description of the "Messiah Craze" among the Dakota (Sioux) in 1889–1890, this includes one musical example along with two song texts and translations (p. 140).

Cooper, John M.

(1957)   *The Gros Ventre of Montana, Part II: Religion and Ritual* edited by Regina Flannery. Anthropological Series no. 16. Washington: Catholic University of America Press. Original edition, 1949.

This is the second part of a general ethnography seeking to reconstruct an image of Gros Ventre life as it existed before the disappearance of the buffalo during the 1880s. Part I (covering other aspects of culture) is by Regina Flannery. This portion on religion and ritual is based on Cooper's interviews with Gros Ventre elders circa 1938–1940. It contains chapters on "The Flat Pipe Ritual" (pp. 77–129), "The Sacred Dances" (pp. 173–256), and "Miscellaneous Private Rites and Observances" (pp. 364–423). Contains no musical notations but includes many references to songs and the religious contexts of singing.

See **Curtis** (1907–1930) in the General bibliography. *Volume Three* contains the following: five Teton melodies, texts, and translations (pp. 79–84); three Assiniboin melodies, texts, and translations (pp. 129–132); and seven Dakota melodies, texts, and translations (pp. 143–150). *Volume Four* contains the following: 16 Crow melodies, one with text and three with translations only (pp. 13–14, 16, 28, 32–34, 37, 62, 64, 73, 81–83, 85, 88, 107, and 117); and nine Hidatsa melodies plus 13 texts and translations (pp. 149–152 and 186–189). *Volume Five* contains the following: two Mandan melodies, plus one text (pp. 37–38 and 50); 14 Arikara melodies, 13 with English texts (pp.155–163); and five Atsina (Gros Ventre) melodies (pp. 164–169). *Volume Six* contains the following: 12 Piegan melodies, 11 with texts and translations (pp. 32–33, 35, 38, 47–49, 55–56, 57, 60–62, and 63); nine Piegan song texts and translations (pp. 35–36, 43, 57–58, and 62); 13 Cheyenne melodies, seven with texts and translations (pp. 106–107, 120–122, and 132–134); and four Arapaho melodies, two with texts and translations (pp. 160–164). *Volume Eighteen* contains five translations of Blackfoot songs (p. 197). *Volume Nineteen* contains four Oto melodies and texts (pp. 205–210), one Oto text in English (p. 176), and two Ponca melodies and texts (pp. 216–220).

Deloria, Ella C.

1929   The Sun Dance of the Oglala Sioux. *Journal of American Folklore* 42(166): 354–413.
This is a revised version of a manuscript collected by J. R. Walker from an Oglala Sioux Indian named Sword. Deloria revised the manuscript with help from several elders. The narrative describes the Sun Dance ritual and gives texts and translations for eight songs. See also Walker (1917 below).

Dempsey, Hugh A.

1956   Social Dances of the Blood Indians of Alberta, Canada. *Journal of American Folklore* 69:47–52.
This focuses mainly on the Owl Dance, which was brought into Canada around 1915 by Blood Indians who had been visiting in the United States. The dance possibly originated among Crow Indians of southern Montana. Dempsey describes various aspects of the dance and also comments on the singing (pp. 49 and 51). No musical examples.

Densmore, Frances

1918   *Teton Sioux Music.* Bureau of American Ethnology
Bulletin (Anthropological Papers) no. 61. Reprinted
by Da Capo Press (New York, 1972).

Contains musical notations (with texts and translations) for
240 Teton songs collected between 1911 and 1914. In this study
Densmore attempts to compare the style of older Teton songs with
that of more recent ones. 240 Teton songs are also compared with
360 Chippewa songs using a tabular analysis showing the relative
occurrence of intervals, rhythmic units, etc. A form of schematic
graph notation is also used here to illustrate several melodic types.
See the reviews by Boas (1925), Kroeber (1918), and Roberts
(1919). This is also an important source of information on the Sun
Dance and its music. See Walker (1917 below) for information on
the Sun Dance.

1923   *Mandan and Hidatsa Music.* Bureau of American
Ethnology Bulletin (Anthropological Papers) no. 80.
Reprinted by Da Capo Press (New York, 1972).

Contains musical notations (some with native texts and translations) for 110 Mandan and Hidatsa songs collected in 1912,
1915, and 1918. Individual songs are analyzed and various genres
or groups of songs are also discussed in terms of style and cultural
background. There is a tabular (quantitative) comparative analysis
similar to that used in Densmore's study of Teton Sioux music
(1918) and other writings, and the author again uses schematic
graph notations to illustrate certain melodic types.

1929   *Pawnee Music.* Bureau of American Ethnology
Bulletin no. 93. Reprinted by Da Capo Press (New
York, 1972).

Contains musical notations (some with texts and translations)
for 86 songs collected by Densmore in 1919 and 1920. There is
musical analysis and cultural commentary for each song, and various genres or groups of songs are also analyzed and discussed. The
melodic and rhythmic aspects of Pawnee songs are compared with
987 songs from other tribes using the tabular (quantitative) method
of earlier studies.

1936   *Cheyenne and Arapaho Music.* Southwest Museum
Papers, no. 10.

Contains musical notations for 44 Cheyenne songs and 28
Arapaho songs collected by Densmore in 1935. There are English

translations for some, but native texts are not given. There is musical analysis and other commentary for each song, and various genres or types of songs are also discussed. The melodic and rhythmic aspects of Pawnee songs are compared with those of other tribes the author had studied using quantitative tables.

1944   The Survival of Omaha Songs. *American Anthropologist* 46:418–420.

This discusses three songs that were originally recorded by Alice Fletcher (see writings below) and recorded again by Densmore in 1941.

1951a   (Recording and liner notes) "Songs of the Sioux." Library of Congress, Music Division, Recorded Sound Section (AAFS L 23).

Contents are identified as follows: Sun Dance Songs (6), War Songs (4), Grass Dance Songs (3), Society Songs (3), Song Concerning the Sacred Stones, Songs Used for Treatment of the Sick (3), and Miscellaneous (7).

1951b   (Recording and liner notes) "Songs of the Pawnee and Northern Ute." Library of Congress, Music Division, Recorded Sound Section (AAFS L 25).

Contents are identified as follows: Ghost Dance Songs (4), Buffalo and Lance Dance Songs (3), Hand Game Songs (2), Wolf Society Songs (2), War Songs (4), Bear Dance Song, Sun Dance Song, Social Dance Songs (4), Parade Songs (4), Songs for Treatment of the Sick (2), and Miscellaneous (4).

1952   (Recording and liner notes) "Songs of the Menomini, Mandan, and Hidatsa." Library of Congress, Music Division, Recorded Sound Section (AAFS L 33).

Contents are identified as follows: Menomini Song of an Adoption Dance, Menomini Songs of Hunting and War Bundles (3), Menomini Dream Songs (3), Menomini Songs for Treatment of the Sick (4), Menomini Songs of the Drum Religion (4), Menomini War Songs (4), Menomini Legend Songs (2), Menomini Miscellaneous Songs (2), Mandan Song of Goose Woman Society, Hidatsa Song in the Gardens, Mandan Song of the Eagle-Catching Camp, Mandan Song of the Dog Society, and Hidatsa War Songs (3).

Dorsey, George Amos

1903   *The Arapaho Sun Dance: The Ceremony of the Offerings Lodge*. Field Columbian Museum Publications (Anthropological Series), no. 75. Also published in Field Museum of Natural History Publications, vol. 4.

The section on "Offerings-Lodge Songs" (pp. 178–179) describes music in the ceremony and includes translations of several song texts. Contains other verbal descriptions of singing (*passim*).

1905a   *The Cheyenne*. 2 vols. Field Columbian Museum Publications (Anthropological Series), nos. 99 and 103. Also published in Field Museum of Natural History Publications, vol. 9, nos. 1–2.

Volume one describes music of the "hoof-rattle warriors" (pp. 18–19), and the second volume contains a description of Sun Dance songs (pp. 126–129).

1905b   The Ponca Sun Dance. *Field Museum of Natural History Publication No. 102*. Anthropological Series 7(2): 67–88.

The text portion (pp. 67–88) describes the sequence of events in the five-day ceremony. Songs and dances are mentioned throughout, but Dorsey mainly discusses the body painting and costumes. This is followed by unnumbered pages containing about 60 photographs and drawings.

Dorsey, James Owen

1884   *Omaha Sociology*. Bureau of American Ethnology, Annual Report (1881–1882) 3: 205–370.

Contains 18 song texts and translations along with three translations only (pp. 290–291, 320, 322–323, and 331). Also includes brief discussion of musicians among the Omaha (pp. 341–342). Information here is from Hickerson (General bibliography, 1961:205).

1885   Mourning and War Customs of the Kansas. *American Naturalist* 19:670–680.

Includes one song text and translation along with descriptions of songs and singing among the Kansas tribe. Could not be obtained. Information here is from Hickerson (General bibliography, 1961:205).

1888   Songs of the Heducka Society. *Journal of American Folklore* 1:65–68.
Contains three musical examples, plus texts and translations for seven songs collected among the Omaha. Could not be obtained. Information given here is from Hickerson (General bibliography, 1961:205).

1888   Abstracts of Omaha and Pawnee Myths. *Journal of American Folklore* 1:204–208.
Includes native texts and translations for three Omaha Indian songs, two of which are also given in musical staff notations. Could not be obtained. Information from Hickerson (General bibliography, 1961:205).

1888   Omaha Songs. *Journal of American Folklore* 1:209–213.
Gives texts and translations for ten songs of various types. Dorsey also discusses differences between spoken and sung versions of the texts.

1889   Ponka and Omaha Songs. *Journal of American Folklore* 2:271–276.
Provides texts and translations of four Ponka songs, three of which are also given in musical staff notations (pp. 271–273). This also gives musical notations for eight Omaha songs, one with text and translation and five with native texts only (pp. 273–276). Six other Omaha Indian song texts are given, two with translations. Could not be obtained. Information given here is from Hickerson (General bibliography, 1961:206).

1892   Siouan Onomatopes. *American Anthropologist* (Old Series) 5:1–8
Discusses seven classes of onomatopoetic structures that occur in the Siuan languages. One type is illustrated by the text of an Omaha song from a story (about a fawn whose mother was killed by hunters). Includes a musical notation of the song, with text and translation.

1894   *A Study of Siouan Cults*. Bureau of American Ethnology, Annual Report (1889–1890), vol. 11, pp. 351–544.
Contains musical notations for two songs with texts and translations (pp.472 and 480). Also includes four other song texts, three of which are translated (pp. 382, 385, 464, and 470). Information given here is from Hickerson (General bibliography, 1961:206).

Farrer, Claire R.

1984   Review of *Yuwipi: Vision and Experience in Oglala Ritual* by William Powers (1982). *Ethnomusicology* 28(2): 338–339.

A mixed review stating that Powers's combination of ethnography and fictionalized narrative left many unanswered questions and failed to meet the reviewer's expectations.

Flannery, Regina

1947   The Changing Form and Functions of the Gros Ventre Grass Dance. *Primitive Man* 20(3): 39–70.

The Gros Ventre received the Grass Dance from the Assiniboin between 1875 and 1880. In this paper Flannery describes early forms of the dance (circa 1875–1890) and transformations which occurred from 1890 to 1916. There are many references to songs, with interesting comments on changing performance practices and musical values (pp. 65–67).

Fletcher, Alice Cunningham

1884a   The Elk Mystery or Festival. Ogallala Sioux. *16th and 17th Annual Reports of the Peabody Museum of American Archaeology and Ethnology* 3(3–4): 276–288.

Describes use of songs in the ceremony and includes one Omaha melody (arranged) with text and translation. Could not be obtained. Information given here is from Hickerson (General bibliography, 1961:222).

1884b   The "Wawan" or Pipe Dance of the Omahas. *16th and 17th Annual Reports of the Peabody Museum of American Archaeology and Ethnology* 3(3–4): 308–333.

Includes musical notations and texts for ten Omaha songs. Could not be obtained. Information from Hickerson (General bibliography, 1961:223).

1892   The Hae-thu-ska Society of the Omaha Tribe. *Journal of American Folklore* 5:135–144.

Gives texts and translations for three ceremonial songs (pp. 139–141). Also contains other information on music and dance, as for example how the society would decide (by group) whether a song should be composed to commemorate a particular heroic deed

(p. 141). If consent was given, the song was commissioned and then later learned by other members of the society. Includes no musical examples.

1899   Leaves from My Omaha Note-Book. *Journal of American Folklore* 2:219–226.
A rather romantic account of Omaha courtship and marriage customs written as if for a personal diary. Contains one musical notation of a man's love song without text or translation.

1904   *The Hako: A Pawnee Ceremony.* Bureau of American Ethnology, Annual Report (1900–1901), vol. 22, no. 2.
This contains musical notations, texts, and translations for 104 songs. The transcriptions are by Edwin Tracy. Includes a rhythmic analysis of the songs. Information from Hickerson (General bibliography, 1961:226).

Fletcher, Alice Cunningham, and Francis La Flesche

1893   *A Study of Omaha Indian Music. With a Report on the Structural Peculiarities of the Music by John Comfort Fillmore.* Archaelogical and Ethnological Papers of the Peabody Museum (Harvard University), vol. 1, no. 5. Reprint. New York: Kraus Reprint Corp., 1967.
Fillmore's analysis (pp. 59–77) focuses mainly on scales and tonality, stressing his views on the natural "harmonic" basis of all Indian music. The monograph contains notations for 92 songs with harmonizations by Fillmore (pp. 79–151). Texts are included for most of the songs. Nearly all the examples are from the Omaha Indians but also represented are the Oto (four songs), Pawnee (2), and Ponca (1). See also the critical review by Wead (General bibliography, 1900b).

1911   *The Omaha Tribe.* Bureau of American Ethnology, Annual Report (1905–1906) 27:17–672.
Contains musical notations, texts, and translations for 128 songs. The transcriptions are by Fletcher, John Fillmore, and Edwin Tracy. 28 of the melodies are harmonized by Fillmore (posthumous). The section on "Music" (pp. 371–401) covers instruments and general characteristics of the style. Could not be obtained. Information given here is from Hickerson (General bibliography, 1961:229).

Fryett, Jere Thomas

1977   The Musical Culture of the Crow Indians of Montana. Doctoral dissertation (Music). University of Colorado at Boulder.

A fairly comprehensive musical ethnography. A lengthy core chapter on "Crow Musical Culture" (chapter three, pp. 40–95) contains sections on the following subjects: earlier musical genres (emphasizing the use of songs for various practical functions), modern song types, musical values, and references to music in Crow mythology. There are also chapters on musical instruments (pp. 96–109) and on musical transcription and analysis (pp. 110–117). Chapter seven (following appendices) contains many notations of songs recorded by Fryett or from commercial recordings.

Gamble, John M.

1949   Changing Patterns in Kiowa Indian Dances. Pp. 94–104 in *Acculturation in the Americas*. Volume two of *Selected Papers of the 29th International Congress of Americanists (New York)* edited by Sol Tax. Chicago: University of Chicago Press.

Gamble notes that formerly religious dances are becoming more secular in character and that there is increased participation of women in dances that were previously men's dances. Also observes that modern dance steps (introduced 20 or 30 years ago) are more homogeneous than previous ones.

Giglio, Virginia

1994   *Southern Cheyenne Women's Songs*. Norman: University of Oklahoma Press.

Focuses mainly on 32 songs, giving transcriptions, analyses, and commentary concerning the meaning and social contexts of the songs as described by the female singers interviewed by Giglio. The following song types are represented: lullabies and children's songs, handgame songs, social songs, and Christian spiritual songs. The songs can be heard on a cassette tape which accompanies the book. Chapter one (pp. 7–42) also gives information on Cheyenne culture and history. The review by Vennum (1995) is highly critical.

Gillis, Verna

1979   (Recording) "Comanche Flute Music." Ethnic Folkways (FE 4328).
The album contains flute music and spoken segments by Doc Tate Nevaquaya. The spoken explanations focus on the meaning of the songs and give other information on the Plains Indian courting flute. Includes liner notes by Verna Gillis and Jamake Highwater.

Goddard, Pliny Earle

1914   Dancing Societies of the Sarsi Indians. *Anthropological Papers of the American Museum of Natural History* 11(5): 461–474.
This gives brief descriptions of five dance organizations (Mosquitoes, Dogs, Police, Preventers, and Dawo). Also describes a dog-meat feast which is sponsored as a pledge in return for spiritual assistance (pp. 473–474). Based on Goddard's interviews with an elderly Indian man in 1911 and 1913.

1919   Notes on the Sun Dance of the Cree in Alberta. *Anthropological Papers of the American Museum of Natural History* 16:295–310.
Could not be obtained for inspection of contents nor could information be gotten from other sources.

Grinnell, George Bird

1903   Notes on Some Cheyenne Songs. *American Anthropologist* 5:312–322.
Begins by describing various types and uses of songs (pp. 312–315). Grinnell then gives texts and translations for 28 songs. These include Wolf Songs (14 songs), War Songs (4 songs), Medicine Lodge Songs (2 songs), Doctoring Songs (2 songs), and others. No musical notations.

Haefer, J. Richard

1986   Blackfoot (Music). Pp. 225–226 in *The New Grove Dictionary of American Music*, vol. 1 (A–D). Edited by H. Wiley Hitchcock and Stanley Sadie. London: Macmillan.
Begins by discussing supernatural origin of songs, musical values, and various ceremonial and social contexts for traditional music. Describes an earlier repertory (connected with ceremonies

such as the Sun Dance and medicine bundle rituals) and a contemporary repertory associated with the intertribal powwow as first established during the 1940s. Discusses musical instruments and concludes by mentioning various types of "white music" performed by contemporary Blackfoot musicians.

Hatton, Orin Thomas

1974   Performance Practices of Northern Plains Pow-wow Singing Groups. *Yearbook of Inter-American Musical Research* 10:123–137.

Focuses on modern forms of the Grass Dance or War Dance among various tribes of the northern Plains. The section entitled "Background Information" (pp. 123–127) gives basic historical data and also touches on musical norms or performance criteria. The core section "Performance Practices and the Four Style Areas" (pp. 127–134) outlines basic features of the style and distinguishes regional variants. Finally, a section entitled "Repertory, Participation of Women, and Other Information" (pp. 134–137) deals with various topics such as drumming techniques and things that singers do to improve their voices.

1986   In the Tradition: Grass Dance Musical Style and Female Pow-wow Singers. *Ethnomusicology* 30(2): 197–221.

Hatton characterizes music of the Grass Dance as an example of what Herzog called "special song types" (General bibliography, 1935). That is, this is a genre of music which has crossed various cultural boundaries and occurs in wide distribution. The author discusses regional variations and focuses on the recent participation of women as singers and drummers. This includes sections on the origin and diffusion of the Grass Dance (pp. 198–200) and a general description of the style (pp. 203–208).

1988   "We Caused Them to Cry": Power and Performance in Gros Ventre War Expedition Songs. Master's thesis. Catholic University of America, Washington, D.C.

An interpretation of Gros Ventre music based on mainly on songs recorded by John Cooper at Fort Belknap (Montana) in 1940. Hatton attempts to move beyond the comparative and functional approaches of previous researchers in order to explore the connections between music and spiritual power in more culturally specific terms. The chapter on "Cultural Analysis of Music" (chapter four, pp. 80–94) discusses various levels of relationship between singing, crying, and speech as vehicles for spiritual communication. Includes notations and analysis for three songs (pp. 95–101).

1989   Gender and Musical Style in Gros Ventre War Expedition Songs. Pages 39–54 in *Women in North American Indian Music* edited by Richard Keeling. Ann Arbor: Society for Ethnomusicology.
Discusses gender relationships in connection with two modes of Gros Ventre singing: a solemn vocal style associated with the Flat Pipe Ritual and a more intense style (with vocal pulsations) identified with the warrior tradition. Hatton finds that historical recordings of male and female singing tend to cross categories and that gender divisions in music are overshadowed by ethnicity and other factors.

1990   *Power and Performance in Gros Ventre War Expedition Songs.* Mercury Series, Paper No. 114. Canadian Ethnology Service. Ottawa: National Museum of Canada.
This is a revised version of Hatton's master's thesis (1988 above). According to the author's abstract: "This study provides a cultural analysis of power and performance in Gros Ventre War Expedition songs. Symbolic content of Gros Ventre myth and ritual is elicited as a tool for analyzing the particular social relations that motivate war expeditions as action and value. Mythological and musical analysis combine in an investigation of structural and performative devices that frame a song as a system of metacommunication" (p. ii).

Howard, James H.

1951   Notes on the Dakota Grass Dance. *Southwestern Journal of Anthropology* 7:82–85.
Howard first discusses various theories of how the Grass Dance (also called the Omaha Dance) came to the Dakota (Sioux) tribe, then describes earlier versions and related current practices. This includes a description of the musical style (p. 84) but no musical examples.

See Howard (1966) in Northeast bibliography. This focuses on an Ojibwa Drum Religion or Dream Dance that is related to the Plains Grass Dance.

1972   John F. Lenger: Music Man among the Santee. *Nebraska History* 53(Summer): 195–215.
Could not be obtained for inspection of contents. Listed in Maguire et al. (General bibliography, 1983:18).

1976   The Plains Gourd Dance as a Revitalization Movement. *American Ethnologist* 3(2): 243–260.
Howard begins by describing earlier forms of the Gourd Dance as performed by warrior societies among various tribes (pp. 243–249). He then describes the recent spread of a more secularized (Pan-Indian) Gourd Dance and discusses some reasons for its popularity.

Howard, James H., and Gertrude P. Kurath

1959   Ponca Dances, Ceremonies and Music. *Ethnomusicology* 3(1): 1–14.
This focuses on three major dances: (1) the Sun Dance, (2) the Wá-wa or Pipe Dance, and (3) the Hethuska or War Dance. The authors also mention the Coyote Dance, the Night Dance, the Ghost Dance, the Stomp Dance, and some others. They discuss historical relationships between northern and southern divisions of the Ponca, and also between the Ponca and other tribes (particularly as related to acquisition of dances from other groups). This contains four musical examples (pp. 7–8) and a summary of musical characteristics (pp. 11–13). Choreographic styles are also analyzed.

Huenemann, Lynn

See Huenemann (1978) in the General bibliography for general information on Plains Indian music (including musical transcriptions for 29 songs).

1980   Record reviews of (1) "Comanche Flute Music" played by Doc Tate Nevaquaya (Folkways FE 4328) and (2) "Flute Songs of the Kiowa and Comanche: Tom Mauchahty-Ware" (Indian House IH 2512). *Ethnomusicology* 24(2): 339–341.
Huenemann considers these to be excellent recordings by two of the best contemporary flute players. Also discusses the increasing popularity of the instrument, the styles of both players, and the important contribution of a non-Indian player and flute-maker, Dr. Richard Payne.

1988   Dakota/Lakota Music and Dance: An Introduction. In
              The Arts of South Dakota edited by R. McIntyre and
              R. L. Bell. Sioux Falls: Center for Western Studies.
       Could not be obtained for inspection of contents nor could in-
       formation be gotten from others sources.

1992   Northern Plains Dance Pp. 125–148 in *Native
              American Dance: Ceremonies and Social Traditions*
              edited by Charlotte Heth. Washington: National
              Museum of the American Indian, Smithsonian
              Institution.
       This contains contemporary descriptions and historical infor-
       mation relating to the Sun Dance and various powwow dances
       mainly as practiced among the Lakota and Dakota (Sioux).

See **Hultkrantz** (1967) in the General bibliography. This contains descriptions of an Arapaho Spirit Lodge Ceremony and other
Sioux rituals of similar (shamanistic) character.

Jenness, Diamond

1938   *The Sarci Indians of Alberta.* Bulletin 90,
              Anthropology Series no. 23, Department of Mines
              and Resources. Ottawa: National Museums of
              Canada.
       Includes chapters on "The Sun Dance" (pp. 47–57) and "Grass
       Dances" (pp. 58–67), the latter giving historical information on the
       Grass Dance and containing several references to songs. Another
       chapter on "Religion" (pp. 68–75) discusses the use of songs got-
       ten in visions and also mentions Jenness's having recorded 80
       medicine songs of this type (p. 71). Based on research conducted in
       1921. No musical examples.

Kavanagh, Thomas W.

1992   Southern Plains Dance: Tradition and Dynamics Pp.
              105–124 in *Native American Dance: Ceremonies and
              Social Traditions* edited by Charlotte Heth.
              Washington: National Museum of the American
              Indian, Smithsonian Institution.
       This describes dances and other events at a modern powwow
       and gives historical information on the origin and regional diversi-
       fication of various dance and costume styles. Contains excellent
       color photographs.

Kennan, William R., and L. Brooks Hill

1980   Kiowa Forty-Nine Singing: A Communication
            Perspective. *International Journal of Intercultural
            Relations* 4(2): 149–165.
Focuses on the textual content of the songs and how the texts
relate to patterns of interaction in the actual performance setting
and in Kiowa culture at large. Eight (English) song texts are discussed. Employs an ethnomethodological approach and related
terminology.

Kilpatrick, Jack Frederick

1946   The Possible Relationship of Content to Form in
            Certain Gros Ventres Songs. Master's thesis (Music).
            Catholic University of America, Washington, D.C.
Focuses on nine Gros Ventre songs recorded by earlier researchers in 1935 and 1940. Attempts to identify connections between the musical structure and the textual content of the songs,
using methods based on those employed in various writings of
Frances Densmore. Includes transcriptions and analyses of the following types of songs: war songs (2), sacred songs (3), children's
songs (3), and a dream song (1).

Kroeber, Alfred Louis

1907   *Ethnography of the Gros Ventre.* Anthropological
            Papers of the American Museum of Natural History
            1:145–281.
The chapter on "Tribal Ceremonial Organization" (pp. 224–
267) gives general information on age-graded dance societies, and
this is followed by sections describing particular events such as the
Fly Dance, Crazy Dance, Kit-Fox Dance, Sun Dance, and others.
Songs are mentioned throughout but no musical examples are
given. Based on research conducted in 1901.

1918   Review of *Teton Sioux Music* by Frances Densmore
            (1918). *American Anthropologist* 20:446–450.
Criticizes the insularity of Densmore's work and particularly
her lack of familiarity with collections of Indian music other than
her own.

See **Kurath** (1951a) in the Northeast bibliography. This mentions the
    spread of the Eastern Stomp Dance to the Osage and
    Comanche tribes (p. 131).

La Flesche, Francis

1890   Death and Funeral Customs Among Omahas. *Journal of American Folklore* 2:3–11.
This includes one musical notation and (vocable) text for a funeral song which La Flesche considers to be the principal funeral song of the Omaha tribe and quite ancient (p. 8). Notated by La Flesche from memory.

1890   The Omaha Buffalo Medicine Man: An Account of Their Method of Practice. *Journal of American Folklore* 3:215–221.
Contains a description of curing songs as sung by one principal (Buffalo) medicine man who is accompanied by twenty or thirty other doctors (singing in unison) and the sound of a bone whistle (p. 217). Includes musical notations (with texts and translations) for two of the songs (pp. 218–219).

1921   *The Osage Tribe: Rite of the Chiefs; Sayings of the Ancient Men.* Bureau of American Ethnology, Annual Report (1914–1915) 36:35–604.
This provides detailed accounts of two major ceremonies as described by Osage elders circa 1914–1915. Contains musical notations, texts, translations, and commentary for about 30 songs performed in the rituals. The musical examples were transcribed from cylinders by Alice Fletcher.

1925   *The Osage Tribe: The Rite of Vigil.* Bureau of American Ethnology, Annual Report (1917–1918) 39: 31–636.
Another superb account of a major ritual based on explanations given by elders. Contains 175 musical examples (with texts and translations) transcribed from cylinders by Alice Fletcher.

1930   *The Osage Tribe: The Rite of Wa-xo'-be.* Bureau of American Ethnology, Annual Report (1927–1928) 45:523–833.
Contains 79 musical examples (with texts and translations) transcribed from cylinders by Charles Cadman. Could not be obtained. Information given here is from Hickerson (General bibliography, 1961:279).

1939   *War Ceremony and Peace Ceremony of the Osage Indians.* Bureau of American Ethnology Bulletin no. 101.

Contains 69 musical examples (with texts and translations) transcribed from cylinders by Alice Fletcher. Could not be obtained. Information given here is from Hickerson (General bibliography, 1961:279).

Lah, Ronald L.

1980   Ethnoaesthetics of Northern Arapaho Indian Music. Doctoral dissertation (Anthropology), Northwestern University.

The author uses a questionnaire to elicit information on musical activities, musical knowledge, beliefs about music, musical values, etc. The verbal responses of contemporary northern Arapaho speakers are discussed in chapters on musical aesthetics and transformations that have occurred as a result of western influences. The chapter on "Contemporary Arapaho Musical Contacts" (pp. 93–124) gives an overview of religious and secular musical activities. Based on research conducted circa 1973–1975.

See the catalogue by **Lee** (1979) in the General bibliography. This lists historical and recent recordings at the Indiana University Archives of Traditional Music. The holdings include collections from the following Plains groups: Arapaho, Arikara, Assiniboin, Blackfoot, Blood, Caddo, Cheyenne, Comanche, Cree, Crow, Dakota/Sioux, Gros Ventre, Hidatsa, Kiowa, Mandan, Omaha, Osage, Oto, Pawnee, Piegan, Ponca, Quapaw, Sarsi, Tonkawa, and Wichita.

Lesser, Alexander

(1933)   *The Pawnee Ghost Dance Hand Game: A Study in Cultural Change.* New York: Columbia University Press. Reprinted by AMS Press (New York, 1969).

The section on "Ghost Dance Songs" (pp. 100–105) contains texts and translations for seven songs. There are also descriptions of Hand Game songs (pp. 134 and 253) but no musical notations. A connection between songs and crying is mentioned (p. 253).

Levine, Victoria Lindsay

1992   Review of *War Dance: Plains Indian Musical Performance*, by William Powers (1990). *Ethnomusicology* 36(3): 426–428.

Basically favorable but the reviewer does question Powers's ideas on the subject of Pan-Indianism. Powers rejects the concept of Pan-Indianism as defined by Howard (General bibliography, 1983); Levine argues that it is not only valid but deserves more attention by researchers.

Lowie, Robert H.

1909   *The Northern Shoshone.* Anthropological Papers of the American Museum of Natural History 2(2): 165–306.

The section on "Dances" (pp. 216–223) contains information on the Sun Dance, the Cree Dance, and an older dance called Nu'akin, which was held to ensure a plentiful supply of food. Lowie gives the text and translation for one Nu'akin song, also commenting on the resemblance of the style to that of later Ghost Dance songs (p. 218). Other dances are also mentioned.

1910   *The Assiniboine.* Anthropological Papers of the American Museum of Natural History 4(1): 1–270.

The section on "Music" (p. 26–27) only gives brief comments on instruments. The section on "War" (pp. 28–33) contains a description of War Dances and a Scalp Dance, also including comments on songs (with one text and translation). The section on "Ceremonial Organization" (pp. 56–74) gives descriptions of the Horse Dance, Sun Dance, Fool Dance, Grass Dance, and some others. This also incudes texts and translations for eight songs.

1913a   *Dance Associations of the Eastern Dakota.* Anthropological Papers of the American Museum of Natural History 11(2): 101–142.

Could not be obtained for inspection of contents nor could information be gotten from other sources.

1913b   *Societies of the Crow, Hidatsa, and Mandan Indians.* Anthropological Papers of the American Museum of Natural History 11(3): 143–358.

Lowie first discusses military and age-grade societies among the Crow (pp. 145–217), then focuses on similar societies of the Mandan and Hidatsa (pp. 219–358). This includes texts and translations for 31 songs in all. Also contains a description of the Crow "Hot Dance" (pp. 200–206).

1915   *Dance Societies of the Plains Shoshone.* Anthropo-
            logical Papers of the American Museum of Natural
            History 11(10).
    This actually gives brief descriptions of dances and societies in
three tribes: the Comanche (pp. 809–812), the Wind River
Shoshone (pp. 813–822), and the Ute (pp. 823–835). Of particular
interest are Lowie's comments on an older Shoshone dance called
"Naroya" (p. 817) and his lengthy account of the Ute "Bear Dance"
(pp. 823–832).

1916   *Plains Indian Age-Societies: Historical and Compar-
            ative Summary.* Anthropological Papers of the Ameri-
            can Museum of Natural History 11(13): 877–1031.
    Lowie's findings are summarized in a section on "Historical
Conclusions" (pp. 946–954). The article also contains an index
listing more than one hundred references to music-related topics in
various editions of Volume 11 (all of which focus on the topic of
Plains Indian societies).

1935   *The Crow Indians.* New York: Farrar and Rinehart.
    This includes chapters or sections on "Rites and Festivals"
(pp. 256–263), "The Bear Song Dance" (pp. 164–168), and "The
Sun Dance" (pp. 297–326). Songs are often mentioned but not discussed in detail. No musical examples.

1959   The Oral Literature of the Crow Indians. *Journal of
            American Folklore* 72:97–106.
    Mainly deals with speeches and prayers but also includes
comments on songs. Includes texts and translations for 13 songs of
various types.

McAllester, David P.

See McAllester (1949) in the General bibliography. This discusses
        Peyote songs among the Comanche, Dakota, Cheyenne,
        Pawnee, Kiowa, Tonkawa, and Arapaho.

1977   Record review of "Cheyenne Peyote Songs," vols. 1–
            2 (Indian House IH 2201–2202). *Ethnomusicology*
            21(1): 161–163.
    A highly favorable review. McAllester describes the spiritual
intent of the songs and also draws attention to subtle variations
which endow this apparently repetitive form with considerable
grace and vitality.

MacLean, John

1888   *The Blackfoot Sun-Dance.* Proceedings of the Canadian Institute (Toronto) Series 3. Vol. 4, pp. 231–237.
Could not be obtained for inspection of contents. Listed in Guédon (General bibliography 1972:472).

McClintock, Walter

1910   *The Old North Trail, or Life, Legends, and Religion of the Blackfoot Indians.* London.
According to Wissler (1918:267 below) this contains a musical notation of an important song for the Sun Dance on page 311. Could not be obtained.

1937   *Dances of the Blackfoot Indians.* Los Angeles: Southwest Museum.
This 22-page booklet describes Grass Dances, a Scalp Dance, and a Blacktail Deer Dance as observed by McClintock in northwestern Montana in 1898. The Blacktail Deer Dance is described as a hunting medicine dance from the Kutenai (of the adjacent Plateau region).

Mails, Thomas E.

1973   *Dog Soldiers, Bear Men, and Buffalo Women: A Study of the Societies and Cults of the Plains Indians.* Englewood Cliffs, New Jersey: Prentice-Hall.
An oversized volume illustrated with paintings and drawings by the author. This begins with introductory chapters on the origin of military and other societies (pp. 9–40), the nature of the societies (pp. 41–58), and society regalia (pp. 59–76). The 13 chapters which follow (pp. 77–368) each describe the societies and cults of a specific tribe. Based on early ethnographies and other secondary sources. No musical examples.

1978   *Sundancing at Rosebud and Pine Ridge.* Sioux Falls, South Dakota: Augustana College; Lincoln: University of Nebraska Press.
Contains no musical analysis but describes essential features of the ceremony and contains many paintings, drawings, and photographs. There are 426 photographs, of which 383 provide a pictorial record of Sun Dances on the Rosebud Reservation in 1974 and 1975. The written portions are based on interviews with elders

and standard ethnographic sources. The review by Powers (1982 below) is highly critical.

Montgomery, Guy

1922   A Method of Studying the Structure of Primitive Verse Applied to the Songs of the Teton-Sioux. The Charles Mills Gayley Anniversary Papers. *University of California Publications in Modern Philology* 11:267–283.

Examines the rhythmic structure of songs in Densmore's extensive study of Teton Sioux music (1918 above). Montgomery identifies five categories of rhythmic patterning (pp. 279–282). Includes one musical notation; gives texts, translations, and rhythmic analysis for eight songs.

Mooney, James

1896   *The Ghost-Dance Religion and the Sioux Outbreak of 1890*. Bureau of American Ethnology, Annual Report (1892–1893) 14(2). Washington: U. S. Government Printing Office. Also see the later abridged edition with an Introduction by Anthony F.C. Wallace. Chicago: University of Chicago Press, 1965.

A classic study of the Ghost Dance religion and its spread from the Great Basin to the Plains area. The early chapters provide information on the doctrines of the Ghost Dance and other comparable prophetic or messianic movements of the nineteenth century. Chapter 15 describes the Ghost Dance ceremony (pp. 915–928). There is extensive information on songs, with texts and translations for 161 songs from various tribes (pp. 953–1103). Includes musical notations for 14 Ghost Dance songs from the following tribes: Arapaho (8 songs), Comanche (1), Kiowa (2), and Caddo (3).

Murie, James R.

1914   *Pawnee Indian Societies*. Anthropological Papers of the American Museum of Natural History 11(7): 543–644.

Could not be obtained for inspection of contents nor could information be gotten from other sources.

(1981)   *Ceremonies of the Pawnee*. Edited by Douglas R. Parks. Smithsonian Contributions to Anthropology, No. 27. Washington: Smithsonian Institution Press.

Reprinted by the University of Nebraska Press
(Lincoln and London, 1989).
James Murie (1862–1921) was a Pawnee of mixed blood. This
posthumous publication of his notes provides an overview of
Pawnee ceremonial life, which was unusually complex. Part One
(pp. 29–182) presents the annual ritual cycle of the Skiri band, including detailed descriptions of major ceremonies and medicine
bundle rituals. Part Two (pp. 183–459) describes three doctors'
ceremonies as practiced among the southern bands: (1) the White
Beaver Ceremony, (2) the Bear Dance, and (3) the Buffalo Dance.
Song texts and translations are given throughout, and there is an
appendix entitled "Notes on Native Songs and Their Composers"
(pp. 467–470).

Myers, Helen

1986   Sioux (Music). Pp. 235–237 in *The New Grove
              Dictionary of American Music*, vol. 4 (R–Z). Edited
              by H. Wiley Hitchcock and Stanley Sadie. London:
              Macmillan.
The section on "Traditional Repertory" is based mainly on
Densmore (1918 above). This discusses various types of songs,
concepts of ownership and origin of songs in dreams, and basic elements of musical style. It also includes information on use of
songs in the Sun Dance. Another section on the "Modern
Repertory" is based largely on the writings of William Powers
(listed below). This describes song types and elements of the musical style but also contains information on technical vocabulary relating to music.

Nettl, Bruno

1951   Musical Culture of the Arapaho. Master's thesis.
              Indiana University.
Based mainly on recordings and fieldnotes of Zdenek
Salzmann. Chapter two (pp. 8–35) describes various functions of
music in Arapaho culture, and chapter three (pp. 36–42) deals with
musical instruments. Chapter four (pp. 43–67) focuses on musical
analysis, describing the basic characteristics of Arapaho music and
distinguishing various "functional song groups." Chapter five (pp.
68–80) discusses song texts and vocables. Musical transcriptions
are given in an appendix.

See Nettl (1954a) in the General bibliography. This discusses general characteristics of music in the "Plains-Pueblo Area" (pp. 24–33).

See Nettl (1954b) in the General bibliography. This discusses compositional practices of an Arapaho singer.

1954   Text-Music Relations in Arapaho Songs. *Southwestern Journal of Anthropology* 10:192–199.

Describes basic characteristics of Arapaho music, classifies songs on the basis of texts, and analyzes the relationship between songs and texts. Nettl's analysis focuses mainly on the correlation of musical stress and length with linguistic high tone and length. Includes one notation (with text).

1955   Musical Culture of the Arapaho. *Musical Quarterly* 41(July): 325–331.

Gives a comparative analysis of Arapaho music. Six groups or classes of songs are delineated, and Nettl speculates on the historical relationships between them. The Arapaho musical style is then briefly compared with that of other Plains tribes. Includes six musical examples.

1966   Zur Kompositionstechnik der Arapaho ("Techniques of Musical Composition among the Arapaho"). *Jahrbuch für musikalische Volks- und Völkerkunde* 2:114–118. Berlin: De Gruyter.

Nettl discusses the use of melodic and rhythmic formulas in various types of songs. Includes four musical notations: New Dance Song, Game Song, War Song, and Wolf Dance Song.

1967a   Blackfoot Music in Browning, 1965: Functions and Attitudes. Pp. 593–598 in *Festschrift für Walter Wiora zum 30 Dezember 1966*. Edited by Ludwig Finscher and Christoph-Hellmut Mahling. Kassel: Bärenreiter.

A portrait of contemporary musical life among Blackfoot Indians of Montana. Nettl begins by describing modern contexts for traditional music, as for example the "North American Indian Days" held in July or social dances that are sponsored by local businesses. He then discusses the attitudes and musical activities of seven Blackfoot individuals.

1967b   Studies in Blackfoot Indian Musical Culture, Part I:
             Traditional Uses and Functions. *Ethnomusicology*
             11(2): 141–160.
Describes the social contexts of Blackfoot music in the nineteenth century as documented by Wissler and other ethnographers. This contains sections on the Sun Dance (pp. 143–145) and on medicine bundle rituals (pp. 145–149). A section on "Other Uses of Music" (pp. 149–150) discusses secular genres of various types. Also includes descriptions of instruments (pp. 150–152) and comments on musical concepts and values (pp. 152–159).

1967c   Studies in Blackfoot Musical Culture, Part II:
             Musical Life of the Montana Blackfoot, 1966.
             Ethnomusicology 11(3): 293–309.
Examines contemporary musical activities and attitudes towards music. Contains a calendar of musical events which includes descriptions of eight types of music-making (pp. 295–298). Nettl also discusses musical values and ideas and practices relating to composition of songs. Gives musical profiles of seven Blackfoot persons who also figure in another paper by Nettl (1967a above).

1968   Biography of a Blackfoot Indian Singer. *Musical
             Quarterly* 54(2): 199–207 (April).
Describes the life and musical activities of an unidentified fullblood man (born in 1916). The biography becomes a vehicle for explaining major transformations which affected Blackfoot culture during the 1930s, 1940s, 1950s, and 1960s.

1968   Studies in Blackfoot Musical Culture, Part IV: Notes
             on Composition, Text-Settings, and Performance.
             Ethnomusicology 12(2): 192–207.
The section on "Tune Relationships" (pp. 192–196) examines melodic themes in the songs of one individual (Tom Many-Guns) and then discusses the melodic form of medicine bundle songs sung by another person. The section on "Text-Settings" (pp. 196–203) analyzes use of words and vocables in seven songs. In his discussion of "Performance Practices" (pp. 203–207) Nettl focuses on tempo, loudness, and various aspects of vocal quality. Includes nine musical examples.

1979   (Recording editor and author of liner notes) "An
             Historical Album of Blackfoot Indian Music." Ethnic
             Folkways (FE 34001).

Contains historical recordings spanning the years from 1903 to 1966. Includes the following song types: Grass Dance Songs (5), Gambling Songs (4), Owl Dance Songs (3), Sun Dance Songs (3), Medicine Pipe Songs (5), Beaver Medicine Songs (3), Lullabies (2), Song of Crazy Dog Society, and some others in the category of "traditional war music."

1986 Arapaho (Music). Pp. 62–63 in *The New Grove Dictionary of American Music*, vol. 1 (A–D). Edited by H. Wiley Hitchcock and Stanley Sadie. London: Macmillan.

Contains a summary of traditional musical genres, emphasizing the central importance of religious songs for the Sun Dance, Flat Pipe ritual, and age-grade societies. Lists basic characteristics of the musical style. Also mentions songs of the Ghost Dance, Peyote religion, and other historical developments.

1989 *Blackfoot Musical Thought: Comparative Perspectives*. Kent, Ohio: Kent State University Press.

An extensive study which attempts to provide a comprehensive model for describing relationships between music and other domains of culture. An opening chapter ("Background," pp. 1–45) provides basic ethnographic information and summarizes the history of research on Blackfoot music. Chapter Two ("Fundamentals," pp. 46–89) discusses musical concepts, often by comparison with those of other world cultures. Chapter Three ("History," pp. 89–115) addresses related issues such as the mythological origins of music, speculations on music and culture history in pre-contact times, and changes in the twentieth century. Chapter Four ("Music in Human and Supernatural Societies," pp. 116–146) focuses on the uses and functions of music, while the final chapter ("Musicianship," pp. 147–173) gives an ethnography of performance practices and discusses Blackfoot musical values. Based on fieldwork conducted by Nettl (circa 1950, 1967, and 1984) and on earlier research by Wissler and others.

Nettl, Bruno, and Stephen Blum

1968 Studies in Blackfoot Indian Musical Culture, Part III: Three Genres of Song. *Ethnomusicology* 12(1): 11–48.

The authors distinguish three major stylistic categories in the repertory as a whole: (1) War dance songs in the "typical Plains form" as defined by Nettl in a previous study (General bibliography, 1954:24–29); (2) Another style, often conforming to the latter but different in some respects, in Medicine Bundle songs; and (3) a distinctly different style in gambling songs. Includes 42 musical notations. Based on recordings collected by Nettl in 1952 and 1966 and on earlier archival recordings. The section on Medicine Pipe songs is by Blum.

O'Brodovich, Lloyd

1968   Plains Cree Sun Dance. *Western Canadian Journal of Anthropology: Cree Studies Issue* 1(1): 71–87.
          Could not be obtained for inspection of contents nor could information be gotten from other sources.

Paige, Harry W.

1970   *Songs of the Teton Sioux.* Los Angeles: Westernlore Press.
          Focuses on poetry (song texts) rather than other aspects of the music. The book expresses some obsolete ideas on the nature of "primitive" music, but still contains useful information and scores of texts and translations. See the sections entitled "Individual Songs" (pp. 59–72), "Ceremonial Songs" (pp. 73–132), and "Modern Songs of Cultural Change" (pp. 133–179).

Pantaleoni, Hewitt

1987   One of Densmore's Dakota Rhythms Reconsidered. *Ethnomusicology* 31(1): 35–55.
          Employs slowed-speed analysis to examine the rhythmic detail in a song recorded by Densmore in 1911. Includes her notation of the song with two other notations intended to illustrate the character of vocal pulsations and congruencies of rhythmic detail between successive phrases. Pantaleoni questions Densmore's assumption that the drum accompaniment is in a different and unrelated tempo from the voice. Rather, according to him, they are synchronized by a pulse at least three times as fast as westerners are accustomed to hearing (p. 52).

Parker, Mrs. Z.A.

1891   Ghost Dance at Pine Ridge. *Journal of American Folklore* 4(13): 160–162.
          A poignant eyewitness account which was originally published in the *New York Evening Post* (April 18, 1891).

Parthun, Paul

1978   Plains War Dance Songs: A Metamorphosis. *Anthropological Journal of Canada* 16(4): 22–26.

Examines stable and changing elements in Ojibwe War Dance songs by comparing modern musical practices with those described by Densmore (1910–1913 above). Considers the following musical elements: function and language, pitch analysis, durational analysis, and vocal mannerisms. The "Summary" (p. 25) lists seven types of changes that have occurred and five characteristics that have remained the same.

Parthun's writings on Ojibwe music are listed in the Northeast bibliography.

Payne, Richard W.

1988   The Plains Flute. *The Flutist Quarterly* 13(4): 11–14.

Despite its brevity, this is the single most informative source I could find on the subject. Payne first describes the design and construction and then goes on to describe playing techniques and aesthetics. He gives terms for parts of the flute and for techniques such as "warbling" and "dog barks." The article includes a discography and an address for requesting further bibliographic information. Also see Gillis (1979 above) and Wapp (General bibliography, 1984).

Peacock, Ken

1955   (Recording and liner notes) "Indian Music of the Canadian Plains." Smithsonian-Folkways Recordings (FE 4464).

Currently available on cassette, this includes songs of the Cree, Assiniboin, Blood and Blackfoot tribes. Contains the following types of songs: War Song (for World War II), Prisoner's Song, Bear Ceremony Song, Big Dog Dance Songs, Hand Game Songs, Warrior's Death Song (for Sitting Bull), Owl Dance Songs (2), Grass Dance Songs (2), and other powwow songs.

Powers, William K.

See Powers (1960, 1961a, 1961b, and 1961c) in the General bibliography for essays on social dance songs and War Dance songs as performed by tribes of the Plains culture area and in Oklahoma.

1961a   American Indian Music, Part Five: Contemporary
             Music and Dance of the Western Sioux. *American
             Indian Tradition* 7(5): 158–165.
Focuses on music of the Teton Sioux or Lakota. The article
gives three main types of information: (1) a description of the
phonology and vocal techniques; (2) a discussion on the social role
of the singer, compositional practices, and requirements of a good
singer; and (3) a classification of the general categories of songs
according to function.

1961b   American Indian Music, Part Six: The Sioux Omaha
             Dance. *American Indian Tradition* 8(1): 24–33.
A concise summary of information on the Omaha Dance (also
called Grass Dance) as practiced in Sioux communities during the
early 1960s. Powers discusses the origins of the dance, which was
borrowed from the Omaha, and how various elements have
changed in early and recent times. This contains descriptions of the
dance style, costumes, dancing area, and various types of songs.
Analyzes the musical structure of the songs, giving texts and translations for several examples. No musical notations.

1962a   American Indian Music, Part Seven: The Rabbit
             Dance. *American Indian Tradition* 8(3): 133–188.
Focuses on a popular social dance in which men and women
dance together as couples. Powers calls this the most prominent
social dance among the western Sioux. The article begins by discussing the origins of the dance, which was borrowed from the
Cree (via the Gros Ventres), then describes the steps and the musical structure of the songs. Includes texts and translations for twelve
songs but no musical notations.

1962b   American Indian Music, Part Eight: Sneak-Up Dance,
             Drum Dance, and Flag Dance. *American Indian
             Tradition* 8(4): 166–171.
Deals with three "specialty dances" performed among the
western Sioux. These originated in warrior society ceremonials but
are subject to constant modification, so that current forms may be
quite different from earlier practices. Of these, only the Sneak-Up
Dance was still being performed at the time the article was written.
Powers describes the dance steps, musical form, and drum patterns
for each of the three dances. Musical form is described in terms of
text and vocable analysis. No musical notations.

1968a   Contemporary Oglala Music and Dance: Pan-Indian-
               ism versus Pan-Tetonism. *Ethnomusicology* 12(3):
               352–372.
Distinguishes the Plains elements in Pan-Indian music from
non-tribal elements as occurring in Oklahoma powwow culture.
Powers first describes basic elements of Oklahoma Pan-Indianism
(pp. 354–358) and lists various Pan-Teton elements as found
among the Oglala Sioux (pp. 358–366). He then discusses
(Oklahoman) Pan-Indian elements that have infiltrated the Pan-
Teton complex and distinguishes other aspects in which the Oglala
seem to be adhering to "Sioux" patterns rather than Pan-Indian
ones.

1968b   Diffusion of the Plains War Dance. *Pow-wow Trails*
               5(6): 68–72.
Could not be obtained for inspection of contents nor could information be gotten from other sources.

1969   Music and Dance. Pp. 165–182 in *Indians of the
               Northern Plains* edited by William K. Powers. New
               York: Putnam.
An introductory essay for general readers. Focuses on cultural
functions of music, the history of the Grass Dance, and contemporary songs. Includes English translations of several Sioux songs
about World War I, World War II, and the Korean War.

1971   Music and Dance. Pp. 161–174 in *Indians of the
               Southern Plains* edited by William K. Powers. New
               York: Putnam.
Could not be obtained for inspection of contents nor could information be gotten from other sources.

1971   Record Review of "Sioux Favorites" (Canyon
               Records ARP 6059). *Ethnomusicology* 15(1): 154–
               160.
Favorable review of an album containing reissues of selected
"favorites" originally recorded on 78 rpm discs. Powers gives
background information on the singers and describes each of the
recorded items in some detail. The review includes translations for
the following: (1) Sioux National Anthem and Victory Dance, (2)
Sioux Flag Song, (3) Scouting Dance Song, (4) Chief's Honoring
Song, and (5) Korea Memorial Song. Powers also notes that the
singing of more recent singers is less dissonant than that of some of
the older singers heard here (p. 155).

1976   Record review of "Kiowa Gourd Dance," recording
              and notes by Tony Issacs, vols. 1–2. (Indian House
              IH 2503 and 2504).
  A favorable review in which Powers also gives historical and
other background information on the Gourd Dance and its recent
resurgence. Other writings and recordings of Gourd Dance songs
are cited.

1977   Record reviews of "Ho Hwo Sju Lakota Singers:
              Traditional Songs of the Sioux" (Indian House IH
              4301) and "Sound of the Badlands Singers" (Indian
              House IH 4012). *Ethnomusicology* 21(1): 163–165.
  Another basically favorable review of both records. Powers
points out that the albums illustrate two contrasting styles from the
northern Plains. The first one (performed by a group from South
Dakota) represents what Powers calls the "traditional" style of
Sioux singing. The second features a "northern style" of singing
from Montana, North Dakota, and the Canadian Prairie Provinces.
The terms are discussed in Powers (1968a above).

1978   Record review of "War Dance Songs of the Kiowa,"
              recording and notes by Tony Issacs, vols. 1–2.
              (Indian House IH 2508 and 2509). *Ethnomusicology*
              22(1): 206–207.
  Very favorable review describing the O-ho-mah Lodge
Singers as "exemplary performers of Southern Plains music" (p.
207). Powers also discusses the history of the O-ho-mah Dance
Society in the larger context of earlier dance complexes and institu-
tions that became incorporated in the contemporary powwow.

1980   Oglala Song Terminology. *Selected Reports in
              Ethnomusicology* 3(2): 23–42. Los Angeles: Program
              in Ethnomusicology, Department of Music, UCLA.
  Examines the general issue of how we should interpret verbal-
izations about music as given by non-western peoples. Powers criticizes the "analytical model" of previous researchers and proposes
a "synthetic model" which incorporates references to other (non-
musical) domains. He illustrates the concept through linguistic
analysis of Lakota words relating to music and concludes that the
Oglala verbalize about songs in a manner analogous to speech
about other bodily functions. Contains several references to the
work of Lucien Lévy-Bruhl.

1980   Plains Indian Music and Dance. Pp. 212–229 in *Anthropology on the Great Plains*, edited by Raymond Wood and Margaret Liberty. Lincoln: University of Nebraska Press.

Focuses on four main topics or problems: (1) the history and character of previous research (pp. 212–214); (2) delineation ("typology") of various musical areas (pp. 214–216); (3) musical diffusion as related to the dynamics of "tribalism" and "intertribalism" (pp. 216–219); and (4) recent developments in music and dance since 1900 (pp. 219–224).

1981   Record reviews of "Kiowa Church Songs," vols. 1 and 2 (Indian House IH 2506 and 2507); and "Yankton Sioux Peyote Songs," vols. 1–4 (Indian House IH 4371–4374). *Ethnomusicology* 25(1): 159–162.

The church songs are not missionary translations into a local dialect but rather Kiowa-composed songs based on Christian themes and sung in a style similar to that of Plains War Dance songs. These were recorded at Carnegie, Oklahoma in 1971. The Yankton Sioux peyote songs, some of which are sung in a harmonic style that was also influenced by Christian hymn singing, were recorded in South Dakota in 1976. The albums both contain photographs and notes with free translations. Powers points out the need for better documentation and gives background information on the musical genres and styles. Also discusses issues relating to musical acculturation.

1981   (Record review-essay) Have Drum, Will Travel: The Professionalization of Native American Singers. *Ethnomusicology* 25(2): 343–346.

Discusses various changes in the organization and style of powwow singing groups which have occurred since the 1950s. Powers gives various explanations for the emergence of professionalized groups and comments on ten recent recordings (all from the 1970s) from this perspective. The albums reviewed here feature the following groups: the Ashland Singers (Cheyenne), the Badlands Singers (Assiniboin-Sioux), the Old Agency Singers (Blood), the Red Earth Singers (Mesquakie, Chippewa, Cree, and Pottawatomie), and a Kiowa group led by Bill Koomsa Sr.

1982   *Yuwipi: Vision and Experience in Oglala Ritual.* Lincoln: University of Oklahoma Press.

The introduction gives background information and explains Powers's thesis that the yuwipi curing ritual cannot be properly understood unless one also considers related ceremonies of the vision quest and sweat lodge. This is followed by a 78-page "narrative exposition" describing the yuwipi ritual held for a certain man and the vision quest which was undertaken by his son as part of the cure. The quasi-fictional style is criticized in a review by Farrer (1984 above).

1982   Review of *Sundancing at Rosebud and Pine Ridge* by Thomas Mails (1978). *Ethnomusicology* 26(1): 163–164.
            Criticizes the author for failing to cite previous works and for a general tone which Powers considers pretentious and patronizing.

1986   *Sacred Language: The Nature of Supernatural Discourse in Lakota*. Norman: University of Oklahoma Press.
            The central thesis is that Oglala Sioux songs represent a form of sacred language. Chapter One ("Incomprehensible Terms") makes the distinction between common and sacred language, the latter used for communicating with spirits and not comprehensible to common (non-shaman) people. Chapter Two focuses on song terminology. Chapter Three ("Song Texts") gives texts and translations for 17 songs used in an important curing ritual. Remaining chapters are basically sociological in content. There is a review by Bahr (1988 above).

1986   Text and Context in Lakota Music. Pp. 139–146 in *Explorations in Ethnomusicology: Essays in Honor of David P. McAllester* edited by Charlotte J. Frisbie. Detroit Monographs in Musicology No. 9. Detroit: Information Coordinators.
            Explores layers of hidden meaning in a song text of the Yuwipi curing ritual as practiced among the Oglala (Sioux). Includes interlinear and free translations along with discussions of the performance context and related beliefs and customs especially concerning transmission of the songs (which are originally gotten by the medicine man in visions).

1990   *War Dance: Plains Indian Musical Performance*. Tucson: University of Arizona Press.
            The book is divided into two parts. The first ("Plains Indian Music and Dance") includes seven chapters based on previously

published articles. The second ("Plains Music in Review") contains four chapters based on record reviews published in the journal *Ethnomusicology*. Contains much information on the origins and development of the powwow, the style of powwow music and dance, and differences between Northern Plains and Southern Plains powwows. There is a review by Levine (1992 above).

1993   Ghost Songs: Echoes from Wounded Knee. *Journal de la Société des Américanistes* 79:9–19. Paris: Musée de l'Homme.

Discusses various aspects of the Ghost Dance among the Lakota which reflect distinctively indigenous (Lakota) patterns as opposed to ideology and ritual patterns associated with the Ghost Dance movement in general. Powers examines the "Lakotafication" of the Ghost Dance mainly through analyzing the texts of 14 Ghost Dance songs. Criticizes the earlier interpretation by Mooney (1896 above).

1990   *Voices from the Spirit World: Translations of Lakota Ghost Dance Songs from 1890–1891. Memorial Tribute to Wounded Knee.* Kendall Park, New Jersey: Lakota Books.

This contains texts, translations, and commentary for 55 songs that were collected by various researchers during the years from 1890 to 1989. The introduction (pp. 8–15) gives a history of the Ghost Dance and also discusses how the Lakota songs reflect indigenous religious feelings as opposed to concepts connected with the Ghost Dance movement in general.

Rhodes, Willard

1954a   (Recording and notes) "Music of the American Indian: Kiowa." Library of Congress, Recorded Sound Division (AFS L35).

From a series of recordings collected by Rhodes circa 1940–1952 and recently reissued with updated liner notes. Contains the following: Sun Dance Songs, Setanke's Death Song, Ghost Dance Songs, Legend Songs, Christian Prayer Songs, Peyote Songs, Round Dance Songs, Rabbit Society Songs, War Dance Songs, Squat Dance Songs, Two Step Songs, and Flag Song.

1954b   (Recording and notes) "Music of the American Indian: Plains: Comanche, Cheyenne, Kiowa, Caddo, Wichita, and Pawnee." American Folklife Center, Library of Congress (AFS L39).

From the same series as the previous recording. This contains several recordings from each of the following tribes: Comanche, Cheyenne, Kiowa, Caddo, Witchita, and Pawnee.

1954c   (Recording and notes) "Music of the American Indian: Sioux." American Folklife Center, Library of Congress (AFS L40).

From the same series as the two previous items. Contents are listed as follows: Sun Dance Songs, Ghost Dance Songs, Christian Hymn, Peyote Song, Lullaby, Hand Game Songs, Love Songs with Flute, Society Songs, Hunka Song, Brave Inspiring Song, Honoring Song, Death Songs, Omaha Dance Songs, and Rabbit Dance Songs.

Richardson, Jane

1937   Review of *Cheyenne and Arapaho Music* by Frances Densmore (1936). *American Anthropologist* 39:675–677.

Richardson observes that some of the Ghost Dance songs and peyote songs notated by Densmore seem to correspond to transcriptions given in Curtis (General bibliography, 1907) and texts published in Mooney (1896 above). She discusses various interpretations and areas for further research. Basically a highly favorable review.

Riemer-Weller, Mary

1986   Crow (Music). Pp. 549–551 in *The New Grove Dictionary of American Music*, vol. 1 (A–D). Edited by H. Wiley Hitchcock and Stanley Sadie. London: Macmillan.

Discusses concepts relating to the supernatural origins of music in Crow culture and use of medicine songs in the vision quest. The author then describes use of songs in military societies, the "Hot Dance" (War Dance), the Sun Dance, the Tobacco Society, and the Sacred Pipe Dance. Gives brief list of instruments (most important being a hand-held frame drum) and summarizes basic elements of the Crow musical style.

1986   Kiowa (Music). Pp. 635–637 in *The New Grove Dictionary of American Music*, vol. 3 (L–Q). Edited by H. Wiley Hitchcock and Stanley Sadie. London: Macmillan.

Begins by discussing the importance of warrior society songs in music of the pre-reservation period. The discussion of recent trends emphasizes that the Kiowa are considered leaders in the southern style of singing and dancing at contemporary Pan-Indian powwows. Mentions other styles of music as connected with the Sun Dance, Ghost Dance, and peyote religion. Describes basic characteristics of the Kiowa musical style.

1986 Pawnee (Music). Pp. 491–492 in *The New Grove Dictionary of American Music*, vol. 3 (L–Q). Edited by H. Wiley Hitchcock and Stanley Sadie. London: Macmillan.

Emphasizes that this is an elaborate religious system involving rituals associated with handling of sacred bundles. Riemer-Weller describes the use of songs in the Thunder Ceremony, agricultural ceremonies, the Calumet ceremony (Hako), and in various medicine societies and warrior societies. Songs of the Thunder Ceremony were evidently quite lengthy, as they involved a system of repetition with word substitutions called "steps." The article also discusses musical instruments, composition of songs, and general characteristics of the Pawnee musical style.

Roberts, Helen Heffron

1919 Review of *Teton Sioux Music* by Frances Densmore (1918). *Journal of American Folklore* 32:523–535.

A lengthy review which criticizes Densmore's notation, analytical methods, and terminology. Includes two notations from the Densmore monograph, one of which is retranscribed by Roberts.

See Roberts (1936) in the General bibliography. This contains a section on general characteristics of Plains Indian music (pp. 34–36).

See **Sanford** (1911) in the General bibliography. Discusses music in Indian missions with examples from the Arapaho and Cheyenne.

Schaefer, C.E.

1969 *Blackfoot Shaking Tent*. Glenbow Institute, Occasional Papers no. 5. Calgary, Alberta.

Could not be obtained for inspection of contents nor could information be gotten elsewhere.

See **Schoolcraft** (1851–1857) in General bibliography. Volume Four contains a brief description of Dakota songs (pp. 71–72). Volume Five contains three Dakota song texts and translations (p. 439).

See the catalogue by **Seeger and Spear** (1987). This contains a listing of early cylinder recordings at the Indiana University Archives of Traditional Music. The collection includes recordings from the following Plains tribes: Arapaho, Arikara, Assiniboin, Blackfoot, Blood, Cheyenne, Comanche, Cree, Crow, Dakota (Sioux), Gros Ventre, Hidatsa, Kiowa, Mandan, Omaha, Oto, Pawnee, Piegan, Ponca, Sarsi, and Wichita.

Skinner, Alanson Buck

1919a   The Sun Dance of the Plains-Cree. *Anthropological Papers of the American Museum of Natural History* 16:283–293.
Could not be obtained for information on contents. Listed in Guédon (General bibliography, 1972:472).

1919b   The Sun Dance of the Plains-Ojibway. *Anthropological Papers of the American Museum of Natural History* 16:311–315.
Could not be obtained for information on contents. Listed in Guédon (General bibliography, 1972:472).

1970   *The Mascoutens or Prairie Potawatomi Indians: Part One, Social Life and Ceremonies.* Bulletin of the Milwaukee Public Museum, vol. 6, no. 1.
The section on "Ceremonial Activities" (pp. 53–210) describes medicine bundle ceremonies for 13 different clans, including texts and translations for 78 songs. There follows another section on "Ceremonies Not Connected with the Rites of the Clans" (pp. 210–246). This gives brief descriptions of other dances and the peyote ceremony (pp. 232–246). No musical examples.

Smith, Harry E.

1965, 1973   (Recording and liner notes) "The Kiowa Peyote Meeting." Smithsonian-Folkways (FE 4601).
Currently reissued on (3) cassettes, this three-record set contains songs recorded at Anadarko Oklahoma in 1964–1965. It gives a complete survey of the types of songs that are heard at actual peyote meetings. Also includes spoken prayers and explanations of

what goes on at the meetings, the origin of peyote, and other related subjects.

Spier, Leslie

1921   The Sun Dance of the Plains Indians: Its Development and Diffusion. *Anthropological Papers of the American Museum of Natural History* 16(7): 453–527. New York.

Could not be obtained for inspection of contents nor could information be gotten from other sources.

See **Stevenson** (1973b) in the General bibliography. This discusses some early written sources on Indian music of the Plains region (pp. 421–429).

Tarasoff, Koozma J.

1980   *Persistent Ceremonialism: The Plains Cree and Saulteaux.* Canadian Ethnology Service Paper No. 69. National Museum of Man Mercury Series. Ottawa: National Museums of Canada.

Contains transcriptions of interviews collected during the 1960s on the subject of the Rain Dance and the Sweat Bath Feast. Discusses how these events contribute to stability and survival of the native culture.

Theisz, Ronnie D.

1981   Acclamations and Accolades: Honor Songs in Lakota Society Today. *Kansas Quarterly* 13(Spring): 27–43.

Examines the modern use of songs to focus attention on personal accomplishments or other noteworthy events in a person's life. Theisz classifies the song types by rhythm (p. 29) and describes various categories by occasion (as for example veterans' songs, memorial songs, or songs for graduation from school). Includes texts and translations for 28 songs.

Tixier, Victor

[1844]   *Tixier's Travels on the Osage Prairies* [Voyage aux Prairies Osages, Louisiane et Missouri, 1838–1840] edited by John F. McDermott and translated from the original French by Albert Salvan. Norman (Oklahoma), 1940.

This contains descriptions of songs and musical instruments among the Osage. Could not be obtained. Information given here is from Hickerson (General bibliography, 1961:366).

Vennum, Thomas, Jr.

1995   Book review of *Southern Cheyenne Women's Songs* by Virginia Giglio (1994). *Anthropological Linguistics* 37:397–399.
        Vennum criticizes the transcriptions, analytical methods, and Giglio's decision to focus only on songs of one gender.

Walker, J.R.

1917   *The Sun Dance and Other Ceremonies of the Oglala.* Anthropological Papers of the American Museum of Natural History 16(1): 51–221. New York.
        Could not be obtained for inspection of contents nor could information be gotten from other sources.

Wallis, Wilson D.

1947   *The Canadian Dakota.* Anthropological Papers of the American Museum of Natural History 41(1): 1–225. New York.
        A general ethnography based on research conducted in 1914. The chapter on "Dance Societies" (pp. 42–77) gives profiles of ten dances. The chapter on "Medicinemen and Medicinewomen" (pp. 78–110) also contains several references to songs. No musical examples.

Weltfish, Gene

1965   (Recording and liner notes) "Music of the Pawnee." Smithsonian-Folkways Recordings (FE 4334).
        Currently available on cassette, this album contains songs that were originally recorded by Weltfish in 1936. Contents are identified as follows: Bear Song, Hand Game Songs (3), War Dance Songs (2), War Songs (2), Love Songs (5), Peyote Song, Buffalo Dance Songs (2), Hoop and Pole Game Song, Deer Dance Songs (5), Doctor's Hypnotism Song, Sacred Bundle Songs (2), and others (animal songs and society songs).

White, Leslie A., Editor

1959   *The Indian Journals of Lewis Henry Morgan.* Ann Arbor: University of Michigan Press.
This contains a description of the Sun Dance and other ceremonies as practiced by Crow Indians in the nineteenth century (pp. 183–190). No detailed information on music. Listed in Guédon (General bibliography, 1972:472).

Wissler, Clark

1912   *Ceremonial Bundles of the Blackfoot Indians.* Anthropological Papers of the American Museum of Natural History 7(2): 65–289.
The section on "Personal Charms and Medicines" (pp. 91–106) contains many references to songs and several translations of song texts. Some of the songs were recorded, and cylinder numbers are given (p. 100). These are among the holdings at Indiana University Archives of Traditional Music. See the catalogues by Lee (General bibliography, 1979) or by Seeger and Spear (General bibliography, 1987). A section on "Songs" (pp. 263–272) gives information on functions of songs, origin of songs in visions, musical values, use of words and vocables in texts, classification of song types, and comparative remarks on the style. No musical notations.

1913   Societies and Dance Associations of the Blackfoot Indians. *Anthropological Papers of the American Museum of Natural History* 11(4): 359–460.
This includes descriptions of ten ceremonies or dances as practiced by various societies. Songs are mentioned but not discussed in detail.

1916   General Discussion of Shamanistic and Dancing Societies. *Anthropological Papers of the American Museum of Natural History* 11(12): 853–876.
Could not be obtained for inspection of contents nor could information be gotten from other sources.

1918   The Sun Dance of the Blackfoot Indians. *Anthropological Papers of the American Museum of Natural History* 16(3): 225–270.
Contains many references to songs, especially in the following sections: "Ceremony of the Tongues" (pp. 234–240), "The Medicine Woman" (pp. 240–248), and "Sun Dance Songs" (pp.

267–268). Includes translations of six brief song texts (p. 237). No musical notations.

Witmer, Robert

1973   Recent Change in the Musical Culture of the Blood Indians of Alberta, Canada. *Yearbook for InterAmerican Musical Research, vol. 9.* Austin: University of Texas Press.

Focuses on the involvement of contemporary Blood Indians in various types of Euro-American music. Witmer begins by giving background data on the Blood Indian musicians and their exposure to Euro-American music. He then analyzes recordings to describe how their performance practices differ from those of white musicans (pp. 79–83). The musical repertory includes 42 songs in three main categories: (1) country-western, (2) sacred or gospel, and (3) rock and roll. Based on fieldwork conducted in 1968.

1982   *The Musical Life of the Blood Indians.* Mercury Series, Paper no. 86. Canadian Ethnology Service. Ottawa: National Museum of Man.

A musical ethnography illustrating the contemporary occurrence of traditional music (in modern settings) and various forms of acculturated music as described in a previous study (Witmer 1973 above). This is a revised version of Witmer's master's thesis (University of Illinois, 1970). Based on research conducted in 1968.

VIII. Northeast and Great Lakes

See **Baker** (1882) in the General bibliography. This contains musical notations of songs from the Iroquois (10 songs) and Chippewa (3).

Barbeau, C. Marius

1915   *Huron and Wyandot Mythology.* Canadian Department of Mines, Geological Survey Memoirs 80, Anthropological Series no.11.
Contains thirteen musical notations (with texts and some translations) transcribed from cylinders collected in 1911 and 1912. Use of songs in myths is also discussed (pp. 16–17).

Barnouw, Victor

1954   Reminiscences of a Chippewa Mide Priest. *Wisconsin Archeologist* 35:83–112.
Could not be obtained for inspection of contents nor could information be gotten from other sources.

1960   A Chippewa Mide Priest's Description of the Medicine Dance. *Wisconsin Archeologist* 41:77–97.
Could not be obtained for inspection of contents nor could information be gotten from other sources.

Barrett, Samuel A.

1911   *The Dream Dance of the Chippewa and Menominee Indians of Northern Wisconsin.* Bulletin of the Public Museum of the City of Milwaukee 1:251–406.
Contains a brief description of the music (pp. 280–282) and of the drum used in the dance (pp. 261–268).

Beauchamp, William Martin

1893   Notes on Onondaga Dance. *Journal of American Folklore* 6:181–184.

Contains descriptions of the Feast for the Dead and another ceremony called the Night Dance. Also includes comments on curing practices, songs, and recent changes in the Green Corn Dance. No musical notations.

1907   Civil, Religious, and Mourning Councils and Ceremonies of Adoption of the New York Indians. *New York State Museum Bulletin* 113:337–451.

Contains musical notations for seven Iroquois songs (opposite page 378). Also gives texts and translations of other ceremonial songs. Could not be obtained. Information given here is from Hickerson (General bibliography, 1961:141).

Boyle, David

1898a   Mid-Winter Festival. *Ontario Education Department: Archeological Museum Report for 1898*, pp. 82–91.

Describes songs and dances used in the Iroquois Midwinter Ceremony. Could not be obtained for inspection of contents. Listed in Hickerson (General bibliography, 1961:149).

1898b   Iroquois Music. *Ontario Education Department: Archeological Museum Report for 1898*, pp. 143–156.

Discusses Alexander Cringan's work collecting Iroquois songs and gives musical notations for fifteen songs. Could not be obtained. Information given here is from Hickerson (General bibliography, 1961:149).

Burke, Carleton

1937   *Symphony Iroquoian.* Rochester.

A symphonic poem incorporating melodies collected by Burke among the Seneca. The work includes 23 transcriptions (six with texts) and seven other Indian melodies with harmonies added by Burke. There is also a section by the Iroquoian artist Jesse Cornplanter entitled "A Word About Seneca Songs" (pp. 5–6). Information given here is from Hickerson (General bibliography, 1961:153).

See **Burlin** (1907) in the General bibliography. This contains musical notations of the following: six Penobscot songs (pp. 7–9 and 14–21), four Passamaquoddy songs (pp. 7, 10, 16, and 24–26), and 17 Winnebago songs (pp. 249–293 and 548–550).

Burton, Frederick Russell

1907   Music from the Ojibway's Point of View: Art an Unknown Word to These Primitive People, and Song a Part of Everyday Living. *Craftsman* 12:375–381.

Discusses Ojibway musical aesthetics and the relation of song texts to music. Includes two musical notations with texts and translations. Information from Hickerson (General bibliography, 1961:155).

1909   *American Primitive Music: With Especial Attention to the Songs of the Ojibways.* New York: Moffat, Yard, and Co.

Despite the ethnocentric tone and the focus on Ojibwa (Chippewa) music, this is an extensive study containing much information on Indian music and the history of research. Includes lengthy discussions of musical style and also touches on other subjects such as Euro-American influences, functions of music in native culture, and use of Indian themes by composers of Western art music. Includes about 100 musical notations that were transcribed by Burton from cylinders he collected beginning in 1901 (pp. 203–281).

Bushnell, David Ives

1905   An Ojibway Ceremony. *American Anthropologist* 7:69–73.

Describes a ceremony observed by the author in Northern Minnesota in 1899. The ceremony is not identified but seems to have involved a series of dances by six women (one after the other).

Cavanagh, Beverley

1987   The Performance of Hymns in Eastern Woodland Indian Communities. Pp. 45–56 in *Sing Out the Glad News: Hymn Tunes in Canada* edited by John Beckwith. CanMus Documents I. Toronto: Institute for Canadian Music.

Could not be obtained for inspection of contents nor could information be gotten from other sources.

Chafe, Wallace

1961   *Seneca Thanksgiving Rituals.* Bureau of American Ethnology Bulletin no. 183. Washington.
Contains two sets of texts and translations that were recorded at Tonawanda Reservation (New York State) in 1959. Both pertain to the Longhouse Religion or New Religion of Handsome Lake. The first set of texts is a speech in 16 parts (pp. 16–45). The second gives the words to songs and explanations of songs used in the Thanksgiving Dance (pp. 47–145). Includes 43 musical examples (pp. 47–68).

Charlevoix, Pierre François Xavier de

1744   *Histoire et description générale de la Nouvelle-France avec le journal d'un voyage fait par ordre du roit dans l'Amérique Septentrionnale.* 6 vols. Paris.
Could not be obtained for inspection of contents. According to Guédon (General bibliography, 1972: 466), volume three contains descriptions of Huron songs and ceremonies.

Coleman, Bernard

1937   The Religion of the Ojibwa of Northern Minnesota. *Primitive Man* 10:33–57.
Besides explaining spiritual concepts such as manitou and windigo, the article contains information on the Midewiwin (Grand Medicine) Society (pp. 43–50). Based on summer research visits beginning in 1929. No musical notations.

Conklin, Harold C., and William C. Sturtevant

1953   Seneca Indian Singing Tools at Coldspring Longhouse: Musical Instruments of the Modern Iroquois. *Proceedings of the American Philosophical Society* 97(3): 262–292.
Begins by emphasizing the non-use of western instruments. Contains detailed descriptions of the following types: green turtle rattle, bark rattle, tin rattle, wooden turtle rattle, water drum, horn rattle, box turtle rattle, stomping stick, rasping sticks, gourd rattles, and flutes without stops (whistles). Based on the authors' observa-

tions of instruments used during Midwinter Ceremonies held in January and February of 1952.

Converse, Harriet M.

1930   The Seneca New Year Ceremony and Other Customs. *Museum of the American Indian (New York), Indian Notes* 7:69–89.
Reprinted from an unidentified newspaper article published in 1895. The author focuses on a New Year Ceremony in which a white dog is ritually sacrificed. This also describes a War Dance and Dance for the Dead (pp. 86–88), mainly as practiced at Cattaraugus Reservation in New York. No musical notations.

Cornelius, Richard, and Terence J. O'Grady

1987   Reclaiming a Tradition: The Soaring Eagles of Oneida. *Ethnomusicology* 31(2): 261–272.
Originally formed in 1960, this group performs a repertory including intertribal (Pan-Indian) powwow songs and others in a more traditional Iroquois style. The paper discusses their efforts to revive or revitalize the traditional songs and contains many quotations in which the performers reveal their feelings about the music and its meaning for them.

Crawford, David E.

1967   The Jesuit Relations and Allied Documents, Early Sources for an Ethnography of Music among American Indians. *Ethnomusicology* 11(2): 199–206.
French traders and Jesuit missionaries were the earliest Europeans to explore the interior regions of New France and established contacts with various Algonquian and Iroquoian Indians during the early 1600s. Annual reports sent by the missionaries were known as the "Jesuit relations" and were later published in a 73-volume set. They contain much information about early Indian life, and this paper provides a sampling of references to music and related activities. For more information on early sources see Stevenson (General bibliography, 1973a and 1973b).

Cringan, Alexander

1899   Music of the Pagan Iroquois. Archeological Report. Appendix to Report of the Minister of Education. Toronto.

Could not be obtained nor could information on publisher be gotten from other sources. According to Cringan (1900a below) this contains transcriptions of several songs performed by an Iroquois singer. The notations were done by repetition, without benefit of a recording device. Also listed in Guédon (General bibliography, 1972:467).

1900a   Pagan Dance Songs of the Iroquois. *Ontario Education Department: Archeological Report for 1899*, pp. 168–189.
Contains 47 musical examples (without texts) as transcribed from cylinder recordings of two Iroquois singers. Cringan describes general characteristics of the music and also discusses performance contexts for most of the items transcribed.

1900b   Traditional Songs of the Iroquois Indians. *Musical Times* 41:114.
Briefly describes the collecting of songs among the Iroquois. Includes three musical examples.

1903   Iroquois Folk Songs. *Ontario Education Department: Archeological Museum Report for 1902*, pp. 137–152.
Contains 34 musical examples collected from an Onondaga singer. There are comments on each song and general remarks on rhythm and tonality in Iroquois music. Five of the songs are Delaware and seven are Tutelo. Could not be obtained. Information given here is from Hickerson (General bibliography, 1961:165).

Davidson, John F.

1945   Ojibwa Songs. *Journal of American Folklore* 58:303–305.
Contains eight Ojibwa (Chippewa) song texts and translations, six with musical notations. Based on data collected circa 1936–1937.

Densmore, Frances

1910–1913   *Chippewa Music.* 2 vols. Bureau of American Ethnology Bulletin nos. 45 and 53.
Volume One contains musical notations (with texts and translations) for 200 songs collected in northern Minnesota by Densmore from 1907 to 1909. Individual songs and types of songs are described in detail. 180 of the songs are analyzed in tables

showing relative occurrence of intervals, rhythmic units, etc. Densmore also discusses general characteristics of Chippewa music. Volume Two gives musical notations (with texts and translations) for 180 Chippewa songs, and 340 songs are analyzed using statistical tables.

1932   *Menominee Music.* Bureau of American Ethnology Bulletin no. 102.

Contains musical notations for 140 Menominee songs that were collected by Densmore in 1925, 1928, and 1929. There are English translations for many of the songs but native texts are lacking. Includes musical analysis and cultural commentary for each song, and the entire corpus is compared with 1,073 songs from other tribes that Densmore had previously studied.

1950   (Recording and liner notes) "Songs of the Chippewa." Library of Congress, Music Division, Recorded Sound Section (AAFS L 22).

The contents are identified as follows: Dream Songs (6), War Songs (4), Songs Used for Treatment of the Sick (3), Midéwiwin Songs (6), Love Songs (7), and Miscellaneous (4). The liner notes by Densmore (10 pp.) give texts, translations, and other useful information.

Dunning, Robert W.

1958   Iroquois Dance of the Dead, New Style. *Anthropologica* 6:87–118.

Describes a three-day ceremony which took place at the Six Nations Reservation (Ontario, Canada) in 1956. The ceremony was held in order to reconsecrate human remains (bones) from an archeological excavation. According to the author, this represented a revival of a Huron ritual that had not been conducted since the middle of the seventeenth century (pp. 87–88).

Fenton, William N.

1936   *An Outline of Seneca Ceremonies at Coldspring Longhouse.* Yale University Publications in Anthropology no. 9.

Gives an overview of calendric rituals performed at one of the few remaining longhouses in New York State and Canada during the 1930s. Includes descriptions of the following: Midwinter (New Year's) Festival, Maple Ceremony, Corn Planting Ceremony, Thunder Ritual, Green Corn Festival, and False Face curing rituals.

Also discusses social dances and the relation ceremonials to kinship patterns. No musical notations.

1940   Masked Medicine Societies of the Iroquois. *Annual Report of the Smithsonian Institution for 1940*, pp. 397–429.

Focuses on "false face societies" whose members wear wooden masks and travel from house to house driving away sickness. Fenton first discusses various types of masks and the mythic characters they represent. He also reviews archeological and historical evidence to speculate on the origins of masked curing societies. This contains 24 photographs of the masks and a painting of a false face curing ritual by a Seneca artist (Ernest Smith).

1941   Tonowanda Longhouse Ceremonies: Ninety Years after Lewis Henry Morgan. *Bureau of American Ethnology Bulletin no. 128, Anthropological Papers, no. 15*, pp. 139–166.

Based on 30 months of continuous research from 1935 to 1937. Fenton lists the ceremonies conducted at the Tonowanda Reservation (New York) and compares the ceremonial cycle with Seneca ceremonies at Coldspring Longhouse (See Fenton 1936 above). The paper gives a critical review of earlier findings by Lewis Henry Morgan. Appendix B (pp. 153–158) gives descriptions of various ceremonies as excerpted from a letter sent by Ely S. Parker (Iroquois) to Morgan in 1850. No musical examples.

1942   (Recording and liner notes) "Songs from the Iroquois Longhouse." Library of Congress, Music Division, Recorded Sound Section (AAFS L 6).

Recorded in New York and Ontario (Canada) in 1941. The contents are identified as follows: Great Feather Dance, Dream Songs (2), Boasting Chant, Thanksgiving Chant, Throwing Songs of Four Medicine Men, Introductory Songs of the Medicine Men, Medicine Dance (selections), Marching or Dream Song for the Winds, Onondaga Address to the Hunchbacks, Songs of the Hunchbacks or False-Faces, Song of the Bushy Heads or Husk-Faces, Corn Song, Iroquois War Dance, Scalp Dance, Eagle Dance, Warrior's Stomp Dance, and Women's Shuffle Dance.

1948   (Recording and liner notes) "Seneca Songs from Coldspring Longhouse." Library of Congress, Music Division, Recorded Sound Section (AAFS L 17).

Recorded in New York at various dates from 1941 to 1945. The album includes songs or series of songs as performed in the following contexts: Drum Dance (a sacred ritual of thanksgiving), Quavering-Changing-a Rib (a women's ritual about courtship), Bear Society Dance, and Fish Dance. The liner notes (16 pp.) include texts, translations, and other information by Fenton and comments on the musical style by Martha Champion Huot.

Fenton, William N., and Gertrude P. Kurath

1951   The Feast of the Dead, or Ghost Dance at Six Indians Reserve, Canada. Pp. 139–365 in *Symposium on Local Diversity in Iroquois Culture* edited by William Fenton. Bureau of American Ethnology Bulletin no. 149.

Could not be obtained. According to Hickerson (General bibliography, 1961:216), this contains musical notations and commentary for eight songs. Also includes song texts and dance notations.

1953   *The Iroquois Eagle Dance: An Offshoot of the Calumet Dance*. With Analysis of the Iroquois Eagle Dance and Songs by Gertrude P. Kurath. Bureau of American Ethnology Bulletin no 156.

For description of the music-related contents, see Kurath (1953a) below.

Fewkes, Jesse Walter

1890   A Contribution to Passamaquoddy Folklore. *Journal of American Folklore* 3:257–280.

Historically important as the earliest study of Indian music based on field recordings collected with the Edison-type phonograph. Begins by listing songs and spoken texts collected on 35 cylinders. Includes three musical notations (including texts) and descriptions of other songs.

Gagnon, Ernest

1907   Les sauvages de l'Amérique et l'art musical. Pp. 179–189 in *Proceedings of the International Congress of Americanists (1906) no. 15*. Vol. 1 (of 2). Quebec.

According to Hickerson (General bibliography, 1961:230), this contains musical notations and texts for five Huron songs and one song from a tribe identified as the "Otchipoues."

Gray, Judith A., Editor

1985   Northeastern Indian Catalog. Pages 1–328 in *The Federal Cylinder Project: A Guide to Field Cylinder Collections in Federal Agencies, Volume 2: Northeastern Indian Catalog, Southeastern Indian Catalog.* Washington: American Folklife Center, Library of Congress.

Lists and describes early recordings from sixteen collections, the earliest being the Passamaquoddy cylinders collected by Jesse Walter Fewkes in 1890. Each collection is preceded by an introduction providing background information on the recordings and citing translations or other documentation in published sources or manuscripts. The Foreword by Thomas Vennum Jr. (pp. 3–7) discusses the early history of musicological research in the Northeast (circa 1890–1930) and gives other information on ethnography and regional history. Recordings from the following groups are listed: Chippewa, Fox, Iroquois, Kickapoo (Mexican), Menominee, Passamaquoddy, Sauk, Shawnee (Absentee), and Winnebago.

See **Guédon** (1972) in General bibliography. This contains a section listing publications, recordings, and films relating to Indian music of the Northeast region (pp. 466–471).

Hale, Horatio Emmons

1883   *The Iroquois Book of Rites.* Library of Aboriginal American Literature, vol. 11. Philadelphia.

Could not be obtained. According to Hickerson (General bibliography 1961:237), this contains six song texts and translations.

Hallowell, A. Irving

1942   *The Role of Conjuring in Saulteaux Society.* Publications of the Philadelphia Anthropological Society 2:1–96.

Focuses on "shaking tent" rituals among the Ojibwa-speaking Saulteaux of Manitoba, Canada. Hallowell examines the functions of conjuring in Saulteaux society and compares related practices among other Algonkian groups. Chapter seven ("A Conjuring Performance," pp. 35–72) and chapter eight ("The Occasions for Conjuring," pp. 53–72) both contain references to songs but no detailed information on music. This includes photographs of a conjuring lodge and two Saulteaux conjurers (following p. 36).

Based on summer field trips in 1930 and years following. No musical notations.

Herzog, George

See Speck and Herzog (1942 below) for transcriptions and analyses of Tutelo Indian songs by George Herzog.

See **Heth** (1979) in the Southeast bibliography. This emphasizes the similarities in Iroquois and Cherokee music.

Hewitt, J.N.B.

1898   The Term Haii-Haii of Iroquois Mourning and Condolence Songs. *American Anthropologist* 11:286–287.
Hewitt explains the origin of the term on the basis of information supplied by Brebeuf in the Jesuit Relations for 1636. Information given here is from Hickerson (General bibliography, 1961:249). For further information on the Jesuit Relations, see Crawford (1967 above).

Hofmann, Charles

1947   American Indian Music in Wisconsin, Summer 1946. *Journal of American Folklore* 60(237): 289–293.
Focuses on music performed by Indians of five different tribes (Winnebago, Sioux, Chippewa, Zuni, and Acoma) at an intertribal gathering which took place annually at the Upper Dells of the Wisconsin River. The gatherings had been held there every summer for 18 years (since 1928). Contains descriptions of songs and ten song texts in English. No musical notations. Some of the songs are heard on a commercial album by Hofmann (General bibliography, 1964).

Hoffman, Walter James

1888   Pictography and Shamanistic Rites of the Ojibwa. *American Anthropologist* (Old Series) 1:209–229.
Describes the use of mnemonic symbols to represent songs, mythic events, and ritual activities in the Midewiwin and other great medicine societies. Includes 16 illustrations of the pictographs, which were also used to record historical events and even for writing letters. Based on research conducted in 1887. Contains no musical notations.

1891   *The Midewiwin or "Grand Medicine Society" of the
            Ojibwa.* Bureau of American Ethnology, Annual
            Report (1885–1886) 7:143–300.

A comprehensive study based on historical sources and research conducted at various reservations (mainly Red Lake and
White Earth in western Wisconsin). The society is graded into four
degrees, and Hoffman describes initiation ceremonies and other
rituals which occur at each level. The section entitled "First
Degree" (pp. 189–223) contains descriptions of instruments (pp.
190–191) and of songs (pp. 192–196). Three musical examples are
discussed in some detail (pp. 207–217). The sections on the
"Second Degree" (pp. 224–239) and "Third Degree" (pp. 240–255)
both contain many song texts and translations. The section on the
"Fourth Degree" (pp. 255–277) contains musical examples keyed
to pictographic symbols (pp. 266–274). The musical style and
mnemonic symbol system are also discussed in Supplementary
Notes (pp. 289–296).

1893   *The Menomini Indians.* Bureau of American
            Ethnology, Annual Report (1892–1893) 14(1): 3–
            328.

This comprehensive ethnography contains descriptions of
Mitawit (Grand Medicine Society) ceremonies conducted in 1890,
1891, 1892, and 1892 (pp. 66–137). This section includes one musical example (pp. 115). The volume also includes one musical notation of a song (sung by Moose) from a mythological text (p. 193).

Howard, James H.

1966   The Henry Davis Drum Rite: An Unusual Drum
            Religion Variant of the Minnesota Ojibwa. *Plains
            Anthropologist* 11(32): 117–126.

The Drum Religion or Dream Dance was basically a form of
the ceremonial Grass Dance (of the Plains tribes) that was modified
into a religion by the addition of various elements, many stemming
from Christianity. Howard traces the origins of the Drum Religion
and then describes ceremonies practiced by Ojibwa Indians at
Mille Lacs, Minnesota, in 1963. Includes descriptions of songs but
no musical notations.

1981   *Shawnee: The Ceremonialism of a Native American
            Tribe and Its Cultural Background.* Athens, Ohio:
            Ohio University Press.

The first ten chapters rely on earlier sources to construct an ethnographic overview; then chapters eleven through fifteen focus on ceremonial activities as viewed by Howard during the 1970s. The handling of historical perspectives is criticized in a review by Sweet (1984 below).

See **Huenemann** (1978) in the General bibliography for information on Indian music of the Great Lakes region (including 10 musical examples).

James, Edwin

1830   *A Narrative of the Captivity and Adventures of John Tanner (U.S. Interpreter at Saut de Ste. Marie), During Thirty Years Residence among the Indians in the Interior of North America.* London and New York.

Could not be obtained. According to Hickerson (General bibliography, 1961:230–231), the chapter on "Music and Poetry of the Indians" (pp. 334–381) includes ten song texts and translations.

Kohl, J.G.

1860   *Kitchi-Gami: Wanderings Round Lake Superior.* London: Chapman and Hall.

According to Hickerson (General bibliography, 1961:266), this contains a description of music among the Dakota and "Ojibbeway" (pp. 248–253) and translations for three Ojibwa (Chippewa) song texts (pp. 250, 252, and 253).

Krehbiel, Henry Edward

1894   An Iroquois Ritual. *Musical Courier* 29:13 (September 26).

Contains one musical example (with text) and translations of two song texts quoted from Hale (1883 above).

Kurath, Gertrude Prokosch

1950   A New Method of Choreographic Notation. *American Anthropologist* 52:120–123.

Contains one musical notation (with text) and dance notation for a Cayuga song collected by William Fenton in 1941.

1951a   Local Diversity in Iroquois Music and Dance. Pp.
             109–137 in *Symposium on Local Diversity in
             Iroquois Culture* edited by William Fenton. Bureau
             of American Ethnology Bulletin no. 149.
    A comparative study of music and dance in Iroquoian com-
munities from northern New York State to northeastern Oklahoma.
Also considers the relation of these to music and dance of the
Oklahoma Cherokee. Kurath begins with an overview of general
patterns in all Iroquois communities, including a summary of musical characteristics (pp. 115–116); she then discusses variations
occurring in various types of dances, with particular attention to
the origin and dissemination of the Stomp dance (pp. 128–131).
This contains 24 musical examples from the following tribes:
Onondaga (3), Onondaga-Cayuga (3), Seneca (10), Cayuga (4),
Cherokee (2), and other groups of Oklahoma (2). The songs
(transcribed by Kurath) were originally recorded by William
Fenton in 1933, 1941, and 1949.

1951b   The Feast of the Dead, or Ghost Dance, at Six
             Nations Reserve, Canada. Pp. 143–165 in *Symposium
             on Local Diversity in Iroquois Culture* edited by
             William Fenton. Bureau of American Ethnology
             Bulletin no. 149.
    This is an ancient feast to placate the dead and not to be con-
fused with the more recent Ghost Dance as originated in the Great
Basin area. The article contains two contemporary descriptions: (1)
an Onandaga ceremony that was observed by Howard Skye in
1945 (pp. 145–153) and (2) a Cayuga ritual attended by Kurath in
1949 (pp. 153–164). Includes eight musical examples (most with
texts) and a comparative analysis of scales.

1951c   Iroquois Midwinter Medicine Rites. *Journal of the
             International Folk Music Council* 3:96–100.
    Includes musical notations (with texts) and commentary for
five Iroquois songs collected by William Fenton.

1952   Matriarchal Dances of the Iroquois. Pp. 123–130 in
             Indian Tribes of Aboriginal America edited by Sol
             Tax. Selected Papers of the 29th International Con-
             gress of Americanists (1952), vol. 3 (of 3). Chicago.
    Kurath begins by describing the high social status of women
as agriculturalists in pre-contact society and states that they still
continue to govern seasonal rituals related to the planting, growth,
and harvesting of various vegetables, roots, fruits, and berries. She

then describes songs, prayers, and dances for some of the festivals. Men sing most of the songs, though they are joined by women on occasion. Includes nine musical examples transcribed from recordings by Fenton.

1953a   An Analysis of the Iroquois Eagle Dance and Songs. Pp. 223–306 in *The Iroquois Eagle Dance: An Offshoot of the Calumet Dance* by William N. Fenton and Gertrude P. Kurath. Bureau of American Ethnology Bulletin no. 156.

This contains musical transcriptions and fairly detailed analyses of 41 dance songs collected by William Fenton and the author. The comparative analysis deals with tonal material, rhythmic features, melodic contour, and personal style features. Musical examples are from the Seneca (17 songs), Onondaga (15), and Cayuga (9).

1953b   The Tutelo Harvest Rites: A Musical and Choreographic Analysis. *Scientific Monthly* 76(March): 153–162.

Contains transcriptions and analyses for eight songs, with song texts and translations. Corresponding dances are also described and analyzed from a comparative and historical perspective.

1954a   The Tutelo Fourth Night Spirit Release Singing. *Midwest Folklore* 4(2): 87–105.

The Iroquois of Six Nations Reserve (Ontario) have adopted this ceremony and two others from (Siouan) Tutelo Indians who came to the area from North Carolina in the mid-1700s. The Spirit Release Singing is performed after a death to assure passing of the spirit to the abode of the dead. The paper describes 24 songs which Kurath recorded in 1952. This includes a comparative analysis of the musical style (pp. 91–97) and four musical notations (pp. 104–105).

1954b   Chippewa Sacred Songs in Religious Metamorphosis. *Scientific Monthly* 79:311–317.

Discusses some of the causes underlying the acceptance of foreign musical styles by Chippewa (Ojibwa) Indians of Michigan. Includes three musical examples, with texts and translations.

1954c   Onondaga Ritual Parodies. *Journal of American Folklore* 67(266): 404–406.

Describes the activities of false-face society dancers during Midwinter rites on Six Nations Reserve (Ontario) in January 1952.

1955a   Modern Ottawa Dancers. *Midwest Folklore* 5(7):15–
           22.
This describes the creative revival of a Ceremony of the Sun performed for tourists and others by (Algonkian) Ottawa Indians of Michigan in 1953. The original day-long event, which was documented in a source dating from 1703, has been condensed into a one-hour performance. Includes three musical notations and dance diagrams.

1955b   Ceremonies, Songs, and Dances of Michigan Indians.
           Michigan History 39:466–468.
Gives a brief survey of contemporary music and related activities among groups identified as Chippewa, Ottawa, and Potawatomi.

1956a   Antiphonal Songs of Eastern Woodland Indians.
           Musical Quarterly 42:520–526.
This includes musical examples from the Iroquois (6 songs), Cherokee (2), and Meskwaki or Fox tribe (1). Kurath distinguishes various categories of antiphonal singing (monotone, bitonal, melodic) and suggests that call and response patterns in the music reflect interlocking patterns of social and ritual behavior (p. 526).

1956b   (Recording and notes) "Songs and Dances of the
           Great Lakes Indians." Monograph Series of the
           Ethnic Folkways Library. Smithsonian-Folkways
           Recordings (P 1003).
Currently available on cassette, this classic album includes extensive liner notes (18 pp.) providing photographs, texts, translations, musical transcriptions (6), and analysis by Kurath. There is a broad sampling of song-types as performed by singers of the following tribes: Meskwaki, Ojibwa, Ottawa, Onondaga, Onondaga-Tuscarora, and Cayuga-Tutelo.

1957a   Algonquian Ceremonialism and Natural Resources of
           the Great Lakes. *Aryan Path* (Bombay) 28(3): 136–
           140.
This focuses on various Algonquian tribes of the Great Lakes area. Kurath first describes pre-contact subsistence patterns and animistic practices through which the Indians worshipped nature. She then focuses on various surviving ceremonies and discusses how these have become threatened by influences of Christianity and modern economic trends. In this article she also mentions a contrast between (apparently) older songs and newer ones in the

Midewiwin medicine society (p. 139). The songs she regards as being older have simple scales and much repetition.

1957b   Catholic Hymns of Michigan Indians. *Anthropological Quarterly* 3:31–44.

Discusses the history of Catholic hymn singing among Indians of Michigan and the relation between hymns and native song styles. This includes seven musical examples (with texts and translations) from various tribes. The history of Catholic influence is also discussed in Kurath (1959b below).

1957c   Pan-Indianism in Great Lakes Tribal Festivals. *Journal of American Folklore* 70(276):179–182.

Interesting for its historical perspective on the intertribal powwow as a relatively modern development among Algonkian tribes of the region. Kurath lists five basic elements of the powwow repertory as standardized among Indians of Oklahoma (War Dance, Victory Round or Soldier Dance, Indian Swing Dances, Calumet or Pipe Dance, and Snake or Stomp Dances). She then tries to explain why some are not present in powwows among the northeastern tribes. Also discusses the meaning or significance of the intertribal powwow for modern Indians of the Great Lakes region.

1959   Menomini Indian Dance Songs in a Changing Culture. *Midwest Folklore* 9 (1): 31–38.

Based on recordings made by various collectors between 1928 and 1956. The essay considers various types of songs and dances, both religious and social in character, and attempts to sketch a history of music and dance. According to Kurath, early animistic songs and dances were followed by successive styles that were adapted from other tribes, and the musical life was finally shaped by post-contact changes due to the acceptance of Christianity and secularization. Includes seven musical notations.

1959   Blackrobe and Shaman: The Christianization of the Michigan Algonquians. *Papers of the Michigan Academy of Sciences, Arts, and Letters* 44:209–215.

Based mainly on historical sources but also includes comments of modern Indian people interviewed by Kurath. The paper describes aboriginal religious patterns and various stages through which Christian elements entered and transformed the native spiritual life. It contains interesting comments on the following: (1) the Indians' enjoyment of religious songs taught to them by Jesuits

during the seventeenth century (p. 212), (2) the concept of the
Great Spirit and how it developed during the eighteenth century (p.
212), and (3) some hidden similarities between the native religion
and Catholicism (p. 214–215).

1961   Effects of Environment on Cherokee-Iroquois Cere-
            monialism, Music, and Dance. Pp. 177–195 in *Sym-
            posium on Cherokee and Iroquois Culture* edited by
            William Fenton and John Gulick. Bureau of
            American Ethnology Bulletin no. 180. Washington.

    A detailed comparison of ceremonial patterns among the
(northeastern) Iroquois tribes and the (linguistically related)
Cherokee of North Carolina. Kurath begins by noting many parallels between the winter dances, summer ceremonies, and social
dances (pp. 178–180). She then focuses on differences, many of
which she attributes to Algonkian influences on the Iroquois and
Muskogean influences on the Cherokee (pp. 180–187). Some differences in ecology and climate are also considered important (p.
187). Musical similarities and differences are discussed throughout, and the article includes 15 musical examples (pp. 192–195).
According to Kurath, songs of the northern style seem to represent
a more archaic tradition because of their "undulating contour, small
compass, (and) rhapsodic form" (p. 191). The southern style (based
on short antiphonal phrases) is considered less ancient (p. 187).
Kurath also concludes that the southern style seems more homogeneous (p. 186), except that Cherokee songs of the Booger Dance
and Bear Dance tend to follow the archaic northern pattern (p.
182). Some of her conclusions are questioned in a paper by
Sturtevant (1961 below).

1964   *Iroquois Music and Dance: Ceremonial Arts of Two
            Seneca Longhouses.* Bureau of American Ethnology
            Bulletin no. 187. Washington.

    A comprehensive study based on research conducted at the
Coldspring Reservation and the Tonawanda Reservation in New
York State. Most of the songs analyzed here were collected by
William Fenton and Marth Champion Huot (Randle) between 1933
and 1951. Other field research was conducted by Kurath between
1947 and 1949. Part I contains descriptions of various dances (pp.
1–26), and this is followed by detailed comparative analyses of the
music (pp. 27–49) and the choreography (pp. 50–75). Parts II and
III (pp. 100–193) contain song texts and notations of songs. There
are more than 300 musical examples in all.

1966   *Michigan Indian Festivals*. Ann Arbor: Ann Arbor Publishers.
Written in a style intended for scholars and general readers alike, this brief monograph (88 pages of text, followed by photographs) actually gives a history of music and culture among Algonkian tribes of the Great Lakes area. Chapter four ("Echoes of the Past in Dance and Song," pp. 21–37) focuses on aboriginal song-types, including 21 musical examples. Chapter five ("Hybrid Liturgies," pp. 39–46) deals with music related to Catholicism, including notations of four hymns in native languages. Chapter six ("Algonquian Evangelism," pp. 47–52) discusses Protestant influences, including notations for two hymns . Other chapters (7, 8, and 9) describe modern musical activities as related to the Pan-Indian powwow or imported from other tribes. These (latter) chapters contain ten musical examples.

1968   *Dance and Song Rituals of Six Rivers Reserve, Ontario*. Ottawa: National Museum of Canada. Bulletin 220, no. 4. Folklore series.
A general ethnography of music and dance based on field research by Kurath between 1948 and 1964 and by William Fenton circa 1941–1945. This includes chapters on the following: "Midwinter Dream and Medicine Rites" (Ch. 5), "Four Sacred Ceremonies" (Ch. 6), "Food Spirit Dances" (Ch. 7), and "Social Dances" (Ch. 8). Contains 83 musical examples.

1981   *Tutelo Rituals on Six Rivers Reserve, Ontario*. Society for Ethnomusicology Special Monograph Series No. 5. Ann Arbor.
Part I contains chapters describing three major ceremonials: (1) "The Four Nights Harvest Dance" (pp. 9–18), (2) "The Fourth Night Spirit Release Singing" (pp. 19–24), and (3) "The Spirit Adoption Ceremony" (pp. 25–40). Part II focuses on comparative analyses, with chapter titles as follows: "Tutelo Music and Dance Styles" (pp. 41–64), "Tutelo Styles and Intertribal Contacts" (pp. 65–88), and "Processes of Change" (pp. 89–110). Contains more than 100 musical examples.

Lafiteau, Joseph Francois

1724   *Moeurs des Sauvages Amériquains Comparées aux Moeurs des Premier Temps*. 2 vols. Paris.
Contains some early descriptions of instruments, songs, and dances identified as belonging to the "Canadian" Indians. Could

not be obtained. Information given here is from Guédon (General bibliography, 1972:468).

LaFrance, Ron

1992   Inside the Longhouse: Dances of the Haudenosaunee
               Pp. 19–32 in *Native American Dance: Ceremonies
               and Social Traditions* edited by Charlotte Heth.
               Washington: National Museum of the American
               Indian, Smithsonian Institution.
       A native culture-bearer (LaFrance) describes contemporary
social dances among the Iroquois of New York State. Dances mentioned include the Stomp Dance, Alligator Dance, Delaware Skin
Dance, Rabbit Dance, New Women's Shuffle Dance, Older
Ladies' Dance, and several others.

Lambert, R.S.

1956   The Shaking Tent. *Tomorrow* 4(3): 113–128.
       A sensationalistic account of Huron shamanism based mainly
on seventeenth-century writings of the Jesuit Father Paul Le Jeune.
No musical notations.

Landes, Ruth

1968   *Ojibwa Religion and the Midewiwin.* Madison,
               Milwaukee, and London: University of Wisconsin
               Press.
       Based on research conducted in northwestern Minnesota and
western Ontario (Canada) from 1932 to 1936, this provides a useful follow-up to the classic study by Hoffman (1891 above). The
lengthy chapter on "Ritual in the Midéwiwin" (pp. 114–177) contains many references to songs and their use in ceremonies. The
chapter includes English translations for texts of 18 songs. No musical notations.

See the catalogue by **Lee** (1979) in the General bibliography. This lists
       historical and recent recordings at Indiana University Archives
       of Traditional Music. The collection includes items from the
       following Northeastern tribes: Abenaki, Beothuk, Chippewa,
       Delaware, Huron, Iroquois (various groups), Kickapoo,
       Malecite, Menomini, Micmac, Ojibwa (Chippewa), Ottawa,
       Pamunkey, Penobscot, Potawatomi, Shawnee, Tuscarora, and
       Winnebago.

Lescarbot, Marc

[1609]   *History of New France.* 3 vols. Translated from the original French edition by W. L. Grant. Publications of the Champlain Society, vols. 1, 7, and 11 (1907–1914).
Volume Three contains a discussion of music and related customs among the Micmac (pp. 105–108). Lescarbot's description of Micmac doctoring and three of the songs he transcribed are quoted and discussed in Stevenson (General bibliography, 1973a:14–15). This is the earliest publication listed in Hickerson (General bibliography, 1961:283) and presumably the earliest source containing references to Indian music north of Mexico.

McAllester, David Park

See McAllester (1949) in the general bibliography. This contains information on Peyote music among the Fox and Kickapoo.

1952   Menomini Peyote Music. Pp. 681–700 in *Menomini Peyotism* by James S. Slotkin. Transactions of the American Philosophical Society, vol. 42, part 4.
Contains musical transcriptions and analysis (by McAllester) for 24 songs (with texts). Also discusses the central importance of music in the Peyote religion.

Marpurg, Friedrich Wilhelm

1754–1778   *Historisch-Kritische Beyträge zur Aufname der Musik.* Five volumes. Berlin.
Volume 5 contains a section entitled "Anmerkungen über drey Lieder der Irokesen" (pp. 341–346). This describes Iroquois music in relation to three musical examples and two translations of song texts (into German). Could not be obtained. The information given here is from Hickerson (General bibliography, 1961:295).

Merriam, Alan P.

1958   Record Review of "Songs and Dances of the Great Lakes Indians" recorded and annotated by Gertrude P. Kurath (1956). *Journal of the International Folk Music Council* 10:108–109.
Merriam criticizes technical aspects of the recording and questions Kurath's characterization of a distinctive musical style shared by Indians of the Great Lakes area. Despite the flaws he still

acknowledges that the album contains types of music that cannot be heard on other commercial recordings and therefore has great value for Indian music specialists.

Mersenne, Marin

1636   *Harmonie Universelle.* Paris. Édition facsimilé. Paris: Centre national de la recherche scientifique.

Could not be obtained for inspection of contents. This is mentioned by Guédon (General bibliography, 1972:468) as the source of a transcription of a Canadian Indian melody in Rousseau (1768 below). This section from Mersenne (1636) is more fully discussed by Stevenson, who also includes a reprint of the notation (General bibliography, 1973a:16–17). Stevenson points out that Mersenne's purpose in quoting the Indian song (and others) was to prove that diatonic scale patterns were used by all peoples of the world, even those lacking professional musicians.

Michelson, Truman

1925   *The Mythical Origin of the White Buffalo Dance of the Fox Indians: Together with Texts on Four Minor Sacred Packs Appertaining to this Ceremony.* Bureau of American Ethnology, Annual Report (1918–1919) 40: 23–289.

This contains texts that were originally written in phonetic symbols by a native speaker (Alfred Kiyana) and later translated by Michelson with help from various native interpretors. The Introduction (pp. 37–45) gives a description of the White Buffalo Dance, which involves singing and flute playing, as performed in June 1924. The monograph includes texts and translations for 43 songs (pp. 97–115). No musical notations.

1927–1930   *Contributions to Fox Ethnology.* 2 vols. Bureau of American Ethnology nos. 85 and 95. Washington.

Like the previous entry (1925 above) these volumes contain texts and translations produced largely by native speakers and interpreters. Volume 85 (1927) contains texts and translations for 17 songs, while 20 other song texts are given only in translation. Volume 95 (1930) contains texts and translations for nine songs, and 19 other song texts are given in English only. Most of the texts pertain to medicine bundle rituals, though some focus on dances. No musical examples.

Morgan, Lewis Henry

[1851]   *League of the Ho-Dé-No-Sau-Nee, or Iroquois.* 2 volumes. Rochester, New York. Second edition edited by Herbert M. Lloyd (New York, 1901).
Volume I, Chapter 2 (pp. 175–216) contains descriptions of the following ceremonies: Maple Dance (pp. 180–186), Planting Festival (pp. 186–189), Berry Festival (pp. 189–190), Green Corn Festival (pp. 190–197), Harvest Festival (pp. 197–199), and a New Year Festival involving the sacrifice of a white dog (pp. 199–208). Volume II, Chapter 4 (pp. 249–279) includes descriptions of musical instruments and various other dances (War Dance, Great Feather Dance, Trotting Dance, Fish Dance, and Dance for the Dead). These is also one musical example which illustrates the sound of an Iroquois war-whoop (p. 261). Otherwise no musical notations.

Myrand, Ernest

1899   *Noëls Anciens de la Nouvelle France.* Québec.
Could not be obtained. According to Guédon (General bibliography, 1972:468), the book "contains Franco-Iroquois Christmas carols." This would seem to indicate that there are notations, but there is no further information concerning number of examples or name of publisher.

Nettl, Bruno

1953   The Shawnee Musical Style: Historical Perspective in Primitive Music. *Southwestern Journal of Anthropology* 9:277–285.
Discusses the stylistic variety in Shawnee music and seeks to explain the existence of sub-styles in terms of historical contacts and migrations. Four distinct styles or "layers" are suggested: (1) an early style heard in story songs and lullabies; (2) a predominant style, heard in various contexts, which Nettl considers similar to other southeastern styles; (3) a later style, heard in Green Corn Dance songs, with wider melodic ranges and greater rhythmic complexity (possibly reflecting musical influences from the southern Plains); and (4) the most recent style, heard in Peyote songs and typical of peyote music in general.

See Nettl (1954a) in the General bibliography. This discusses the general characteristics of music in "The Eastern Area" (pp. 33–36).

328 North American Indian Music

Osburn, Mary Russell

1946   Prehistoric Musical Instruments in Ohio. *Ohio State Archeology and Historical Quarterly* 55:12–20.
According to Hickerson (General bibliography, 1961: 316), this gives a survey of published literature on the subject. Could not be obtained.

Parker, Arthur C.

[1913]   *Parker on the Iroquois.* Edited by William Fenton. Reprint. Syracuse: Syracuse University Press, 1968.
Parker (1881–1955) was an Iroquois who became an anthropologist and museum curator. He was also the grand-nephew of Ely S. Parker, another distinguished Iroquois who collaborated with Lewis Morgan (1851 above) and later became a general in the Union Army. This volume contains three books or parts, each with separate pagination. Book Two ("The Code of Handsome Lake, the Seneca Prophet") contains much information on dances and rituals. See especially the section entitled "Field Notes on the Rites and Ceremonies of the Ganiodaio Religion" (pp. 81–85). There is also a description of the white dog sacrifice (pp. 85–94). The volume includes historical photographs (including one of the dog sacrifice) and drawings by Jesse Cornplanter (Iroquois).

Parthun, Paul

1976   Ojibwe Music in Minnesota. Ph.D. dissertation. University of Minnesota.
This is a general music ethnography in three main parts. Part One ("Anthropology of Ojibwe Music," pp. 2–80) contains separate chapters on ideas about music, musical instruments, and uses and functions of music. Part Two ("Ethnomusicology of Ojibwe Music," pp. 81–268) begins with a critical survey of earlier musicological research (Ch. 5) and then gives notations, analysis, and commentary for 111 songs recorded by Parthun during the early 1970s (Ch. 6). Part Three ("Musico-Social Change," pp. 269–300) deals with the changing style of War Dance songs (Ch. 7) and other historical developments such as peyote songs and the singing of Christian hymns (Ch. 8).

1977   (Recording and liner notes) "Songs of the Chippewa, Volume I: Game and Social Dance Songs." Smithsonian-Folkways (FE 4392).

Currently available on cassette, this album contains songs recorded at various places in Minnesota and Wisconsin in 1976. Contents include the following: Moccasin Game Songs (2), Round Dance Song, War Dance Song, Forty-Nine Dance Song, Air Force Song, "Old" War Dance Song, Buffalo Dance Song, and various types of powwow songs.

1978   Conceptualization of Traditional Music among the Ojibwe of Manitoba and Minnesota. *Anthropological Journal of Canada* 16(3): 27–32.

Contains texts transcribed from taped interviews in juxtaposition with interpretive comments by Parthun. The following subjects are discussed: composition of new songs, musical values, old and new songs, aids for the singer's voice, techniques of cueing in musical performance, and changes in musical style.

Radin, Paul

1911   The Ritual and Significance of the Winnebago Medicine Dance. *Journal of American Folklore* 24(92): 149–208.

Gives fairly detailed description of a Winnebago medicine society and compares it with the Midewiwin societies of the Ojibwa and the Menominee. This contains a classification of songs in the Winnebago rituals (p. 156) but no musical examples. Towards the end Radin traces historical connections between these and other initiatory societies (also found among the Omaha). Also discusses psychological factors and social functions of the rituals.

Reade, John

1887   Some Wabanaki Songs. *Transactions of the Royal Society of Canada* 5(2): 1–8.

Could not be obtained for inspection of contents. Listed in Guédon (General bibliography, 1972:468).

Reagan, Albert

1922   The Medicine Songs of George Farmer. *American Anthropologist* 24:332–369.

Gives texts, translations, and commentary for 25 Chippewa songs as performed in the Midewiwin medicine society. Farmer, who was a medicine man and police officer among the the Bois Fort Indians of Minnesota, had originally written out the texts himself. Reagan, who served as an Indian agent at the time, found the notebooks and obtained translations from Farmer. Also includes a description of the Midewiwin society and its functions (pp. 366–369).

See **Roberts** (1936) in the General bibliography. This describes general characteristics of vocal music among tribes of the Eastern Woodlands region (pp. 36–38).

See **Rhodes** (1954) in the Southeast bibliography for commercial record album containing songs from the Delaware tribe.

Riemer, Mary Frances (See also Mary Frances Riemer-Weller)

1980   (Recording and liner notes) "Seneca Social Dance Music." Smithsonian Folkways Recordings (FE 4072).
Currently available on cassette, this album features music recorded on the Allegany Reservation in New York between 1977 and 1980. Contents are listed as follows: Stomp Dance songs, Moccasin Dance songs, Robin Dance songs, Shaking-the-Bush Dance songs, Raccoon Dance songs, Alligator Dance songs, Smoke Dance song, Ladies' Dance songs, Rabbit Dance songs, Round Dance songs, Farewell Song, and Seneca Anthem.

Riemer-Weller, Mary Frances

1986   Iroquois (Music). Pp. 497–500 in *The New Grove Dictionary of American Music*, vol. 2 (E–K). Edited by H. Wiley Hitchcock and Stanley Sadie. London: Macmillan.
Begins by discussing early history of the Iroquois and the New Religion of Handsome Lake, a Seneca prophet who began preaching among the Iroquois in 1799. A section on the "Ceremonial Calendar and Music" (p. 98) discusses the Midwinter Ceremony and various harvest ceremonies. The author then discusses medicine societies (such as the False Face Society), social dance music, and basic elements of the Iroquois musical style.

Rothenberg, Jerome

1971   Chronicle: A Seneca Songman. *Alcheringa* 3:82–93.
Could not be obtained for inspection of contents. Listed in Guédon (General bibliography, 1972:468).

Rousseau, Jean Jacques

[1768]   *A Complete Dictionary of Music.* Second edition. Translated from the original French edition by William Waring. London (1779).
This includes one notation of an Indian song from Canada (p. 266) that is quoted from Mersenne (1636 above). Could not be obtained. Information given here is from Hickerson (General bibliography, 1961:333).

Sagard Theodat, F. Gabriel

[1632]   *The Long Journey to the Country of the Hurons.* Translated from the French second edition of 1865 (Paris) by H. H. Langton. Edited by George Wrong. Publications of the Champlain Society 15 (1939).
The chapter entitled "Their Dances, Songs, and Other Silly Ceremonies" (chapter ten, pp. 115–120) includes descriptions of singing and notations for seven songs. Two melodies are given in staff notation (four parts) and five are in solfège only. Three of the songs are identified as Micmac. Some of the data is from Lescarbot (1609 above). Information given here is from Hickerson (General bibliography, 1961:336).

Sargent, Margaret

1950   Seven Songs from Lorette. *Journal of American Folklore* 63:175–180.
Contains notations (with texts) for seven Huron songs collected by Marius Barbeau in 1911. Also discusses characteristics of the music.

See **Schoolcraft** (1851–1857) in General bibliography. Volume One gives texts and translations for 15 Chippewa (Ojibwa) songs (pp. 358–380, 398–404). Volume Two contains texts and translations for nine Chippewa songs (pp. 59–62, 223) and also includes sections on "Mnemonic Symbols for Music" (pp. 226–228) and "Musical Instruments" (p. 514) among the Chippewa. Volume Three includes a general description of Chippewa poetry and music (pp. 325–330).

See the catalogue by **Seeger and Spear** (1987). This contains a listing of early cylinder recordings at the Indiana University Archives of Traditional Music. The collection includes recordings from the following tribes of the Northeast area: Abenaki, Beothuk, Chippewa (Ojibwa), Delaware, Huron, Iroquois, Kickapoo, Malecite, Menomini, Micmac, Pamunkey, Penobscot, Potawatomi, Shawnee, Tuscarora, and Winnebago.

Skinner, Alanson Buck

1911   Notes on the Eastern Cree and Northern Saulteaux. *Anthropological Papers of the American Museum of Natural History* 9(1): 1–173.
The section on the Eastern Cree contains a description of musical instruments (pp. 41–43) and one song text and translation (p. 112). This also gives descriptions of dances and instruments of the Northern Saulteaux (pp. 142–143) and translations for three Saulteaux song texts (pp. 155, 174).

1913   Social Life and Ceremonial Bundles of the Menomini Indians. *Anthropological Papers of the American Museum of Natural History* 13(1): 1–165.
Could not be obtained for inspection of contents. According to Hickerson (General bibliography, 1961:346), this contains about 50 song texts and translations (passim).

1915   Associations and Ceremonies of the Menomini Indians. *Anthropological Papers of the American Museum of Natural History* 13(2): 167–215.
Could not be obtained for inspection of contents. According to Hickerson (General bibliography, 1961:346), this contains texts and translations for 12 songs (passim).

1920   *Medicine Ceremony of the Menominee, Iowa, and Wahpeton, Dakota, with Notes on the Ceremony among the Ponca, Bungi, Ojibwa, and Potawatomi.* Indian Notes and Monographs, vol. 4. New York.
Focuses on complex medicine societies that were analogous to the Ojibwa Midewiwin as described by Hoffman (1891 above). Skinner describes basic concepts, organizational structures, and initiation rituals of medicine societies among the Menomini (pp. 15–188), the Iowa (pp. 189–261), and the Wahpeton Dakota (pp. 190–265). He also discusses the distribution and history of these medicine societies in a Preface (pp. 9–14). This contains several song texts and translations but no musical examples.

1925   Songs of the Menomini Medicine Ceremony. *American Anthropologist* 27:290–314.

Gives texts and translations for 44 songs, also including comments on the mythological contents of songs and when they are used in (Mitawen) medicine society rituals. No musical notations. This is based on research conducted near Keshena, Wisconsin, in June 1919. Skinner's recordings of the songs were originally deposited at the Museum of the American Indian, Heye Foundation (New York). They are currently available at the Library of Congress and are listed in the catalogue by Gray (1985:212–220 above).

Slotkin, James S.

1957   *The Menominee Powwow: A Study in Cultural Decay.* Public Museum of the City of Milwaukee Publications in Anthropology 4:1–166.
This does not deal with the Pan-Indian powwow but rather with the more localized Drum Religion, the ritual of which is locally referred to as a "powwow" by English-speaking Menominee. The subtitle refers to the fact that this is a relatively recent (white-influenced) religion compared to the earlier Mitawin medicine society. Slotkin provides much information on the history and mythological basis of the religion. A chapter (7) entitled "The Powwow Rites" (pp. 81–154) contains descriptions of various rituals, including lengthy quotations from native practitioners. There is also an outline of "Song Services for the Day Dance" (pp. 160–163). Includes many descriptions of songs but no musical notations. Based on research conducted in Wisconsin from 1949 to 1951.

Smith, Nicholas N.

1962   St. Francis Indian Dances—1960. *Ethnomusicology* 6(1): 15–18.
This describes a revitalization of Wabanaki dances which occurred in connection with a public program that was given in 1960. Smith describes the dances and gives additional information from ethnographic sources. Dances mentioned include the following: Snake Dance, Friendly Dance, Blanket Dance, War Dance, Tomahawk Dance, Calumet Dance, and Eagle Dance. No musical notations.

Speck, Frank Gouldsmith

1919   *Penobscot Shamanism. American Anthropological Association Memoirs*, vol. 6, pp. 238–288.

Describes shamanistic singing and playing of a hoop-shaped drum with a buzzing snare (pp. 240–242). Concepts relating to the supernatural power of the drum are illustrated by a song text given in a footnote (pp. 241–242). Speck discusses Penobscot shamanism and also gives comparative data from other northeast Algonkian groups, particularly in the section entitled "The Older Algonkian Shamanism" (pp. 273–279). No musical examples.

1922   *Beothuc and Micmac*. New York: Museum of the American Indian, Heye Foundation. Indian Notes and Monographs, Miscellaneous Series 22.
        This is a general ethnography without much information on music. It does contain one musical transcription (by Jacob Sapir) of a song collected on phonograph from a Micmac woman named Santu in 1910 (pp. 67–68).

1931   *A Study of the Delaware Indian Bighouse Ceremony*. Publications of the Pennsylvania Historical Commission, vol. 2.
        According to Hickerson (General bibliography, 1961:348), this contains many descriptions of songs and instruments and also includes texts and translations for five songs. Could not be obtained.

1937   *Oklahoma Delaware Ceremonies, Feasts, and Dances*. Memoirs of the American Philosophical Society, vol. 7.
        This includes descriptions of 20 ceremonies or rituals, many of which are given as Delaware-language texts with interlinear translations. Speck interprets the significance of the rituals as invocations to various spiritual powers, particularly in family cult rituals dedicated to animals. Secular stomp dances and games are also discussed. Contains references to music and dance throughout but no musical notations. Based on research conducted between 1928 and 1932.

1940   *Penobscot Man: The Life History of a Forest Tribe in Maine*. Philadelphia: University of Pennsylvania Press.
        The section "Singing and Musical Instruments" (pp. 163–173) contains 12 musical examples with texts, translations, and commentary on the songs. The section on "Dances and Ceremonies" (pp. 272–300) contains 33 more musical examples, all with native

texts and some translated. Three other songs are also notated (pp. 260–261). Transcriptions are by Jacob Sapir.

1945a   *The Celestial Bear Comes Down to Earth: The Bear Sacrifice Ceremony of the Munsee-Mahican in Canada as Related by Nekatcit.* Reading, Pennsylvania: Reading Public Museum and Art Gallery, Science Publication 7.

Gives a detailed description of the Bear Sacrifice Festival based mainly on information gotten from a Delaware-Mahican man (Nekatcit) whose Christian name was Nicodemus Peters (1859–1938). Also contains texts and translations for five song recitatives acquired by spiritual men in dreams or visions (Appendix II, pp. 85–89).

1945b   *The Iroquois: A Study in Cultural Evolution.* Cranbrook Institute of Science Bulletin no. 23.

A booklet prepared in connection with museum exhibits at the Cranbrook Institute of Science (Bloomfield Hills, Michigan). The section on musical instruments (pp. 78–82) includes several photographs.

1949   *Midwinter Rites of the Cayuga Longhouse.* Philadelphia: University of Pennsylvania Press.

A comprehensive study of Cayuga religion based on research conducted at various times from 1931 to 1947. Chapter 4 ("The Annual Ceremonial Cycle," pp. 34–38) gives an overview of rituals and dances. Many of these are described in later chapters titled as follows: "Timing and Preparatory Rites of the Midwinter Ceremony" (Ch. 6), "The Medicine Societies" (Ch. 7), "The Restricted Medicine Societies and Their Rites" (Ch. 8), "Unrestricted Societies: Curing Rites and Dances" (Ch. 9), "The Four Sacred Ceremonial Rites" (Ch. 10), "Worship Rites Addressed to Food Spirits" (Ch. 11), and "Social Dances" (Ch. 12). More than 50 dances or rituals are described though music is not discussed in detail.

Speck, Frank G., and George Herzog

1942   *The Tutelo Adoption Ceremony: Reclothing the Living in the Name of the Dead. Transcriptions and Analysis of Tutelo Music.* Harrisburg: Pennsylvania Historical Commission.

This monograph (125 pp.) gives an ethnography of the ceremony based on historical sources and evidence collected in 1938 and 1939. The section entitled "Transcriptions and Analysis of Tutelo Music" (pp. 83–117) contains Herzog's analyses of 27 songs recorded on cylinders by Speck. The songs fall into four categories: (1) individual chants; (2) songs of a four-night harvest ceremony; (3) songs of the Bean Dance, a social dance; and (4) a medicine song for hunting (muskrat). Herzog comments on the similarity of the musical style to that of the Iroquois and (to a lesser extent) that of the southeastern tribes (p. 89).

See **Stevenson** (1973a and 1973b) in the General bibliography. These discuss several early sources relating to Indian music of the Northeast region.

Sturtevant, William C.

1961   Comment on G. Kurath's paper, "Effects of environment on Cherokee-Iroquois Ceremonialism, Music, and Dance." Pp. 197–204 in *Symposium on Cherokee and Iroquois Culture* edited by William Fenton and J. Gulick. Washington: Bureau of American Ethnology Bulletin no. 180.

Sturtevant commends the use of musicological comparison as a method for historical reconstruction and also agrees that Kurath has identified meaningful parallels in Iroquois and Cherokee musical life. However, he questions her conclusions relating to the distinction between an archaic northern style and a less ancient style borrowed from the southeastern (Muskogean) tribes and associated with agriculturalism. He gives several reasons to suggest that her view on this point is overly simplistic.

Sweet, Jill Drayson

1984   Review of *Shawnee: The Ceremonialism of a Native American Tribe* by James Howard (1981). *Ethnomusicology* 28(1): 140–141.

Criticizes Howard for insisting on the fact that Shawnee ceremonial life has changed little in modern times even though he presents contradictory evidence himself. Sweet argues that Howard makes no attempt to deal with processes of culture change and ignores current theory relating to ritual and ceremonialism.

Thwaites, Reuben Gold

1896–1901   *The Jesuit Relations and Allied Documents: Travels and Explorations of the Jesuit Missionaries in New France, 1610–1791.* 73 vols. Cleveland. Reprint. New York: Pageant Books, 1959.
These volumes contain many descriptions of Indian music and dance as observed by French missionaries in the seventeenth and eighteenth centuries. For more information see Crawford (1967 above).

Tooker, Elizabeth

1970   *The Iroquois Ceremonial of Midwinter.* Syracuse: Syracuse University Press.
Part I ("Principles of Iroquois Ritualism," pp. 7–38) gives information on musical instruments and dances (pp. 27–30). Part II ("The Structure of the Midwinter Ceremonial," pp. 39–82) provides a comparative analysis of longhouse ceremonies as practiced in six different communities. Part III ("The Midwinter Ceremonial in Historical Perspective," pp. 83–155) presents Tooker's hypotheses concerning how various elements of the Midwinter ceremonial may have evolved since the 1600s. Does not contain detailed information on music but the historical analysis is most interesting. For more information, see the review by Wallace (1972 below).

Vecsey, Christopher

1983   *Traditional Ojibwa Religion and Its Historical Changes.* American Philosophical Society Memoirs, vol. 152. Philadelphia: The American Philosophical Society.
An ethnohistorical study based on secondary sources. Vecsey attempts to show that the Midewiwin (Grand Medicine Society) and the concept of a Supreme Being were both post-contact developments and not aboriginal. The original (animistic) belief system of the Ojibwas is sketched in a chapter entitled "The Manitos" (pp. 72–83). Shaking Tent rituals and the use of medicine songs are discussed in the chapters entitled "Ojibwa Relations with the Manitos" (pp. 101–120) and "Puberty Fasting and Visions" (pp. 121–143). A chapter on the Midewiwin society (pp. 174–190) focuses on Christian influences which shaped its development, and another chapter entitled "Diverse Religious Movements" (pp. 191–198) gives descriptions of more recent developments such as the

Wabano Movement, the Shawnee Prophet Religion, the Dream
Dance, the Ghost Dance, and Peyotism. Does not contain detailed
information on music.

Vennum, Thomas, Jr.

1978   Ojibwa Origin-Migration Songs of the Mitewiwin.
            Journal of American Folklore 91(361): 753–791.
Focuses on song texts which Frank K. Blessing collected at
White Earth Reservation and Milles Lacs (Minnesota) in 1946.
Vennum gives texts, translations, and comments on songs in sections entitled "Origin-Migration Song Series" (pp. 781–786) and
"Ceremonial Use of Origin-Migration Songs" (pp. 787–791). This
is based mainly on Blessing's unpublished manuscripts, but also
includes information from Densmore (1910 above), Hoffman
(1891 above), and Landes (1968 above). Does not contain musical
notations.

1980   A History of Ojibwa Song Form. *Selected Reports in
            Ethnomusicology* 3(2): 43–75. Los Angeles: Program
            in Ethnomusicology, Department of Music, UCLA.
Focuses on the predominant public style of Ojibwa music,
without considering other genres such as love songs, Midewiwin
medicine songs, peyote songs, or Christian hymns with Ojibwa
texts. Compares the form of modern songs (circa 1970) with that of
songs recorded by Densmore and others around 1910. Vennum
concludes that nearly all modern songs are in the so-called
"incomplete repetition" form (pp. 47–55) while earlier song forms
(pp. 55–66) were more varied and probably represent a period of
stylistic transition. Includes six musical examples.

1982   *The Ojibwa Dance Drum: Its History and
            Construction.* Smithsonian Folklife Studies no. 2.
            Washington: Smithsonian Institution.
The first part of the book (pp. 14–155) gives a comprehensive
history of the Drum Dance including its origins (circa 1870s), its
transmission to the Ojibwa from the Santee Sioux, and its gradual
decline in the 1930s. Vennum then describes the construction of
the drum in detail, relying primarily on information from drummaker William Bineshi Baker (Ojibwa). The book was published
in conjunction with a 42-minute film ("The Drummaker") shot on
location at Lac Court Oreilles Reservation in Wisconsin.

See Gray (1985 above). This includes a history of ethnomusicological
research in the Northeast region by Vennum (pp. 3–7).

1986   Ojibwe (Music). Pp. 404–405 in *The New Grove Dictionary of American Music*, vol. 3 (L–Q). Edited by H. Wiley Hitchcock and Stanley Sadie. London: Macmillan.

Vennum begins by describing the wide variety of contexts for music in earlier Ojibwe culture, also observing how the style of songs for the Grand Medicine Society (Midewiwin) differed from that of other musical genres. He then discusses musical instruments and historical developments, noting that War Dance songs now constitute the greatest portion of the repertory.

1989   The Changing Role of Women in Ojibwa Music History. Pp. 13–21 in *Women in North American Indian Music*, edited by Richard Keeling. Ann Arbor: Society for Ethnomusicology.

Notes that males and females were about equally represented in early recordings of (Midewiwin) medicine songs and love songs but states that a reduced role for women came with the adoption of the Grass Dance from Plains tribes to the west. Relies on early writings by Burton (1909 above) and especially Densmore (1910 and 1913 above).

1991   The Alice Fletcher Ojibwe Indian Recordings. Pp. 73–103 in *Discourse in Ethnomusicology III: Essays in Honor of Frank J. Gillis* edited by Nancy Cassell McEntire. Bloomington: Ethnomusicology Publications Group. Archives of Traditional Music, Indiana University.

Gives musical notations and commentary for six songs recorded by Fletcher in January of 1899. The titles are as follows: (1) Women's Dance Song, (2) Moccasin Game Song, (3) Mide Medicine Song, (4) Drum Dance Song, (5) Love Song, and (6) War Song. The singer is an Ojibwe woman named Swift Flying Feather. See Gray (1985:134–135 above) for more information on the recordings.

Wallace, Anthony F.C.

1972   Book review of *The Iroquois Ceremonial of Midwinter* by Elizabeth Tooker (1970). *Journal of American Folklore* 85(337): 286–287.

A very positive review containing a useful summary of Tooker's comparative and historical analysis of midwinter ceremonials. Tooker classifies the rituals into three categories: (1)

"Renewal Rites," (2) "Sacred Ceremonies," and (3) "Life Supporter Ceremonies." She identifies the renewal rituals with early hunting culture and connects "Life Supporter Ceremonies" with a later subsistence pattern based on agriculture. The so-called "Sacred Ceremonies" are associated (according to Tooker) with influences of the nineteenth-century prophet Handsome Lake.

Wheeler-Voegelin, Erminie

1942   Shawnee Musical Instruments. *American Anthropologist* 44:463–475.
The author begins by noting the absence of European instruments and states this owes at least partly to the primary importance of singing in Shawnee music. She then gives a fairly thorough survey of rattles and other idiophones used as an accompaniment to vocal music. She discusses construction, performance techniques, and methods of "purifying" the instruments before they are used.

See **Witthoft** (1949) in Southeast bibliography for a comparative study of Green Corn ceremonials among tribes of the Northeast and Southeast regions.

IX. Southeast

Adair, James

1775   *The History of the American Indians, Particularly Those Nations Adjoining to the Mississippi, East and West Florida, Georgia, South and North Carolina, and Virginia.* London: Edward and Charles Dilly.

The author seeks to establish that Indians of the New World were descended from the biblical "lost tribes" of Israel. Despite its obsolete thesis, the book has considerable importance for its colorful and authentic descriptions of Indian cultures as viewed by Adair in travels begun as early as 1735. Stevenson discusses the work and gives three quotations from it (General bibliography, 1973b:403–406). It is also mentioned in various writings of Swanton (below). Contains many descriptions of songs and dances but no musical examples.

See **Baker** (1882) in General bibliography. This contains musical examples identified as Cherokee (1), Muskogee (1), and Brotherton Indian (1).

Ballard, W.L.

1978   *The Yuchi Green Corn Ceremonial: Form and Meaning.* Los Angeles: American Indian Studies Center, UCLA.

A study of contemporary ceremonials in northeastern Oklahoma, also including historical perspectives based on writings of Speck (see below) and others. Chapter Two (pp. 6–41) describes activities at the Kellyville square ground. Chapter Three (pp. 42–47) focuses on modern variations from earlier practices. Chapter Four (pp. 48–72) discusses social functions and various levels of symbolism in the ceremonial. This does not contain musical examples but does have many dance diagrams. Based on research conducted between 1970 and 1975.

Bushnell, David I.

1909   *The Choctaws of Bayou Lacomb, St. Tammany Parrish, Louisiana.* Bureau of American Ethnology Bulletin no. 48. Washington: Smithsonian Institution.
Contains musical notations and texts for three songs along with a general description of dances and instruments (pp. 20–22). Could not be obtained. Information given here is from Hickerson (General bibliography, 1961:156).

Capron, Louis

1953   *The Medicine Bundles of the Florida Seminole and the Green Corn Dance.* Bureau of American Ethnology Bulletin no. 151. Anthropological Papers no. 35, pp. 155–210.
Contains one Seminole song text collected in 1936 (p. 203). Information from Hickerson (General bibliography, 1961:156).

DeBaillou, Clemens

1961   A Contribution to the Mythology and Conceptual World of the Cherokee Indians. *Ethnohistory* 8(1): 93–102.
This contains extracts translated from diaries of Moravian missionaries writing in the early 1800s. One extract (dated 1803) describes a Green Corn Dance performed by Cherokees of Georgia (pp. 97–99). No information on music.

Densmore, Frances

1934   A Study of Indian Music in the Gulf States. *American Anthropologist* 36:386–389.
A short report of research conducted circa 1932–1933 among the Alibama (Texas), Chitimacha (Louisiana), Choctaw (Mississippi), and Seminole (Florida). Densmore is looking for examples of "the rise" as noted by Herzog among the Yuman tribes and manages to discover some examples in songs of the Choctaw and Seminole. Densmore also mentions an unusual form of vocal accompaniment (repetitive, in the low range of the voice) used in songs of the Choctaw Snake Dance (p. 387).

1937   The Alabama Indians and Their Music. Pp. 270–293
            in *Straight Texas* edited by J. Frank Dobie.
            Publications of the Texas Folklore Society no. 13.
Description and analysis of 62 songs collected by Densmore in
1933. Includes musical notations for 20 songs. Information from
Hickerson (General bibliography, 1961:194).

1943   *Choctaw Music.* Bureau of American Ethnology
            Bulletin no. 136, Anthropological Papers no. 28.
Contains musical notations for 65 songs classified by
Densmore into the following (functional) categories: war songs,
game songs, Tick Dance songs, Drunken-Man Dance songs, Duck
Dance songs, Snake Dance songs, Bear Dance songs, Stomp Dance
songs, hunting songs, and miscellaneous. Each song is analyzed
and described. The collection is compared with others the author
has previously made using a (quantitative) tabular approach (pp.
181–186).

1956   *Seminole Music.* Bureau of American Ethnology
            Bulletin no. 161.
Contains musical notations and analysis for 243 Seminole
songs collected by Densmore between 1931 and 1933. Background
information for each song is given, and various genres or song
types are identified. The whole corpus is compared with other collections Densmore has studied through use of tables to indicate
melodic and rhythmic features.

1972   (Recording) "Songs of the Seminole Indians of
            Florida." Smithsonian-Folkways Recordings (FE
            4383).
Currently available on cassette, this posthumous release contains recordings collected by Densmore circa 1931–1933. The
contents are as follows: various bird and animal dance songs
(Alligator Dance, Bird Dance, Turkey Dance, Snake Dance),
Calusa Corn Dance Song, Buffalo Dance Songs (4 songs), Songs
for the Story about Opossum and Her Baby, and Songs Used for
the Treatment of the Sick. Includes liner notes (6 pp.) by Charles
Hofmann.

Draper, David E.

1980   Occasions for the Performance of Native Choctaw
            Music. *Selected Reports in Ethnomusicology* 3(2):
            147–174. Los Angeles: Program in Ethnomusicology,
            Department of Music, UCLA).

Provides an overview of musical styles currently being performed among the Choctaw of Mississippi. These include indigenous dance songs, Christian hymns in the Choctaw language, and
instrumental dance music for fiddle and guitar. The indigenous
dances are listed, and five of the songs (for the Jump Dance) are
notated and analyzed (pp. 153–171).

1981   Record Review of "Choctaw-Chickasaw Dance
            Songs," Vols. I and II. (Sweetland Productions; dis-
            tributed by the Choctaw-Chickasaw Heritage
            Committee, Box 44, Mannsville, Oklahoma).
            Ethnomusicology 25(3): 553–555.
The producers are a tribal group dedicated to reviving traditional dances, which were halted in Oklahoma in 1937. Draper
notes various disparities between these musical styles and the presumably older versions of the Mississippi Choctaw. He explains
these as the result of musical influences from the Pan-Indian powwow and from other tribes such as the Natchez-Creek of
Oklahoma. His review points up the need for comparative studies
concerning the musical changes that have taken place.

1982   Abba Isht Tuluwa: The Christian Hymns of the
            Mississippi Choctaw. *American Indian Culture and
            Research Journal* 6(1): 43–62.
Draper first gives historical information on missions established in the early nineteenth century and describes published editions with Choctaw versions of Christian hymns. The section on
"Musical Characteristics" (pp. 48–50) focuses mainly on correspondences with Euro-American tunes and formal structures.
Another section entitled "Comparison with Native Repertories"
(pp. 50–53) gives more information on the style. This includes four
musical examples with texts and translations (pp. 57–61).

1986   Choctaw (Music). Page 429 in *The New Grove
            Dictionary of American Music*, vol. 1 (A–D). Edited
            by H. Wiley Hitchcock and Stanley Sadie. London:
            Macmillan.
Begins by listing types of songs in the Mississippi Choctaw
repertory. Draper then describes musical events in a night of indigenous dance songs (First Song, song cycles, Jump Dance, and
concluding Walk Dance). He also discusses musical style characteristics and historical changes in style as based on comparison
with information given in Densmore (1943 above).

1992   Book review of *Choctaw Music and Dance* by James Howard and Victoria Levine (1990). *Ethnomusicology* 36(3): 416–418.

Draper mentions several discrepancies between the information given by Howard and his own data on the Mississippi Choctaw and their dances. He also criticizes the musical analysis by Levine and suggests the authors should have focused on one of the Choctaw groups in more depth.

Fogelson, Raymond D.

1961   Change, Persistence, and Accommodation in Cherokee Medico-Magical Beliefs. Pp. 213–225 in *Symposium on Cherokee and Iroquois Culture* edited by William N. Fenton and John Gulick. Bureau of American Ethnology Bulletin no. 180. Washington.

This focuses on relatively isolated groups of Eastern Cherokee which were not greatly influenced by white civilization until the early years of the twentieth century. Fogelson describes use of the Cherokee syllabary to preserve cultural knowledge (pp. 216–218) and discusses how Cherokee conjuring was accommodated to concepts based on Christianity and western medicine (pp. 219–222). He then describes medicine for hunting, fishing, agriculture, divination, sorcery, and love magic (pp. 222–225). Based on earlier sources, especially the work of Mooney, and on fieldwork conducted during the summers of 1957 and 1958. Contains no information on songs.

1962   The Cherokee Ball Game: A Study in Southeastern Ethnology. Ph.D. dissertation (Anthropology). University of Pennsylvania.

Could not be obtained for inspection of contents nor could information be gotten from other sources.

1971   The Cherokee Ballgame Cycle: An Ethnographer's View. *Ethnomusicology* 15(3): 327–338.

This was written in collaboration with a more music-oriented study of the same subject by Herndon (1971 below). Fogelson's paper is based on documentary sources and research conducted in 1959 and 1960. This essay begins with a section on traditional Cherokee social structure (pp. 327–330). Fogelson then discusses the relation of the game to warfare, planning and rituals preceding the game, and post-game rituals (pp. 330–332). He also describes an all-night dance which is held on the eve of the game and constitutes the central focus of the ballgame cycle (pp. 332–337). The "transformative character" of the all-night dance is discussed on three levels: (1) social organization, (2) ritual symbols, and (3) psychological interpretation.

See **Frisbie** (1981) in the General bibliography for review of video-tapes containing interviews with Creek and Cherokee Indian singers.

Gatschet, Albert S.

1891   *The Karankawa Indians: The Coast People of Texas.* Archeological and Ethnological Papers of the Peabody Museum (Harvard University). Vol. 1, no. 2.
Contains texts and translations for three songs and a description of Karankawa singing (pp. 18 and 81). Could not be obtained. Information given here is from Hickerson (General bibliography, 1961:231)

Gilbert, William Harlen, Jr.

1943   *The Eastern Cherokees.* Bureau of American Ethnology Bulletin 133(23): 169–414.
A comprehensive ethnography based on published sources and fieldwork conducted on the Eastern Cherokee Reservation (North Carolina) in 1932. The part which focuses on contemporary culture (pp. 177–312) contains sections describing dances (pp. 257–267), the social function of dances (p. 281), and the use of magical formulas or prayers (pp. 286–300). Gilbert also analyzes historical sources to speculate on the character of pre-contact culture (pp. 313–370). This historical reconstruction contains descriptions of early ceremonies (pp. 325–335) and other sections entitled "Symbolism of the Ceremonies" (pp. 358–360) and "Ceremonial Change" (pp. 367–370). Contains no information on music as such.

1957   The Cherokees of North Carolina. *Annual Report of the Smithsonian Institution for 1956*, pp. 529–556.
Contains comments on Cherokee dances (pp. 543–544) and a section on the use of formulas and songs for medicine-making (pp. 544–547).

Gillespie, John D.

1961   Some Eastern Cherokee Dances Today. *Southern Indian Studies* 13(1): 29–43.

Could not be obtained for inspection of contents nor could information be gotten from other sources.

Herndon, Marcia

1971   The Cherokee Ballgame Cycle: An Ethnomusicologist's View. *Ethnomusicology* 15(3): 339–352.

This was published in conjunction with another study of the same subject by Fogelson (1971 above). Herndon begins by identifying the ballgame cycle as a "cultural performance," a concept borrowed from the anthropologist Milton Singer (pp. 339–341). She then discusses musical aspects of the all-night dance held prior to the game itself (pp. 341–351). She attempts to show various respects in which the style can be viewed as "an encapsulation of cognitive values and forms" (p. 341). Herndon also discusses Cherokee concepts of power in relation to various types of medicine formulas that may be thought, spoken, or sung (pp. 349–350). Includes three musical examples.

1980   Fox, Owl, and Raven. *Selected Reports in Ethnomusicology* 3(2): 175–192. Los Angeles: Program in Ethnomusicology, Department of Music, UCLA.

Focuses on animal spirit songs of the Eastern Cherokee. Herndon discusses the concept of the spirit animal as a messenger and the mythic origins of curing and divination. She then describes beliefs relating to three specific spirit animals and songs for communicating with them. This includes notations and analysis for two songs (Raven Song and Song to the Nameless Spirit of Water).

1986   Sound, Danger, and Balanced Response. Pp. 129–138 in *Explorations in Ethnomusicology: Essays in Honor of David P. McAllester*, edited by Charlotte J. Frisbie. Detroit Monographs in Musicology No. 9. Detroit: Information Coordinators.

Explores use of song in medicine formulas of the Eastern Cherokee. Herndon begins by describing sources of sacred formulas (especially certain documents that were originally written in the Cherokee syllabary) and gives the general pattern of spoken formulas as noted in Mooney and Olbrechts (1932 below). She then gives musical notations and interlinear translations for two medicine songs, for bruise (injury) and for snakebite. Herndon argues that the sung form of formulas carries greater power than spoken or muttered formulas, thus explaining the importance of sung formulas in situations of perceived danger. The source of the

songs is not identified but there is a comment (p. 130) which
suggests that they were recorded within the past 25 years.

See **Herzog** (1944) in the General bibliography. This essay discusses
his ideas concerning possible African American influences on
Indian music among the southeastern tribes.

Heth, Charlotte Wilson

1975   The Stomp Dance of the Oklahoma Cherokee: A
            Study of Contemporary Practice with Special
            Reference to the Illinois District Council Ground.
            Ph.D. dissertation (Music). University of California,
            Los Angeles.
            A musical ethnography based on fieldwork conducted at vari-
ous periods from 1971 to 1974. The opening chapters give ethnographic and historical information. Chapter three (pp. 57–93) describes the ceremonial context of the music, and chapter four (pp.
93–117) deals with instruments. The main musical analyses are
found in chapters five (song texts and vocables), six (musical form
and rhythm), and seven (tonal structures). For the most part, the
musical genres described here are song cycles with a musical texture based on leader-chorus antiphony. The appendices contain
many transcriptions of the music and song texts.

1979   Stylistic Similarities in Cherokee and Iroquois Music.
            Journal of Cherokee Studies 4(3): 128–162.
            This focuses on parallels between Cherokee Stomp Dance mu-
sic and Seneca Longhouse music as recorded by Heth in Oklahoma
(1971–1977) and on the Alleghenny Reservation in New York
(1975). Heth criticizes George Herzog's hypothesis concerning
African American influences on Indian music of the southeastern
area (1944 below) and also discusses various commonalities that
are evident in Cherokee and Seneca songs. Includes twelve musical
examples. Also see Kurath (Northeast bibliography, 1961) for
more information on Cherokee-Iroquois parallels.

1986   Cherokee (Music). Pp. 414–416 in *The New Grove
            Dictionary of American Music*, vol. 1 (A–D). Edited
            by H. Wiley Hitchcock and Stanley Sadie. London:
            Macmillan.
            Begins by listing musical genres or contexts in historical and
recent times, then discusses the similarities between Cherokee and
Iroquois music. She gives a general description of the musical

style, including five musical examples to illustrate her comments on scales and rhythmic organization. These are partial transcriptions, not complete songs. Toward the end, she discusses (3) musical events which occur during a Stomp Dance among the Oklahoma Cherokee. These are as follows: (1) the opening Friendship Dance, (2) the Stomp Dances, and (3) a closing Old Folks' Dance.

1986   Seminole (Music). Pp. 187–188 in *The New Grove Dictionary of American Music*, vol. 4 (R–Z). Edited by H. Wiley Hitchcock and Stanley Sadie. London: Macmillan.

Gives a list of musical genres based on information from Densmore (1956 above). Heth then describes musical and other elements of the Corn Dance (also called Green Corn Dance or Busk Dance by the Creek) and outlines some basic characteristics of the Seminole musical style.

Howard, James H.

1959   Altamaha Cherokee Folklore and Customs. *Journal of American Folklore* 72:134–138.

This focuses on a little-known Cherokee group of Georgia and includes a brief section on "Dances and Ceremonies" (p. 137). Based on information given by a Cherokee man of Albion, Michigan, circa 1954–1956.

1968   *The Southeastern Ceremonial Complex and Its Interpretation*. Memoir of the Missouri Archeological Society No. 6. Columbia, Missouri.

Could not be obtained nor could information on the contents be gotten from other sources.

1984   *Oklahoma Seminoles: Medicines, Magic, and Religion*. Norman: University of Oklahoma Press.

Could not be obtained nor could information on the contents be gotten from other sources.

Howard, James H., and Victoria Lindsay Levine

1990   *Choctaw Music and Dance*. Norman: University of Oklahoma Press.

This focuses on contemporary dance songs (circa 1965–1982) among Choctaw groups in Mississippi and Oklahoma. Howard begins by discussing historical factors which led to the separation of the two populations and related issues (chapter One). He then describes dances, instruments, and costumes of Choctaw groups in both areas (chapters Two and Three). Chapter Four contains analysis and discussion of the musical styles by Levine. 30 musical transcriptions by Levine are found in an appendix. The review by Draper (1992 above) is rather critical.

Hudson, Charles

1975   Vomiting for Purity: Ritual Emesis in the Aboriginal Southeastern United States. Pp. 91–102 in *Symbols and Society, Essays on Belief Systems in Action* edited by Carole Hill. Southern Anthropological Society Proceedings no. 9.
    Could not be obtained nor could information on the contents be gotten from other sources.

Jones, Charles C., Jr.

1873   *Antiquities of the Southern Indians, Particularly of the Georgia Tribes.* New York: Appleton.
    Could not be obtained. According to Hickerson (General bibliography, 1961:261) this contains a chapter on "Music and Musical Instruments" (Chapter Four).

Kilpatrick, Jack F., and Anna G. Kilpatrick

1962   Plains Indian Motifs in Cherokee Culture. *Plains Anthropologist* 7(16): 136–137.
    This contains some brief comments on the current state of Cherokee music in Oklahoma. The authors comment on the tenuous survival of traditional genres and a flourishing tradition of Christian hymn singing. They also note that Cherokee music shows no evidence of Plains influence whatever (p. 137).

1964   Cherokee Rituals Pertaining to Medicinal Roots. *Southern Indian Studies* 16(October): 24–28.
    This contains texts, translations, and explanations for three medicine formulas. Songs are not mentioned.

1965   *Walk in Your Soul: Love Incantations of the Oklahoma Cherokee.* Dallas: Southern Methodist University Press.
    Contains translations and commentary for 90 formulas relating to love magic. The authors make it clear that formulas such as

these could be sung, spoken, or even only thought (pp. 4–5), but there is no information on the musical style.

1967   *Muskogean Charm Songs Among the Oklahoma Cherokees.* Smithsonian Contributions to Anthropology, vol. 2, no. 3.

Contains musical notations, translations, and commentary for ten medicine songs collected from a Cherokee shaman of eastern Cherokee County (Oklahoma) in 1963 and 1964. The songs themselves are identified as being Creek or Natchez in derivation (p. 30). They include hunting songs, love medicine songs, and curing songs for various illnesses or wounds. The authors note that the musical style seems to differ from that of songs given in Densmore (1956 above) and Speck (1911 below). The transcriptions were evidently done in an interview setting (without being recorded), but rhythmic aspects of the music are notated in some detail.

1967   *Run Toward the Nightland: Music of the Oklahoma Cherokee.* Dallas: Southern Methodist University Press.

Could not be obtained nor could information on the contents be gotten from other sources.

1970   *Notebook of a Cherokee Shaman.* Smithsonian Contributions to Anthropology, vol. 2, no. 6.

Contains texts, translations, and commentary for 50 medicine formulas that were originally written in the Cherokee syllabary by a Cherokee shaman of Oklahoma. Songs are mentioned in connection with two of the texts (pp. 103 and 110) but not discussed in detail. The information given here is from a notebook (manuscript) that was obtained by the authors in 1961. The formulas derive from an earlier period, as the shaman passed away in 1938.

Kurath, Gertrude Prokosch

See Kurath (1951a) in Northeast bibliography. This contains comparative analyses of music and dances among the Iroquois and various southeastern groups, particularly the Oklahoma Cherokee.

1952   Book review of *Cherokee Dance and Drama* by Frank G. Speck and Leonard Broom, with Will West Long (1951). *Journal of American Folklore* 65(255): 105–106.

This is basically a positive review, but Kurath does criticize the lack of musical notations and analysis. Citing personal correspondence, she notes that a body of related (Cherokee) songs were recorded and transcribed by George Herzog (p. 106) but that the notations were not included in the publication. The recordings (and possibly the transcriptions) are likely to be found at the Indiana University Archives of Traditional Music. See the catalogue by Lee (General bibliography, 1979). Also see Speck and Broom (1951 below).

1956   Antiphonal Songs of the Eastern Woodland Indians. *Musical Quarterly* 42(4): 520–526.

This focuses on responsorial techniques associated with Stomp Dances in both the Southeast and Northeast areas. Kurath describes three styles of antiphony (monotonal, bitonal, and melodic) and illustrates the types with nine brief musical examples. She suggests that there may be a connection between antiphonal singing and patterns of social organization (especially clan and moiety divisions) among tribes of the Southeast. Also, some of the musical examples correspond to Iroquoian dance songs that are heard on a commercial album produced by Kurath (Northeast bibliography, 1956b).

See Kurath (1956) in the Mesoamerican bibliography. This contains comments on the relation of Aztec circle dances to those of the Cherokee and other tribes of the southeastern United States.

See Kurath (1961) in Northeast bibliography. This compares music and ceremonial practices among the Cherokee of North Carolina and Iroquoian tribes to the north.

Lee, Dorothy Sara

See Lee (1979) in the General bibliography. This is a catalogue of early cylinder recordings and more recent recordings at the Indiana University Archives of Traditional Music. The collection includes recordings from the following Southeastern groups: Cherokee, Creek, Natchez, Seminole, Tunica, and Yuchi.

1985   Southeastern Indian Catalog. Pages 329–419 in *The Federal Cylinder Project: A Guide to Field Cylinder Collections in Federal Agencies, Volume 2: Northeastern Indian Catalog, Southeastern Indian Catalog*. Washington: American Folklife Center, Library of Congress.

Lists and describes the contents of wax cylinder recordings from six different collections, the largest being a group of Seminole (and Calusa) recordings made by Densmore between 1931 and 1933. Each collection is preceded by an introductory essay giving background information on the recordings and on translations or other documentation in published sources or manuscripts. Early recordings from the following groups are represented: Alabama, Catawba, Cherokee, Chitimacha, Choctaw, and Seminole (including Calusa).

Levine, Victoria Lindsay

1991   Arzelie Langley and a Lost Pantribal Tradition. Pp. 190–206 in *Ethnomusicology and Modern Music History* edited by Stephen Blum, Philip Bohlman, and Daniel Neuman. Urbana: University of Illinois Press.

Based on recordings and oral data collected by a Choctaw man, Claude Medford (1942–1989). The paper begins with biographical information on his mother, Arzelie Langley, who was a medicine woman. Levine then describes an intertribal music culture that was shared by Indians of the following tribes (of Louisiana and Texas): Coushatta, Alabama, Tunica, and Choctaw. She gives an inventory of dances (p. 196) and discusses general characteristics of the musical style (pp. 197–203. This intertribal tradition was discontinued during the 1940s. Includes four musical examples.

1991b   Feathers in Native American Ceremony and Society. *Expedition: The University Museum Magazine of Archeology and Anthropology, University of Pennsylvania* 33(2): 3–11.

Discusses the mythological significance of birds and ritual use of feathers among various southeastern Indian peoples, with comments on related archeological evidence from early Mississippian culture. Includes brief descriptions of the following: the Green Corn Ceremony, Ball Game, and Cherokee Eagle Dance. No musical notations.

1993   Musical Revitalization Among the Choctaw. *American Music* 11(4): 391–411.

Levine begins by defining "musical revitalization" as occurring in modern Indian societies. She discusses various issues it raises for scholars and argues that revitalization should be viewed as an authentic extension of traditional cultures, rather than as a stage in the process of assimilation. The core section (pp. 393–405) focuses on social and musical aspects of musical revitalization as occurring among the Choctaw of Ardmore, Oklahoma. Similar developments among Choctaw groups of Mississippi and Louisiana are discussed more briefly (pp. 405–409).

Longe, Alexander

[1725]   A Small Postscript on the Ways and Manners of the Indians Called Cherokees. Edited by David H. Corkran. *Southern Indian Studies* 21(October 1969): 6–49.

The writer was an adventurous character who traded and lived among the Cherokee and other nearby tribes since 1710. Various dances are described in a section entitled "The Feasts of the First Fruits" (pp. 14–26). No information on music.

MacCauley, Clay

1887   *The Seminole Indians of Florida.* Bureau of American Ethnology, Annual Report (1883–1884) 5:469–531.

This contains comments on music (pp. 498–519), including notations of two songs as the author later remembered them. Could not be obtained. Information here is from Hickerson (General bibliography, 1961:292).

McCoy, George, and H.F. Fulling

1961   *The History of the Stomp Dance or the Sacred Fire of the Cherokee Indian Nation.* Edited and published by Marshall Walker. Blackgum, Oklahoma.

Could not be obtained nor could information on the contents be gotten from other sources.

Mooney, James

1890   The Cherokee Ball Play. *American Anthropologist* (Old Series) 3(2): 105–132.

Contains description of songs and two musical examples (pp. 118–119). Information is from Hickerson (General bibliography, 1961:304).

1891   *Sacred Formulas of the Cherokees.* Bureau of American Ethnology, Annual Report (1885–1886) 7:301–409.

An extensive study of medicine formulas as recorded in the Sequoyah syllabary by "Swimmer" and other medicine men of the tribe for their own use. The study begins with an ethnography of Cherokee medicine making (pp. 317–345). Mooney then gives texts, translations, and commentary for 28 formulas or prayers (pp. 346–409). Six of the texts are identified as songs, to be used as follows: for curing (three songs), for hunting bear (one song), and for love medicine (two songs). The formulas given here were selected from a total collection of 600 written texts obtained on the Cherokee reservation in North Carolina during the 1880s.

1900a   The Cherokee River Cult. *Journal of American Folklore* 13:1–10.

This describes ceremonies and prayers for ritual bathing and related mythological concepts. Music is not discussed. Also includes no information on the date or location of the research.

1900b   *Myths of the Cherokee.* Bureau of American Ethnology, Annual Report (1897–1898) 19:3–548.

A comprehensive study based on research conducted on the Qualla reservation in North Carolina between 1897 and 1898. This contains translations and commentary for 126 texts. Among them are the following songs: two bear hunting songs (pp. 326 and 327), song from a story about mother bear and cubs (pp. 400–401), baby song to please children (p. 401), and a deer hunting song (p. 435). The style of hunting songs is briefly discussed (p. 472). No musical notations.

Mooney, James, and Frans Olbrechts, Editors

1932   *The Swimmer Manuscript: Cherokee Sacred and Medicinal Prescriptions.* Bureau of American Ethnology Bulletin no. 99. Washington: Smithsonian Institution.

"Swimmer" is a translation of the Cherokee name of the man who was Mooney's principal informant and a renowned practitioner of traditional medicine. He died in 1899 at the age of 65. This monograph is based on medicine formulas which Swimmer himself recorded using the Cherokee syllabary. The book contains an ethnographic description of Cherokee medicine (pp. 1–165) followed by texts and translations for 96 texts for curing various maladies or wounds (pp. 166–311). Some of the formulas were recited, while others were supposed to be sung. There are some comments on "How the Formulas Are Recited or Sung" (pp. 155–156) but no other information on the musical style. Fifteen cylinder recordings of songs and spoken texts were collected in connection with this research (mentioned on p. 155). These are currently available at the Library of Congress and are listed in the catalogue by Lee (1985:348–354 above).

See **Nettl** (1954a) in the General bibliography. This discusses the general characteristics of music in "The Eastern Area" (pp. 33–36).

Olbrechts, Frans M.

1926   Cherokee Dances. Manuscript found among 28 boxes of papers in the Olbrechts (Cherokee) collection. National Anthropological Archives, Smithsonian Institution.
        Could not be obtained for inspection of contents. The entire collection of Olbrecht's papers are identified as catalogue no. 4600.

Payne, Richard W.

1990–1991   Medicine and Music: Whistles of Eastern Oklahoma Indians. *The Chronicles of Oklahoma* 68(4): 424–433.
        This describes cane whistles and block flutes as used during the earliest periods of contact. There are separate sections on instruments used among the following tribes: Choctaw, Chickasaw, Creek, Seminole, and Cherokee. The author describes specimens from collections and discusses references to the music in historical sources. Includes five photographs.

Randolph, J. Ralph

1973   *British Travelers Among the Southern Indians, 1660–1763*. Norman: Oklahoma University Press.
        This is based on written accounts left by nearly 50 British subjects who traveled among Indians of the Southeast region during this period. Randolph focuses more on the travelers and their impressions than on the Indian cultures that they observed. There are some references to music and dance (pp. 136–137, 146–147, and 158–160) but little of substance. Contains no musical notations.

Rhodes, Willard

1954   (Recording and liner notes) "Music of the American Indian: Delaware, Cherokee, Choctaw, Creek." Library of Congress, Recorded Sound Division (AFS L37).

One of a series of recordings collected by Rhodes circa 1940–1952 and recently reissued on cassette with updated liner notes. Contents are as follows: Songs of the Delaware Big House, Delaware Peyote Song, Delaware War Dance Song, Cherokee Lullaby, Cherokee Stomp Dance Songs, Cherokee Christian Hymn, Cherokee Horse Dance Song, Cherokee Quail Dance Song, Cherokee Pumpkin Dance Song, Choctaw Hymn, Creek Ball Game Songs, Creek Lullaby, Creek Counting Song, Creek Christian Hymns, Creek Ribbon Dance Song, Creek Stomp Dance Songs.

1958   Review of *Seminole Music* by Frances Densmore (1956). *Ethnomusicology* 2(2): 83–84.

Basically a highly favorable review, though Rhodes does question the non-indication of song texts in Densmore's transcriptions and her use of European key signatures. He also notes that Densmore does not mention the presumably antiphonal performance style of the Stomp Dance songs.

See **Roberts** (1936) in the General bibliography. This describes general characteristics of vocal music among tribes of the Southeast area (pp. 36–38).

See **Schoolcraft** (1851–1857) in General bibliography. Volume Five contains one Cherokee song text and translation (p. 564).

Schupman, Edwin

1984   Current Musical Practices of the Creek Indians as Examined Through the Green Corn Ceremonies of the Tulsa Cedar River and Fish Pond Stomp Grounds. Master's thesis (Music), Miami University (Ohio).

An ambitious thesis project based on research conducted in 1983–1984. Chapter Two (pp. 22–43) gives descriptions of 1983 Green Corn ceremonials at two locations. Chapter Three (pp. 44–75) discusses basic characteristics of the music, including a summary of stylistic characteristics (pp. 73–75). Includes 22 shorter musical examples in the text and nine (rather lengthy) complete transcriptions in an appendix (pp. 81–116).

See the catalogue by **Seeger and Spear** (1987). This contains a listing of early cylinder recordings at the Indiana University Archives of Traditional Music. The collection includes recordings from the following Indian tribes of the Southeast area: Cherokee, Creek, Natchez, Tunica, and Yuchi.

Speck, Frank Gouldsmith

1907   The Creek Indians of Taskigi Town. *Memoirs of the American Anthropological Association*, vol. 2, pp. 99–164.
      The section on "Formulistic Songs" (pp. 124–133) includes 10 song texts and translations. It also contains an interesting description of animal dances that figure in Green Corn rituals (pp. 135–136). These dances are propitiatory in character and comparable in function to medicine songs and formulas for hunting.

1909   *Ethnology of the Yuchi Indians.* University of Pennsylvania: The University Museum; Anthropological Publications 1(1): 1–154.
      A section on "Music" (pp. 61–66) discusses instruments and musical characteristics. Includes one transcription and two melodic fragments. Information from Hickerson (General bibliography, 1961:347).

1911   *Ceremonial Songs of the Creek and Yuchi Indians.* University of Pennsylvania: The University Museum; Anthropological Publications 50(2): 157–245.
      This contains notations (with texts and translations) and commentary for 48 songs identified as Creek (39 songs), Yuchi (7), and Shawnee (2). The transcriptions and musical analysis are by Jacob Sapir. The songs were recorded by Speck in 1904 and 1905. Also contains descriptions of musical instruments.

1939   Catawba Religious Beliefs: Mortuary Customs and Dances. *Primitive Man* 12:21–57.
      This contains a section on "Instruments for Musical Accompaniment" (pp. 50–53). Listed in Hickerson (General bibliography, 1961:348–349).

1941   *Gourds of the Southeastern Indians.* Boston: New England Gourd Society.
      The chapter on "Categories of Use" (pp. 25–51) gives information on various functions for gourds, including their use as rattles, whistles, and ceremonial masks.

Speck, Frank Gouldsmith, and Leonard Broom, with Will West Long

1951   *Cherokee Dance and Drama.* Berkeley and Los Angeles: University of California Press.

Focuses on contemporary dances of the Eastern Cherokee at Qualla Reservation in North Carolina. Based mainly on research conducted by Speck in the years from 1929 to 1944. An introductory chapter (pp. 1–18) gives background information and discusses the mythological origins of music and dance in connection with the slaying of a monster called Stone Coat. The core chapter two ("The Repertory of Dances," pp. 18–94) contains descriptions of 25 dances, grouped into the following categories: Winter Dances, Summer Dances, War Rites, Formal Rites, and Animal Rites. Chapter three ("Animal Hunting Formulas and Rites," pp. 84–98) contains much information on medicine songs. In all, there are translations of ten song texts (pp. 66–67, 68, 87, 88–89, 91, 92, 93, and 94). This also includes excellent historical photographs. See the review by Kurath (1952 above).

Speck, Frank Gouldsmith, and George Herzog

1942   *The Tutelo Spirit Adoption Ceremony: Reclothing the Living in the Name of the Dead.* Philadelphia.

The section "Transcription and Analysis of Tutelo Music" (pp. 85–117) contains a study by George Herzog of 27 Tutelo songs recorded by Speck in 1938 and 1939. There is also a section on musical instruments (pp. 22–26). Could not be obtained. Information given here is from Hickerson (General bibliography, 1961:350).

See **Stevenson** (1973a) in the General bibliography. This discusses early written sources (originally in Spanish) on Indian music of the Southeast region (pp. 4–6).

See Stevenson (1973b) in General bibliography. This discusses other early sources (in English) on Indian music of the Southeast (pp. 403–405). This includes an interesting reference to a large (banjo-like) stringed instrument observed among the Natchez of Mississippi in 1746 (p. 404).

Stevenson, George William

1977   The Hymnody of the Choctaw Indians of Oklahoma.
              Doctoral dissertation (Music), Southern Baptist
              Theological Seminary. Louisville, Kentucky.
       Could not be obtained nor could information on the contents
be gotten from other sources.

Swanton, John R.

1929   *Myths and Tales of the Southeastern Indians.* Bureau
              of American Ethnology Bulletin no. 88.
       Contains translations for 305 texts collected among various
tribes (Creek, Hitchiti, Alabama, Koasati, and Natchez) between
1908 and 1914. Songs are mentioned in some of the texts, but musical notations are lacking.

1931   *Source Material for the Social and Ceremonial Life
              of the Choctaw Indians.* Bureau of American Ethnol-
              ogy Bulletin no. 103. Washington: Smithsonian
              Institution.
       This is actually an ethnography of pre-contact Choctaw soci-
ety based on historical sources. The section on "Games" (pp. 140–
160) gives information on the ball game and related ceremonies.
There is also another section on "Ceremonials and Dances" (pp.
221–226). Includes paintings of the Ball Game Play (p. 142) and
the Eagle Dance (p. 222). No information on music.

1946   *The Indians of the Southeastern United States.*
              Bureau of American Ethnology Bulletin no. 137.
       This comprehensive study (857 pp.) gives brief sketches of
176 local tribes (pp. 81–216) and then discusses general aspects of
regional culture. The section entitled "Religious Beliefs and
Usages" (pp. 742–782) contains many descriptions of dances and
songs, mainly as described in earlier historical sources. The book
contains a section on "Musical Instruments" (pp. 624–629). No
musical examples.

Thomas, Robert K.

1961   The Redbird Smith Movement. In *Symposium on
              Cherokee and Iroquois Culture* edited by William
              Fenton and John Gulick. Bureau of American
              Ethnology Bulletin no. 180.

Could not be obtained nor could further information be gotten from other sources.

Witthoft, John

1946a   Bird Lore of the Eastern Cherokees. *Journal of the Washington Academy of Sciences* 36(11): 372–384.

Contains descriptions of the Pigeon Dance (p. 375) and the Eagle Dance (pp. 376–377). Also gives (onomatopoetic) Cherokee versions of the sounds made by various birds. Based on data collected on the Qualla Reservation in North Carolina in 1945 and 1946.

1946b   The Cherokee Green Corn Medicine and the Green Corn Festival. *Journal of the Washington Academy of Sciences* 36(7): 213–219.

Contains information on the Green Corn festival (pp. 213–215) and on the Green Corn medicine and plants used to make it (pp. 215–217). Also includes two versions of a myth about the origins of corn (pp. 217–219). Based mainly on secondary sources. No information on music.

1949   *Green Corn Ceremonialism in the Eastern Woodlands.* Occasional Contributions from the Museum of Anthropology of the University of Michigan, no. 13. Ann Arbor: University of Michigan Press.

Originally produced as a master's thesis in Anthropology at the University of Pennsylvania (1946). Gives a comparative survey of Green Corn ceremonies among various tribes of the Northeast and Southeast areas. Based mainly on secondary sources. Songs and dances are often mentioned but not discussed in detail.

X. Mexico

The creation of this bibliography was assisted by Helena Simonett.

Alderson, Richard

1975   (Recording and liner notes) "Modern Maya: The Indian Music of Chiapas, Mexico." Ethnic Folkways (FE 4377).

Focuses on various groups (Chol, Tzotzil, Tzeltal, and Tojolobal) which are presumed to be descended from the ancient Mayans. The contents include chanted prayers, songs, dances, and processional music. The concept of musical performance as a religious duty or obligation is mentioned in the notes. For more information, see the reviews by Stevenson (1980 below) and Yurchenco (1976 below).

1977   (Recording and liner notes) "Modern Maya, Vol. II: Indian Music of Chiapas, Mexico." Smithsonian Folkways (FE 4379).

Currently reissued on cassette, the album features music recorded at various actual Indian fiestas circa 1972–1974. The performance contexts and/or locations are identified as follows: Metontic Christmas, Chalchiuitan carnival, San Bartolo Venustiano carranza, Huistan, Tenejapa carnival, Tenango, Petalcingo, Tila, and Guacitepec.

Anderson, Arthur J. O.

1954   Aztec Music. *Western Humanities Review* 8(2): 131–137.

This summary begins by describing Aztec instruments (pp. 131–132), then gives descriptions of songs and orchestral music from the writings of Durán, Torquemada, and other sixteenth-century observers (pp. 132–136). The author emphasizes the extensive training required for Aztec musicians and dancers. Anderson and Charles Dibble are the translators of Sahagún (1950–1969 below).

Anonymous

1912   The Fiesta of the Pinole at Azquetlán. *University of Pennsylvania Museum Journal* 3(3): 44–50.
This focuses on a peyote ceremony observed in January 1912 among Tepehuan Indians of northern Jalisco. The article describes songs that are accompanied by a musical bow played with two sticks (pp. 46–48). Includes a drawing of the main singer with bow in playing position (p. 47).

Barker, G. C.

1957   The Yaqui Easter Ceremony at Hermosillo. *Western Folklore* 16:256–262.
Focuses on the fusion of aboriginal and Catholic elements in a religious drama based on the Passion of Jesus. The ritual originated from improvised plays which the Jesuit missionaries used in order to indoctrinate the Yaquis toward Catholicism. Barker describes Holy Week events observed among Yaquis of northwestern Sonora in 1956 and 1957.

Barlow, Robert

1949   El Códice Azcatitlán. *Journal de la Société des Américanistes* 38:101–135 and Supplement.
The codex is reproduced in the Supplement (a separate volume). It was originally drawn and painted on 56 pages of European notebook paper and seems to contain several images of musical instrument playing and dances or rituals. The (Spanish) text by Barlow (pp. 101–135) discusses the images depicted in each of the 29 illustrations contained in the codex.

Beals, Ralph L.

1932–1933   The Comparative Ethnology of Northern Mexico Before 1750. *Ibero-Americana* 2: 93–225.
Beals argues that it is impossible to draw clear boundaries between the cultures of the Pueblos and those of southern Mexico. The paper explores historical relationships through comparative ethnographic data, Spanish colonial writings, and archeological evidence. Instruments such as the musical bow, kettle drum and teponaztli (slit-drum) are mentioned.

Beyer, Herman

1934   Mexican Bone Rattles. New Orleans: Tulane
University. *Middle American Research Series* 5(7):
329–349.
Focuses on a type of bone rasp known as omichicahuaztli
among the Aztecs. Beyer discusses the use of the instrument (to
accompany songs) among the Aztecs and describes its use among
contemporary tribes of Mexico (Tarahumara, Huichol, Yaqui) and
the southwestern United States (Pima, Papago, Hopi, Yaqui).
Includes several illustrations of instruments from museum collections and reproductions from codices in which the rasp is pictured.

Bierhorst, John

1974   Quetzalcoatl. Pp. 17–108 in *Four Masterworks of
American Literature* edited by John Bierhorst. New
York: Farrar, Straus, and Giroux.
Contains Bierhorst's translations of Nahuatl (Aztec) texts relating to the deity Quetzalcoatl. Fragment E ("A Song of
Survival") is a song from the sixteenth-century manuscript identified as "Cantares Mexicanos." The translation (pp. 63–66) seems
to indicate responsorial singing between a soloist and chorus. The
likelihood of solo-chorus alternation in Aztec music is mentioned
in Roberts (1936:38) and Hague (1934:11 and 13).

1985   *Cantares Mexicanos: Songs of the Aztecs.* Palo Alto:
Stanford University Press.
The "Cantares Mexicanos" is a codex containing 91 Nahuatl
(Aztec) songs which were transcribed by Catholic scribes during
the sixteenth century. Many of the texts are prefaced by syllables
(as for example, "tico tico toco toto") which indicate the rhythm
and relative pitches of the *teponaztli* (drum) accompaniment. This
study provides native texts, free translations, and commentary for
each of the songs. All belong to a ritual genre in which warrior-
singers poetically summon the ghosts of ancestors. Bierhorst's introduction (130 pp.) gives information on the ritual itself and other
aspects of Aztec history and poetics. The section called "Ghost
Songs in Performance" (pp. 70–82) includes a thoughtful discussion of what can be gathered about the musical style on the basis of
historical sources and comparative evidence.

Bogert, Charles M., and Martha R. Bogert

1958   (Recording and liner notes) "Songs and Dances of the
            Mexican Plateau: Tarascan and Other Music of
            Mexico." Folkways Records, FW 8867.
This contains a survey of indigenous styles from Nayarit,
Chihuahua, and the Lake Pátzcuaro region of Michoacán. The
notes (12 pages) include song texts and English translations.

Boilés, Charles Lafayette

1965   La Flauta Triple de Tenenexpan. *La Palabra y el
            Hombre* 34:213–222.
This focuses on a flute with three tubes from the collection of
the Institute for Anthropology at the University of Veracruz. The
artifact is presumed to date from between the sixth and the eighth
century AD. Boilés gives tonal measurements and speculates on
the scales and other aspects of the music that was played on the instrument.

1966   The Pipe and Tabor in Mesoamerica. *Yearbook of the
            Inter-American Institute of Musical Research* 2:43–
            74.
The flute and drum music of Mesoamerican tribes is generally
assumed to be derived from Spanish prototypes, but Boilés presents various types of evidence that the unusual combination (with
one player) is indigenous. He discusses archeological specimens
(figurines) and depictions in some early codices, then compares
(four) contemporary Indian recordings collected in Veracruz
(between 1960 and 1965) with a Spanish example of pipe and tabor
music. Boilés uses an analytic chart to illustrate significant differences between the Spanish and Mesoamerican musical styles.
Includes photos, drawings, and five musical transcriptions.

1966   Review of *Dances of Anáhuac* by Gertrude Kurath
            and Samuel Martí (1964). *Yearbook of Inter-Ameri-
            can Music Research* 2:173–177.
Boilés praises the methodology used in reconstructing images
of Aztec music and dance of the pre-contact period, but he also has
some important criticisms. He agrees with Martí's generalizations
about the music but also notes that they are unsupported by notations of any particular pieces. The same objection is also made
with respect to Kurath's analyses of the dances. Boilés also criticizes Martí's translations of Spanish texts (from Durán and
Sahagún) and points out problems with the English translations

which were relied upon by Kurath. See Kurath and Martí (1964 below).

1967a   El arco musical: Una pervivencia? *La Palabra y el Hombre* 39:383–403.

Boilés describes musical bows from various regions of Mexico and compares them with instruments from Africa and Brazil. He speculates on the origins of the instrument and concludes that it is probably indigenous rather than derived from Old World prototypes. This includes drawings, photographs, and two musical examples.

1967b   Tepehua Thought-Song: A Case of Semantic Signaling. *Ethnomusicology* 11(3): 267–292.

Contains detailed semiotic analyses of instrumental pieces used in compulsive rituals for curing and other purposes. Each piece corresponds to a verbal text which is known to all the participants but not sung in the ritual itself (nor could it be sung without melodic modifications). The six violin pieces analyzed here are drawn from a collection of 45 such songs recorded by the author in northern Veracruz in 1966.

1976   Review of *María Sabina and Her Mazatec Mushroom Velada* by R. Gordon Wasson, George Cowan, Florence Cowan, and Willard Rhodes (1974). *Ethnomusicology* 20 (3): 606–607.

Basically a favorable review but Boilés does raise questions concerning Rhodes' analysis of the music. He points out how the transcriptions could have been improved and suggests that a syntactic approach should have been used to analyze the correspondences between language pitch patterns and melodic formulae. See the approach used in Boilés (1967b above).

1978   Review of *Chamulas in the World of the Sun* by Gary Gossen (1974). *Ethnomusicology* 22(2): 345–346.

Basically positive but Boilés criticizes the non-musicologist Gossen for relying on Harrison and Harrison (1968 below) and accepting their idea that the Chamula songs are derived from sixteenth and seventeenth century songs of Spanish origin. Boilés argues that the degree of acculturation in Mexican Indian music has been overestimated by Mexican musicologists and others.

Boulton, Laura

1957   (Recording and liner notes) "Indian Music of
            Mexico." Smithsonian-Folkways (FE 8851).
Currently reissued on cassette, this contains music from the
Zapotec, Otomi, Yaqui, and Maya. The recordings were made at
various locations in Mexico in 1941. This contains songs and instrumental music for the Deer Dance, Matachines, and Pascolas.

Brinton, Daniel G.

(1887)   *Ancient Nahuatl Poetry.* Brinton's Library of
            Aboriginal American Literature no. 7. Philadelphia:
            D. G. Brinton. Reprint. New York: AMS Press, 1969.
This contains translations and commentary for 27 poems.
Brinton emphasizes the importance of music and dance in ancient
Nahua life. He also mentions an instrument known as the
tecomapiloa ("suspended vase"), presuming that it was derived
from the Aztec *teponaztli* (slit-drum) and was probably an an-
tecedent of the marimba (p. 23).

1890   *Rig Veda Americanus: Sacred Songs of the Ancient
            Mexicans, with a Gloss in Nahuatl.* Brinton's Library
            of Aboriginal American Literature, no. 8. Philadel-
            phia: D. G. Brinton.
This gives texts and translations for 20 Nahua hymns. Brinton
uses the expression "Rig Veda Americanus" because he considers
they are analogous to Aryan sacred hymns.

Castellanos, Pablo

1970   *Horizontes de la música precortesiana.* Mexico City:
            Fondo de Cultura Económica.
Discusses archeological evidence for music during the following periods: (1) Pre-Agricultural (10,000–5,000 BC); (2) Proto-
Agricultural (5,000–2,000 BC); (3) Pre-Classic (2,000 BC–0 AD);
(4) Classic (0–800 AD); and (5) Post-Classic (800–1521 AD). The
last chapter discusses surviving elements of native music among
contemporary Indian peoples.

Castañeda, Daniel

1942   Una flauta de la cultura Tarasca. *Revista musical
            mexicana* 1(5):110–113.

This focuses on a clay flute found at Tarímbaro (Michoacán) in 1938. Castañeda gives a fairly detailed description of the instrument, including a drawing. He also discusses the Tarascan word *cuiraxetacua*, which literally means "a long instrument for the song."

Castañeda, Daniel, and Vicente T. Mendoza

1933   Los Teponaztlis, Los Percutores Precortesianos, and Los Huehuetls (3 articles). In *Anales del Museo Nacional de Arqueología, Historia, y Etnografía* (4a Época), vol. 8.

These articles describe instruments among the holdings in the National Museum of Archeology (Mexico City). Images from early codices and other sources are used to describe construction methods and playing techniques.

Castillo, Jesús

1977   *La Música Maya Quiché, región de Guatemala: Recuento de la primera investigación Eenofonistica de Guatemala.* Guatemala: Editorial P. Santa.

Castillo (1877–1949) is mainly known as a composer, but he also became involved in research on indigenous music beginning around 1900. Calling himself an "ethnophonist," he traveled throughout Guatemala collecting musical data and often used the melodies in his compositions. Castillo discusses the complexity of local musical repertories and attributes this to contacts between the Mayas, Quichés, and Toltecs. Includes drawings of instruments and musical examples quoted from the author's compositions.

Chamorro, Jorge Arturo

1991   Sones de la Guerra: Purépecha Music and Its Audience Responses as Audible Symbols of Rivalry and Emotion in Northern Michoacán, Mexico. Doctoral dissertation (Ethnomusicology), University of Texas at Austin.

A contemporary study of inter-ethnic factionalism as expressed through music at local fiestas. Chamorro focuses on competitions between brass bands and other confrontational songs in the Purépecha language. He also discusses other aggressive sounds such as whistles, gritos (shouts), and fireworks. Chamorro views the fiestas as competitive celebrations and interprets the meanings of musical symbols and events in relation to local traditions and conflicts created by a peasant society in crisis.

Charters, Samuel B.

1957   (Recording and liner notes) "Yaqui Dances: The Pascola Music of the Yaqui Indians of Northern Mexico." Notes by Jean Zeiger and Samuel Charters (6 pages). Folkways Records, FW 957.

Recorded in 1956 in Guaymas (Sonora). The music is performed by Maximiliano Valencia (harp) and Raymondo Lori (violin). Valencia, a Yaqui man who was imprisoned in Veracruz in the late 1920s, is believed to have learned to play the harp there and brought it later to Sonora. It has since become so popular there that the harp and violin duo have almost replaced the older combination of flute and drum in Yaqui music.

Chenoweth, Vida

1964   *The Marimbas of Guatemala.* Lexington: University of Kentucky Press.

Based on research conducted circa 1957–1960. Three types of marimbas are identified: (1) the commercially manufactured chromatic marimba (*marimba doble*), (2) an older gourd marimba (*marimba con tecomates*), and (3) a transitional type (*marimba sencilla*), which is still being used. Chenoweth discusses details of construction, typical musical styles, playing techniques, and related customs and practices. The final chapter explores the history of the instrument, concluding that it was most likely imported originally from Africa. Includes drawings, musical staff notations, and transcriptions of rhythmic patterns.

Christensen, Bodil

1939   The Acatlaxqui Dance of Mexico. *Ethnos* 4:133–136. Stockholm: The Ethnographic Museum of Sweden.

According to Christensen, this dance is performed by Aztec Indians in the northwestern region of the Sierra de Puebla around Saint Catherine's day (November 25). The article mainly focuses on the dance, and music is only mentioned in passing. Includes four photographs.

Collaer, Paul

1959   Cariban and Mayan Music. Pp. 123–140 in *Studia Memoriae Belae Bartók Sacra*. Third edition. London: Boosey and Hawkes.

This is a comparative study based on recordings obtained from the Library of Congress, the Instituto Nacional de Antropología e Historia (Mexico), and the Museé de l'Homme (Paris). Through analysis of melodic patterns and scales, Collaer determines that the music of the Maya-Quiché of Guatemala is likely to be related to that of certain Venezuelan Indian tribes, despite the geographical distance involved. Taking a diffusionist position, he also discusses similarities to the Javanese pelog scale.

Cornyn, John Hubert

1932   An Aztec Master Musician. *Maya Society Quarterly* 1:182–187.

Focuses on a poem about a celebrated musician named Quecholcohuatzin who served in the court of an Aztec ruler. The text (dated around 1521) is given in Nahuatl and in English. It describes the outstanding skills of this drummer, who was able to please the king and make him dance.

Correa, Gustavo, and Calvin Cannon

1961   La Loa en Guatemala. Pp. 1–96 in *The Native Theatre in Middle America* edited by Gustavo Correa et al. New Orleans: Middle American Research Institute, Tulane University .

The *loa* is a short dramatic work of religious character, designed for presentation on certain Catholic holy days. The authors discuss its Spanish origins and its relation to other cults and rituals of Mexico and Guatemala. There is a brief summary in English (pp. 5–9).

Cresson, H.T.

1884   Aztec Music. *Proceedings of the Academy of Natural Sciences of Philadelphia* 35 (1883): 86–94.

The author emphasizes that Aztec music seems quite sophisticated by comparison with that of other "primitive" peoples. Cresson suggests that these "children of nature" were influenced by animal sounds and tried to imitate the sounds and even the shapes of the animals with their musical instruments. He then describes various instruments. Cresson notes that some of the four-holed clay flutes can produce the whole diatonic scale and even chromatic intervals, thus challenging previous writers who insisted Aztec music was mainly pentatonic.

Crossley-Holland, Peter

1980   *Musical Artifacts of Pre-Hispanic West Mexico: Towards an Interdisciplinary Approach.* Monograph Series in Ethnomusicology, No. 1. Los Angeles: Program in Ethnomusicology, Department of Music, UCLA.

This mainly focuses on flutes but also encompasses other instruments such as turtle shells, drums, rattles, ocarinas, whistles, and trumpets. The author discusses issues such as the following: raw materials and methods of construction, performance positions and playing techniques, range of possible sound production, occasions for performance, and iconography or symbolism in the exterior decoration or shape of instruments.

Crumrine, N. Ross

1969   Capokoba, the Mayo Easter Ceremonial Impersonator: Explanations of Ritual Clowning. *Journal for the Scientific Study of Religion* 8(1): 1–22.

Deals with Lenten season rituals among the Mayo Indians of southern Sonora. In these ceremonies there are masked clowns who capture and crucify Christ in symbolic fashion. Crumrine discusses various possible explanations (historical, psychological/affective, and sociological) and finally focuses on a "cultural cognitive" approach (pp. 17–21). Music is mentioned throughout the paper but not discussed in detail.

d'Harcourt, Raoul

1930   *L'ocarina à cinq sons dans l'Amérique prehispanique.* Journal de la Société des Américanistes 22(2).

This describes mesoamerican ocarinas from various museum collections and also includes a brief report by Erich von Hornbostel and Curt Sachs on some specimens at the Museum für Völkerkunde in Berlin. According to d'Harcourt, the Italian term *ocarina* ("little goose") was coined by Giuseppe Donati in 1880. Includes photographs of 64 ocarinas.

1941   *Sifflets et ocarinas du Nicaragua et du Mexique.*
            Journal de la Société des Américanistes 33.
            Gives detailed descriptions of nine ocarinas from museum col-
            lections. Each of the instruments has four holes and an anthro-
            pomorphic animal shape. According to d'Harcourt the ocarinas
            could produce 6–8 tones. Includes several photographs.

Díaz del Castillo, Bernal

1956   *The Discovery and Conquest of Mexico.* New York:
            Grove Press. Translated from the original edition en-
            titled *Historia verdadera de la conqvista de la
            Nueva-España* (Madrid, 1632).
            Contains unfavorable comments on Aztec music and also de-
            scribes the ritual sacrifice of Spanish prisoners as witnessed by
            Díaz. Otherwise this deals mainly with the history of exploration
            and military conflicts.

Durán, Diego

[1964]   *The Aztecs: The History of the Indies of New Spain.*
            Translated and edited from the first edition (1867–
            1880) of the original manuscript (1581) by Doris
            Heyden and Fernando Horcasitas. New York: Orion
            Press. Originally entitled *Historia de las indias de
            Nueva-España e islas de tierra firme.*
            This chronicle of pre-Conquest Mexico deals not only with
            historical matters but with Indian culture in general. Though born
            in Seville, Durán grew up in Texcoco and had excellent knowledge
            of the Nahuatl language. Like other historian-ethnographers of his
            time, he used two main sources: native manuscripts in pictographic
            writing and information obtained from living informants. Part two
            contains 23 chapters on Aztec deities, rituals, feasts, and temples.

1971   *Book of the Gods and Rites of the Ancient Calendar.*
            Translated and edited by Fernando Horcasitas and
            Doris Heyden. Norman: University of Oklahoma
            Press.
            Contains much information on religion and other aspects of
            culture among Aztecs of the pre-contact period. Chapter 21 dis-
            cusses music-related topics such as the God of Dance, schools of
            dance in the Aztec temples, and various dances performed in pub-
            lic. This also contains descriptions of musical instruments (drums,
            flutes, conch shells, trumpets, and rattles).

Edmunson, Munro S., Translator and Editor

1971   *The Book of Counsel: The Popol Vuh of the Quiche Maya of Guatemala.* New Orleans: Middle American Research Institute, Tulane University.
This is the translation of a manuscript dated circa 1550. The original text (in the Quiché-Maya language) was either based on oral traditions or on an earlier pictographic manuscript. The book discusses various aspects of native cosmology (especially the successive creations of human beings) and the rise and fall of Mayan civilization.

Estrada, Alvaro

1981   *María Sabina: Her Life and Chants.* With translations by Henry Munn. Santa Barbara, California: Ross-Erikson.
María Sabina is a Mazatec Indian religious practitioner who was born in Huautla de Jiménez (Oaxaca) in 1894. She performs a shamanic healing ceremony which involves the use of hallucinogenic mushrooms and the recitation of sacred chants. The editor of this particular autobiography (Estrada) is also Mazatec himself. This only gives texts and translations for the chants. For musical notations and other related information see Wasson et al. (1974). Also see the recording by Wasson and Wasson (1957).

Fernández de Oviedo y Valdés, Gonzalo

1535   *La historia general de las Indias.* Seville: Juan Cromberger.
This is possibly the earliest publication containing a reference to indigenous music in the Americas. The author describes an instrument like the Aztec *teponaztli* on the island of Hispaniola. For more information see Stevenson (General bibliography 1973a:1).

Foster, Elizabeth A., Translator and Editor

1950   *Motolinía's History of the Indians of New Spain.* Berkeley: The Cortés Society.
The Franciscan scholar Toribio de Motolinía originally wrote his two principal works (*Historia de los Indios* and *Memoriales*) in the years from 1536 to 1542. This book contains much information on the role and status of musicians in Aztec society. It also includes descriptions of instruments and performances of songs and

dances. Motolinía's writings are considered particularly valuable because he arrived in Mexico quite early (in 1524).

Gallop, Rodney

1939   The Music of Indian Mexico. *Musical Quarterly* 25(2): 210–225.

The author questions the extent to which authentic indigenous music has survived, except for some rare exceptions, and suggests that the most prevalent forms of Indian music are Spanish-influenced (mestizo) styles. Gallop does note that some native instruments, especially the *teponaztli*, were kept in Indian villages and generally concealed from strangers. In this paper he describes music of the Yaqui Deer Dance and the Volador (Flying Pole) Ritual of the Otomí and Totonac Indians. This contains musical notations and photographs .

1940   Otomí Indian Music from Mexico. *Musical Quarterly* 26(1): 87–100.

As in the previous entry (1939 above), Gallop begins by noting that truly indigenous music is rare except in connection with a few surviving rituals. This paper focuses on some indigenous secular music that he did manage to find among the Otomí of eastern Hidalgo. Gallop discusses the problems he had communicating with the women who performed these drinking songs. Apparently (because of their drunkenness) they were not able to repeat the same song twice with the same words. This contains musical notations for the songs along with descriptions of some other Otomí ceremonies.

See **Galpin** (1902–1903) in General bibliography. Discusses Aztec influence on musical instruments of other American Indian groups.

Génin, Auguste

1922   Notes on the Dances, Music, and Songs of the Ancient and Modern Mexicans. *Annual Report of the Smithsonian Institution for 1920*. Pp. 657–658. Washington.

Génin criticizes the tendency of some to identify contemporary musical practices with those of the remote past. He also warns against presuming that various tribes have similar or related musical traditions, especially in cases where the tribes are geographically distant from one another.

Goetz, Delia, and Sylvanus G. Morley

1950   *Popol Vuh: The Sacred Book of the Ancient Quiché*
            Maya. Norman: University of Oklahoma Press.
            This is an English version based on the Spanish translation
published by Adrián Recinos in1947. It is considered to be less accurate than the translation by Edmunson (1971 above), but it does
have a comprehensive introduction. The book describes various
aspects of Mayan cosmology, mythology, and history.

Gossen, Gary

1974   *Chamulas in the World of the Sun.* Cambridge,
            Massachusetts: Harvard University Press.
            Spoken texts serve as the basis for an interpretation of
Chamula Indian world view in this comprehensive study. Gossen is
not a music specialist, but the book does include a chapter on songs
(pp. 216–229). See the review by Boilés (1978 above).

Gray, Judith A.

See Gray (1984) in the General bibliography. This gives information on
            early cylinder recordings collected among the Huichol and
            Cora Indians.

1990   (Editor) Middle and South American Catalogue. Pp.
            329–382 in *The Federal Cylinder Project, Volume 5:*
            California Indian Catalogue, Middle and South
            American Catalogue, Southwestern Catalogue.
            Edited by Judith Gray and Edwin Schupman.
            Washington: American Folklife Center, Library of
            Congress.
            Lists and describes the contents of cylinder recordings from
eight separate collections, including those of Karl Theodor Preuss,
(Cora and Huichol), Carl Lumholtz (Huichol), and Edgar Lee
Hewitt (Nahuatl). The list for each collection is preceded by an introduction giving information on the recordings and the circumstances under which they were collected. Other documentation
from published sources and/or manuscripts is cited for each collection.

Hague, Eleanor

1934   *Latin American Music: Past and Present.* Santa Ana,
            California: The Fine Arts Press.

Mentioned by Roberts (General bibliography, 1936:38), who evidently agrees with Hague's assertion that early Aztec vocal techniques included alternate singing between a soloist and chorus. Chapters one and two deal with pre-contact music and Spanish influences during the colonial period. Chapters three and four focus on contemporary Indian music.

Hammond, Norman

1972   *Classic Maya Music*. Working Papers No. 4. Cambridge, England: Centre of Latin American Studies, University of Cambridge.
Contains a survey of Mayan instruments as known through various types of archeological evidence, surviving codices, and early documentary accounts. Contains several (24) drawings copied from archeological sites, pottery decorations, or depictions in the Dresden Codex and others. Also contains photographs of instruments and a fresco from Bonampak.

Harrison, Frank, and Joan Harrison

1968   Spanish Elements in the Music of Two Maya Groups in Chiapas. *Selected Reports in Ethnomusicology* 1(2): 1–44. Los Angeles: Program in Ethnomusicology, Department of Music, UCLA.
This focuses on festival music among two Mayan groups identified as the Zinacanteco and Chamula. The authors argue that the (syncretistic) music and the instruments are derived from genres of colonial music which were current in the sixteenth and seventeenth centuries but no longer survive in Spain. This includes numerous musical examples (23 pages). The hypothesis is criticized by Boilés (1978 above) in a review of Gossen (1974 above).

Hellmer, José Raúl

1964   Los Antiguos Mexicanos y su Música. *Boletín Bibliográfico de la Secretária de Hacienda y Crédito Público*, X/286 (January): 12–17.
Discusses instruments in museum collections and argues against the notion that pre-Cortesian music was primitive. Hellmer suggests that study of contemporary Indian music could give clues for better understanding of ancient musical styles. Includes photographs of instruments.

1973   (Recording and notes) "Musiques Mexicaines." With notes in French and English by Serge Roterman (6 pages). Ocora, OCR 73.

This includes a variety of genres from groups identified as follows: Zapotec, Huichol, Nahuatl, Séri, Tarahumara, Maya, Chontal, Purépecha, Mixtec, and Lacandon. The liner notes argue that stringed instruments existed before the arrival of the Spaniards and that African influences did not penetrate into remote areas. Reviewed by Stevenson (1974 below).

Hornbostel, Erich M. von, and Karl Theodor Preuss

1912   Zwei Gesänge der Cora Indianer. Pages 367–381 in *Die Nayarit-Expedition* (vol. 1), by Karl Theodor Preuss. Leipzig: B. G. Teubner.

This gives texts, translations, musical notations, and musical analyses for two songs recorded by Preuss in 1906. The recordings are also discussed in Gray (1990:333–336 above).

Horspool, Glen Arvel

1982   The Music of the Quiché Maya of Momostenango in Its Cultural Setting. Doctoral dissertation (Music), University of California, Los Angeles.

This focuses on contemporary musical life in a Quiché Mayan community of Guatemala. Horspool distinguishes two basic styles of music: (1) strophic songs based on European tonal practices and (2) an indigenous style with wide-ranged melodies and predominantly descending contours. He also discusses how the music reflects community attitudes and social patterns. The contexts for music include dance-dramas, church services, processions, and other festivities. Various instrumental groupings are described, and the (largely informal) training of musicians is discussed.

Kaptain, Laurence

1992   *The Wood That Sings: The Marimba in Chiapas, Mexico.* Everett, Pennsylvania: Honey Rock Press.

The author is a classical marimba performer, and the book focuses mainly on elite marimba groups which compete in government-sponsored competitions in the urban centers of Chiapas. Kaptain discusses the musical repertories, construction of the instruments, and history of their origin and development. Training techniques and various aspects of performance practice are described in some detail. Also gives biographical information on some important performers and family marimba groups.

Kissam, Edward

1971   Aztec Poems. *Antaeus* 4 (Winter): 7–17.
Contains seven poems (actually Aztec, Otomí, and Huichol) translated into English from earlier Spanish renditions.

Kurath, Gertrude Prokosch

1946   Los Concheros. *Journal of American Folklore* 59 (234): 387–399.
Historical account and descriptive analysis of a dance widely performed among Indians at Fiestas in Central Mexico, particularly by descendants of the Aztecs in the Mexico City area. The dance is named after a stringed instrument which is played by the dancers and made from the shell (concha) of an armadillo. Kurath speculates on the origins of the dance, concluding it represents a hybrid of northerly Indian and European elements superimposed on a basically indigenous core.

1947   Los Arrieros of Acopilco, Mexico. *Western Folklore* 6(3): 232–236.
Charming description of an Indian dance and ritual drama performed (along with Los Concheros and Los Vaqueros) at a small town just beyond the southwestern limits of Mexico City. Includes brief transcription of an apparently non-Indian melody played on a fiddle which is handmade but also basically European in character (p. 233).

1949   Mexican Moriscas: A Problem in Dance Acculturation. *Journal of American Folklore* 62(244): 87–106.
Describes and compares ritual dances of Indians from various parts of Mexico. Types of dances discussed include Moros, Santiagos, and Matachini, among others. Though spectacular and entertaining, the function of the dances is religious, often involving the fulfillment of a personal vow. Kurath traces the origin of the dances to Europe, where similar dances are known as Morisca (Spain), Mouriscada (Portugal), and Morris (England). The European versions are also compared in this excellent study, which analyzes the complex blending of foreign and indigenous elements in the Mexican dances. Contains three notations (pp. 102–103) and comparative tables (pp. 105–106).

1952   Dance Acculturation. Pp. 232–242 in *Heritage of Conquest: The Ethnology of Middle America* edited by Sol Tax. Glencoe, Illinois: Free Press of Glencoe.

Kurath argues that a significant core of indigenous ritual and dance has remained functional in various remote highland locations. She makes a major distinction between religious and secular dances, also noting that they are identified by different terms in Spanish (danza and baile). While the native religious dances (*danzas*) tend to transcend tribal boundaries, the European-influenced bailes have more limited regional distributions.

1956   Dance Rituals of Mid-Europe and Middle America. *Journal of American Folklore* 69(673): 286–298.

This comparative study views dances of Central Europe and Central Mexico (respectively) under three main categories: (1) couple dances, (2) ceremonial round dances, and (3) ancient male combat dances. Kurath finds that Mexican couple dances such as the *bailes* and *jarabes* came from Europe, probably brought by nineteenth-century immigrants (p. 292). Mexican circle dances such as the *mitote* have Aztec prototypes and resemblance to European forms is considered coincidental (pp. 292–293). Mexican ritual combat dances also have antecedents but are also influenced by Spanish moriscas and other European ritual dramas (pp. 293–294). In both areas (Europe and Mexico) the three dance categories are assigned to analogous historical "layers" (pp. 295–296). Also contains interesting comments on the relation of Aztec circle dances to those of North American Indian groups (pp. 293 and 295–296).

1960   The Sena'asom Rattle of the Yaqui Indian Pascolas. *Ethnomusicology* 4(2): 60–63.

Describes an instrument resembling the sistrum which is played by ritual clowns in Pascola dances among the Yaquis of Sonora. Kurath gives a physical description and photograph, gives notations for the rhythms played, and speculates on the origins of the instrument.

1967   La Danza de los Matachines entre los Indios y los Mestizos. *Revista Mexicana de Estudios Antropológicos* 21:261–285. Mexico City.

Compares versions of the Matachines dances among Pueblo Indians of New Mexico, Yaqui Indians of Sonora (Mexico), and mestizos of Durango, Chihuahua, and Nuevo León (Mexico). Examines various aspects of music, dance, and costume in order to distinguish indigenous elements from those which are due to European influence or local innovation. The description of mestizo dances is written by Froylán Saldaña.

1967   Drama, Dance, Music. Pp. 158–190 in *Handbook of the Middle American Indians, Volume 6: Social Anthropology.* Volume edited by Manning Nash. Austin: University of Texas.

Kurath classifies indigenous events and fiestas according to three types of calendrical system: (1) ecological, (2) ecclesiastical, and (3) secular. In general, religious dances conform to ecological or ecclesiastical calendars while the recreational dances are observed according to secular calendars. She discusses various survivals of pre-contact rituals and dances according to this system. Kurath also classifies syncretistic dance-dramas deriving from the colonial period into three main categories: (1) *moriscas,* which relate to the Spanish-Moorish confrontation; (2) passion plays, which dramatize the Crucifixion; and (3) *posadas, pastorelas,* and (Guatemalan) *loas* which are performed during the season of Christmas and Epiphany.

Kurath, Gertrude Prokosch, and Samuel Martí

1964   *Dances of Anáhuac.* Viking Fund Publications in Anthropology no. 38. Chicago: Aldine Publishing Co.

An ambitious attempt to reconstruct what can be known about Aztec music of the precortesian era based on (1) archeological evidence, (2) images in codices, (3) descriptions left by sixteenth-century Spanish chroniclers, and (4) comparison with surviving elements of music and dance among contemporary Indian peoples. Kurath focuses on dances while Martí deals with the music. Includes a synopsis which shows the organization of the Aztec ritual calendar and indicates the music and dance elements connected with various ceremonies.

Larsen, Helga

1937   Notes on the Volador and Its Associated Ceremonies and Superstitions. *Ethnos* 2(4): 179–189.

Based on research among Indians of the Sierra Madre region. Larsen considers the Volador ceremony to be a rare survival of pre-conquest life which has not been influenced by European traditions. In earlier times (according to her), the voladores were intended as human sacrifices which symbolically fertilized the soil with their blood. Today, the meaning of the ceremony is not so clear. This describes various elements of the ceremony, from beginning to end. The music for the ceremony is performed by one individual who plays the flute and drum at the same time.

Lazar, Alan, Compiler

1975   (Recording) "Anthology of Central and South American Music." Smithsonian-Folkways Records (FE 4542).
        Currently available as a two-cassette set, this incorporates recordings from earlier Folkways and Asch recordings that are less readily obtained. Side A of the first cassette contains ten examples from the following groups: Yaqui, Huichol, Cora, Tarascan, Mayan (Tzotzil), Mayan (Chol), Mayan (Ixil), and Mayan (Chuj). Liner notes contain brief descriptive comments quoted from Charters, Yurchenco, and other collectors.

See the catalogue by **Lee** (1979) in the General bibliography. This lists historical and recent recordings at the Indiana University Archives of Traditional Music. The holdings include important Mesoamerican collections by Laura Boulton, Gordon Wasson, Karl Theodor Preuss, Carl Lumholtz, E. Thomas Stanford, Arturo Warman, and Henrietta Yurchenco (among others). Tribal groups are identified as follows: Aztec, Chiapanic, Chichimec, Cora, Huastec, Huave, Huichol, Lacandon, Maya, Mayo, Mazatec, Mixe Mixtec, Nahuatl, Otomi, Seri, Tarahumara, Tarascan, Totonac, Tzotzil, Tzutuhil, Zapotec, and Zoque.

León-Portilla, Miguel

1980   *Native Mesoamerican Spirituality: Ancient Myths, Discourses, Stories, Doctrines, Hymns, Poems from the Aztec, Yucatec, Quiché-Maya, and Other Sacred Traditions.* New York: Paulist Press.
        Contains interpretations of early religion among the Mayans and Aztecs based on selected texts from the Popol Vuh, Cantares Mexicanos, the Book of Chilam Balam, and other major codices and documents. Does not discuss the music which might have accompanied the songs and poems.

Lumholtz, Carl Sofus

1898   The Huichol Indians of Mexico. *Bulletin of the American Museum of Natural History* 10:1–14.

This is a report on research conducted by Lumholtz circa 1894–1897 among the Cora Indians of Nayarit and the Huichol of northwestern Jalisco. Apparently, he gained the confidence of the hostile Huichol community by learning to sing the shaman's songs at a feast for making rain. This gives brief descriptions of ceremonies and religious objects. Also discusses use of hallucinogenic plants and preparation of alcoholic drinks. Includes two photographs and one drawing of a Huichol distillery.

1900   *Symbolism of the Huichol Indians.* Memoirs of the American Museum of Natural History 3 (May): 1–228. Reprinted with the new title *A Nation of Shamans.* Oakland: Bruce I. Finson, 1988.

An ethnography based on early research among the Huichol Indians of west-central Mexico (Jalisco). This contains detailed descriptions of various rituals and Lumholtz's interpretations concerning the symbolic meaning of the ceremonies and related sacred objects.

1902   *Unknown Mexico* (2 volumes). New York: Charles Scribner's Sons. Reprinted with an introduction by Evon Z. Vogt. New York: AMS Press, 1962.

As the subtitle states, this contains "A Record of Five Years' Exploration among the Tribes of the Western Sierra Madre; in the Tierra Caliente of Tepic and Jalisco; and among the Tarascos of Michoacán." The Norwegian Lumholtz traveled widely through these areas and collected ethnographic data on virtually all of the major tribes. He apparently expected to find descendants of cliff-dwelling peoples from the southwestern United States in northwestern Mexico. Music and dance are only sporadically mentioned. Includes drawings, photographs, and some music transcriptions.

1903   The Huichol Indians of Mexico. *Bulletin of the American Geographical Society of New York* 35(1): 79–93.

Lumholtz argues that advanced cultures such as the ancient Aztecs and Mayans lived side by side with more primitive tribes. While the so-called "high cultures" were destroyed by the Spaniards, the Huichol and other more "primitive" groups have continued to survive. Here Lumholtz reports again on his experiences with the initially distrustful Huichol. Impressed by their voices, he began to learn their songs and eventually came to be accepted by them. This describes the *hikuli* (small cactus) ceremony and some other beliefs and myths. Although he was basically an evolutionist, Lumholtz's report on the Huichol is very favorable and sensitive.

Mace, Carroll Edward

1966   Three Quiché Dance Dramas of Rabinal Guatemala. Ph.D. dissertation (Spanish and Portuguese), Tulane University.

Theater plays an important role in the social and religious life of the Rabinal Quiché. The three dance-dramas studied in this dissertation thus provide interesting insights on their culture: (1) the Patzcá reveals the complexity of their religious life; (2) the Charamiyesh includes elements of humor and satire; and (3) the Baile de Cortés expresses the Indians' reaction to the conquering Spaniards. Each section includes the Quiché (Mayan) text, a Spanish translation, and interpretive comments by the author.

1970   *Two Spanish-Quiché Dance Dramas of Rabinal.* Tulane Studies in Romance Languages and Literature, no. 3. New Orleans: Tulane University.

This gives texts, translations, and commentary for two of the dramatic texts considered in Mace's earlier dissertation (1966 above). Included here are (1) the Baile de Patzcá ("The Dance that Made the Divine Laugh") and (2) Charamiyex ("The Chirimía Player").

Martí, Samuel

1954   Precortesian Music. *Ethnos* 19:69–78.

Emphasizes the sophistication of Aztec music for its artistic effects and advanced instrumental acoustics. Summarizes much information from sixteenth-century observers, also giving information on musical aesthetics among modern Mexican tribes and historical relationships between the Aztecs and other ethnic groups. Unfortunately, Martí does not generally include references to the authors he quotes nor is there a bibliography. Several characteristics of the music are listed (pp. 77–78), and there is also a classification of styles by genre or function (p. 78).

1955   *Instrumentos musicales precortesianos.* Mexico City: Instituto Nacional de Antropología e Historia. Revised second edition, 1968.

This includes 25 chapters on various Aztec instruments. Martí argues that the variety and technical sophistication of the instruments serves to refute any stereotypic notion that pre-Hispanic music was primitive and monotonous. He indicates that some of the flutes could produce as many as 17 different pitches and harmonies of three or four tones. In a chapter on the musical bow, Martí calls this the only indigenous stringed instrument that was known in the New World before the arrival of the Europeans; thus he contradicts other writers who had claimed it was African in origin. Includes photographs, drawings, and musical notations.

1961   *Canto, danza, y música precortesianos.* Mexico City: Fondo de Cultura Económica.

This comprehensive study of pre-contact music is based mainly on historical sources, but the chapter on "Survivals of Dance" (pp. 271–303) also considers contemporary Indian practices. This contains a chapter on music of the early Mayan and Mixtec-Zapotec civilizations (pp. 305–330) and another on Mayan musical instruments (pp. 331–346). Includes numerous photographs and drawings.

Mendizábal, Miguel Othón de

1923   La Poesía indigena y las canciones populares. *Boletín del Museo Nacional de Arqueología, Historia, y Ethnografía* 2(4): 79–84.

The author laments that indigenous music, dance, and poetry have received such little attention from scholars, even though there is much evidence for interpreting the history and development of these artforms. In this paper he uses sources from the colonial period to speculate on the performance of pre-contact songs and their musical accompaniment.

1929   Los Cantares y la música indígena. *Mexican Folkways* 3(2): 109–121.

Mendizábal argues that the study of contemporary Indian music can help to fill the gaps in our knowledge of pre-Conquest music and dance. Relying mainly on historical sources from the colonial period, he attempts to reconstruct an image of earlier musical practices. This is a revised and expanded version of his previous article (Mendizábal 1923 above).

Mendoza, Vicente T.

1941   Tres instrumentos musicales prehispánicos. *Annales del Instituto de Investigaciones Estéticas* 7:71–86.

The article contends that the variety and sophistication of pre-contact aerophones has been greatly underestimated. Mendoza describes three trumpet-like instruments used among the early Aztecs and focuses on the complexity of their acoustical design. Includes photographs and drawings.

1950   Música indígena de México. *México en el Arte* 9:55–64.

Focusing on pre-Cortesian civilizations, Mendoza argues that major cultural centers had schools for music, dance, and instruments in order to maintain public performances of calendrical ceremonies. He analyzes various musical examples (based on melodic, rhythmic, and textual criteria) and identifies one Mayan song as being particularly archaic in character.

1951   *Música Indígena Otomí: Investigación Musical en el Valle del Mezquital (1936).* Mendoza: Universidad Nacional de Cuyo.

Focuses on research conducted in the Valle del Mezquital (Hidalgo) in collaboration with Gabriel Saldívar. Mendoza and Saldívar collected various versions of fourteen songs from more than 30 Otomí Indian singers. Much of the book describes general aspects of Otomí Indian life, but there is also much information on music and dance. Includes many musical examples.

1956   *Panorama de la Música Tradicional de México.* Mexico City: Imprenta Universitaria.

This historical survey of traditional music in Mexico begins with a chapter on indigenous music (pp. 17–34). The main focus is on mestizo music, but Mendoza also discusses the texts of songs from a sixteenth-century Aztec codex which is generally known as "Cantares Mexicanos." The song texts are preceded by various syllabic patterns which apparently indicated the rhythm and relative pitch of the musical accompaniment provided on drums or slit-drums. For related information see Bierhorst (1985 above).

1959   La Música y la Danza. Pp. 323–354 in *Esplendor del México Antiguo*, Volume 1. Edited by Jorge Acosta. Mexico: Centro de Investigaciones Antropológicas de México.

This article contains basically the same information as the first chapter in the previous entry (Mendoza 1956 above).

Myerhoff, Barbara

1974   *Peyote Hunt: The Sacred Journey of the Huichol Indians.* Ithaca, New York: Cornell University Press. An interpretative study of Huichol religion and cosmology as shown through their annual pilgrimage to gather peyote buttons. The Huichol live in the western Sierra Madres but travel several hundred miles to a high desert location which they consider their mythological homeland. The author accompanied them once and describes the trip as a quest for spiritual renewal. Songs are mentioned but not discussed in detail.

Nowotny, Karl Anton

1956   Die Notation des Tono in den aztekischen Cantares. *Baessler-Archiv, Neue Folge* 4(2): 185–189. Focuses on syllabic indications of rhythmic patterns which precede song texts in the manuscript known as "Cantares Mexicanos." According to Nowotny, the four syllables (ti, qui, to, co) can be combined in various ways to produce 758 possible rhythmic patterns. Also see Bierhorst (1985 above) and Peñafiel (1899 below) for related information.

Nuttall, Zelia

1903   *The Book of Life of the Ancient Mexicans.* Berkeley and Los Angeles: University of California Press. This contains the reproduced facsimile of a manuscript preserved at the Biblioteca Nazionale Centrale in Florence, Italy. The manuscript contains pictographs painted by a Mexican (Aztec) artist, probably in the second half of the sixteenth century. Nuttall gives a detailed description of the manuscript in her introduction and also provides commentaries for each page of the codex. The book includes an illustration of the Panquetzaliztli festival and many images of musical instruments.

O'Brien, Linda

1975   Songs of the Face of the Earth: Ancestor Songs of the Tzutuhil-Maya of Santiago Atitlán, Guatemala. Ph.D. dissertation (Music), University of California, Los Angeles.

The guitar-accompanied songs of the Tzutuhil-Maya in the midwestern highlands of Guatemala are vehicles for the transmission of traditional Tzutuhil teaching. The singers are considered to be ritual specialists, chosen and taught in dreams by ancestral spirits. Their improvised texts are integral to rituals and also contain the essentials of Tzutuhil religion. In this study, O'Brien transcribes and analyzes several of the lengthy songs and provides other information on Tzutuhil mythology and the social role of the singer as educator.

1979   Record review of "Music of the Maya-Guichés of Guatemala: The Rabinal Achí and Baile de la Canastas," recording and notes by Henrietta Yurchenco (Folkways FE 4226, 1978). *Ethnomusicology* 23(3): 475–477.

Criticizes the notes for editorial mistakes and other inaccuracies but mainly praises the album for its unique contents. These are the earliest examples of Guatemalan Indian music commercially available and were recorded by Yurchenco in 1945. With two exceptions, the album contains instrumental music in three main categories: (1) music to accompany dance-dramas such as the "Rabinal Achí" or "Baile de la Canastas," (2) music for *cofradía* rituals honoring images of the saints, and (3) music for popular dances. O'Brien's review gives much background information and discusses musical style of various items.

1980   Record review of "En Busca de la música Maya (Maya no ongaku o tazunete)," produced by Mabuchi Usaburo (1976). Three 12-inch discs. King Records GXH (K) 5001–5003. *Ethnomusicology* 24(3): 624–628.

Highly favorable review of recordings produced by a Japanese research team, with notes in Japanese including 68 pages of musical transcriptions. The recordings feature 41 songs of the forest Lacandón (Maya) and other music of the Mazatec Indians (Oaxaca) and Tzotzil Mayan Indians. O'Brien describes the rarity of commercial recordings of the Lacandón and gives much background information, including a classification of the song types represented and a description of the vocal style (pp. 625–626). Similar information is also provided for the other (Mazatec and Tzotzil Mayan) recordings (pp. 626–628). A partial translation of the notes is available from the Ethnomusicology Archive, University of California, Los Angeles.

See **Parmentier** (1979) in the Southwest bibliography. Discusses the relations of Pueblo mythology and ritual to Mesoamerican cultures.

Payne, Richard W.

1992   Pre-Columbian Flutes of Mesoamerica. *Journal of the American Musical Instrument Society* 18:22–61.

Payne first discusses flute-related mythology among the Aztecs, then gives a survey of archeological specimens from museum collections by region. The instruments are classified into six categories: (1) true flutes, (2) duct flutes, (3) ocarinas, (4) whistle pots, (5) bitonal whistles, and (6) chamberduct ocarinas. Flutes from the following culture areas are then described in separate sections: Central Mexico, Mayan cultures, Gulf Coast, western cultures, and other Mesoamerican aerophones. Contains 23 photographs or other illustrations.

Peñafiel, Antonio, Editor

1899   *Cantares en Idioma Mexicano*. Mexico City. Secretária de Fomento. Reprinted by same publisher, 1904.

This is another reproduction of the manuscript generally known as "Cantares Mexicanos." Also see Bierhorst (1985 above). The introduction by Peñafiel (pp. 2–27) gives useful background information.

Preuss, Karl Theodor

1906   Beobachtungen über die Religion der Cora-Indianer. *Archiv für Religionswissenschaft* 9:464–480.

Preuss conducted research among the Cora and Huichol for about one year (circa 1906–1907). This research report gives detailed descriptions of Cora ceremonies and interpretations concerning their symbolic meanings. Preuss considered that the ceremonies (and particularly the mitote songs) were the major sources for understanding Cora religion.

1906   Weiteres über die religiösen Gebräuche der Coraindianer, insbesondere über die Phallophoren des Osterfestes. *Globus (Illustrierte Zeitschrift für Länder und Völkerkunde)* 90:165–169.

This describes religious ceremonies of Cora Indians living in the town of Jesús María in northern Nayarit. Preuss observes that influences of the Catholic church on indigenous culture were minimal, but he also notes that the Cora religious dances were generally performed on church holy days. The Easter celebration and the "danza de los moros" (Dance of the Moors) are described in some detail, and Preuss also discusses their symbolic meaning. Music for the Easter celebration was accompanied by reed flutes and drums.

1907   Die Hochzeit des Maizes und andere Geschichten der Huichol-Indianer. *Globus (Illustrierte Zeitschrift für Länder und Völkerkunde)* 91:185–192.

Preuss describes his field research and difficulties he encountered, particularly problems with the indigenous translators and the Indians' refusal to collaborate. He discusses collecting song texts and spoken narratives and gives translations (in German) of two narratives based on the magical power of nature. These are entitled "The Marriage of the Maize" and "The Origin of the Cloud."

1909   Dialoglieder des Rigveda im Lichte der religiösen Gesänge mexicanischer Indianer. *Globus (Illustrierte Zeitschrift für Länder und Völkerkunde)* 95:41–46.

The title does not refer to Aryan (Vedic) sacred hymns but rather to Aztec (Nahuatl) songs as published for example in Brinton (1890 above). Preuss argues that research on existing "primitive" cultures is useful for understanding the ancient Aztec song texts. He suggests that there are parallels between the responsorial songs of the Aztecs and Cora and Huichol ceremonies such as the wine feast or the ritual for rain.

1910   Das Fest des Erwachens (Weinfest) bei den Cora-Indianern. *International Congress of Americanists* 16(2): 489–512.

Could not be obtained for inspection of contents nor could information be gotten from other sources.

1932   Au sujet du caractère des myths et des chants Huichols. *Revista del Instituto de Etnología (Tucumán)* 2(2): 445–457.

This focuses on differences between the religious practices of the Cora and the neighboring Huichol Indians. The Huichols celebrate more than ten rituals during the course of a year while the Coras have fewer deities and only three annual celebrations.

Accordingly, Preuss describes myths and songs of the Huichol in more detail.

Provost, Paul, and Alan R. Sandstrom

1977   (Recording and liner notes) "Sacred Guitar and Violin Music of the Modern Aztecs." Folkways Records, FE 4358.

This contains religious music of Aztec descendants living in a remote area of northern Veracruz. This is instrumental music (scored for guitar, violin, and gourd rattle) used in rituals and dances connected with annual fertility ceremonies. All the recordings were made in actual context circa 1972–1973. The notes (7 pp.) include photographs of the ceremonies.

1979   (Recording and liner notes) "Carnival in the Huasteca: Guitar and Violin Huapangos of the Modern Aztecs." Ethnodisc Journal of Recorded Sound, Volume 11. Pachart, ER 45181.

Like the previous entry, these recordings were collected among modern Aztecs of northern Veracruz in research conducted circa 1972–1973. This album features music for the Nanawatili ceremony. While the ceremony derives from pre-contact religious practices, it has also been syncretized with the Catholic celebration of Carnival. The liner notes (19 pp.) contain seven pages of musical notations.

Redfield, Robert

1930   *Tepoztlán, a Mexican Village: A Study of Folk Life.* Chicago: University of Chicago Press.

This is an ethnography focusing on contemporary changes in Indian village life as observed in fieldwork conducted circa 1926–1927. Redfield notes that the Indians distinguish Mestizo music from indigenous ritual music, which is ordinarily not regarded as music. Instruments used for the ritual music are the teponaztli, the chirimía (small flageolet), and a small drum a small drum. In chapter six ("A Tepoztecan Book of Days") Redfield discusses the cycle of ceremonies which are performed annually. Contains many photographs.

Riley, Carroll L., and John Hobgood

1959   A Recent Nativistic Movement among the Southern
          Tepehuan Indians. *Southwestern Journal of Anthro-
          pology* 15(4): 355–360.
          This focuses on (two) apparitions of the Virgen de Guadalupe
which resulted in a nativistic movement among the Tepehuan
Indians of southern Durango. In both of the visions, the Virgen or-
dered the people to continue celebrating their native customs, especially a fertility and thanksgiving dance known as the mitote.

Rodríguez Rouanet, Francisco

1962   Notas sobre una representación actual del Rabinal
          Achí o el baile del tun. *Guatemala indigena* 2(1): 45–
          56.
          This describes a Mayan dance-drama presumed by many to be
extinct but observed by the author in 1955. The ritual features music by valveless metal trumpets and a slit-drum(*tun*). For a recording of the music see the album by Yurchenco (1978 below).

See **Roberts** (1936) in the General bibliography for comments on pos-
          sible connections between Mexican Indian music and dance
          and those of more northerly tribes (pp. 34 and 38).

Rosoff, Nancy, and Olivia Cadaval

1992   The Fiesta: Rhythm of Life in the Sierras of Mexico
          and the Altiplano of Bolivia. Pp. 33–64 in *Native
          American Dance: Ceremonies and Social Traditions*
          edited by Charlotte Heth. Washington: National Mu-
          seum of the American Indian, Smithsonian Institu-
          tion.
          This contains sections describing contemporary dances among
the Zapotec of Oaxaca and the Tzotzil and Tzeltal Maya of
Highland Chiapas. The authors emphasize various levels of
spiritual significance which the fiestas have for native culture-
bearers. This includes short essays by Manuel Ríos Morales, a
Zapotec anthropologist (p. 38), and by Jaime Torres Burguete, a
Tzotzil ethnolinguist (pp. 49–51). Also includes excellent color
photos.

Roys, Ralph L.

(1933) *The Book of Chilam Balam of Chumayel.* Washington: Carnegie Institution. New revised edition. Norman: University of Oklahoma Press, 1967.

The Chilams were high-ranking Mayan priests who often served as teachers and prophets. *Balam* means "jaguar," but it was also the name of the last and greatest prophet (living around 1500), who foretold the coming of the strangers from the east. The original Chumayel manuscript was written in a romanic script which the sixteenth-century missionaries adapted for writing the Maya language of Yucatan. This provides a translation of the Mayan text with extensive explanatory comments.

Sahagún, Bernardino de

[1950–1969] *Florentine Codex, or General History of the Things of New Spain.* Translated and edited by Arthur J. O. Anderson and Charles E. Dibble. 13 vols. Second revised edition. Monographs of the School of American Research. Santa Fe, New Mexico.

Fray Bernardino Ribeira from Sahagún, Spain, arrived in New Spain in 1529. Interested in languages, he compiled information on virtually every aspect of Aztec life and produced an exhaustive dictionary of the Nahuatl language (1558–1585). The manuscript known generally as the Florentine Codex was written in Mexico City. For music-related contents see especially Volume 3, Book 2 (entitled "The Ceremonies").

Saville, Marshall H.

1898 The Musical Bow in Ancient Mexico. *American Anthropologist* 11(9):280–284.

Attempts to show that the musical bow was an indigenous instrument in North America (rather than having been introduced from Africa). Saville claims that a musician pictured in an early Aztec manuscript (the so-called Codex Becker) is playing a musical bow. For an opposing interpretation of the same figure, see Seler (1899 below).

1925 *The Wood-Carver's Art in Ancient Mexico.* New York: Museum of the American Indian.

A comprehensive study of indigenous wood-carving, including that of instruments such as the Aztec *teponaztli* (slit-drum).

See the catalogue by **Seeger and Spear** (1987). This contains a listing of early cylinder recordings at the Indiana University Archives of Traditional Music. The collection includes early recordings from the Huichol and Tarahumara Indians.

Seler, Eduard

1899   Mittelamerikanische Musikinstrumente. *Globus (Illustrierte Zeitschrift für Länder und Völkerkunde)* 76:109–113.

Seler takes issue with Saville's interpretation (1898 above) of the instrument played by one of the priests portrayed in the Codex Becker. In his opinion the figure is holding a tortoise shell. Seler also discusses other instruments pictured in this and other codices. He argues that the marimba and the musical bow are both of African origin.

Sheehy, Daniel

1979   Record reviews of "Indian Music of Northwest Mexico: Tarahumara, Warihio, Mayo" (Canyon Records C-8801); and "Raramuri Tagiara: Music of the Tarahumar" (Stuff that Kountz 3). *Ethnomusicology* 23(2): 352–354.

Criticizes the lack of adequate documentation for both records. The Canyon recording features 32 performers who performed at an exhibit at the Heard Museum (Phoenix, Arizona) in 1977. Sheehy gives background on the tribes and on the genres, mainly dance music including Tarahumara matachín dances and Mayo pascola and deer dances. Side one of the other recording (Raramuri Tagiara) contains a sampling of musical instruments and four short female solo songs. Side two contains 17 minutes of unbanded excerpts from the Tarahumara "Easter Pageant." The latter features music played on locally made instruments and was recorded in the Sierra Madre mountains of Chihuahua.

1980   Record reviews of "Bats'i Son: Música indígena de Chiapas" (Na-Bolom LPNB-24576); and "Bats'i Vom: La Música chamula de los altos de Chiapas" (Centro de Estudios Científicos, Chiapas, Mexico). *Ethnomusicology* 24(2): 337–338.

Begins by mentioning five other recent commercial recordings of Mayan Indian music from Chiapas. Notes that these two are unique for focusing only on the Tzotzil- and Tzeltal-speaking peoples and provide a greater variety of material than the others. The first album (Bats'i Son) contains mainly religious and other music recorded at actual festivals. The other (Bats'i Vom) contains instrumental music. Two types of ensemble are represented: (1) various combinations of locally-made harps, guitars, and violins; and (2) a pairing of a three-holed flute with a double headed drum. The liner notes are very brief but Sheehy provides additional information and references.

Sorenson, E. Richard, and Philip R. Lenna

1966   (Recording and liner notes) "Cora Indian Festive Music." Folkways Records (FE 4327).

Currently reissued on cassette, the album features recordings made in the mountains of northwestern Nayarit. Contents are identified as follows: Knife Dance, violin improvisation and flute accompaniment, spontaneous singing, music and revelry, flute solo, violin improvisation, music and revelry with a Mexican song, flute solo, mass singing and revelry, and ceremonial dance at San Pedro de Honor. The liner notes (4 pp.) include photographs.

Stanford, E. Thomas

1966   A Linguistic Analysis of Music and Dance Terms from Three Sixteenth-Century Dictionaries of Mexican Indian Languages. *Yearbook of the Inter-American Institute for Musical Research* 2:101–159.

This contains analyses of Mixtec, Nahuatl, and Tarascan words relating to music, musical instruments, and dance. Stanford begins by discussing methodological issues. He feels that the differences between pre-contact cultures have been exaggerated and that various cultures actually had close contacts with each other. The analysis produces three main conclusions: (1) there was only one term for music and dance in the three languages considered here; (2) favored sound qualities in music were high pitched, loud, and clear; and (3) that common people participated in dancing.

1966   Three Mexican Indian Carnival Songs. *Ethnomusicology* 10(1): 58–69.

The three carnival songs that Stanford examines here are each indigenous interpretations of the Spanish romance "El Señor Don Gato." They were collected in the states of Veracruz, Oaxaca, and Guerrero. The author argues that the wide distribution of this Spanish romance shows that it probably came to the New World when these territories were still controlled by Spain. According to historical documents, the celebration of Carnival was introduced in Mexico a few years after the Spanish conquest and became popular very quickly. Includes translations of the various song texts (pp. 62–69).

1974   Record Review of "Music of the Tarascan Indians of Mexico," recording and notes by Henrietta Yurchenco (1970). *Ethnomusicology* 18(2): 349–350.
This is a highly unfavorable review. Stanford criticizes the sound quality of the recordings, the liner notes, and the choice of performers.

Starr, Frederick

1896   Popular Celebrations in Mexico. *Journal of American Folklore* 9(34): 161–169.
Starr distinguishes three elements in popular celebrations: (1) aspects deriving from authentic indigenous ceremonies; (2) elements derived from medieval European celebrations; and (3) purely Catholic elements. In the second category (medieval celebrations), indigenous instruments as well as modifications of European instruments are used. He then describes five events (either dances, dramas, or celebrations) to illustrate his thesis.

1903   Notes on Mexican Musical Instruments Past and Present: What Was the Tecomapiloa? *American Antiquarian and Oriental Journal* 25(5):303–310.
Describes the surviving forms of ten Aztec instruments which are mentioned in an ancient Nahuatl poem. The term *tecomapiloa* literally means "the suspended vase" or "hanging gourd." This was apparently a woman's instrument. It was attached to a small *teponaztli* or slit-drum (from which it hung) and evidently served as a resonator.

Stevenson, Robert

1952   *Music in Mexico: A Historical Survey*. New York: Crowell.
Chapter one discusses the history of research on Mexican Indian music as inspired in part by an "Aztec renaissance" movement among composers and musicians of the 1920s. Stevenson also suggests three main directions for research on Aztec music, which he addresses more thoroughly in the entry which follows. Contains an extensive bibliography.

1968   *Music in Aztec and Inca Territory.* Berkeley and Los
            Angeles: University of California.
A comprehensive study depicting early Aztec music as a sophisticated tradition in which members of a professional caste provided music and dance for sacrificial rituals and other public events
sponsored by a ruling religious elite. The chapters on precortesian
music approach the subject in three separate discussions: (1) a survey of Aztec musical instruments as known through archeological
evidence, painted images in early codices, and contemporary descriptions by Spanish observers; (2) a summary of references to
music and dance events in the writings of Durán, Sahagún,
Motolinía, and other sixteenth-century chroniclers; and (3) a discussion of research conducted among more recent Mexican Indian
peoples whose music may still preserve evidence of earlier practices. Notations of songs from the following tribes are provided
and discussed: Tarahumara (3), Tepehuane (1), and Huichol (4).
The survey of historical references is prefaced by Stevenson's listing of 16 general assertions about Aztec music (pp. 89–91). There
is also a fairly lengthy chapter describing musical acculturation
during the colonial period, as Indians became involved in various
forms of church music and use of European instruments. The bibliography lists about 700 titles.

1974   Record Review of "Musiques Mexicaines," recording
            and notes by José Raúl Hellmer (1973). *Ethnomusi-
            cology* 18(3): 486.
Stevenson criticizes the brevity of the selections and lack of
adequate documentation in the liner notes. Also see Hellmer (1973
above).

1980   Aztec Music. Pp. 760–761 in *The New Grove
            Dictionary of Music and Musicians*, Volume 1.
            Edited by Stanley Sadie. London: Macmillan.
Contains useful information on the social contexts of music,
the role of musicians, and musical instruments. Includes basic bibliography and one photograph of an early Aztec drum (*huehuetl*),
carved from wood with extensive decorations in bas relief.

1980   Maya Music. Pp. 852–854 in *The New Grove
            Dictionary of Music and Musicians*, Volume 10.
            Edited by Stanley Sadie. London: Macmillan.
Gives an overview emphasizing the historical dimensions of
Mayan music and methods of research on the subject. Contains
information on musical instruments. Includes a bibliography and

illustrations of musical scenes depicted in a wall-painting (dated circa 775 AD) and in an early manuscript.

1980   Record reviews of "Sacred and Profane Music of the Ika," recording and notes by Jim Billipp (Folkways FE 4055); "Sacred Guitar and Violin Music of the Modern Aztec," recording and notes by Paul Provost and Alan Sandstrom (Folkways FE 4358); and "Modern Maya: The Indian Music of Chiapas," Volume 2, recording and notes by Richard Alderson (Folkways FE 4379). *Ethnomusicology* 24(1): 138–139.

Stevenson mainly describes the contents of the recordings. He also notes that the use of the words "Aztec" and "Mayan" in the latter titles is questionable since the instruments (except for percussion) and chordal style are European-derived.

Thompson, John Eric S.

(1954)   *The Rise and Fall of Maya Civilization.* Second edition. Norman: University of Oklahoma Press (1966).

Includes a chapter on religious ceremonies and dances (pp. 293–296). This is based mainly on Spanish colonial sources and paintings on the Bonampak murals.

Tozzer, Alfred M.

1907   *A Comparative Study of the Mayas and the Lacadones.* New York.

According to Hammond (1972 above), this contains several references to early Mayan musical instruments still being used among Lacandon groups. Could not be obtained for inspection of contents.

Varela, Leticia R.

1986   *La Música en la vida de los Yaquis.* Hermosillo: Secretaría de Fomento Educativo y Cultura, Gobierno del Estado de Sonora.

This is based on the author's doctoral dissertation, completed in 1982. In chapter 1 Varela makes a distinction between liturgical and para-liturgical dances, the latter including indigenous elements. Chapter 2 describes the social functions of the music, and chapter 3 deals with musical instruments. Chapter 4 ("Structural Principles") gives a fairly detailed analysis of Yaqui music (including several musical transcriptions). The book closes with a brief chapter on music and cosmology.

Warman, Arturo

1969   (Recording and liner notes) "Música indígena del noroeste." Museo Nacional de Antropología, MNA 05.
This contains dance music of the Yaqui and Mayo Indians of Sonora. The recordings were collected by Arturo Warman and Thomas Stanford in 1964. Contains selections of music for the Pascola, Matachines, and Deer Dances. Includes liner notes (3 pages) in Spanish.

1970   (Recording and liner notes) "Banda de Tlayacapan," Volume 5. Museo Nacional de Antropología, MNA 09.
This contains music by an 18-piece military band which plays in a clearly indigenous style. Side one ("La danza de los chinelos") contains a series of marches interspersed with brief trumpet calls. Side two ("Sones o jarabes para los toros") contains eight pieces for use at bullfights.

1972   (Recording and liner notes) "Musica del Istmo de Tehuantepec: Oaxaca." Museo Nacional de Antropologia, MNA 11.
Could not be obtained for inspection of contents nor could information be gotten from other sources.

1974   (Recording and liner notes) "Música de los Huaves o Mareños." Instituto Nacional de Antropología e Historia, INAH 14.
The celebrations of the Huaves follow the Catholic calendar, but their dances are also related to animal spirit-beings such as the Fish, Serpent, and Tortoise. The recordings were made in Oaxaca circa 1971–1972. Includes liner notes (2 pages) in Spanish.

Wasson, R. Gordon, and Valentina P. Wasson

1957   (Recording and liner notes) "Mushroom Ceremony of the Mazatec Indians of Mexico." Smithsonian Folkways (FR 8975).
Currently reissued on cassette, the album features various types of music sung by Maria Sabina (Mazatec) during a curing ceremony. This was recorded at Huantla de Jiménez in northern

Oaxaca in 1956. The liner notes (7 pp.) include song texts in the
Mazatec language and English translations.

**Wasson, R. Gordon, George Cowan, Florence Cowan, and Willard
Rhodes**

1974   *María Sabina and Her Mazatec Mushroom Velada.*
New York and London: Harcourt, Brace, and
Jovanovich.
Describes a curing ceremony performed in the late 1950s.
Describes the use of hallucinogenic mushrooms and discusses parallels in the language used by ancient and contemporary ritualists.
George Cowan describes the Mazatec language and a whistle language based on its tone patterns. The musical sections of the ceremony are transcribed by Rhodes. Rhodes also discusses possible
influences of Catholic church music (pp. 256–257) and the relation
between pitch patterns of the spoken language and melodic patterns in the music (pp. 263–265). Reviewed by Boilés (1976
above).

Yurchenco, Henrietta

1947   (Recording and liner notes). "Folk Music of Mexico."
Library of Congress, Recorded Sound Division, L 19.
Contains songs and instrumental music from the following
tribes: Cora, Seri, Yaqui, Tarahumara, Huichol, Tzotzil, and
Tzeltal. These groups were selected because they were presumed to
be among the least influenced by modern civilization. Recorded at
various locations circa 1944–1946. Includes liner notes (6 pp.) with
illustrations.

1952   (Recording and liner notes) "Indian Music of
Mexico." Ethnic Folkways Recordings, FE 4413
(P413).
Contains music of the following groups: Yaqui, Huichol, Cora,
and Tzotzil. In the Cora harvest chants the singer (a shaman) accompanies himself on a musical bow. Includes liner notes (4
pages) by Gordon Ekholm and Henrietta Yurchenco.

1963   Survivals of Pre-Hispanic Music in New Mexico.
Journal of the International Folk Music Council 15
(June): 15–18.
This begins with a short historical background on the Spanish
conquest and its devastating consequences for indigenous music.
Yurchenco then discusses some forms of pre-contact music which

have survived among "primitive" agricultural tribes. She also describes the Yaqui Deer Dance as deriving from an even earlier (pre-acricultural) period. Includes three musical examples, transcribed from recordings made during the 1940s.

1963–1964   *Investigación folklórico-musical en Nayarit y Jalisco.* Cuadernos de Bellas Artes 4(6) through 5(3).

This contains information on field research conducted by Yurchenco among the Cora Indians of Nayarit and the Huichol of Jalisco in 1944. The report is given in a series of articles spread over nine successive issues of the journal. Contains musical transcriptions by Jorge González Avila.

1970   (Recording and liner notes) "Music of the Tarascan Indians of Mexico." Smithsonian Folkways, Asch Records (AHM 4217).

Currently reissued on cassette, the album features music recorded by Yurchenco in Michoacan (Mexico). Contents are described as follows: Tarascan string music, pirecuas, abajenos, music for religious festivals, and Mestizo music. The liner notes by Yurchenco (8 pp.) contain descriptions of the musical genres. Recorded in 1942 and 1965.

1976   Record Review of "Modern Maya: The Indian Music of Chiapas, Mexico." Recording and notes by Richard Alderson (Folkways FE 4377). *Ethnomusicology* 20(3): 616–617.

Basically a favorable review. Yurchenco notices that one of the processional pieces is polyphonic and mentions various other forms of indigenous polyphony towards the end of the review. She spells the collector's name "Anderson," but "Alderson" is correct.

1978   (Recording and liner notes) "Music of the Maya-Quichés of Guatemala: The Rabinal Achí and Baile de la Canastas." Smithsonian-Folkways (FE 4226).

Currently reissued on cassette, the album features music recorded by Yurchenco on location in 1945. Tribes represented are Quiché and Ixil. Contents are listed as follows: Rabinal Achi, Baile de las Canastas, Finale del Baile de las Canastas, flute solos, Baile del Venado, Son de Cuaresmo, Baile de la Conquista, Baile de Ajitz, marimba music, and Son de San Gaspar. Reviewed by O'Brien (1979 above).

Zingg, Robert Mowry

1938   *The Huichols: Primitive Artists* (Report of the Mr.
            and Mrs. Henry Pfeiffer Expedition for Huichol
            Ethnography). New York: G. E. Stechert.
    This was the first extensive study of Huichol culture to appear
after the early publications by Lumholtz (listed above). A lengthy
section entitled "The Sacred Art of the Huichol" (pp. 383–502)
contains much information on music, dance, and drama. Does not
include notations or analysis.

Author Index

Tribes and Languages Index

Abenaki, 324

Achomawi, 162, 167, 182

Achumawi, 139

Acoma, 6, 29, 40, 205, 208, 225, 232, 243, 245, 315

Aleut, 68, 69, 78, 92, 96, 110

Algonkian (Algonquian), 74, 88, 89, 309, 314, 320–323, 334

Alibama, 342

Apache, 6, 28, 30, 34, 45, 47, 50, 61, 92, 95, 154, 199, 200, 202, 203, 205, 206, 210, 216, 217, 220, 224, 231, 235, 236, 238–240, 244, 247, 249, 251, 252, 261, 262

Arapaho, 6, 8, 17, 24, 26, 30, 40, 43, 44, 46, 179, 264, 266, 268, 269, 278, 281, 284, 286, 287, 289, 298, 299

Arikara, 8, 266, 281

Assiniboin, 8, 266, 271, 281, 282, 291, 296

Athabascan, 44, 45, 67, 79, 87–89, 92, 94, 96, 98, 112, 243, 262

Athapaskan, 21, 30, 65, 78, 94, 98

Atsugewi, 139

Aztec, 14, 19, 31, 43, 121, 202, 203, 206, 210, 233, 245, 352, 363, 365, 366, 368, 370–374, 377, 379–

387, 389–391, 393, 396–398

Bannock, 180, 181, 187

Beaver Indians (Also see Dunne-Za), 105

Bella Coola, 115, 118, 119, 127, 129, 131, 136

Beothuk (Beothuc), 94, 106, 324, 332, 334

Blackfoot, 49, 266, 275, 281, 284, 287–291, 300, 303, 304

Blood, 266, 267, 281, 291, 296, 304

Brotherton, 341

Caddo, 30, 62, 281, 286, 298

Cahuilla, 151, 155, 164, 167

Carrier, 20, 32, 67, 79, 89, 112, 123

Catawba, 353, 358

Cayuga, 35, 317, 318, 319, 320, 335

Chemehuevi, 28, 160, 161, 180, 181, 226

Cherokee, 18, 25, 26, 28, 53, 57, 315, 318, 320, 322, 336, 341, 342, 345, 346, 348, 350–355, 357, 359, 360

Cheyenne, 6, 8, 12, 40, 43, 179, 261, 264, 266, 268, 269, 273, 274, 281, 284, 296, 298, 299, 302

Chichimec, 382

Chinook, 8, 57, 114, 117, 123, 127, 131, 133, 135–137

Chippewa, 6, 10, 11, 12, 21, 29, 37, 46, 49, 57, 59, 176, 267, 296, 305, 307, 310, 311, 314, 315, 317, 319, 324, 328, 329, 331, 332

Chitimacha, 342, 353

Choctaw, 12, 44, 48, 52, 342–345, 349, 353, 356, 357, 360

Chumash, 142, 151, 153, 156, 164, 168

Clallam (Klallam), 8, 59, 113, 117, 120, 131, 133, 136, 224

Clayoquot, 118, 123, 131, 136

Comanche, 15, 37, 40, 43, 182, 193, 249, 261, 274, 277, 280, 281, 283, 284, 286, 298, 300

Concow, 140, 143, 166

Cora, 20, 376, 378, 382, 383, 389, 390, 395, 400

Costanoan, 58, 149, 151, 161, 164, 169

Cowichan, 8, 117, 131, 136

Cree, 9, 30, 66, 74, 78, 79, 88, 93, 94, 103, 105, 107, 109, 177, 190, 274, 281, 290–292, 296, 300, 301, 332

Subject Index

vocal game, 67, 96, 98–
100, 107

vocal quality, 12, 17, 23,
50, 159, 219, 225, 289

vocal techniques, 292, 377

volador, 375, 381

waila, 202, 220

war, 11, 29, 41, 47, 52, 53,
91, 97, 119, 122, 124, 126,
140, 208, 223, 240, 244,
268, 269, 274–276, 279,
281, 282, 287, 289, 291,
293, 303, 311, 327, 339,
343, 359

war dance, 51, 143, 145,
146, 158, 184, 191, 192,
194, 218, 222, 249, 263,
264, 275, 277, 282, 290–
295, 297, 298, 302, 309,
312, 321, 327, 328, 329,
333, 339, 357

wealth, 146, 151, 158

whale, 73, 82, 92, 103, 109,
120, 125, 126, 134

whistle, 8, 21, 121, 157,
168, 171, 179, 182, 246,
280, 308, 356, 358, 369,
372, 389, 400

wolf, 13, 84, 85, 91, 120,
122, 124, 125, 129, 135,
190, 268, 274, 287

women, 12, 23, 33, 37, 55,
72, 74–76, 81, 90, 99, 100,
104, 111, 146, 158, 164,
179, 190, 193, 194, 212,
213, 217, 225, 230, 249,
256, 273, 275, 276, 284,
292, 302, 307, 312, 313,
318, 319, 324, 339, 375

world renewal, 145, 161